PERSPECTIVES ON HIGHER EDUCATION

PERSPECTIVES ON HIGHER EDUCATION

EIGHT DISCIPLINARY AND COMPARATIVE VIEWS

EDITED BY

BURTON R. CLARK

UNIVERSITY OF CALIFORNIA PRESS
Berkeley, Los Angeles, London

University of California Press
Berkeley and Los Angeles, California
University of California Press, Ltd.
London, England
Copyright © 1984 by The Regents of the University of California

Library of Congress Cataloging in Publication Data

Main entry under title:

Perspectives on higher education.

   Papers presented at the 1982 summer seminar at the University of California, Los Angeles.
   Includes index.
   1. Education, Higher—History—Congresses.   2. Universities and colleges—Administration—Congresses.   3. Higher education and state—Congresses.   4. Educational innovations—Congresses.   5. Social change—Congresses.
I. Clark, Burton R.
LA174.P47   1984   378   83-24342
ISBN 0-520-05151-3

Printed in the United States of America

1 2 3 4 5 6 7 8 9

CONTENTS

ACKNOWLEDGMENTS

The primary debts accumulated in the preparation of this volume nest in three circles. The Editor is particularly indebted to the seven colleagues in Brazil, France, the United Kingdom, and the United States who joined me in preparing the basic papers and, after critical review, revising them for publication. The eight authors collectively are indebted to the entire group of twenty-five scholars, drawn from seven countries, who examined the prepared essays during a four-day seminar held at the University of California, Los Angeles, in July, 1982, particularly to the two colleagues who, in each case, prepared critiques that stimulated discussion. The participants are listed at the end of this volume. In turn, all who were involved are indebted to the Exxon Education Foundation for the funds that made the meeting and the volume possible.

In the organizing of the topics and the experts for this collective effort, I was joined particularly by Maurice Kogan and Ladislav Cerych. Patricia Carlson helped organize the UCLA Seminar and typed the final copy of the integrated manuscript. Adele Halitsky Clark provided the general editing that aided considerably our wish to shape a volume that would deserve to reach a large audience; Grace Stimson did the careful final editing. It is a pleasure to thank all the above for their contribution.

Burton R. Clark

Santa Monica, California
December 1982

CONTRIBUTORS

Tony Becher is professor of education at the University of Sussex, England. He served for some years on the editorial staff of Cambridge University Press, while teaching at Cambridge, and later served as director of the Nuffield Higher Education Group which studied innovations in undergraduate teaching. His principal publications include: (with Jack Embling and Maurice Kogan) *Systems of Higher Education: United Kingdom*, 1978; (with S. MacLure) *The Politics of Curriculum Change*, 1978, and *Accountability in Education*, 1979; and (with Maurice Kogan) *Process and Structure in Higher Education*, 1980.

Ladislav Cerych is director of the Institute of Education and Social Policy of the European Cultural Foundation, Paris. Born in Czechoslovakia, now a French citizen, he served for some years as head of the Higher Education Programme in the Organisation for Economic Co-operation and Development (OECD). His publications include: (with OECD staff) *Development of Higher Education, 1950–1967*, 2 volumes, 1970–1971; (with Ignace Hecquet and Christiane Verniers) *Recent Student Flows in Higher Education*, 1976; and (with Paul Sabatier) *Implementation of Higher Education Reforms*, forthcoming.

Burton R. Clark is Allan M. Cartter professor of higher education and sociology, and chairman of the Comparative Higher Education Research Group, University of California, Los Angeles. He taught previously at Stanford University, Harvard University, University of California, Berkeley, and Yale University in departments of sociology and schools of education, serving as chairman of the Sociology Department at Yale from 1969 to 1972, and as chairman of the Yale Higher Education Research Group from 1974 to 1980. His publications include: *The Open Door College*, 1960; *The Distinctive College*, 1970; *Academic Power in Italy*, 1977; and *The Higher Education System*, 1983.

Maurice Kogan is now professor of government and social administration and head of the Department of Government, Brunel University, England. After graduating from Christ's College, Cambridge, he served for fifteen years in various posts in the Department of Education in the British government. His numerous publications include: *The Politics of Education*, 1971; *Educational Policy-Making*, 1975; (with Tony Becher and Jack Embling) *Systems of Higher Education: United Kingdom*, 1978; and (with Tony Becher) *Process and Structure in Higher Education*, 1980.

Harold Perkin is professor of social history and director of the Centre for Social History, University of Lancaster, England. A graduate of Jesus College, Cambridge, he has taught at the University of Manchester, served as president of the British Association of University Teachers (A.U.T.) in 1970–71, and has also served as editor of Studies in Social History for Routledge and Kegan Paul since 1957. His publications include: *The Origins of Modern English Society, 1780–1880*, 1969; *Key Profession: The History of the A.U.T.*, 1969; and *New Universities in the United Kingdom*, 1970.

Simon Schwartzman is professor in the Instituto Universitario de Pesquisas do Rio de Janeiro and researcher in the Centro de Resquisa e Documentação em História Contemporânea do Brasil da Fundação Getulio Vargas. Brazilian by birth, he did undergraduate work in Brazil and pursued graduate studies in sociology and political science in Chile and the United States. His publications include: (editor) *Metodos Avanzados en Ciencias Sociales*, 1977; *Formação da Comunidade Científica no Brasil*, 1979; and *Bases do Autoritarismo Brasileiro*, 1982.

Martin Trow is professor of sociology in the Graduate School of Public Policy and director of the Center for Studies in Higher Education at the University of California, Berkeley. He taught at Columbia University and Bennington College before joining the Berkeley faculty in 1957. Between 1969 and 1972, and again from 1974 to 1976, he directed major surveys of American higher education for the Carnegie Commission and the Carnegie Council on Policy Studies in Higher Education. His major publications include: (with S. M. Lipset and James Coleman) *Union Democracy*, 1956; (with A. H. Halsey) *The British Academics*, 1971; and (editor) *Teachers and Students*, 1975.

Gareth Williams is professor of educational planning and director of the Institute for Research and Development in Post-Compulsory Education, University of Lancaster, England. Before joining the Lancaster faculty, he served for six years as principal administrator in the Directorate for Scientific Affairs, Organisation for Economic Co-operation and Development (OECD), and five years as associate director of the Higher Education Research Unit at the London School of Economics. His publications include: (with T. A. V. Blackstone and D. Metcalfe) *The Academic Labour Market in Britain*, 1974; *Towards Lifelong Learning*, 1978; (with Zabalza and Turnbull) *The Economics of Teacher Supply*, 1979.

INTRODUCTION

We know much more about higher education than we did a quarter of a century ago. But what we need to know has grown geometrically, racing ahead of pursuing knowledge. This disturbing gap has numerous sources. Throughout the many organized sectors of modern society, tasks proliferate and responsibilities become more ambiguous. Observers and analysts speak with some alarm of increasing complexity and uncertainty. Within higher education itself, the driving imperatives of research and scholarship rapidly create new fields of knowledge as well as arcane specialties within the old, fragmenting the foundations of universities and colleges in the leading institutions of the international centers of learning and then spreading downward to other universities and colleges within their own countries and outward to other nations. On these grounds alone there is each year more to be comprehended if we are to grasp what academics do. Complexity and uncertainty have been increased even more by the greatly expanded scale of modern higher education, changes in size and scope which are indicated by increased numbers of students and faculty, reflected in the piling of administrative echelon upon administrative echelon, and witnessed by a growing sense that those at the top and the bottom, on the inside and the outside, are out of touch with one another. At the same time the ambition to comprehend and control has grown. Citizens, officials, and many participants have been subject to a rising tide of expectations that we should be able to order educational affairs and control educational change. Analysts believe they ought to find answers and think they will manage to do so if they redouble their efforts and devise the right theories. Simplicities should be found among the ambiguities that confuse us. Meanwhile, the gap grows larger.

What is to be done? There is no way to slow the growing complexity, for the empirical world is not within anyone's control. The payoffs of invention, specialization, and competition, within science and higher education in each country and especially among countries, alone ensure that the future will not be simpler. From the side of analysis, researchers are not likely to amass the resources and personnel that will greatly accelerate their progress and broaden their reach and thereby close the gap. As elsewhere, relative scarcity is their lot. What is left is the opportunity to attend selectively and to moderate expectations. We have never really needed to know everything about the functioning of higher education, and those who seek complete accounts of modern systems are asking for the impossible and pushing attention in the wrong direction. The strategic decision is to be selective, more conscious of distinguishing between the significant and the trivial. If analysts cannot do it all, what most needs to be done and what can be done well? Can researchers sensibly adjust the objectives of analysis and critical thought to the limited resources that sustain those activities? Answers to such questions must always be partial and temporary rather than definitive and permanent. But to hold such queries before us is to concentrate attention in ways that help turn laundry lists of research topics into agendas that have a point.

In pursuing selectively the complex realities of higher education, there is considerable gain at the present time in turning to the most relevant disciplines and the perspectives that they cultivate and bring to bear. The various analytical specialties are selective ways of knowing, tunnels of vision that make analysts simultaneously more knowledgeable and more ignorant. An illuminating perspective is like a spotlight in the theatre, concentrating attention as it highlights certain actions at the front of the stage while relegating other features to background and periphery. No one approach can reveal all; broad accounts are necessarily multidisciplinary, with all the lights turned up and the eye wandering back and forth across the broad stage. But the disciplinary view is compellingly necessary, since it is in the power of approaches and ideas developed by specialists that we find the cutting edge. And so it is in the study of higher education. If we did not have at hand different analytical visions for that study, the ways of looking provided by history and political science and economics and organizational theory and so on, we would have to invent them.

As research on higher education accelerated during the past two decades, we have indeed seen the disciplinarians go to work. Sociologists have developed a major body of work on questions of access and equality; economists have turned to theories of human capital and the economic behavior of universities. Policy analysts have isolated key areas of decision making and pursued the implementation as well as the formation of policy. Historians have helped us understand the flow of events and how the past conditions the present. As they have done so, the attending specialties naturally mind their own knitting: the rewards of the separate disciplines ensure that scholarly actions will push along different tracks. The specialists have various vocabularies and have difficulty understanding one another's language: Who can fathom an econometrician when he or she is under full steam? The disciplinarians occupy separate cultural houses, publishing in different journals, attending different meetings, and belonging to different networks of colleagues. And because they say widely different things, each with a certain amount of conviction, they confuse one another as well as the practitioner and the layman.

Thus it becomes useful to pursue the disciplinary experts as they pursue higher education, asking them to explain what their spotlights reveal and introducing them again to one another. Occasional collective efforts can be highly instructive. They may strengthen the sense that those who fragment knowledge have some responsibility for integrating it. They may help clear the minds of specialists in any one area by having colleagues from other areas insist on seeing more of a forest among the trees. They can provide some simultaneous translation, turning the jargon of the specialist back into a shared language. They can add sophistication to any one group of specialists by making them more aware of what bordering experts have found out and are capable of explicating. They can even reduce the arrogance of specialists, raising the value of modesty in scholarly work, as the limitations of one's vision and the value of others' are simultaneously revealed. With special exertion, collective efforts can bring some small amount of conceptual and analytical order to the chaos of loosely coupled inquiry, not to control research tightly but to suggest which directions of effort are most promising. And, properly reported, a coming together of diverse specialists can help generalists grasp the distinctive contributions of the specialties and meld those contributions into larger understandings.

Such are the hopes and purposes of the contributors to this volume. The central chapters are designed to clarify eight perspectives: the historical, the political, the economic, the organizational, the sociological interest in status, the cultural, the scientific, and the policy-centered. The specialists were asked to state what a national system of higher education looks like as seen through the lenses of their fields. To what aspects of systems of higher education does the perspective draw attention? What does one thereby imagine or see which others are not likely to conceive or emphasize? What does it mean to think of higher education as a political system, an economic system, or a scientific system, the latter drawing upon the conceptions of historians and sociologists of science who have created a lively, cumulative literature during the past two decades? How does the perspective under review relate to the approaches that guide analysis in other fields? Can the perspectives of the nonhistorians come to grips with long-run developments in higher education, or must they remain basically ahistorical? Are there discernible overlaps or gaps?

The papers that follow were planned from the outset to allow eight scholars to speak divergently, each in a distinctive mode. Yet we also sought some sense of convergence in common topics, bordering explanations, and approaches that give aid and comfort to others. During four days of intense discussion at a 1982 summer seminar at the University of California, Los Angeles, the eight papers were critically assessed by twenty-five specialists, all selected for disciplinary competence and comparative experience that would ensure informed judgment from within and without the field in question. The papers were then revised and edited for publication in this volume.

Chapters 1 through 8 are not primarily theoretical formulations or methodological exercises or reviews of the literature. Rather, each author has been asked to highlight the better aspects of the craft of his field, in the broad sense of approach and perspective, and then to go on at greater length to indicate the yield in illuminating materials already in hand. What is the best scholarship offered by that particular approach to the understanding of higher education? In addition, the contributors had the liberty of playing to their own particular analytical interests and strengths. The study of higher education is a relatively new as well as a diffuse area of inquiry, with individual voyagers having an important role in exploring different paths of explanation. The subject is a "soft" one, a field in which individual style and interpretation will continue to have an important role. Hence the voices in the chapters are those of eight individuals as well as of eight disciplinary perspectives.

Selected as well for their cross-national experience, the authors were asked to draw together materials from two or more countries, engaging in comparative analysis as fully as possible. In exploring the workings of several national systems, an established perspective can best show its value in accounts of what is thereby uncovered. If a relatively new perspective has little research upon which to draw, then it helps to know the promise of what will be highlighted when more work is done. For either old or new approaches, to such macrolevel phenomena as educational systems, cross-cultural comparison becomes the one broad method in the search for common features and recurrent patterns, with a concurrent isolating of the unique. The study of higher education needs access to the fullest possible range of information on commonalities and diversities. Hence, the cross-national dimension is useful in all the perspectives that we apply. At the same time, the working knowledge of leading experts is only gradually extended to continents around the world. The chapters that follow primarily reflect expertise on systems in advanced industrial democracies, with modest attention to developing societies and only occasional comment on higher education in Communist nations.

Taken together, these eight statements are also an effort to raise the standards of discussion in comparative higher education. Some progress has been made during the past two decades, as earlier noted, in exploring systematically the complex realities of different systems of higher education. But such analysis, relatively new, lacks firm footing in universities. It is greatly outweighed by the vast amount of comment made by participants who are otherwise preoccupied. Learned professors, studious and rigorous in their own fields, often discuss higher education without much preparation, much as busy medical doctors offer opinions on hospital organization and the state of their profession. Able administrators meet to engage in shoptalk on the latest problems, tackling issues on an ad hoc basis, first clinging to one post and then another as they lurch down the road of understanding. It is often deemed sufficient to have a philosopher-statesman restate the ideals of higher education, with all those assembled warmed by affect rather than informed by analysis. There is typically less there than meets the eye. Amateurism has its points, but it becomes injurious when it stalls understanding and almost willfully contributes to the gap between what we know and what we need to know. In short, even at this early stage, there are perspectives to be grasped and materials to be mastered. And there is still the need to separate as much as possible the descriptive and analytical from the normative, the "is" from the "ought to be," particularly in a realm where romantic images abound and analysts have vested interests.

We may state confidently that from the contemplation of contemporary higher education the materials that last and have the highest value will be those that come from the work of scholars and observers who turn the same cold, steady eye on this sector of activity as they would use in the study of politics or the economy, the social-class system or the cultures of others. Imagination and craft are as necessary here as elsewhere. And, at their best, disciplinary perspectives are large acts of imagination rooted in collective crafts. Any effort to clarify and assemble relevant perspectives should help steady the base from which we advance.

A word is necessary about the murky term "system," an idea we can hardly do without in any of the social sciences even when bothered by its multiple uses, shifting meanings, and extended ambiguities. We may properly refer to systems in higher education at quite different levels of size and complexity: for example, the social system of the classroom, the university as a system, all postsecondary enterprises in a country viewed as a national system of higher education. The latter is the common usage in this volume, with the smaller entities then becoming subsystems. We may also properly vary the actors and actions that we include at any level, arbitrarily fashioning boundaries that define an inside and an outside. The different perspectives make different cuts. An economic perspective sees economic activities; other activities are outside "the economic system." It sees people as economic actors, engaged in the distribution of resources or the exchange of goods and services; when the same persons engage in other activities they are outside the system.

Third, even when we focus on one level and work from a single perspective, it is often useful in analysis to switch from one usage of "system" to another. Thus, in using an organizational approach to a national system we may begin by depending on the conventional definition in which we point to the aggregate of universities and colleges, along with such formal means of coordination as the ministry of education. All other entities and groups are then outside the system and become part of its environment. But it is soon worthwhile to extend the boundaries, properly to portray actors and actions as parts of the system when they are seriously engaged in educational activities: trustees when acting as trustees, the committees of the legislature when attending to higher education. To do otherwise is to place outside the system some of its most important participants and institutions. When "outside" interest groups occupy designated positions on various boards of influence and control, as in Sweden, they clearly have moved inside the system. Thus, even within one analysis, loose and varied usage of "system" may be useful. In fact, when boundaries are so problematic and so subject to analytical variation it makes sense not to worry a great deal whether particular persons and agencies sit on one side or the other of an arbitrary line, but instead focus on how well-located groups, nominally inside or outside the system, involve themselves and use educational activities for their own purposes.

In introducing the chapters that follow, it is helpful to stress in summary form the distinctive point of view presented by each one and to note one or two central findings. It is also useful to point to a few linkages that connect one discussion to another. The concluding chapter pursues four major topics upon which these eight perspectives converge: political economy, institution and culture, science and higher education, and implications for administrative policy. These broad themes lead toward integration of separate subjects. They may also help to integrate the interests of scholars and practitioners, serving as bridges between the specific topics of scholars and the specific concerns of those who, come next Monday morning, will be practicing in a system of higher education.

The historical perspective.—Historians ensure that we pursue the dimension of time, that we see successive stages in the form of one leading to another. To work historically is also to provide comparisons that may aid current understanding: the conception of the university today is illuminated by conceptions of it in the past; decline and recovery in earlier centuries will perhaps help us understand the problems of decline today and the possibilities of recovery tomorrow. Key questions become: In what ways, if any, is higher education always the same? When changes occur, are they unilinear, moving on to new states of being, or do they often double back upon old forms, reinventing the wheel? Historical accounts help us get to the basics, both in properties of the system and their causes and effects. History becomes a concern with change and stability, particularly that which is unacknowledged and unforeseen. In this regard historians allow themselves to be particular, often concentrating on the flow of events in a particular place at a particular time, where many factors, studied separately by others, converge. They provide relatively full accounts, less guided by selective theory, while others deliberately accentuate one or another facet.

Thus, Harold Perkin provides an overview of four critical phases in the evolution of higher education. In the first phase, a unique institution—the Western university—was born. Out of those early centuries came the guildlike values and structures that became the key to longevity and adaptability. In the second period, there was a long decline in higher education in England and Scotland between the mid-seventeenth and the mid-nineteenth centuries, with recovery initiated in new alternatives to the old universities: scientific academies, mechanics' institutes, and a set of new universities, somewhat differently constituted from the old, which originated with the University of London and the University of Durham. In the third phase, we witness "the German transformation" during the nineteenth century in which the key device became the single-discipline professor who emphasized highly specialized research and taught from that basis. Upon this footing, German scholarship raced ahead and the system became for a long time the accepted international model. Finally, in the fourth and current phase, higher education becomes a corporate bureaucracy to a significant degree, more fully a part of the state or very close to it, and, in general, "the axial institution of modern society."

The historical review shows that higher education is capable of both enormous change and deadening inertia. Particularly impressive is the stubbornness of certain underlying forms, notably faculty members' ways of organizing themselves which are guildlike in nature. Also prominent is the underlying tension between freedom and control which has characterized this sector of society from its beginning. In the past, that tension pitted academics primarily against church officials and political rulers. Now, bureaucratic control becomes the more serious threat to the freedoms that academics claim they must have to function effectively. State power over this sector becomes newly and deeply institutionalized in the bureaucratic form.

The political view.—The historian's emphasis on state power in the contemporary period is picked up and extended in the analysis by Maurice Kogan of the more political aspects of modern higher education. He distinguishes between micro- and macropolitics, with the former referring primarily to the internal politics of the university, shading upward into the internal politics of the higher education system at large, whereas macropolitics refers primarily to state-level politics, shading downward into the relations of the state officials with universities and colleges. As we move from one level to another we often need different political theories and approaches. Political matters change qualitatively as we move up the scale of size from dyadic relations to those of a world system, and hence different concepts must be employed. When we tackle the university and its internal operations we must understand collegial forms of authority as well as portray departments and faculties as contending interest groups. When we turn directly to the bearing of state-level politics on higher education, we need to go armed with ideas about emerging corporatist relations in which major external interest groups—the organized arms of big labor and big business, for example—become systematically involved in the control of higher education, as well as to utilize the capacity of political scientists to analyze political parties, legislatures, executives, and public bureaus. "Politics" stretches from the top to the bottom, from the most externally relevant actions to the most internally insistent behaviors.

Kogan gives empirical flesh to these conceptions by examining recent events in Britain, first at the lower and then at the higher level. The British university remains decidedly less managerial than the American, less influenced by the government than the Swedish. Institutional autonomy has been high; collegial controls have been strong. But the efforts of central government to contract the system may cause a change in the internal political alignments. The "collegial mode" is placed under heavy strain; more "management" seems inevitable. At the state level in Britain, much decision making by elite groups has been secret, hence largely contra-academic in style, and has entailed some co-optation of academic oligarchs by the political-bureaucratic system. Recent efforts by the state to contract the system, sharply and quickly, have deepened this latter engrained tendency.

Kogan in his chapter suggests the many rich veins of action which can be mined by political analysis. The higher education system is "an intensely political complex." Yet, political science has been the least attentive of the social sciences to date and has only recently begun to focus upon what is clearly an attractive agenda for research. Alternative and competing forms of authority abound. External and internal interest groups transact and trade off in various ways. Group freedom is both enhanced and diminished under a variety of state controls and types of regimes. Pluralism, federalism, statism, authoritarianism, corporatism—issues of legitimate control in general—may be explored to great advantage in a realm that is at the cutting edge of expertise and influence based upon it. The references cited by Kogan are a good start in building a literature, especially from the detailed work of young scholars. The coming decade should see a larger contribution by political analysis to our understanding of higher education.

The economic approach.—Economists have been more concerned than political scientists in the study of higher education and have come armed with more theory and method. The concept of human capital has been a major contribution by economists to general thought about education. As Gareth Williams points out, the idea is an old one, to be found in the classic writings of Adam Smith; and, stated anew in the early 1960s, it has dominated the economics of higher education for two decades. The idea that education is a productive investment in human resources will undoubtedly continue to be part of informed conventional wisdom. But as economists and then sociologists have probed the evidence of the returns to individuals and society from different levels and types of education, analysis has become exceedingly complicated, with competing explanations and interpretations that range from the optimistic to the pessimistic. A debate rages over whether higher education mainly screens individuals, selecting those with characteristics that will prove useful in later employment, or whether it affects people directly by investing them with useful knowledge and skills.

What else can economists do for us? Specifically, they can turn from individual behavior to institutional behavior, in the approach laid out by Gareth Williams, to the modes and mechanisms of finance which affect the operation of universities and colleges, departments and institutes. The old saying that he who pays the piper calls the tune needs a discriminating revision, because it is the way payment is made which determines how the tune is played. Governments may have quite different ways of allocating funds, ways that influence the behavior of institutions and professors. One government may leave the money on the stump, working by lump-sum allocation from one level to the next, thereby promoting institutional and departmental autonomy and discretion. A second may have a finely tuned system of segmental allocation, with moneys fixed within a large number of specific categories—from civil service rank for professors' salaries to budgets for typewriters—thereby increasing central systemwide controls. Also, as Williams notes, most of the intermediate decisions that affect the day-to-day life of academics are taken under a variety of administrative arrangements.

The way in which Williams pursues the financing of higher education is highly institutional. He refers to the historical origins of present-day practices. He enters the world of modern political economy to compare the workings and effects of bureaucratic structures with those of markets. He notes the role of interest groups and politics. His approach is a model of how economic perspectives can be broadened to interact effectively with non-economic approaches. At the same time, a powerful argument is presented on the centrality and specificity of financing mechanisms, phenomena that economists are well equipped to study. Since these mechanisms are also relatively manipulable, analysis of the way they operate and the effects they produce moves scholarly analysis close to the interests of those who shape educational policies.

The organizational conception.—Organizational analysis has exploded during the past quarter century, becoming a congeries of approaches with quite different emphases. Organizational analysts function in psychology, sociology, economics, and political science, as well as in business and public administration. Their interests range from the most basic to the most applied, and from the societal level to the psychology of leadership. They have begun to show interest in historical explanations, working into history as they seek to determine how earlier forms of organization give rise to and condition later ones. During the 1970s theorizing about organizations began to take institutions of higher education into account. Analysts studying universities and colleges developed new concepts, or revised and applied old ones, which were appropriate to this domain: loosely coupled systems, organized anarchies, collegial authority, the political or interest-group model. The 1970s also saw organizational analysis applied to entire national systems of higher education, including direct cross-national comparison.

Chapter 4 stresses the latter interest, specifying three broad categories for cross-national comparison: how work is divided among and within institutions; how diverse beliefs are generated and maintained; and how authority is distributed. Following these broad properties, one can observe ever expanding complexity in one national system after another. Central to a complex internal composition is an intersecting of disciplines with enterprises which affiliates academics with two quite different forms of organization and places them under dual authority. Much authoritativeness is then located at the departmental or operational level, where academics represent their fields of study as well as work for a particular institution.

From this peculiar internal configuration, around which national systems vary, come many of the peculiar features of national coordination. Here a widened organizational imagination stretches into the concepts of political economy, allowing us to juxtapose market forms of linkage against bureaucratic, political, and oligarchical forms. The underlying matrix of disciplines and institutions also conditions reform and change. The system as a whole is peculiarly difficult to change wholesale and by top-down command. It is likely to exhibit much grass-roots innovation, with changes occurring incrementally and often in ways difficult to discern from outside the system and even from within it.

An organizational awareness sensitizes observers to the many ways in which organization shapes outcomes, including the fate of contending bodies of ideas. It makes a difference whether a national system of higher education has only one major sector, or two, or half a dozen; whether the boundaries between institutions, and between sectors, are airtight or permit students to transfer and faculty members to move from one to another; whether there are graduate schools or not; whether the operating level is constituted by chairs or departments or residential colleges. Such anatomical features affect commitment to teaching, competence in research, student access, faculty morale, program emphases, and so on. They are likely to affect the very viability of the many bundles of knowledge, the subjects, upon and around which the system is constituted. A particular task for the near future is research on the departmental or operational level, where the structures and cultures of the disciplines and the professions converge with the institutions and larger sectors thereof. The later chapters on academic culture and scientific activity provide two ways of probing this nexus of academic affairs.

The sociological analysis of status.—Sociologists have long focused on the stratification of society and attendant problems of mobility and inequality. In so doing they have done research mainly on the status of individuals, building a large literature on "status attainment," particularly in the United States and Great Britain. They have then examined educational structures chiefly for correlates of changes in the social position of individuals. This focus has caused them to pay little attention to phenomena of institutional status, the relative social standing and academic ranking of the larger units making up a system. In his chapter on higher education as a status system, Martin A. Trow turns squarely toward this latter much needed form of macroanalysis, to the phenomena that comparative students of higher education study under the concept of "institutional hierarchy."

All systems of higher education have some institutional hierarchy, in which prestige plays a key role in the allocation of resources and the attraction of faculty and students. But the hierarchies vary considerably in degree and form, as shown by Trow in comparison of national structures of sectors in such countries as Germany, France, England, the United States, and Australia. The hierarchies may be quite peaked, or moderately scaled, or relatively flat. They clearly exhibit much stability over time, yet they are subject to some change. Differences in the status of institutions within such large sectors as American state colleges or British universities may well sharpen even while differences between sectors are decreasing. The nature of the status hierarchy may be determined largely by government, through its allocation of functions and resources, or mainly by institutional interaction, through competition. And sharp questions may be posed: Does state control mean a leveling down of prestige hierarchies, while market interaction leads to a leveling up? If not, what are the conditions that promote the opposite outcomes? How are enclaves of excellence maintained in "mass" institutions? What is the role of leadership in the status attainment of universities and colleges? How crucial is historical priority, since in so many countries the highest-ranked institutions are the ones that came first?

The focus on institutional status also leads toward broad questions of public policy in maintaining the strength of universities and colleges and promoting diversity and adaptability. Status deprivation seems to make institutions insecure and vulnerable; the search for respected, dignified roles, or places, in the larger division of labor then becomes critical. The effort to form comprehensive universities, including more functions under one formal entity, may produce such units as parts of a diversified system or make them a substitute for one. Status plays an unusually strong role in academic systems, replacing money as the primary coin of exchange, and virtually all major policy deliberations need to be sensitive to its use and especially its redistribution. Chapter 5 isolates the matter of status as a central topic much in need of more research and as one that has a decided bearing on the unintended and undesired effects of policies and reforms.

The cultural view.—The effort to comprehend the cultures of higher education is the newest of the eight approaches. Tony Becher, in chapter 6, draws directly upon the anthropological tradition of analyzing culture as "a shared way of thinking and a collective way of behaving." He also picks up on the more humanistic use of the concept—"culture as the shaping of the individual mind"—as an appropriate meaning for academic culture, thereby blending two powerful and distinct usages of an old and hallowed term.

Academics live by many subcultures that inhere in their system of work: those of an individual discipline, a particular university or college, the academic profession at large, and even an entire national system. Students develop separate cultures, usually many of them, and administrators build their own values and norms whenever they become numerous. Among the main types the disciplinary form has clearly ascended in recent decades. Hence, Becher appropriately focuses on disciplinary cultures, there to draw upon his own pathbreaking work. The arguments are new and insightful. Dominant thought in the sociology of science has portrayed academic culture as socially determined. Becher builds into that conception the argument that the respective bodies of knowledge of the different fields make a difference in the disciplinary cultures. To be located in a particular discipline is first of all to be embedded in a particular body of knowledge which contains particular theories, analytical approaches, methodologies, and specific techniques. Disciplines are thought groups that have individual thought styles.

Becher goes further, noting that each major discipline is a set of sub-specialties that become somewhat different cultural houses for their members. From his own research on biology, engineering, history, law, physics, and sociology, he then observes that there are some similarities and differences among the subspecialties that cut across disciplinary boundaries. At one level the discipline is an adequate basis for cultural analysis. At a second and more specific level the discipline is no longer "a viable framework for such an analysis, and the boundaries have to be drawn along different lines."

As in the study of organizational features generally, we can observe researchers and observers becoming more sensitive to the symbolic side of academic life. And while the study of academic culture seems remote from policy management, Becher points out that policies could often be better tuned than they are now to the working conditions of higher education if politicians and administrators were to gain from cultural research "a more sophisticated awareness of the different varieties of academic life and their associated functions of teaching and research." Initially low on glamour for funding agencies, and high on hard grind for researchers, the cultural approach is highly promising, not least for those who must make decisions next Monday morning.

The focus on scientific activity.—The propensity of analytical specialties to run on different tracks is well illustrated in the odd separation between those who study "higher education" and those who study "science." Those in the first group study the history of universities and colleges, the economics and politics of higher education systems, issues of access and inequality, academic management, faculty tenure and unionization, student development, and so on, with hardly a word about scientific activity per se. Those in the second group, historians and sociologists of science, study scientific activity as a system in itself, specifying the general orientation and norms of science, studying particular "scientific communities," and debating whether science is driven primarily by its internal logic or by external forces, with hardly a word about the obvious fact that the principal institutional location of science for well over a century has been within systems of higher education, there to be conditioned by the characteristics of those systems. Simon Schwartzman points to the virtually unbelievable fact that two recent major volumes in the sociology of science and the study of science, technology, and society refer to universities on seven out of 600 pages and on twenty out of 600, respectively; neither makes any mention of systems of higher education in a broader sense. A first-class example of tunnel vision! The need has grown for bridges between these two literatures, for those who study higher education to take seriously the primary role of the disciplines and their research orientations (as done in several chapters in this volume), and for those who study science to take seriously the primary role of higher education in the support and development of science.

The contribution by Schwartzman helps to construct the needed bridge. He provides a historical overview of the development of science in Britain, France, Germany, and the United States, with specific reference to the conditions of their systems of higher education. As reviewed earlier by Harold Perkin, science came into these systems in a major way in the nineteenth century, with the new German model of university organization proving to be the more powerful stimulant to scientific development. In the twentieth century the United States model of university organization became "an absolute innovation" in making scientific research a goal of its own, specifically by providing the graduate school as an upper tier, separate from undergraduate teaching, and thus giving science "much more room than it ever had in other countries and places."

A Latin American expert, Schwartzman also reports on the specific attitudes and conditions in various Latin countries, specifically within their systems of higher education, which impede or favor scientific progress. He describes institution building and the changeover from older European images to more Americanized forms and styles. Notable has been the huge, rapid investment in graduate schools in Brazil, along with the creation of new elite universities and institutes, intent on high quality, to operate outside the mainstream of the higher education system. The Latin American examples provide quite different contexts for scientific progress, inside and outside higher education, from those of the most developed countries. Schwartzman notes that the educational systems of these countries have been more amenable to change and growth than have other institutions, including the incorporation of science at the advanced level. In return, science now plays an important legitimizing role for the universities in their claims for resources, prestige, and autonomy.

Departmental organization, graduate school organization, special schools, and a host of other specific structures in higher education can decisively affect science in developing as well as in developed societies. The disciplines provide direct contact across national boundaries, thus favoring the flow of advanced knowledge. Schwartzman concludes that more differentiation and complexity are needed within the less developed systems to permit the simultaneous operation of different and frequently contradictory functions.

The policy perspective.—Scholars in various social sciences, particularly political science, have increasingly turned their attention in recent years to "policy studies," primarily to studies of public policies. An interdisciplinary subfield has rapidly emerged, particularly in Britain and the United States, with journals, meetings, and invisible colleges. Policy analysts turned first to the formation of policy, with all the exciting problems of interest-group pressure and legislative and executive enactment. What happened after a policy was announced seemed uninteresting, a matter of bureaucratic routine. But attention soon turned, in the early 1970s, to the implementation of policy, to all the conditions and processes that make for success or failure in the carrying out of policies. Much has been learned in a few short years, if only to make us aware of the increasing difficulties of implementing public policies in complex sectors of society.

In chapter 8 Ladislav Cerych, working extensively from his own major research, applies this perspective to the study of higher education. He searches for the features that help account for relative success or failure in a number of major reforms attempted in continental Europe in the 1960s and 1970s. One must identify the support or resistance of powerful groups, especially those within the system, such as senior professors, who occupy the key sites through which implementation must flow. One must grasp several dimensions of the change that is sought, such as its "depth"—departure from existing values and rules—its "breadth"—the number of activities to be affected—and its "level"—change in the whole system, a subsector, a single institution, or a subunit. Since policy-directed reforms are usually carried out over a number of years, policy analysts must also confront changes in the environment which may swing support to or away from the reform. And the time frame for judging success and effectiveness may be a decade or longer in a sector as complex as higher education, with unanticipated and undesired efforts possibly looming larger than the anticipated and the desired.

In linking the fate of our most purposive collective actions—that is, governmental policies—to the internal workings of higher education and its environmental conditions, the policy perspective offers a promising focus. It links naturally to the study of leadership: Under what conditions do one or two individuals make a difference in effecting a policy? It leads us to think historically and developmentally as we follow the path of a policy over a number of years. It causes us to contemplate the flow of unplanned changes as we discern what has happened to changes that are planned. As an interdisciplinary field, policy analysis will continue to embrace a loose assortment of analysts with divergent interests. But its interdisciplinary nature allows it wide freedom to borrow and test ideas from a number of sources. And thus it relates to various of the other approaches covered in this volume, particularly the political, the economic, and the organizational. Finally, research on specific policies is close to the interests of policymakers and administrators, even if they often shun "evaluation" that may bring them bad news. The study of higher education policies, already catching the attention of able young scholars, should progress well in the coming decade.

* * * *

What has been left out? We have not considered the social psychology of higher education, a perspective centered on properties of individuals which has led to extensive research on student characteristics. This concern has been mainly an American preoccupation, one little developed in other countries, and has not been focused on macro system-level phenomena. For similar reasons, we have said little about the status attainment of individuals, a major industry in American and British social science, as it would require a separate volume. We have not directly pursued a political economy approach, which is indeed one that proceeds at a macro level and hence comes close in level and style of analysis to our eight interests. But several chapters edge into political economy, particularly in the triangulation provided by the political, the economic, and the organizational, and I return to that subject in the concluding chapter. The eight chapters, while not exhaustive of approaches, cover a large part of the analytical territory.

And so we begin with history and end with policy studies, eight ways of imagining and penetrating systems of higher education to understand better how they operate and why they operate as they do, and how and why they connect to certain other sectors of society. These presentations should interest professors, students, administrators, and laymen who are curious about the policies of nations in developing and disseminating their higher knowledge. For the most part only recently applied to higher education, the points of view are broad tools that will remain with us. This is the first time they are brought together, but it is not the last time they should be made accessible to specialists and generalists alike.

1. THE HISTORICAL PERSPECTIVE

Harold Perkin

History is the maverick among disciplines, the misfit, the bull in the china shop. Since everything has a history and history, potentially at least, deals with everything that has ever happened in human society, the historian is a kind of licensed rustler who wanders at will across his scholarly neighbors' fields, poaching their stock and purloining their crops and breaking down their hedges. In a very real sense it is not a discipline at all, but the sum or, perhaps, the lowest common denominator of all the other disciplines. The historian is not a respectable specialist but a sort of mongrel generalist who scavenges the spoil heaps of the contemporary sciences for old, forgotten, cast-off scraps of insight and information which, to him, will make the past intelligible and the future less surprising.

For, contrary to popular opinion, history as a discipline is not an ordered sequence of chronological facts or a mine of carefully authenticated information for others to draw on and theorize about. It is not narrative, a dirty word in the historian's vocabulary, nor is it antiquarianism, the skeleton in the historian's cupboard. True history is a problem-solving discipline which poses questions to the real, or once real, world and is forced to follow the questions wherever they lead. The historian can never say, like the physicist or the economist or the theologian, "That is not my subject." Anything that may throw light on his particular problem is his business, and he cannot afford to ignore it. If, to take a problem with which I have been much concerned and to which higher education is by no means irrelevant, he wants to know why the industrial revolution occurred when and where it did and how it came to spread to certain countries and not to others, he may begin with purely economic, geographical, and technological answers but he will soon be driven back to political, cultural, intellectual, even (in the Weber thesis) to religious ones, and indeed to the whole nature and social structure of those comparatively few preindustrial societies that found it possible to industrialize. Education comes into the revolution not only because clever inventors, imaginative entrepreneurs, and a skilled labor force are obvious prerequisites of industrialism, but because historical experience has shown that without a certain cultural attitude on the part of important sections of a community toward material progress, which can only come from education in its broadest sense, no injections of capital and technology, however massive, can move a reluctant society to change. And higher education comes into it because, unless the educated elites welcome such change and, where it does not exist, make provision for the necessary higher technical and professional instruction, the economy will remain earthbound.

This holistic approach to the past is, of course, merely an ideal and a method, a perspective and a process, not a boasted accomplishment of actual historians. It is certainly not a substitute for the contemporary analytical disciplines and their more specialized theoretical approaches to particular aspects of human endeavor, though it can offer them a context and a perspective in which to operate. If one is forced, however, to isolate what it is that the historical approach can offer which other disciplines do not provide—except, as it were, by historical accident—it may best be described as a concern with change and stability. More specifically, it is a concern with change that is unacknowledged and unforeseen as well as with change that is planned and intended, with the underlying processes of decay and renewal which affect all human institutions, and with the stubborn resistances to change which, despite external pressures and internal mutation, maintain a tenacious continuity over time. The slogan inscribed on the historian's banner as he goes into battle with the intractable past is, or should be, "Things change but names remain the same."

In no area of human experience is this concept truer than in the history of higher education. The uniqueness of the university, that peculiarly European invention whose meaning and purpose have changed from age to age and from society to society from its birth in twelfth-century Italy and France to its colonization of the whole modern non-European world, lies in its protean capacity to change its shape and function to suit its temporal and sociopolitical environment while retaining enough continuity to deserve its unchanging name. History, to use a familiar if oversimplified distinction, is an idiographic rather than a nomothetic discipline. It seeks its insights and interpretations of the changing world in concrete situations rather than in abstract generalizations or so-called scientific covering laws.[1] Nevertheless, it is no less informative about the nature of the real world. Some entities in the real world are better understood by idiographic than by nomothetic interrogation: they define themselves in action. The university is one of those entities. Though we can easily say what it ought to be—for example, a community of mature and apprentice scholars dedicated to the pursuit of knowledge by means of teaching and research and, less obviously, to the service of the wider society—we can understand what these terms mean only by looking at what they have meant in different times and places.

---

[1] For a critique of the distinction between idiographic and nomothetic disciplines and of the inaptitude of "covering laws" to history and the social sciences, see Perkin, "On Being a Centipede."

Knowledge is power, but power for what purpose? If there is one anachronistic metaphor we can apply to the university to illustrate its continuity through all its vicissitudes, its triumphs, declines, recoveries, and renewals from its medieval birth out of the union of sacred and profane knowledge to its central role in knowledge-based, science-oriented, technological, postindustrial society, it is that of the powerhouse of human society. But a powerhouse meant one kind of thing to a medieval society that saw its vital interest in reconciling revelation and reason, God's writings with God's much more practical and earthy world; it meant quite another thing to a society whose God was progress or posterity, yet another to one that saw mastery of the world in scientific discovery unlocking not only the secrets but the abundance of nature, and still another to one that fears the destruction of the world by the abuse of science or the wasteful folly of a self-defeating material abundance. Sometimes the power was self-destructive, as in the Renaissance and Reformation when humanism, the union of Christian and classical learning which held the intellectual world together, itself turned upon the precarious balance of church and state and tore it asunder. Sometimes the power weakened and had to be rekindled outside the university, as in the scientific and early industrial revolutions, when most of the new science and technology had to be generated by ad hoc academies and societies and taught in new institutions of technical instruction. Sometimes the demand for power outstripped the capacity, as in the late industrial and now postindustrial period, when new powerhouses of different shapes and sizes had to be built to meet the calls for more expertise and for mass higher education demanded by the age of the masses and of the uncommon expert. But always the powerhouse of the university was able, at least with a time lag, to adjust itself to the demands of society for more, and more appropriate, knowledge and for the trained personnel capable of applying it.

To demonstrate this idea fully would require a universal history of the universities and their role in society, a kind that has never yet been attempted. In this paper I merely try to illustrate it by concentrating on four critical phases or turning points in the evolution of higher education:

1) the origins of a peculiarly European institution which both helped to create and to destroy the medieval world order;
2) its decline and recovery in early modern Europe, illustrated by a case study of English and Scottish universities;
3) its German transformation in the nineteenth century, largely unintended, into an instrument for the discovery of new knowledge; and German influence, equally different from that intended, on its admirers in Britain, America, and Japan;
4) its apotheosis in the mid-twentieth century as the "axial institution" of "postindustrial society," the service-oriented society resting on

science-based industries and new university-educated elites, and the dilemma produced by the built-in contradiction between elite and mass higher education.

Connecting these four points is an underlying central theme, the tension between freedom and control. Insofar as the university needs freedom in which to pursue and disseminate knowledge, it thrived intellectually when the forces of control were decentralized and weak. Insofar as it needed resources to fuel its operations and depended on the support of the wealthy and powerful in church, state, or marketplace, it thrived materially when the forces of control were strong, but these very forces might, and frequently did, attempt to exercise control in ways inimical to the freedom of teaching and research. Hence the paradox that when the university was most free it had least resources and when it had most resources it was least free. (This is not to say that freedom automatically produced good scholarship and control inhibited it. The freedom of the eighteenth-century English university encouraged lethargy and hedonism; the state-controlled nineteenth-century German professoriat, despite rather than because of the Humboldtian theory of *Lehrfreiheit*, produced works of remarkable scholarship.) The university came to birth in a civilization that, almost uniquely, was politically, spiritually, and intellectually divided and decentralized. It has come to its largest size and its greatest prosperity in societies that, though divided among themselves, are increasingly subject to the all-embracing control of the bureaucratic state. Whether the necessary corner of freedom in which the university can maintain its independent pursuit of knowledge will persist remains to be seen.

THE BIRTH OF A UNIQUE INSTITUTION

The university was the accidental product of a uniquely divided and decentralized society. All civilized societies need institutions of higher learning to meet their need for esoteric knowledge and its keepers and practitioners: Veblen's "select body of adepts or specialists—scientists, scholars, savants, clerks, priests, shamans, medicinemen—whatever designation may fit the given case."[2] But most civilizations, or at least the major societies within them—with the notable exception of the Greeks—have been centrally organized and dominated by a unified elite of secular or theocratic rulers, or sometimes both in the same person, who tightly controlled the training of their literary, bureaucratic, scientific, and technical experts. Thus imperial Chinese mandarins were trained in Confucian

---

[2]Veblen, *Higher Learning in America*, p. 1.

schools (some of them private cram schools) of good manners and administration, Islamic theocrats in Koran colleges, Inca calendarists in temple schools of mathematics, Tokugawa samurai in Hanko schools of Bushido and Han service, and so on—all professional schools dependent on and controlled by the ruling elite.

The one exception was Greece, where a fragmented collection of city-states and an even more fragmented polytheistic religion had little need of full-time bureaucrats or powerful priests; instead it developed informal schools of philosophy for a free but aristocratic citizenry whose somewhat casual teachers could migrate to wherever learning was practiced most freely and so could escape the control of the state. (There were penalties for those who failed to escape in time, as Socrates discovered.) Although there were also professional temple schools for priests and medical men, like the temple of Aeschylus for Hippocrates and his healing art, the philosophical schools of Athens, Plato's grove of academe, and Aristotle's garden of lyceum, and their imitators, were to have enormous importance for the medieval university because the free speculative thought encouraged by the lack of political or theocratic control held a powerful attraction for later communities of scholars who similarly benefited, though for different reasons, from a weakness of control by Church or state and had a similar ability to vote with their feet.

The Greek school of philosophy was as little like the medieval university, however, as the voluntary debating society of the Athenian agora was like a parliament, another unique medieval European invention. The difference lay not in the degree of freedom but in the structure. Just as the medieval parliament was a community of communes, of representatives of community-minded boroughs and counties, so the university was a community of scholars, with an articulated organization and a corporate personality, its own statutes and a common seal, which enabled it to persist through time as a continuing entity whatever teachers and scholars came and went. This element of organic continuity is encapsulated in its very name. "*Universitas* was a general word of wide application in the twelfth, thirteenth, and fourteenth centuries and was used to denote any kind of aggregate or body of persons with common interests and independent legal status: it indicated a defined group whether a craft guild or a municipal corporation."[3] Its nearest translation was guild, and as such it was a very medieval concept indeed and gives us a clue as to why, when it finally came to be attached to the guild or community of scholars, it could have appeared only in medieval Europe.

Medieval Europe was a highly fragmented and decentralized civilization.

---

[3]Cobban, *Medieval Universities*, p. 23. See also Rashdall, *Universities of Europe in the Middle Ages*; Haskins, *Rise of the Universities*; Murray, *Reason and Society in the Middle Ages*, esp. Part III; Reeves, "European University from Medieval Times," pp. 61–84.

Unlike most of its predecessors, unlike even that other heir of the Roman Empire, Byzantium, in which the Christian patriarch of Constantinople was unquestionably subordinate to the emperor's control, the medieval West had no single center of overriding authority and power. At the heart of its political and intellectual consciousness was a dualism that rested on the Gelasian doctrine of the two swords, temporal and spiritual, imperial and papal, both the Holy Roman Empire and the bishopric of Rome claiming authority as successor to the ancient Roman emperors.[4] This dualism split medieval society from top to bottom, from emperor and pope through king and archbishop, baron and abbot, down to manorial lord and parish priest. It created two forms of law, lay and canon law, to both of which men and women owed obedience, and two sets of courts, one for offenses against king, neighbors, and property, one for offenses against God and his Church, which might include anything from heresy or blasphemy to adultery or washing clothes on Sunday. It led to material and military struggles for power, not only between empire and papacy but among their followers and allies right down the political and social scale, who could always play one side off against the other and appeal to a distant power against a local tyrant, as Becket appealed to the pope against King Henry II or the barons obtained an interdict against King John. The fragmentation of authority which always appears when central power is weak took the form of feudalism in secular politics and, more subtly, of royal or noble appointment of bishops and abbots in the Church and, at the lowest level, the system of advowson, or lay ownership of the right to appoint a parish priest. When the towns revived at the end of the Dark Ages they, too, demanded their autonomy, which they bought from king, baron, bishop, or abbot in the form of a charter giving them freedom from feudal obligations. And inside the towns, groups of merchants and carftsmen in turn demanded their corporate independence, in the shape of merchant or craft guilds.

The universities grew up within this decentralized, community-minded ethos as "primarily vocational schools for the professions, affording only a minimal expression for the concept of a study *per se*"; "they evolved as institutional responses to the pressures to harness educational forces to the professional, ecclesiastical and governmental requirements of society."[5] They grew spontaneously out of the cathedral and urban schools of the eleventh and twelfth centuries which, despite the clerical status of their teachers and students, "were secular in intent, catering for the needs of an increasingly urbanized society with a steadily growing population," many

---

[4]From Pope Gelasius II, A.D. 494: "the two powers by which this world is chiefly ruled—viz. the sacred authority of the priests and the imperial power." Cf. Leff, *Medieval Thought from St. Augustine to Ockham*, p. 74 and, for the dualism between empire and papacy and the respective propagandists, passim.

[5]Cobban, *Medieval Universities*, pp. 218–219, 8–9.

of them specializing in theology, law, rhetoric, or the liberal arts and sciences which were deemed appropriate training for professional clergy, lawyers, and clerical and lay administrators.[6] There is little doubt as to what attracted the students to them: "ambition" and "avarice" according to critics like Bernard of Clairvaux and John of Salisbury—the hope, among poor and not so poor boys unlikely to inherit land or feudal lordship, of rising in the world and making money through high office or the lucrative professions of clergy, law, and medicine.[7] The spontaneous gatherings of ambitious students who flocked to leading teachers of theology such as Peter Abelard or Gerald of Wales in Paris, to those of medicine such as the legendary doctors of Salerno, or to those of Roman and canon law such as Irnerius and Gratian at Bologna, were originally as volatile and geographically mobile as the philosophical schools of ancient Greece, but in the communitarian ambience of medieval Europe they rapidly developed the guild form of organization which gave strength, permanence, and a measure of autonomy to the medieval university.[8]

There were, to be sure, two main forms of scholastic guild: the lay, student-centered, market-oriented Italian university based on the model of Bologna in which the student guilds paid the lecturers' fees and had wide powers of discipline over them; and the more orthodox clerical magisterial model of Paris, where the masters controlled the students and the guild succession of apprentice (undergraduate), journeyman (bachelor), and master became the norm. The extreme form of student control at Bologna and Padua was soon whittled down, however, even in Italy, by the pressures of the city authorities and the establishment of a salaried professoriat and, although medieval universities were as varied as their independence readily allowed them to be and Italian students retained a robust tradition of student participation, most universities converged toward the orthodox model of guild organization, which was the key to their adaptability and longevity.[9]

This institutional form was so successful that the four universities of the twelfth century, Parma, Bologna, Paris, and Oxford, had grown to sixteen in Italy, France, Spain, and England by 1300, by another fourteen all over central Europe as far as Austria, Poland, and Bohemia by 1400, and by a further twenty-eight as far afield as Scotland, Hungary, and Scandinavia

---

[6]Ibid., p. 8.

[7]Murray, *Reason and Society*, chap. 9, pp. 213–233, "The University Ladder," esp. sec. 2, "University Careerism: The 'Lucrative Sciences,' " pp. 218–227.

[8]Cobban, *Medieval Universities*, chap. 2, sec. 1, "The Concept of a University," pp. 21–36; chap. 8, "The Academic Community," pp. 196–217. See also Rashdall, *Universities of Europe*; Haskins, *Rise of the Universities*.

[9]Cobban, *Medieval Universities*, chap. 3, "Bologna: Student Archetype," pp. 48–74; chap. 4, "Paris: Magisterial Archetype," pp. 75–95; chap. 7, "Medieval Student Power," pp. 163–195, esp. pp. 174–175.

by 1500.[10] They were truly cosmopolitan institutions, taking scholars and students from far and wide and teaching the seven arts and, most of them, the three postgraduate disciplines in the lingua franca of medieval Europe, Latin. They thus anticipated another feature of the modern university, the immensely strong interinstitutional and cross-national bonds of the discipline (of which Burton R. Clark writes in his contribution to this volume), which came to be more powerful than the local loyalties even to the university itself.

Like other privileged communities, urban communes and guilds, monasteries and religious or knightly brotherhoods, the university needed a charter or license from some superior authority, emperor, pope, king, bishop, or, at least and lowest, the city commune. The best and highest was the papal or imperial grant of a *studium generale*, which gave the university international status, and the *ius ubique docendi*, the right of teaching everywhere, which was meant to give its degrees international recognition (but did not always succeed).[11] But the most important privilege was the right of voting with one's feet, the effective threat to any overbearing authority, whether city commune, bishop, king, or pope, of migration, of taking the university's prestige and local custom elsewhere. In this way Vicenza (1204) and Padua (1220) were founded by migrations from Bologna, and Oxford (before 1167) and Cambridge (1209) by migrations from Paris and Oxford respectively. The power of this threat is shown by the strenuous efforts of city authorities, and sometimes of the universities themselves, to prevent migration, often appealing to king and/or pope.[12]

What marked off the university as a teaching institution from other professional training schools were two multidisciplinary features: first, that the lucrative professional disciplines that became the postgraduate faculties of theology, law, and medicine were all taught side by side in the same institution (and an institution where this did not happen, like the medical school at Salerno, did not achieve full university status); second, that these advanced professional courses were preceded by a common curriculum in the seven liberal arts. The latter were divided into the trivium, the undergraduate or apprentice's course in grammar, logic, and rhetoric, the basic tools of further study, and the quadrivium, the bachelor's or journeyman's course in arithmetic, geometry, astronomy, and music, the foundations (in a Ptolemaic cosmology) of natural science. It would be misleading to

---

[10]Kerr, "Comparative Effectiveness of Systems," table 1, "Enduring Universities of the Western World," pp. 166–167. Also private information from the Standing Conference of Rectors of European Universities, Geneva: "Liste chronologique des universités concernées," 16 February 1982.

[11]Cobban, *Medieval Universities*, pp. 26–33.

[12]Ibid., pp. 73, 97–99, 111; Armytage, *Civic Universities*, pp. 35–36. Migration was all the easier because scholarship was largely oral and literary and its paraphernalia therefore highly portable, as Sheldon Rothblatt has pointed out to me.

suggest that the arts faculty, as it became, was any less utilitarian or vocational than the professional faculties, and for what was probably a majority of students who stayed no longer, it provided a useful training in literacy, logical argument, persuasive reasoning, computation, mensuration, and the elements of observational science, which fitted them for a variety of careers in church and lay administration.[13] The method of teaching, mainly by dialectical demonstration and disputation, prepared students for a mainly oral culture in which men made their mark in sermons, court hearings, and administrative discussions by force of verbal argument. Dialectic, epitomized by Peter Abelard's book *Sic et Non* ("Yes and No"), which taught the method of creative analysis and progressive criticism (hypothesis, antithesis, higher and more imaginative synthesis), laid the foundations of rational deductive thinking practiced down to Hegel, Marx, and beyond.

Yet this common course of education as it developed became much more than vocational or professional training. In its mature form it offered a unification of the medieval universe of thought which could counteract the fragmentation and decentralization of medieval society and hold its centrifugal tendencies together in a single, coherent world view. The power of knowledge which it sought was no less than a reconciliation of the two incompatible interpretations of this world, that of the Holy Scriptures and that of nature as revealed by the best and most reliable observers. The first was represented by the Bible and the early church fathers; the second, surprisingly for a society that hated and persecuted heresy, by the pagan literature of the ancient Greeks and Romans.

Here we come upon the most surprising difference between medieval Europe and most other civilizations: despite its religious faith and its intolerance of other beliefs it lacked self-confidence in its own intellectual capacity. When faced by the manifest contradictions within Holy Writ and between it and the observed world, it could call to its aid only the power of reasoning of the ancient pagans whose speculative philosophy had not been stultified by an authoritarian revelation. As Sir Richard Southern has expressed it,

the medieval scholastic curriculum met an urgent need for order in the intellectual outlook of a Europe first rising to independent thought. At that time the only available instrument of intellectual order was a thorough command of the sciences and techniques of the Greco-Roman world so far as they had been preserved in the West. This command was achieved, and it brought intellectual order into human life in a wonderfully short space of time.[14]

---

[13]Cobban, *Medieval Universities*, pp. 9—13; Murray, *Reason and Society*, pp. 219—222.
[14]Southern, *Medieval Humanism and other Studies*, p. 39.

The new humanists of the twelfth-century renaissance—so called because they dealt in *literae humaniores*, more human or profane as distinct from sacred letters—not only recovered, largely through translations from the Arabs, the most important writings of Aristotle and to a lesser extent those of Plato, but they raised the self-confidence of human reason to a far higher plane. As one of the leading twelfth-century humanists, William of Conches, put it:

The dignity of our mind is its capacity to know all things. . . . We who have been endowed by nature with genius must seek through philosophy the stature of our primeval nature. . . . In the solitude of this life the chief solace of our minds is the study of wisdom. . . . We have joined together science and letters, that from this marriage there may come forth a free nation of philosophers.[15]

It is not surprising that the Church and sometimes the secular state were suspicious of this dangerously heretical movement and occasionally tried to suppress it, as when Bernard of Clairvaux harassed Peter Abelard into monastic exile in Brittany.[16] But neither church nor state could manage without the services of the universities and their products, least of all in the propaganda battles against each other. And in the safer hands of the great schoolmen of the thirteenth century, through whom "virtually the whole corpus of Greek science was made available to the western world," above all in Thomas Aquinas who patiently reconciled Aristotle with the Bible in the greatest syncretism of Christianity and Hellenism, medieval humanism created a unified world order which lasted until its destruction by the more corrosive humanism of the great Renaissance and the Reformation.[17]

For the intellectuals who created that world order could also, in the arrogance that is the besetting sin of the educated professional, come to challenge it. The men of learning who filled the proliferating universities of the last two medieval centuries came to think of themselves as a separate "intellectual estate," safe in their autonomous fortress of the university, from which they could assail both the authority of the priesthood up to, eventually, the pope himself, and the hereditary status of the lay nobility up to, occasionally, king and emperor.[18] This is not the place to pursue the role of university-based propagandists in the struggle between the empire and the papacy, in which they learned how to marshal arguments destructive of the authority of both. Suffice it to say that late medieval academic assailants

---

[15]William of Conches, *Philosophia Mundi*, quoted in Southern, *Medieval Humanism*, p. 40.

[16]Southern, *Medieval Humanism*, chap. 6, "The Letters of Abelard and Heloise," pp. 86–104; Waddell, *Peter Abelard*; Waddell, *Wandering Scholars*.

[17]Southern, *Medieval Humanism*, pp. 48–60; Murray, *Reason and Society*, chap. 7, esp. pp. 211–224.

[18]Murray, *Reason and Society*, chap. 10, "The Intellectual Elite," pp. 234–257; chap. 11, "The Assault on the Citadel: Theory," pp. 258–281, esp. sec. 1, "The theoretical assault on priestly authority," and sec. 2, "The theoretical assault on the nobility."

of the papacy, such as William of Ockham, Marsilius of Padua, William Wycliffe, and John Hus, paved the way for the great sixteenth-century academic humanists and reformers—Erasmus, Luther, Zwingli, and Calvin—who made the Reformation.[19]

When Martin Luther nailed his ninety-five theses to the church door at Wittenberg University in 1517, he was, in a sense, hammering home the triumph of the university over the medieval Church and with it the demise of the medieval world order. What the university had given the university had taken away. But its triumph paved the way for the rise of the secular nation-state which was to be a more serious threat to the independence of the university than ever the medieval Church had been.

DECLINE AND RECOVERY: ENGLAND AND SCOTLAND

The power of intellectual thought has no better example than the dissolution of the English monasteries. The Reformation was about many theological disputes, about the means of grace, salvation by faith or by works, the two or the seven sacraments, the omniscience and omnipotence of God and their implications for the predestination of man's soul, and so on, all of them fought with weapons forged in the universities. None had so many implications for a thousand-year-old way of life and the transfer of a large mass of property as did the destruction, in Protestant countries, of the doctrine of purgatory. Monasteries existed to pray for souls. If there was no purgatory, there was no point in praying for the souls of the dead, which had already departed to everlasting heaven or hell, and whose stay in purgatory could not be shortened by prayer. Ergo, the monasteries had no raison d'être. Out of the collapse of the doctrine of purgatory came the largest land grab since the Norman Conquest. Such was the firepower of the university militant.

Yet the Reformation was a Pyrrhic victory for the universities. They forged the weapon, but the secular state took the spoils, though it squandered them on royal favorites, war, and luxuries. The universities, which had tried and failed to provide Henry VIII with pope-proof arguments for his "divorce," did not escape the fallout of his anticlerical wrath. The first effect on them was the ban, by Thomas Cromwell in 1535, on the study of canon law, abolishing at a stroke the largest postgraduate faculty, which produced two-thirds of the higher degrees awarded to the superior clergy

[19]Cf. Leff, *Medieval Thought*, chap. 9, esp. pp. 279–294, 302–303; Potter, ed., *The Renaissance*, chap. 4, "The Papacy and the Catholic Church," pp. 76–94; chap. 5, "Learning and Education in Western Europe from 1470 to 1520," pp. 95–126; Elton, ed., *The Reformation*, chap. 3, "Luther and the German Reformation"; chap. 4, "The Swiss Reformers"; chap. 12, "Intellectual Tendencies"; chap. 13, "Schools and Universities."

and to most of the traditional administrators of the Church.[20] There was some talk of abolishing Oxford and Cambridge themselves as quasi-monastic establishments, but the king intervened personally to save them: "I judge no land in England better bestowed than that which is given to our Universities, for by their maintenance our land shall be well-governed when we be dead and rotten."[21] And he founded the Regius professorships and the two academic palaces of Trinity College, Cambridge, and Christ Church, Oxford.[22] But what were the universities to do? Common law was taught in the Inns of Court, the "legal university" in London, while medicine at Oxford and Cambridge had become an outworn theoretical subject studied by the smallest, most prestigious, but least effective group of practitioners, the physicians, and most treatment was given by surgeons and apothecaries.[23] Little more remained to the universities than the liberal arts and the faculty of theology, devoted to the education of a depleted clergy shorn of the regular orders of monks and friars, destined for the service of a now much smaller, state-controlled church and largely excluded from the once lucrative bureaucracy of the secular state.

The answer was to change the whole social and intellectual character of the two universities, which slipped sideways to educate, alongside the secular clergy, a new lay clientele. As Hugh Kearney has pointed out, "Some time between 1530 and 1570 laymen from the gentry class began to go up to Oxford and Cambridge in large numbers. The universities ceased to be merely the educational organs of the Church. They began to cater in part at least for the educational needs of the lay ruling elite."[24] The change was aided by the decline of the halls, which had catered mainly to the now defunct canon lawyers, and the rise of the colleges which, though intended for the clergy and still manned by clerical fellows, were readily adapted to the general and moral education of a lay ruling class on whom the state came increasingly to rely for central administration and still more for the amateur system of government and social control in the localities.[25]

Student numbers leaped from an annual intake of about 150 at each university before the Reformation to 300 or 400 afterward and to record heights of 400 to 500 in the decades around the Civil War, levels not to be

---

[20]Kearney, *Scholars and Gentlemen*, pp. 16–20.

[21]Mansbridge, *Older Universities of Oxford and Cambridge*, p. 50.

[22]Kearney, *Scholars and Gentlemen*, p. 21.

[23]Physicians were required to be graduates of Oxford or Cambridge, a rule confirmed by an act of 1522 empowering the Royal College of Physicians, chartered in 1518, to examine and license all physicians practicing within seven miles of London; but it had become the practice for the most skillful physicians to be educated at foreign universities and then to be "incorporated" by a short residence and payment of a fee at Oxford or Cambridge. Meanwhile, physicians were rare, and most medical practitioners were surgeons and apothecaries trained by apprenticeship. See Carr-Saunders and Wilson, *The Professions*, pp. 65–69.

[24]Kearney, *Scholars and Gentlemen*, p. 23.

[25]Ibid., pp. 20, 22–28.

seen again before the nineteenth century.[26] Some of these students were sons of wealthy gentry and nobility who were looking for a polished education to fit them for patronage in royal or noble service; many more, sons of smaller gentry, merchants, and yeomen, probably came to raise or confirm their status as gentlemen by education; a few may even have been attracted by the education for its own sake, based as it was on the new Platonic humanism introduced on the eve of the Reformation by men such as More, Colet, and Erasmus; and increasing numbers, sons of gentry, merchants, and yeomen as well as of the newly married clergy, came to train for the church, whose ministers seem to have been rising modestly in wealth and status between the Reformation and the Civil War, when the parson was becoming the second gentleman of the parish next only to the squire.[27] The parson was also, like the lay justice of the peace, an instrument of social control. Under both the Elizabethan and Laudian churches the homilies he read on Sunday were an important part of the propaganda of the state. To quote Kearney again, "the universities between 1500 and 1600 underwent a change of social function. They were transformed from being institutions geared to training for a particular profession into institutions which acted as instruments of social control."[28]

Alas for the universities. With the decline of the Tudor and early Stuart authoritarian state, the boom in student numbers did not last. After the Civil War, more specifically from the 1670s, numbers fell away. By 1685 Oxford was "very dead for want of scholars" and remained so until the nineteenth century.[29] Annual intakes at each university declined steadily from 400 or more in the 1660s to less than 250 at Oxford and less than 200 at Cambridge in the mid-eighteenth century, where they remained beyond 1800, when the population of England and Wales was double that of 1660.[30] Poor boys almost disappeared altogether, as they were squeezed out of scholarships and jobs in the church by the competition of wealthy gentry and clergymen's sons and were repelled by the increasing costs of college residence, which rose from about thirty to forty pounds in the early seventeenth century to about eighty to a hundred pounds in the mid-eighteenth century and to two hundred pounds in the early nineteenth. The rise in costs was not owing to the basic cost of living but to the competitive

[26]Ibid., pp. 22, 401 (graph); Stone, "Size and Composition of the Oxford Student Body, 1580–1909," pp. 91–92, tables 1A (Oxford admissions), 1B (Cambridge admissions).
[27]Kearney, *Scholars and Gentlemen*, pp. 26–28; Stone, "Educational Revolution in England, 1560–1640," esp. pp. 68–80; Hexter, "Education of the Aristocracy during the Renaissance"; Curtis, *Oxford and Cambridge in Transition*; Charlton, *Education in Renaissance England*, chap. 5, "The Universities," pp. 131–168; McConica, "Scholars and Commoners in Renaissance Oxford"; Morgan, "Cambridge University and 'The Country,' 1560–1640."
[28]Kearney, *Scholars and Gentlemen*, p. 33.
[29]Wood, *Life and Times*, quoted in Stone, ed., *University in Society*, I:37, 91–92.
[30]Ibid., pp. 91–92.

extravagance of gentlemen undergraduates in wining and dining, in acquiring fine clothes and furniture, in keeping horses, and in living high.[31]

The nobility and gentry no longer came in large numbers, for very different reasons. For those who could afford them the private tutor and the grand tour of the continent became the fashionable mode of education, and only those who could not were "schooled in public" at the boarding school and the university.[32] Whether the decline of humanism into a boring and routine scholasticism and the decay of lecturing and disputation caused or were caused by this change in educational fashions it is difficult to say, but John Aubrey's jibe in the late seventeenth century that the universities taught "the learning of a Benedictine monk" was echoed by Edward Gibbon's, a hundred years later, about "the monks of Magdalen."[33] In the former's day Anthony Wood wrote in his Oxford diary: "Our Colleges grow elegantly dull. Our schools are empty and our taverns full"; and in the latter's, Vicesimus Knox less pithily wrote: "In no places of education are men more extravagant; in none do they learn to drink sooner; in none do they more effectively shake off the firm sensibilities of shame and learn to glory in debauchery."[34]

Worse than debauchery was the suspicion of treason, rebellion, and Jacobitism at the universities. Thomas Hobbes blamed them for the Civil War: "The core of rebellion are the universities." His pupil, the Duke of Newcastle, told Charles II: "Your Majesty knows by too woeful experience that these lecturers have preached Your Majesty out of your kingdoms."[35] After the Hanoverian succession Oxford openly sympathized with the Jacobite rebellion of 1715, and for many of the loyal Anglican nobility and gentry it remained "that idle, ignorant, ill-bred, debauched, Popish University of Oxford."[36]

Recovery of reputation and student numbers did not come until the early nineteenth century, and then only slowly, not permanently overtaking the annual admissions of the 1660s until the 1860s, when the population of England and Wales was more than four times as large as it had been in the mid-seventeenth century, and the drastic parliamentary reforms of Oxford and Cambridge in the 1850s had opened the two universities to dissenters and to a burgeoning new professional middle class.[37] But by then, for the

---

[31] Ibid., pp. 37–46.

[32] Ibid., pp. 46–51.

[33] Aubrey, "Idea of the Education of a Young Gentlemen," quoted in Wood, *Life and Times*, p. 50; Gibbon, *Autobiography*, pp. 36, 40.

[34] Wood, *Strephon's Revenge*, p. 6; Knox, *Works*, p. 163; both quoted in *University in Society*, ed. Stone. Stone, ed., *University in Society*, I:52.

[35] Hobbes, *Behemoth, or the Long Parliament*; Strong, *Catalogue of Documents . . . at Welbeck*; both quoted in Stone, ed., *University in Society*, I:54.

[36] Penton, *Guardian's Instruction*, p. 2, repr. in Stone, ed., *University in Society*, I:56.

[37] Ibid., pp. 91–92; Rothblatt, *Revolution of the Dons*, passim; Ward, *Victorian Oxford*; Engel, "Emerging Concept of the Academic Profession at Oxford, 1800–54"; Engel, "From Clergyman to Don."

first time since the Middle Ages, new universities and colleges had begun to appear in England, and to understand the demand and the need for these we have to go back to the eighteenth century, to an England where modern knowledge, science, and technology had perforce to be generated outside the university, and to a Scotland where the university proved, miraculously, capable of absorbing them.

The true recovery in English higher education began in new institutions of teaching and research which owed little to the universities, illustrating the principle that if society cannot get what it wants from an existing institution it will call alternatives into existence. The scientific revolution, for example, owed nothing to the universities apart from the accidents that Trinity College, Cambridge, provided house room for Isaac Newton and that Robert Boyle had his private laboratory at Oxford. The Royal Society of 1662, founded admittedly by Bishop Wilkins and his Wadham College, Oxford, circle, came into existence to supply the deficiencies of the Aristotelian scholasticism still taught by the universities, and the scientific impulse was forwarded in the next century by such bodies as the Royal Society of arts of 1754 "for the encouragement of arts, manufactures and commerce in Great Britain," the Lunar Society of Birmingham whose beginnings as a scientific discussion group can be traced back to 1765, the provincial literary and philosophical societies beginning with Manchester in 1781, and the laboratories of Count Rumford's Royal Institution of 1799.[38] The Dissenters, excluded from Oxford and Cambridge, came in the mid-eighteenth century to found their own public academies, at Hoxton (London), Northampton, Daventry, Warrington, and elsewhere, which were able to produce philosophers and economists like Richard Price and chemists like Joseph Priestley.[39] From the 1820s date the mechanics' institutes, the first pioneered by George Birkbeck, a Glasgow professor, in London in 1824, many of which much later, like those in London, Manchester, and Glasgow, grew into technical colleges and eventually into university institutions.[40] Finally came the founding of new English universities themselves (the first since the abortive foundations of Stamford in 1334 and Durham in 1657), University and King's colleges, London, founded in 1828 and 1829 and joined together as the federal University of London in 1836, and the Anglican University of Durham in 1832. By 1851 no less than twenty-nine general colleges and nearly sixty medical colleges all over the country, including a few in the empire, had affiliated with

[38]Sprat, *History of the Royal Society*; Wood, *History of the Royal Society of Arts*; Jones, *Royal Institution*; Martin, *Royal Institution*; Manchester Literary and Philosophical Society, *Memoirs*; Schofield, *Lunar Society of Birmingham*; Musson and Robinson, "Science and Industry in the 18th Century"; Armytage, *Civic Universities*, chap. 6.

[39]Hans, *New Trends in 18th-Century Education*; Armytage, *Civic Universities*, pp. 123–132, 153–156; MacLachlan, *English Education under the Test Acts*.

[40]Hudson, *History of Adult Education*; Tylecote, *Mechanics Institutes of Lancashire and Yorkshire before 1851*; Harrison, *Learning and Living, 1790–1960*.

London University, most of them founded in the preceding quarter century, the most prolific period of college building since the Middle Ages.[41] Such was the impact of the industrial revolution and a new pullulating urban society on the middle-class hunger for higher education.

The impulse for London University and many other English colleges and medical schools came from Scotland. Henry Brougham, Thomas Campbell, and several other founders of University College were graduates of Edinburgh and Glasgow and thus of the Scottish Enlightenment. The four Scottish universities at St. Andrews, Glasgow, Aberdeen (two separate colleges), and Edinburgh had suffered, if anything, a worse decline than their English counterparts and, despite the boisterous efforts of post-Reformation educational reformers like Andrew Melville, nicknamed "the Blast," they had become, and to some extent remained down to the nineteenth century, little more than secondary schools for a poverty-stricken society which, though it valued education to the extent of providing a village school in every parish by the Act of 1696, could not afford a full array of grammar schools.[42] Yet its very poverty proved a blessing to higher education and encouraged it during the eighteenth century to pioneer a new kind of university which combined teaching and research in a way that anticipated the modern university. Eighteenth-century Scotland also pioneered new disciplines that gave it some claim to be the birthplace of the modern physical and social sciences.

The new system began with a typically Scottish device for saving money, first tried by Andrew Melville in late sixteenth-century Glasgow and St. Andrews but not widely adopted till the eighteenth century. This was the substitution for the traditional "regent masters," the general tutors each of whom covered the whole syllabus, of a smaller number of professors responsible for single disciplines. The establishment of separate chairs of mathematics, medicine, astronomy, natural philosophy (physical science), moral philosophy (social science), law, humanity (classics), and so on, had an almost magical effect on the advancement of knowledge.[43] The specialist professors, men like Colin Maclaurin, Newton's pupil and professor of mathematics at nineteen; Joseph Black, chemist and patron of James Watt of the steam engine, in medicine; Francis Hutcheson, David Hume, and Dugald Stewart in philosophy; William Robertson in history; Adam Smith in moral philosophy which he interpreted broadly enough to found the university discipline of economics; and his pupil John Millar in law, whose work under Smith enabled him to supply the economic interpretation of history—all developed their subjects to a level that made Scotland the

---

[41]Harte and North, *World of University College London, 1828–1978*; Huelin, *King's College London, 1828–1978*; Armytage, *Civic Universities*, pp. 171–176.

[42]Scotland, *History of Scottish Education*, chap. 11.

[43]Ibid., pp. 144–149.

advance guard of the European intellectual enlightenment. Scottish medical education and its offshoots in biology and chemistry became proverbial, and "the Scottish historical school of philosophy," which invented, among other organizing concepts, the evolutionary scheme of mankind's development from hunting and food gathering to settled agriculture and the metal-using civilizations, was in effect the mother of modern social sciences.[44] Although the original momentum did not last, and "the democratic intellect" faded for a time in the nineteenth century,[45] the Scottish professorial system with its emphasis on the advancement of knowledge in departmental disciplines had a profound effect elsewhere, notably in the new universities of England and the United States. By an almost accidental internal metamorphosis the university in Scotland, not the most prosperous or economically progressive of societies, had adapted itself more appropriately to the needs of the modern world.

THE GERMAN TRANSFORMATION AND ITS BEMUSED ADMIRERS

The German university went through a similar transformation in the nineteenth century and, also for reasons that owe more to accident than to real understanding of what was being imitated, had more influence than the Scots on the worldwide dispersion of the research ideal. The new German idea of the university owed nothing to Scottish example. It was provoked into existence by the French Revolution and Napoleon's defeat of Prussia at Jena in 1806. Germany, before Napoleon, was as fragmented as medieval Europe, and its many universities, almost one for every state and independent city, had a similar function: to provide in the absence of a single political authority a unifying intellectual link for its wandering scholars and students. Some eighteenth-century universities, notably Göttingen and Halle, had pioneered the teaching, in German rather than in Latin, of a peculiarly German philosophy of Platonic idealism, an organic view of society and the state which opposed the atomic individualism of the French Revolution.[46]

When the university at Halle was suppressed by Napoleon and appealed to King Frederick William III to restore it elsewhere, he replied: "Das ist recht! Das ist brav! Der Staat muss durch geistige Kräfte ersetzen, was er an physischen verloren hat." ("That's right! That's fine! The state must re-

---

[44]Rendall, ed., *Origins of the Scottish Enlightenment, 1707–76.*
[45]Davie, *Democratic Intellect.*
[46]Scott, *Wilhelm von Humboldt and the Idea of a University*; Van de Graaff, "Federal Republic of Germany," p. 15; Ashby, "Future of the 19th-Century Idea of a University," pp. 3–17.

place by intellectual powers what it has lost in material ones.")[47] And so he appointed Wilhelm von Humboldt to a post in the Ministry of the Interior to reform the Prussian education system and to found the University of Berlin. Humboldt, brother of the famous scientist, had studied at Göttingen and saw the university as the moral soul of society, "the summit where everything that happens directly in the interest of the moral culture of the nation comes together . . . where learning in the deepest sense of the word may be cultivated."[48] To ensure the purest and highest form of knowledge (*Wissenschaft*), absolute freedom of teaching and learning (*Lehrfreiheit* and *Lernfreiheit*), was central to the ideal. But *Wissenschaft*, often translated as "science," was not, as came to be thought later, the research-oriented and especially the natural science suited to an industrial Germany that did not yet exist. It was not a thing but a process, an approach to learning, an attitude of mind, a skill and a capacity to think rather than a specialized form of knowledge:

> It is not a matter of ensuring that this or that should be learnt, but that in the process of learning the memory must be exercised, the intellect sharpened, the faculty of judgment corrected, the moral feeling refined. Only thus will the skill, the freedom, the power be attained, which are necessary to take up any profession from free inclination and for its own sake—and not to keep body and soul together.[49]

Wissenschaft, far from denoting natural science, lay much nearer to the traditional humanism inherited from the medieval university, reborn once again in the form of the Platonic idealism represented by Berlin's first professor of philosophy, Hegel. Hegel raised medieval dialectic into the motive force of history, driven by the dialectical spiral of thought which embodied itself in human institutions culminating in its most perfect form, the state.[50] So "pure" was *Wissenschaft*, and so far from practical knowledge or applied science, that, for example, German medical professors were not allowed to treat patients, and engineering and other technologies were excluded from the universities until the very end of the nineteenth century and had to be taught in new institutions, the *Technische Hochschule* (technical college or high school) and the *Gewerbe Institut* (trade school), both established from the 1820s onward in Prussia and in other German states to meet the demand for engineers and skilled technicians for the developing German economy.[51]

Yet such was the flexibility of the university as an institution and such the internal logic of its development that, despite rather than because of the

---

[47]Scott, *Wilhelm von Humboldt*, p. 7.
[48]Cowen, trans., *Humanist without Portfolio*, p. 132.
[49]Scott, *Wilhelm von Humboldt*, p. 15.
[50]Ibid., pp. 12–16.
[51]Lundgreen, "Differentiation in German Higher Education."

Humboldtian ideal, the German university became the embodiment of the specialized research-oriented ideal and the model for the progressive system of higher education in other advanced societies. This happened in much the same way as in eighteenth-century Scotland, through the device of the specialized, single-discipline professor whose whole prestige and promotion came to depend on single-minded dedication to the advancement of his subject. Professors like Liebig in chemistry, Wundt in experimental psychology, and Ranke in history established the fame of the German universities as the leading centers of research. According to Joseph Ben-David,

> By about 1860 the original four faculties of theology, philosophy, law and medicine, comprising just about all higher knowledge existing at the beginning of the century, had been transformed beyond all recognition. A host of new disciplines had found their place within the loose frame of the faculties, none of which—with the exception of theology—seems to have been averse to incorporating new fields.[52]

On the contrary, given the structure of the German university, built around the autonomous chair holder (*Ordinarius*) with his private research institute and his acolytes (the *Privatdozent* and research students), it was easier to proliferate new professorships and new disciplines or subdisciplines than to expand old ones by appointing to second and third chairs. Indeed, in the second half of the century the system may have become counterproductive as the creation of new disciplines, each with its own chair, became more difficult and slowed down, and the rigidly separate and isolated research institutes, each under the personal control of a single professor, may have discouraged new blood, innovation, and competition.[53]

There can be no gainsaying, however, the enormous success of German higher education in the nineteenth century, whether in terms of the proliferation of disciplines, the founding of new universities and technical and teacher training colleges, or the explosion in student numbers (from about 13,000 in 1850 to 64,657 in 1914), so much so that there were, down to the end of the empire and into the Weimar Republic, recurrent complaints about the oversupply of graduates.[54] The students, drawn originally from the educated elite of high government officials, the clergy, and the professions, and to a smaller extent from the landlords and the old bourgeoisie of artisans and shopkeepers, were intended mainly for the state bureaucracy, the church, and the professions. As time went on, however, they were drawn increasingly from the business class and from the new lower middle

---

[52]Ben-David and Zloczower, "Universities and Academic Systems in Modern Societies," p. 49.

[53]Cf. Titze, "Enrollment Expansion and Academic Overcrowding in Germany"; Jarausch, "Social Transformation of the University."

[54]Titze, "Enrollment Expansion"; 1850 figure from Craig, "Higher Education and Social Mobility in Germany," p. 109; 1914 figure calculated from Ben-David, *Fundamental Research and the Universities*, p. 40.

class of middle-ranking government officials and other white-collar workers and the lesser professions and schoolteachers, and they went less into law and theology in preparation for the state administration and the church and more into science and engineering, medicine, and other vocational subjects, even when they intended to work as public employees, as nearly two-thirds of them did.[55]

The state, especially the Prussian state, and from 1871 the imperial state, played the leading role in the development of the German university, as founder and financier, as employer of the professors who were state officials, and as potential employer (along with the church, the state schools, local government, and the largely state-controlled professions) of most of the graduates.[56] *Lehrfreiheit* and *Lernfreiheit* were, paradoxically, guaranteed by the state, which thus had a psychological leverage on both professors and students and an expectation of loyalty and patriotism in which, down to 1918 and, in some instances, 1933 and beyond, it was not disappointed.

The German model of the modern, progressive, research-oriented university which came to be admired and emulated all over the world was not quite what it seemed. Those who imitated it, notably the British, the Americans, and the Japanese, borrowed very selectively, without always understanding what they were taking. If the university was a flexible institution that could change in the hands of its incumbents while its name reassured them that it remained substantially the same, in nothing was this so true as in the migration of the European, and more specifically the German, model abroad.

The British borrowing, despite the Victorians' deep admiration for and even envy of most things German, from philosophy and history to chemistry and engineering, was fairly modest. Although all the new English universities and university colleges adopted the professorial system, they did so more because of Scottish influence via London than of German influence,[57] and British professors never had the same independence and private research institutes as did their German counterparts, nor were they civil servants appointed and paid by the state. In the English system the professor was primus inter pares, and his departmental lecturers were colleagues, not his unpaid assistants like the *Dozent*, and the students stayed put instead of wandering from university to university as the Germans did. The German example was used by reformers like the Oxford and Cam-

[55]Ben-David, *Fundamental Research*, p. 40; 64.3 percent of university and *Technische Hochschule* students studied science, engineering, agriculture, and medicine, only 21.2 percent, humanities, and 14.5 percent, law. See Craig, "Higher Education and Social Mobility," p. 110.

[56]McClelland, "Professionalization and Higher Education in Germany."

[57]Armytage, *Civic Universities*, pp. 171–175; Harte and North, *World of University College London*, p. 10; Huelin, *King's College London*, chap. 1.

bridge commissioners of the 1850s to advocate a strong professoriat,[58] but their purpose was mainly to aid a strong university as a counterpoise to the fissiparous colleges, and Oxbridge professors remained powerless compared with the collectively organized college fellows.[59] Research certainly revived in both new and old universities in late nineteenth-century Britain, owing more to indigenous causes, including the internal logic of disciplinary progress and the demands of the new industrial society, than to German example, though the advocates of reform made good use of the latter.[60]

The German model was most self-consciously admired and followed in the United States, with the least Germanic of results. Nothing could be further from the German state-controlled and -financed university than the buccaneering, free-market system of American higher education in the nineteenth century, where any educational entrepreneur could open a college anywhere and teach whatever the student customers were prepared to pay for.[61] Even the older foundations, like Yale, Harvard, and Princeton, which had originated to provide general education for denominational ministers and "Christian gentlemen," were acutely aware of the market in which they operated,[62] whereas the state colleges, originating in the Morrill Land Grant College Act of 1862, were consciously geared to meeting the local demand for instruction in agriculture and the mechanical arts "in order to promote the liberal and practical education of the industrial classes in the several pursuits and professions of life."[63] The greatest of them, Ezra Cornell's university at Ithaca, New York, expressed the American ideal of higher education perfectly: "an institution where any person can find instruction in any study."[64] What most American colleges provided in the middle decades of the nineteenth century, however, was a general education in a range of liberal arts and sciences, a tradition that, quite unconsciously, was a modernized version of the medieval trivium and quadrivium. It is a tradition that American higher education has maintained, quite different from the more specialized "honours" degrees of Britain and Europe, down to the present day in the liberal arts college and in the

---

[58]*Report of the Royal Commission on the University of Oxford, 1852*, p. 94; Engel, "Emerging Concept of the Academic Profession," pp. 330–335; Armytage, *Civic Universities*, pp. 199–200.

[59]For the difference between the two traditions of English university teaching, the dominance at Oxbridge of the college fellows and that at other universities of the professors, see Perkin, *Key Profession*, esp. pp. 14–16.

[60]Cf. Sanderson, *Universities and British Industry, 1850–1970*, esp. chaps. 2–7; Armytage, *Civic Universities*, pp. 233–234.

[61]Ashby, *Any Person, Any Study*; Clark, "United States."

[62]Ben-David, *Centers of Learning*, pp. 59–60.

[63]Morrill Land Grant College Act, 7 U.S.C. 304, July 2, 1862, sec. 4.

[64]Cornell, *Cornell University Register, 1869–70*, p. 17.

"college" tier of the university, with the four-year general training for life and the professions which is the envy of other less prosperous and expensive systems.[65]

Yet, surprisingly, the Americans in that age and down to the interwar period had an inferiority complex about their higher education when they compared it with European and especially German education. This feeling related specifically to advanced professional training and to scientific research, for both of which Americans sent their most promising students to Europe. In many ways they were misled:

Aspiring Americans who visited Germany and returned with the phrase "scientific research" on their lips compounded this phrase from elements of German theory and practice which had very different contexts in their original habitat. The German ideal of "pure" learning, largely unaffected by utilitarian demands, became for many Americans the notion of "pure science," with methodological connotations which the concept had often lacked in Germany. The larger, almost contemplative implications of *Wissenschaft* were missed by the Americans, who seem almost always to have assumed that "investigation" meant something specifically scientific.[66]

Mistaken or not, the American belief that a college could not be a university unless a considerable part of its resources was devoted to specialized research had an immense impact on American higher education, both on its very un-Germanic organization and on its contribution to the advancement of knowledge. To that prize academic snob, Abraham Flexner, who endlessly belittled the greatest academic achievement of his countrymen, the democratization of higher education, "a university is essentially a seat of learning, devoted to the conservation of knowledge, the increase of systematic knowledge and the training of students well above the secondary level," and in achievement of this goal almost all American universities were behind the great European universities.[67] The graduate school was not only "the most meritorious part of the American university"; it was the only part that justified the name of university.[68] Such thinking (of which Flexner, writing in 1930, was merely the residuary legatee) led, in 1876, to the foundation of what he considered to be the first true university in the United States, the Johns Hopkins, with its pioneering graduate courses and its outstanding medical school.[69] Competition forced Harvard, Yale, Columbia, the state universities of Michigan, Wisconsin, California, and a great many more to set up or improve their graduate schools in order to

---

[65]Ben-David, *Centers of Learning*, pp. 59–64, 78–87; Clark, *Higher Education System*, chap. 2, esp. pp. 49–53.

[66]Veysey, *Emergence of the American University*, p. 127.

[67]Flexner, *Universities*, pp. 230, 178–179.

[68]Ibid., pp. 42, 73.

[69]Ibid., pp. 73, 86.

claim the status of full university.[70] Fortunately, none of these universities gave up their undergraduate teaching—on the contrary, Johns Hopkins developed an undergraduate program to compete with theirs—and so the top echelon of American universities developed a two-tier system of "college" and "university," undergraduate and graduate stages, which in its systematic organization and size, particularly at the upper level, went beyond anything existing in contemporary Europe.[71] The German influence on American higher education, except for the pedantry of some branches of research, notably in the social sciences, was wholly beneficial, but it was the influence of a Germany that never existed except in the minds of its admirers.

German influence upon Japan was still more deliberate but just as distorted. After the Meiji restoration of 1868 the Japanese revolutionary government consciously and selectively borrowed from the West what its officials felt was most needed to modernize the country and defeat the barbarians at their own game: "Dutch" (meaning general Western) learning, British and American technology, a German and Austrian constitution, French primary education, and German higher education.[72] The latter suited the Japanese admirably because they saw in Germany a similarly authoritarian government and society in which the higher education system was state controlled and had been adapted to the production of bureaucrats, professional men, and engineers for a state-led program of political, military, and economic development. The new Japanese universities, which replaced the Confucian Hanko schools for the samurai warrior-officials of the feudal period, deliberately followed the German model, with faculties of law, medicine, science, and philosophy, the chair system with an authoritarian professor supported by his lecturer-assistants and research students as the basic unit of academic organization, and, at least in the early stages, an emphasis on moral education and the formation of character as well as on scientific research.[73] The prime minister, Ito Hirobumi, told the graduating class at the Imperial University of Tokyo in 1886:

The only way to maintain the nation's strength and to guarantee the welfare of our people in perpetuity is through the results of science. . . . Nations will only prosper

---

[70]Ibid., pp. 73−85; Veysey, *Emergence of the American University*, chap. 3.

[71]Ben-David, *Centers of Learning*, pp. 108−113.

[72]Aso and Amano, *Education and Japan's Modernization*; National Institute for Educational Research, Tokyo, "Modernization of Education in Japan," passim; Ministry of Education, Science and Culture, *Japan's Modern Educational System*, pp. 14−23; Nagai, *Higher Education in Japan*; Kobayashi, *Society, Schools and Progress in Japan*; Perkin, "Britain and Japan."

[73]National Institute for Educational Research, Tokyo, *Research Bulletin*, pp. 15−16, 21−22, 35−40; Bartholomew, "Japanese Modernization and the Imperial Universities, 1876−1920," pp. 251−271.

by applying science. . . . If we wish to place our country on a secure foundation, insure its future prosperity, and make it the equal of the advanced nations, the best way to do it is to increase our knowledge and to waste no time in developing scientific research.[74]

The German research-oriented university seemed to be the ideal model for Japanese higher education.

In practice, the Japanese system could not have been more different from the German. The Japanese could not conceive of *Lehrfreiheit* and *Lernfreiheit* and closely controlled what was taught in the state universities. The concept of *Wissenschaft*, of pure learning or science for its own sake, was a luxury they could not afford, and the emphasis was entirely on practical disciplines and applied science.[75] Engineering, which the German university hived off to the *Technische Hochschule*, was an integral part of the Japanese university almost from the beginning, and the great University of Tokyo was founded by the amalgamation of the Tokyo Kaisei Gakko for law, physics, and literature with the Tokyo Medical School in 1877 and the Imperial College of Engineering in 1886.[76] German professors of medicine, as we have seen, were not allowed to treat patients and general practitioners were not allowed access to university hospitals and their research facilities, whereas in Japan both these practices were actively encouraged. The faculties were not self-governing units but were under the control of the central university administration.[77] The Japanese chair system was quite different: professors did not have individual research institutes; there was often more than one chair per discipline; there was no position of unpaid *Privadozent*; and the salaried lecturer-assistants were colleagues rather than subordinates and often went drinking with the professor, something unheard of in Germany. In the traditional Japanese joke, it was not a chair but a sofa, and a very convivial one at that, in line with Japanese in-group loyalty.[78] Students did not, as in Germany, migrate from one university to another for periods with the best teachers; instead, they competed fiercely to get into the best university and to stay there until graduation and the almost guaranteed career with a connected government department or business firm. The Japanese university was far more concerned than the German with turning out civil servants, factory engineers, and practicing doctors rather than professional research scientists, and such research as it produced was geared to the immediate needs of industry and the state.[79]

[74]Quoted in Bartholomew, "Japanese Modernization," p. 254.
[75]Ibid., pp. 254–259.
[76]National Institute for Educational Research, *Research Bulletin*, pp. 36–40.
[77]Cummings and Amano, "Changing Role of the Professor."
[78]Wheeler, "Japan," p. 129; Bartholomew, "Japanese Modernization," p. 264.
[79]Bartholomew, "Japanese Modernization," passim.

The Japanese still criticize themselves for a lack of interest in pure research, as witnessed by their small number of Nobel prize winners as compared with Sweden, Britain, the United States, and Germany,[80] though it can scarcely be supposed that their lack of innovation in science has held back their technological and economic progress, in which they have shown themselves to be the most tirelessly innovative competitors in the world.

Japanese imitation of the German university, then, was so highly selective as to transform the institution to suit their very different society and national purposes while retaining little more than the name.[81] They were doing much the same as the British and the Americans—and, we might add, as the French, the Scandinavians, the Russians, and many other bemused admirers who emulated the German style—in adapting to their own situations and needs what they took, usually mistakenly, to be the most important features of the German success story. This process illustrates once again the infinite flexibility of the university and its adaptability to changing times and places.

THE AXIAL INSTITUTION OF MODERN SOCIETY

History is at its weakest and least persuasive when it comes to dealing with the recent past and the "specious present," the contemporary scene that has always gone by before we come to examine it. The reason is that historians need hindsight to work their conjuring trick of explaining the past in terms of what happened next or what came of it in the end. But since they also claim, not the ability to forecast the future, but the capacity not to be surprised by it, they have to exercise the most difficult feat of historical imagination: to view the present, or the very recent past which flies away from us so fast, with the same detachment as they examine medieval or ancient history.

The expansion of higher education since 1960, a worldwide phenomenon in all the advanced and developing countries, so recently a thing of joy to most though by no means all academics—"Bliss was it in that dawn to be alive / But to be young was very heaven"—already in the depressed and shrinking 1980s belongs to history. So, too, do the labels that optimistic observers applied to that euphoric period: the age of expansion, the Robbins

---

[80]Arimoto, "Beikoku no Daigaku Kyojushijo no Tokushitsu," p. 28. (I am indebted to Professor Yoshihito Yasuhara of the Research Institute for Education, Tokyo, for a translation of this reference, and to Professor Arimoto for supplying it.)

[81]Although all Japanese universities were state institutions on the German model until 1917, the private sector was always important; it grew from 24.1 percent of all students in higher education in 1880 to 59.1 percent in 1930 and 77.4 percent in 1975 (Ichikawa, "Finance of Higher Education," p. 45).

era, higher education as investment, the age of the masses, and postindustrial society.[82]

The most illuminating of these labels was the last, Daniel Bell's postindustrial society. In relation to higher education it contains or implies four connected ideas:

1) that the codification of theoretical knowledge is the "axial principle" of modern society;
2) that "the class of knowledge workers," the educated, professional elite, are therefore the increasingly central or directing social group;
3) that the key to social, economic, and political progress is to extend advanced education to as many people as can benefit from it;
4) that the higher education system is the "axial structure" and the university (together with the research institute where it is separate) is the "axial institution" of modern society.[83]

It is not necessary to go all the way with Bell's analysis to accept and use the insights contained in his theory. The information explosion, the communications revolution, the electronic global village, automated production, computerized administration, and the threat of high technology warfare and universal destruction have all been generated in the past hundred years in the laboratories of universities and research institutes of the kind developed first in Germany and raised to a still higher power in Britain, America, Soviet Russia, and elsewhere, and they have not suddenly ceased to exist with the oil crisis, world inflation, and depression. The men and women who originate, improve, and service these developments are increasingly trained in universities, or in other institutions of higher education which are universities in everything but name.[84]

These axial institutions, though some of them, as in Britain, the United States, and Japan, are technically private organizations, are too important to the prosperity and the survival of society to be left to their own autonomous devices, and they are increasingly brought under the direct or indirect control of the central government.[85] Since they are increasingly expensive

---

[82]For references, see Perkin, *Professionalism, Property and English Society since 1880*, pp. 3–6; Gouldner, *Future of the Intellectuals and the Rise of the New Class*, pp. 94–101.

[83]Bell, *Coming of Post-Industrial Society*, pp. 116–117.

[84]For the many different institutions that make up different national systems of higher education, see Clark, *Higher Education System*; for the concept of "academic drift" by which nonuniversity institutions tend to seek, and frequently attain, university status, see Pratt and Burgess, *Polytechnics*; for "The Diversification of Institutions" in the period 1860–1930 see Jarausch, ed., *Transformation of Higher Learning, 1860–1930*, Part 2, articles on England, Russia, Germany, and the United States, by Rothblatt, Alston, Lundgreen, and Herbst, respectively.

[85]Cf. Clark, "Co-ordination," pp. 82–83.

institutions, and become more so as they move from small numbers of students to large, from elite to mass higher education, control over them can readily be exercised through government funding which already operates in the public sector and, in the private sector, begins like the Greeks bearing gifts and ends with the triumphal entry of the Trojan horse.[86] In the world economic crisis of the 1980s higher education everywhere is on the defensive against the tightening screw of state control. The traditional autonomy of the university, which has served it well since the twelfth century, is increasingly at the mercy of the bureaucratic corporate state, which, in collaboration with the huge impersonal bureaucracies of private and public industry and the "corporations" of employers' associations, trade unions, and the professions, intervenes more and more in the life of the individual citizen and spends more and more of his money.[87]

In this less optimistic version of postindustrial society, in which, it may be argued, the bureaucrat replaces the capitalist as the dominant social type and chief exploiter, higher education as the axial structure for the production of bureaucrats and technocrats becomes itself a corporate bureaucracy which the state seeks to control and which, like other corporate bureaucracies, seeks in turn to maintain its autonomy and to persuade the state to provide it with ever larger public resources. Those who think that the great private universities of the market-oriented American system are immune from this corporate development should contemplate the large federal research grants they solicit and receive and the fact that it pays Ivy League universities to maintain permanent offices of professional lobbyists in Washington.[88]

Bureaucratic corporatism is not merely the environment in which the university has to operate. It infiltrates higher education itself and tends to set up an opposition between the academics and the full-time administrators. Internal bureaucratization has proceeded less far in those national systems, such as Italy, West Germany, and Britain, with a tradition of academic and especially professorial control,[89] and furthest in the United

---

[86]For the enormous dependence of the higher education systems in West Germany, France, Sweden, the U.K., U.S.A., and Japan on government finance by the 1960s and early 1970s, see Van de Graaff et al., *Academic Power*, pp. 210–211, tables A.2, A.3. In the late 1970s and early 1980s governments everywhere began to use their financial power to constrain and even reverse university expansion.

[87]Cf. Clark, "Coordination," pp. 76–84. There is now an enormous literature on corporatism. See, inter alia, Shonfield, *Modern Capitalism*, esp. pp. 161–163, 220–233; Marris, ed., *Corporate Economy*; Harris, *Competition and the Corporate State*; Hannah, *Rise of the Corporate Economy*; Middlemas, *Politics of Industrial Society*.

[88]Discussed at Conference on Organizational Participation and Public Policy, Center of International Studies, Princeton University, September 1981.

[89]Note, however, the role of Italian, German, and British academics in government and on quasi-governmental bodies (QUANGOs), which increases the external involvement of the universities in the corporate state.

States, where academic administration in some universities is becoming a full-time career with its own promotion ladder "alongside and above" the academic.[90] Yet bureaucratization is not absent anywhere, and it is accelerated especially at the national level by the state's financial squeeze on higher education and the increased leverage it gives to those who are the channels of scarce resources. In Britain, for example, the University Grants Committee, once the buffer between the government and the universities guaranteeing academic autonomy, has become a bureaucratic instrument of state control and of compulsory redundancies in subjects such as the social sciences, minority languages, archaeology, and theater studies which party politicians and their allies, the "co-opted academics," consider "undesirable."[91] In the so-called public sector, where the state, through the local authorities, owns and directly controls the institutions, the polytechnics and other colleges are already run by a hierarchy of full-time administrators to whom the lecturing staff are formally subordinate.[92]

The bureaucratic model with its hierarchy of officials whose goals and values have little or nothing to do with the advancement of knowledge, whose very existence is predicated on the preference for predictable routine procedures rather than on the pursuit of innovation and the unexpected, encroaches with every increase of state funding and state control. The universities everywhere have never been so large, so numerous, so central to the functioning of a knowledge-based society and, despite financial cuts, so well endowed with public funds. Yet as research institutions they have never before been in so much danger of losing the sine qua non of their existence, the freedom to pursue their primary function of conserving, advancing, and disseminating independent knowledge. There is a growing and mistaken belief among politicians and "co-opted academics" that the mutually fertilizing union of teaching and research is an unnecessary myth which can be abandoned without adverse effects on either, as in the English polytechnics. The university thus faces the classic dilemma between freedom and starvation. It may well be tempted to say, with Patrick Henry,

---

[90]The hierarchy of nonteaching deans and other administrators, paid more than full professors and now often appointed at a younger age, is a comparatively recent development in American universities. It strikes European visitors, accustomed to professorial domination and control, as unusual. In Britain, however, a similar but not quite equivalent development is occurring in the nonuniversity (especially polytechnic) sector. See Becher, Embling, and Kogan, *Systems of Higher Education*, pp. 71–72.

[91]The classic example of the transition from the state as benevolent patron to the state as wielder of financial control is that of the British University Grants Committee, traditionally described as the "buffer" against state interference with university autonomy and a "pressure group *for* the universities," but now better described as the channel of "prescriptive guidance" *by* the government, including "guidance," backed by financial constraints, on academic redundancies and the closure of named departments. See Becher, Embling, and Kogan, *Systems of Higher Education*, pp. 21–22, 52–57.

[92]See ibid., pp. 71–72.

"Give me liberty or give me death." It may not be so fortunate in the answer as Patrick Henry was.

As teaching institutions the universities face another dilemma: the incompatibility between the demands of elite and mass higher education. Postindustrial society, whether benevolently meritocratic or malignantly bureaucratic, demands contradictory goals from the university. On the one hand, modern society needs an elite of highly trained specialists, bureaucrats, technocrats, scientists, engineers, communications experts, and so on. On the other hand, it faces a demand for mass higher education partly because the expanding service sector cannot be wholly met from the children of the traditional privileged classes, partly because the talents required by the new elites are widely dispersed throughout society, but mainly because a knowledge-based society and science-based industries and services require a far wider dissemination of training and skill than in any previous age. This situation reflects a wider dichotomy in society at large, between the minority of upwardly mobile meritocrats and the majority of students and potential students who, however fast they run in terms of education and qualifications, find themselves standing in the same place.[93] Mass higher education, although a lofty and worthy ideal, has a self-defeating tendency which increases rather than decreases discontent. When full-time higher education, as at the beginning of the twentieth century, was confined to 1 or 2 percent of the student age-group in most advanced countries, even when only twenty years ago between 4 and 7 percent completed courses of higher education in western Europe and Russia (though 10 percent in Britain and 17 percent in the United States),[94] the university and college-educated could expect to monopolize the elite careers in society (at least in government service and the professions, since business then set less store by advanced qualifications). Now that 14 to 16 percent of the age-group take degree courses in western Europe, 35 percent or more in Japan, Canada, and Australia, and no less than 49 percent in the United States,[95] higher education is no longer the guaranteed door to high status.

The heady plans of the expansionist 1960s which were intended to make the university the instrument of egalitarian social mobility seem to have gone awry. The expansion of student numbers has benefited all classes but has disproportionately benefited the already privileged classes so that the number of students from the "lower stratum," although larger, is still far

---

[93]See Dore, *Diploma Disease*; Collins, *Credential Society*. For the transition from mass to elite higher education see Trow, "Problems in the Transition from Elite to Mass Higher Education," pp. 51–101.

[94]Robbins Committee on Higher Education, *Report*, p. 44.

[95]Bowen, "Measurements of Efficiency," table 7, p. 145. The Japanese figure (38% including higher vocational schools in 1977) has been corrected from Cummings et al., eds., *Changes in the Japanese University*, p. 64.

smaller, proportionately, than the class they represent.[96] (The proportion of women has on the other hand considerably increased, to a third or more in Britain, Europe, and Japan, and near equality in France, Canada, Australia, and the United States.)[97] Meanwhile, far from satisfying the demand even from the middle classes for greater access to the elites, the expansion has sharply reversed expectations, frustrated hopes, and increased student discontent. Although the worst excesses of student protest have subsided to a worried vocationalism or sullen resignation, the upheavals of the 1960s and early 1970s helped to disillusion governments and taxpayers with the promises of higher education and gave a welcome excuse to those who wished to tame the university and bring it under control. In less than twenty years the popular image of the university has moved from that of the vanguard institution of modern society to that of a ghetto for the alienated young which, according to some politicians, causes more trouble than it is worth.

Yet postindustrial society needs the university as much as the university needs postindustrial society. A knowledge-based society depends on both the constant advancement of knowledge and the reproduction of knowledgeable people as much as industrial society depended on the constant investment of capital and the reproduction of skilled managers and workers. Nor does this mean merely the production of pure research and the reproduction of a highly educated elite. That would be to go back to the late medieval "intellectual estate" which helped to destroy the medieval world order or, still worse, to go forward to the year 2033 in Michael Young's *Rise of the Meritocracy* (1958) in which the educated elite finally provoke the unmeritorious majority to rise and destroy them. To adapt Francis Bacon's aphorism about money in early capitalist society, we may say that in postcapitalist society "knowledge is like muck, not good unless it be spread." A knowledge-based society requires educated people throughout its social range, not only because they are needed at all levels to carry on its work but because knowledge is an end as well as a means, a good in itself to be enjoyed by all who want it. Just as wealth in a preindustrial or industrial society does not consist in money or even in goods and services but in the men and women who produce them—so that a people with few or no resources but plenty of resourcefulness, like the ancient Greeks, the eighteenth-century British, or the Germans and the Japanese after World War II, can create wealth with miraculous speed—so in a postindustrial society knowledge and knowledgeable people are both the means to the end and the end itself. Man does not live by bread alone but by the dangerous yet life-giving fruit of the tree of knowledge.

---

[96]Kerr et al., *12 Systems*, Appendix, table 9, p. 175.
[97]Ibid., table 8, p. 174.

In such a society the university becomes the axial institution not merely in the sense of producing an educated elite but in that of providing knowledge for the whole community. This unique and infinitely flexible institution can adapt itself to one final role, that of "the community service station," in W. H. G. Armytage's phrase.[98]

This concept is not a new idea or a blueprint for the utopian future but a product of history, and it is at least a hundred years old. From 1867 James Stuart, a Cambridge tutor, gave public lectures on gravitation to audiences mainly composed of schoolmistresses in Liverpool, Manchester, Sheffield, Leeds, and Nottingham; he dreamed of "a sort of peripatetic university of professors which should circulate in the big towns." Out of Stuart's lectures grew the Cambridge University Extension Movement of the 1870s.[99] In 1903 A. L. Smith, master of Balliol College, Oxford, helped a self-educated man, Albert Mansbridge, to found the Workers' Educational Association (WEA), and four years later another Oxford tutor, R. H. Tawney, began the first WEA university tutorial classes in Rochdale and the Potteries.[100] These were the beginnings of the extramural courses that most British universities came to offer, many of them in conjunction with the WEA. In a similar manner, in the United States in the 1920s, Columbia, Harvard, Chicago, Wisconsin, and even Johns Hopkins, to the horror of Abraham Flexner, began to offer University Extension home study courses and enrolled large numbers of part-time and correspondence students, sometimes more numerous than the full-time students.[101] Many other countries followed suit. Since World War II there has been a marked expansion of part-time education, continuing education, *education permanente*, and so on, and the highly successful British Open University has found imitators in the United States, Australia, Japan, and elsewhere.[102]

This development suggests that there is an almost insatiable demand for advanced education both for vocational purposes and for its own intrinsic value, for "second chance" mature students and for those who wish to build on or diversify from their first chance. As Japan has shown, a country cannot have too much education; it is merely a question of the intelligence

---

[98]Armytage, *Civic Universities*, chap. 11, "Community Service Stations, 1898–1930"; he is referring to the new English provincial universities of that period and their role as "a scientific and cultural service station" and not specifically to their adult education function (which he deals with elsewhere in the book), but it is more apt to the latter role.

[99]Armytage, *Civic Universities*, pp. 225–227. Several new universities, and ultimately all civic universities, owed their origin to the Extension Movement, notably Nottingham, Sheffield, and Reading.

[100]Mansbridge, *University Tutorial Classes*; Mansbridge, *Adventure in Working-Class Education*.

[101]Flexner, *Universities*, pp. 128–147, where he pours scorn not only on the home study courses but on the whole "service" function of the university.

[102]See, inter alia, MacArthur, "Flexibility and Innovation," pp. 102–104.

and the political will to make productive and pleasurable use of it. And as the Americans have shown, perhaps most spectacularly in the University of California, it is not impossible to combine in one flexible university both elite and mass higher education, a community service station that combines both the advancement of knowledge and Ezra Cornell's ideal of "an institution where any person can find instruction in any study."

As for corporatism, the universities, whether as elite institutions or as community service stations, will have to learn to play the bureaucratic game. There are in fact two kinds of corporatism, state or authoritarian corporatism in which collaboration is imposed upon the nongovernmental corporations from the top, Pahl and Winkler's "fascism with a human face," and spontaneous democratic corporatism, Colin Crouch's "bargained corporatism," in which the corporations, perhaps more responsive to their memberships, cooperate voluntarily with the state and bargaining becomes a two-way process.[103] In Margaret Thatcher's Britain and Ronald Reagan's America it seems that bargained corporatism is in retreat before a paradoxically authoritarian revival of the nineteenth-century free market, but in a world of large-scale organization and giant corporations, both business and trade union, it is still there and inescapable. To survive in this world of corporate dinosaurs, higher education may become a dinosaur itself, a bureaucratic giant that can hold its own in the Darwinian struggle. If the university is indeed the axial institution of postindustrial society, it has an evolutionary advantage beyond its rivals: it is a dinosaur with wings.

THE HISTORICAL PERSPECTIVE ON HIGHER EDUCATION

The four phases or turning points in the development of higher education discussed in this paper are meant to illustrate the kind of insight the historical perspective can offer. Perspective is a useful metaphor in the context of higher education which, in Burton Clark's "slight exaggeration," we may view as "a social structure for the control of advanced knowledge,"[104] always remembering, of course, that advanced knowledge means different things to different societies. Disciplines, after all, are only different ways of looking at the same reality. Higher education, like other social structures, looks very different from a political, an economic, an organizational, a sociostructural, a cultural, a scientific, or a policy-oriented point of view, but it is still the same structure and all these perspectives share a common reality. They might all come together, let us say, in a holograph, a

---

[103]Pahl and Winkler, "Coming Corporatism"; Crouch, *Politics of Industrial Relations*, pp. 186–196.

[104]Clark, "Coordination," p. 58.

three-dimensional model projected in light—the light of informed intelligence—and viewable from any direction.

What is there left for the historian to add to this comprehensive, multi-perspective view? Only, it would seem, the time dimension. Change and stability through time, as we have seen in the introductory essay, are the historian's chief concerns. Yet the dimension of time is different in kind from other dimensions, and the perspective it offers is of a different order. It embraces a reality that is not the same as that viewed from other perspectives, but it changes with the depth of focus back to where the lines finally converge, not at the present synchronic horizon but at the point of origin in the more or less distant past.

To take a concrete example, London may look very different from a political, an economic, a sociological, an organizational, a cultural, a scientific, or a policy point of view, but at least it is still London as we know it. For a historian, London is at once the contemporary city and the city of Churchill, Dickens, Boswell, Nell Gwyn, Shakespeare, Chaucer, William the Conqueror, the Emperor Hadrian, and Boadicea, snaking back through time to its pre-Roman origins, at which point it disappears from view. And at every stage in that backward view, the city, though immensely different in size of population, physical shape, and even function, possesses all the aspects, suitably transmuted and scaled down, studied by the contemporary analytical disciplines, whose perspectives would be just as valid then as now. What, then, is the peculiar contribution of the historian? Simply that he can see each successive London in focus and can explain how it was related to the one that came after. Most pertinently, he can show how contemporary London is a palimpsest of all the previously existing Londons, and how one cannot really understand its present form and structure without understanding how it encapsulates and epitomizes the legacies of all the Londons that have gone before.

In the same way one cannot understand the contemporary university without understanding the very different concepts of the university which have existed at different times and different places in the past. Not because the contemporary university is simply the automatic product of an inevitable evolution; far from it, history shows that accidents and unintended consequences of past choices and decisions are often more important than conscious plans and policies. But the hopes and aspirations, expectations and values, of the past are built into the current concept of what a university is and should be far more concretely than the bricks and mortar, libraries and laboratories, which are their visible and outward sign. Even the deficiencies and dissatisfactions of the past are embodied in our present structures: the new universities, polytechnics, *Technische Hochschulen*, folk high schools, liberal arts colleges, and, in some countries, research institutes and academies. They all are expressions of past discontents with the traditional university which may or may not have been resolved by them. And the most powerful but immaterial value of all, the pecking order of institutions in every country, the prestige of Oxford and Cambridge in Britain, of the *grandes écoles* in France, of the Moscow and Leningrad academies in Russia, of the Ivy League and a handful of major state campuses in America, of Tokyo, Kyoto, and Waseda in Japan, and so on, is, as Martin Trow's contribution to this volume shows (chap. 5), a self-perpetuating legacy from the past which defies all efforts at egalitarian reform. Despite the increasing power of the state and its determination in most countries to bring the higher education system under its control, the university can still tap deep reserves of academic pride, alumni loyalty, and student preference. These assets can turn the tables on state policy and, for example, provoke "academic drift" and the demand of state-created alternative institutions for university status.

History is not a straitjacket. It cannot constrain the present generation. The most important thing about a received tradition is not its age but the fact that people now choose to accept it. As its changing concept, purposes, and functions over the past 800 years have shown, the university is capable of enormous change and also of stubborn resistance to change. Although the historian of higher education has no crystal ball, no magic mirror, no videotape recording of the future, he does have one tiny piece of folk wisdom to offer his co-workers in the field: if you want to know where you are going, it helps to know where you have been.

BIBLIOGRAPHY

Arimoto, Akira. "Beikoku no Daigaku Kyojushijo no Tokushitsu" ("A Study of the Characteristics of the Academic Marketplace in the United States"). In *Daigaku Ronshu 6*. Research Institute for Higher Education, Hiroshima University, 1978.

Armytage, W. H. G. *Civic Universities: Aspects of a British Tradition*. London: Ernest Benn, 1955.

Ashby, Eric. "The Future of the 19th-Century Idea of a University." *Minerva 6* (Autumn 1967):3–17.

———. *Any Person, Any Study: An Essay on Higher Education in the United States*. New York: McGraw-Hill, 1971.

Aso, Makoto, and Ikuo Amano. *Education and Japan's Modernization*. Tokyo: Ministry of Foreign Affairs, 1972.

Aubrey, John. "The Idea of the Education of a Young Gentleman." Aubrey MSS, Bodleian Library, Oxford.

Bartholemew, James R. "Japanese Modernization and the Imperial Universities, 1876–1920." *Journal of Asian Studies* 37 (February 1978):251–271.

Becher, Tony, Jack Embling, and Maurice Kogan. *Systems of Higher Education: United Kingdom*. New York: International Council for Educational Development, 1977.

Bell, Daniel. *The Coming of Post-Industrial Society*. Harmondsworth, Middlesex: Penguin Books, 1976.

Ben-David, Joseph. *Fundamental Research and the Universities: Some Comments on International Differences*. Paris: Organisation for Economic Co-operation and Development, 1968.

———. *Centers of Learning: Britain, France Germany, United States*. New York: McGraw-Hill, 1977.

Ben-David, Joseph, and Abraham Zloczower. "Universities and Academic Systems in Modern Societies." *European Journal of Sociology* 3 (1962):45–84.

Bowen, Howard. "Measurements of Efficiency." *In* Clark Kerr, John Millett, Burton R. Clark, Brian MacArthur, and Howard Bowen, *12 Systems of Higher Education: 6 Decisive Issues*. New York: International Council for Educational Development, 1978.

Carr-Saunders, A. M. and P. A. Wilson. *The Professions*. Oxford: Clarendon Press, 1933.

Charlton, Kenneth. *Education in Renaissance England*. London: Routledge and Kegan Paul, 1965.

Clark, Burton R. "Coordination: Patterns and Processes." *In* Clark Kerr, John Millett, Burton R. Clark, Brian MacArthur, and Howard Bowen, *12 Systems of Higher Education: 6 Decisive Issues*. New York: International Council for Educational Development, 1978.

———. "United States." *In* John H. Van de Graaff, Burton R. Clark, Dorotea Furth, Dietrich Goldschmidt, and Donald F. Wheeler, *Academic Power: Patterns of Authority in Seven National Systems of Higher Education*. New York: Praeger, 1978.

———. *The Higher Education System: Academic Organization in Cross-National Perspective*. Berkeley, Los Angeles, London: University of California Press, 1983.

Cobban, A. B. *The Medieval Universities: Their Development and Organization*. London: Methuen, 1975.

Collins, Randall. *The Credential Society*. New York, London: Academic Press, 1980.

Cornell, Ezra. *Cornell University Register, 1869–70*. Ithaca, New York.

Cowen, Marianne, trans. *Humanist without Portfolio: An Anthology of the Writings of Wilhelm von Humboldt*. Detroit: Wayne State University Press, 1963.

Craig, John E. "Higher Education and Social Mobility in Germany." In *The Transformation of Higher Education, 1860–1930*, ed. Konrad H. Jarausch. Stuttgart: Klett-Kotta, 1982.

Crouch, Colin. *The Politics of Industrial Relations*. London: Fontana/Collins, 1979.

Cummings, William K., and Ikuo Amano. "The Changing Role of the Professor." In *Changes in the Japanese University*, ed. William K. Cummings, Ikuo Amano, and Kazuyuki Kitamura. New York: Praeger, 1979.

Curtis, M. *Oxford and Cambridge in Transition*. London: Oxford University Press, 1959.

Davie, G. E. *The Democratic Intellect: Scotland and Her Universities in the 19th Century*. Edinburgh: Edinburgh University Press, 1964.

Dore, Ronald A. *The Diploma Disease: Education, Qualifications and Development*. London: Allen and Unwin, 1976.

Elton, G. R., ed. *The Reformation*. Vol. 2 of *The New Cambridge Modern History*. Cambridge: Cambridge University Press, 1958.

Engel, Arthur. "The Emerging Concept of the Academic Profession at Oxford, 1800–54." In *The University and Society*, ed. Laurence Stone, Vol. I. Princeton: Princeton University Press; London: Oxford University Press, 1975.

———. "From Clergyman to Don: The Rise of the Academic Profession in 19th-Century Oxford." Ph.D. diss., Princeton University, 1975.

Flexner, Abraham. *Universities: American, English, German*. London: Oxford University Press, 1930.

Gibbon, Edward. *Autobiography*. Oxford: World's Classics, 1907.

Gouldner, Alvin. *The Future of the Intellectuals and the Rise of the New Class*. London: Macmillan, 1979.

Hannah, Leslie. *The Rise of the Corporate Economy*. London: Methuen, 1976.

Hans, N. A. *New Trends in 18th-Century Education*. London: Routledge and Kegan Paul, 1951.

Harris, Nigel. *Competition and the Corporate State: British Conservatives, the State and Industry, 1945–64*. London: Methuen 1976.

Harrison, J. F. C. *Learning and Living, 1790–1960*. London: Routledge and Kegan Paul, 1961.

Harte, Negley, and John North. *The World of University College London, 1828–1978*. London: University College London, 1978.

Haskins, C. H. *The Rise of the Universities*. Ithaca: Cornell University Press, 1957.

Hexter, J. H. "The Education of the Aristocracy during the Renaissance." In *Reappraisals in History*, ed. J. H. Hexter. London: Longmans, 1961.

Hobbes, Thomas. *Behemoth, or the Long Parliament*. London: Cass, 1969.

Hudson, J. W. *History of Adult Education*. London, 1851.

Huelin, Gordon. *King's College London, 1828–1978*. London: King's College London, 1978.

Ichikawa, Shogo. "Finance of Higher Education." In *Changes in the Japanese University*, ed. William K. Cummings, Ikuo Amano, and Kazuyuki Kitamura. New York: Praeger, 1979.

Japan. Ministry of Education, Science and Culture. *Japan's Modern Educational System: A History of the First Hundred Years*. Tokyo: Government of Japan, 1980.

———. National Institute for Educational Research, Tokyo. "Modernization of Education in Japan." *Research Bulletin*, no. 17 (October 1978).

Jarausch, Konrad H. "The Social Transformation of the University: The Case of Prussia, 1865–1914." *Journal of Social History* 12 (Summer 1979):609–636.

Jarausch, Konrad H., ed. *The Transformation of Higher Learning, 1860–1930*. Stuttgart: Klett-Kotta, 1982.

Jones, Henry Bence. *The Royal Institution*. London, 1871.

Kearney, Hugh. *Scholars and Gentlemen: Universities and Society in Pre-Industrial Britain*. London: Faber, 1970.

Kerr, Clark. "Comparative Effectiveness of Systems: Unknown and Mostly Unknowable." *In* Clark Kerr, John Millett, Burton R. Clark, Brian MacArthur, and Howard Bowen, *12 Systems of Higher Education: 6 Decisive Issues*. New York: International Council for Educational Development, 1978.

Kerr, Clark, John Millett, Burton R. Clark, Brian MacArthur, and Howard Bowen. *12 Systems of Higher Education: 6 Decisive Issues*. New York: International Council for Educational Development, 1978.

Knox, V. *Works* (1780). Vol. IV.

Kobayashi, Tetsuya. *Society, Schools and Progress in Japan*. Oxford: Pergamon Press, 1976.

Leff, Gordon. *Medieval Thought from St. Augustine to Ockham*. Harmondsworth, Middlesex: Penguin Books, 1958.

Lundgreen, Peter. "Differentiation in German Higher Education." In *The Transformation of Higher Learning, 1860–1930*, ed. Konrad H. Jarausch. Stuttgart: Klett-Kotta, 1982.

MacArthur, Brian. "Flexibility and Innovation." *In* Clark Kerr, John Millett, Burton R. Clark, Brian MacArthur, and Howard Bowen, *12 Systems of Higher Education: 6 Decisive Issues*. New York: International Council for Educational Development, 1978.

McClelland, Charles E. "Professionalization and Higher Education in Germany." In *The Transformation of Higher Learning, 1860–1930*, ed. Konrad H. Jarausch. Stuttgart: Klett-Kotta, 1982.

McConica, James. "Scholars and Commoners in Renaissance Oxford." In *The University in Society*, ed. Laurence Stone. Vol. I. Princeton: Princeton University Press; London: Oxford University Press, 1975.

MacLachlan, H. *English Education under the Test Acts*. Manchester: Manchester University Press, 1931.

Manchester Literary and Philosophical Society. *Memoirs*. Manchester, 1785.

Mansbridge, Albert. *University Tutorial Classes: A Study in the Development of Higher Education among Working Men and Women*. London: Longmans, 1913.

———. *An Adventure in Working-Class Education: The Workers' Educational Association, 1903–15*. London: Longmans, 1920.

———. *The Older Universities of Oxford and Cambridge*. London: Longmans, 1923.

Marris, Robin, ed. *The Corporate Economy*. Cambridge: Harvard University Press, 1971.

Martin, T. *The Royal Institution*. London: Longmans, 1948.

Middlemas, Keith. *The Politics of Industrial Society*. London: Deutsch, 1979.

Morgan, Victor. "Cambridge University and 'The Country,' 1560–1640." In *The University in Society*, ed. Laurence Stone. Vol. I. Princeton: Princeton University Press; London: Oxford University Press, 1975.

Murray, Alexander. *Reason and Society in the Middle Ages*. Oxford: Clarendon Press, 1978.

Musson, A. E., and E. Robinson. "Science in Society in the 18th Century." *Economic History Review*, 13 (1960):222–244.

Nagai, Michio. *Higher Education in Japan*. Tokyo: Tokyo University Press, 1971.

Pahl, R. E., and J. T. Winkler. "The Coming Corporatism." *New Society*, 30 October 1974:72–76.

Penton, S. *The Guardian's Instruction*. London, 1868. Repr. in *The University in Society*, Laurence Stone. Vol. I. Princeton: Princeton University Press; London: Oxford University Press, 1975.

Perkin, Harold. *Key Profession: The History of the Association of University Teachers*. London: Routledge and Kegan Paul, 1969.

———. "Britain and Japan: Two Roads to Higher Education." *Higher Education Review* (Summer 1981):7–16.

———. *Professionalism, Property and English Society since 1880*. Reading: University of Reading Press, 1982.

———. "On Being a Centipede: An Arthropod's Eye-View of Philosophy of History." In *Philosophy of History and Contemporary Historiography*, ed. William H. Dray, David Carr, Theodore Jeraets, Fernand Ouellet, and Hubert Watelet. Ottawa, Canada: Ottawa University Press. In Press.

Potter, G. R., ed. *The Renaissance*. Vol. 3 of *The New Cambridge Modern History*. Cambridge: Cambridge University Press, 1961.

Pratt, John, and Tyrrell Burgess. *Polytechnics: A Report*. London: Pitman, 1974.

Rashdall, Hastings. *The Universities of Europe in the Middle Ages*. London: Oxford University Press, 1957.

Reeves, Marjorie. "The European University from Medieval Times, with Special Reference to Oxford and Cambridge." In *Higher Education: Demand and Response*, ed. W. R. Niblett. London: Tavistock, 1969.

Rendall, Jane L., ed. *The Origins of the Scottish Enlightenment, 1707–76*. London: Macmillan, 1978.

Robbins Committee on Higher Education. *Report*. London: HMSO, Cmnd. 2154 (October 1963).

Rothblatt, Sheldon. *The Revolution of the Dons*. Cambridge: Cambridge University Press, 1981.

Sanderson, Michael. *The Universities and British Industry, 1850–1970*. London: Routledge and Kegan Paul, 1972.

Schofield, R. E. *The Lunar Society of Birmingham*. London: Oxford University Press, 1963.

Scotland, James. *The History of Scottish Education*. Vol. I. London: London University Press, 1969.

Scott, D. F. S. *Wilhelm von Humboldt and the Idea of a University*. Durham: University of Durham, 1960.

Shonfield, Andrew. *Modern Capitalism: The Changing Balance of Public and Private Power*. London: Oxford University Press, 1965.

Southern, R. W. *Medieval Humanism and Other Studies*. Oxford: Blackwell, 1970.

Sprat, Thomas. *History of the Royal Society*. London, 1667.

Stone, Laurence. "The Educational Revolution in England, 1560–1640." *Past and Present*, no. 28 (July 1964):41–80.

———. "The Size and Composition of the Oxford Student Body, 1580–1909." In *The University in Society*, ed. Laurence Stone. Vol. I of 2 vols. Princeton: Princeton University Press; London: Oxford University Press, 1975.

Strong, S. A. *Catalogue of Documents . . . at Welbeck*. London, 1903.

Titze, Hartmut. "Enrollment Expansion and Academic Overcrowding in Germany." In *The Transformation of Higher Learning, 1860–1930*, ed. Konrad H. Jarausch. Stuttgart: Klett-Kotta, 1983.

Trow, Martin. "Problems in the Transition from Elite to Mass Higher Education." In *Policies for Higher Education*. General report of the Conference on Future Structure of Post Secondary Education. Paris: Organisation for Economic Cooperation and Development, 1974.

Tylecote, Mabel. *The Mechanics Institutes of Lancashire and Yorkshire before 1851*. Manchester: Manchester University Press, 1951.

United Kingdom. Royal Commission on the University of Oxford. *Report*. In *The University in Society*, ed. Laurence Stone. Vol. I. Princeton: Princeton University Press; London: Oxford University Press, 1975.

Van de Graaff, John H. "The Federal Republic of Germany." *In* John H. Van de Graaff, Burton R. Clark, Dorotea Furth, Dietrich Goldschmidt, and Donald F. Wheeler, *Academic Power: Patterns of Authority in Seven National Systems of Higher Education*. New York: Praeger, 1978.

Van de Graaff, John H., Burton R. Clark, Dorotea Furth, Dietrich Goldschmidt, and Donald F. Wheeler. *Academic Power: Patterns of Authority in Seven National Systems of Higher Education*. New York: Praeger, 1978.

Veblen, Theodore. *The Higher Learning in America* (1918). Repr. New York: Hill and Wang, 1965.

Veysey, Laurence R. *The Emergence of the American University*. Chicago and London: University of Chicago Press, 1965.

Waddell, Helen. *Peter Abelard*. London: Constable, 1933.

———. *The Wandering Scholars* (1927). Repr. Harmondsworth, Middlesex: Penguin Books, 1954.

Ward, W. R. *Victorian Oxford*. London: Frank Cass, 1965.

Wheeler, Donald F. "Japan." *In* John H. Van de Graaff, Burton R. Clark, Dorotea Furth, Dietrich Goldschmidt, and Donald F. Wheeler, *Academic Power: Patterns of Authority in Seven National Systems of Higher Education*. New York: Praeger, 1978.

William of Conches. *Philosophia Mundi*, c. 1145.

Wood, Anthony. *Life and Times of Anthony Wood*. ed. Andrew Clark. Oxford: Clarendon, 1894.

———. *Strephon's Revenge*. London, 1918.

Wood, H. T. *History of the Royal Society of Arts*. London: Murray, 1913.

2. THE POLITICAL VIEW

Maurice Kogan

The political scientist contemplating higher education has cause to be both frustrated and exhilarated. He must be frustrated because political science has had "very great difficulty in achieving even a limited number of tested generalizations,"[1] creating "a paradigmatic jungle."[2] As a discipline, it has passed through many stages, each of which has opened up valuable perspectives; these perspectives, however, cannot easily be synthesized into a holistic view of the place of politics. There have been decisive shifts from static descriptions of formal institutions toward analysis of action, from conceptualizations of structure toward analysis of function. Yet these many strands of concern, emerging and receding and some emerging again over the past seventy years, themselves indicate the central importance of the political dimension in the life of societies. Just as the modes, processes, and institutions for political action are various, so also are the preoccupations of those who study them.

FOCI AND BOUNDARIES OF THE POLITICAL VIEW

The politics of the world inhabited by higher education are sui generis. There is, perhaps, no other zone of activity where the foci of concern are so public and the modes of operation so private. Yet higher education, even if idiosyncratic, is a testing ground for many of the more important generalizations about social life. In no other area is there so powerful a tension between institutions that are internationally visible and are expected to respond to the highest norms of moral accountability while at the same time being deeply grounded in the rights of individuals to pursue personal and small-group action. Higher education institutions also have particularly diffuse goals which affect their internal and external relations, offering analysts the opportunity to probe the relationships between the nature of goals and patterns of power and authority. This sector also abounds with

---

[1]Mackenzie, *Politics and Social Science*, p. 77.
[2]The phrase is that of James S. Coleman at the Los Angeles seminar.

relationships between institutions dominated by professionals and environments dominated by the politics of irrationality.

If, or perhaps because, political science is an eclectic assembly of descriptions, propositions, and paradigms, the political science of higher education is not well developed. Its literature is profuse, particularly in the United States,[3] but much writing has been devoted to the administration of the system. A few pioneer political analyses of a descriptive kind, often elegantly performed, stand out among the many writings.

Stated briefly, the political science contribution must mainly concern itself with the processes and institutions through which issues emerge and conflicts are presented, negotiated, and converted into policies. The political scientist is thus centrally concerned with the processes as they are conditioned by distributions of power and authority and by the resulting distributions of influence. Political science encompasses not only the formal descriptions of institutions but the analysis of action. Increasingly, too, political scientists are concerning themselves with policy studies, with the impact of policies, and the processes of their implementation.

This definition does not conflict with those of leading contemporary authorities such as Baldridge[4] and Archer.[5] In his studies of the internal politics of universities Baldridge assumes that "complex organizations can be studied as major political systems, with interest group dynamics and conflicts similar to those in the city, state and other political situations." His political model depicts several stages centering in the university's policy-forming processes, because it is they that commit the organization to goals, set strategies, and determine long-range destinies. Baldridge thus describes some of the modes of politics: how inactivity and conflict are normal, participation fluid, authority limited, and institutions fragmented into interest groups. In a later work Baldridge and his colleagues,[6] while sustaining the importance of conflict, bargaining, and negotiating, put more emphasis on structural developments as well as on environmental factors. In doing so they match well Margaret Scotford Archer's definition: "the attempts (conscious and organized to some degree) to influence the inputs, processes, and outputs of education, whether by legislation, pressure group or union action, experimentation, private investment, local transactions, internal innovation or propaganda."[7]

Archer contributes much to the conceptualization of the subject area. In

---

[3]Three bibliographies of higher education are Gove and Floyd, "Research on Higher Education Administration and Policy"; Harman, *Research in the Politics of Higher Education, 1973–1978*; and Hastings, *Study of Politics and Education*.

[4]Baldridge, *Power and Conflict in the University*; Baldridge et al., *Policy Making and Effective Leadership*.

[5]Archer, *Educational Politics*.

[6]Baldridge et al., *Policy Making and Effective Leadership*.

[7]Archer, "Educational Politics"; Archer, *Social Origins of Educational Systems*, p. 29.

her writing we find a great deal about how change occurs through hassle and bargaining, processes that she conceptualizes through the powerful metaphors of exchange theory. She is also interested in the ways in which negotiation, manipulation, and other processual elements lead to the formation of structures, or the phenomenon of "morphogenesis." Inchoate and messy political interactions do indeed produce, cause changes in, and are themselves affected by structure. The routinization of process as a substantive factor in its own right is also noted by Baldridge.

Taking Heed of the Other Disciplines

With any of these definitions it is obvious that political analysis, though it has a life of its own, cannot explain effectively unless it uses concepts drawn from other disciplines. It thus reciprocates the needs of economists and sociologists for "political" explanations of economic and social phenomena. The political scientist, in searching for determinants of policy outcomes,[8] asks "Why?" and must then act as a summative historian. The political scientist, through policy studies concerned with impact, asks "With what result?" but in so doing he must join others to find the answer. (See chap. 8, below.) Once into the questions of what causes what, and with what result, he is in territory inhabited by sociologists, economists, and psychologists.

The international phenomenon of higher education's expansion in the 1960s is an example. Sociologists may chart changes concerning access to higher education and try to analyze their effect on social stratification. Economists may link changing rates of recruitment to manpower demands, the opportunity costs of satisfying them, and the different styles of planning—the latter to be shared with the political scientist—invoked by attempts to change participation rates. The political scientist, however, would be concerned with how the issue emerged in the first place and through what processes of negotiation and institutional changes conclusions were reached. Were demands for access presented as political demands? If so, who presented them and what characteristics did the presenters possess? Through what mechanisms did demands for more skilled manpower reach the policy system? The determinants of these processes are to be found, perhaps in the economy, perhaps in demography, perhaps in movements of social structure, but certainly in changes in social consciousness—"the ideology of expansion." The mechanisms of the emergence of the issue, the creation of coalitions, the ways in which decisions to allocate were made, might all have affected the outcome. And expansion changed the authority and power patterns of higher education. The state found itself footing larger bills. It encountered wider constituencies. The institutions could no longer coast along as the educators of elites and as the

---

[8]Premfors, *Politics of Higher Education*.

repositories of specialized knowledge; they had to face demands for more application and relevance and for access from groups whose credentials were social rather than academic. It is not clear that the expansion of higher education was overtly intended to change the distribution of power in society at large, but, to some extent, power shifts have surely been a consequence of it.

Take other themes and the same point of interdisciplinary dependence emerges: if the political scientist seeks to determine how assumptions about the creation of knowledge affect power and authority, he must draw on the sociology of knowledge. If he wants to assess and explain the behavior of bureaucrats and the nature of negotiation over public expenditure, he must acknowledge debts to the economists for recent developments in "formal" political theory[9] which convert officials into economic men. Indeed, one economist[10] has claimed that the metaphors of incrementalism, polyarchy, and partisan mutual adjustment, so powerful in policy studies, derive at one or other remove from the analog of the market. But of course the market analog is itself a bundle of social-psychological assumptions.

The political scientist must, then, lean on neighboring disciplines. The currency of politics is influence, power, and interest. The political dimension is essentially procedural, processual, and constitutional, and rather less devoted to the substantive contents of policy issues, although it is concerned with the impact of substance on process. These are the categories too easily described, taken for granted, or treated as an explanatory stopgap, rather than closely specified and given analytic weight. Can political scientists move beyond the telling descriptions by C. P. Snow, David Lodge, Malcolm Bradbury, and Mary McCarthy? The answer is "yes." Literature illuminates political behavior. It may even reinforce it. Political science, by contrast, attempts to apply systematic analysis and derive concepts about the interactions embodied in political action.

We can, at this point, state more confidently what political science is able to do which other contributions cannot. First, in its public institutional form, it describes the structures and processes of decision making and policy formation. Berdahl describes the University Grants Committee but he also describes the quality of the political processes in which the committee was engaged.[11] Second, in its newer policy studies format, political science is concerned with the way in which process affects outcomes and how outcomes then help reshape processes and structures.[12] Third, it is concerned with the distribution of power and authority, and here it must

---

[9]Ibid.

[10]Conversation with Robert Levin, deputy director, Congressional Budget Office, 16 June 1976.

[11]Berdahl, *British Universities and the State.*

[12]Premfors, *Politics of Higher Education.*

tap into the rich literature of elites, of pluralism, of neopluralism, and the like.[13] For example, in a study of higher education in California political science would be concerned with the relationship between the professoriat and campus administrations, student unions, and systemwide politics. To take an example in Britain, political science would be concerned with the extent to which higher education has created its own elite of co-opted academics who are both part of the broad-based invisible college and yet part of an elite that helps make allocations. Fourth, it is concerned with analyzing, through normative theory, the moral base and the assumed consequences of key relationships in society and in the polity, such as power, authority, consent, and participation. Such analyses enable us to ask questions as to how far and in what senses a university may be regarded as democratic. What authority does a president or a vice-chancellor or a rector have over a tenured professor?

It will be readily seen that, along with the phenomena being observed, the lines of analysis become more diffuse and more complex. The inner life of institutions becomes more complex as they attempt to reconcile collegiality, managerialism, popularism, and many, often conflicting, forms of participation. Within the larger network of higher education, institutions and their component disciplines find themselves encountering deeper and more complex issues as policymakers and academics reach a period of dissent and possible conflict associated with contraction.[14] The phenomena of political co-optation, alliance making, and networking of otherwise diffuse groups in the policymaking process implied by corporatism are the phenomena that compel simple models of public authority, bureaucracy, and institutionalism to yield to far more subtle forms of interpretation.

The usefulness of the political perspective is best explored by considering how it compares with the economic. Economic pressures or the arguments of economists may influence the expansion or contraction of higher education. Economic constraints affect policy. But there is a large agenda for the political science of higher education, stimulated by economic approaches to the same issues.

Economists can advise policymakers on how to distribute their preferences among competing ways of spending money. Obvious alternatives are between higher education and industrial training or unemployment benefits or between one form of higher education and another. A price may be put on the preferences. Such a calculation would have the enormous advantage of being stated in monetary terms, and these we all understand. But the political scientist does not deal in money. Preferences need to be stated in voting patterns or in descriptions of virtually unaggregatable interest-group behavior. The economic market makes choices visible

[13]Whitaker, *School Governing Bodies.*
[14]Premfors, *Politics of Higher Education.*

through prices sought and paid. By contrast, underlying demands may not even be presented through the political system, which detects unstated wants poorly. When choices are stated they appear as amorphous bundles of policies presented by politicians to electorates at infrequent intervals. The process of presentation is determined by incalculables and the irrationalities of the main actors as much as by a series of advantages and disadvantages which can be weighed and assessed. Given these imprecisions the political scientist may be at a loss to give scientific explanations of why almost every country in the world "decided" to expand higher education. He can only look to fairly gross evidence of the expressions of social preferences.

The central problem of how individual preferences are ascertained and aggregated is, therefore, common to both the political scientist and the economist:

Politics works through a structure of influence. Influence provides for the political scientist a concept somewhat analogous to money for the economist, a measure of the individual's or group's capacity to secure desired results. One can "buy" a desired policy or decision with influence just as one can buy a desired good with money. . . . Opportunity cost is as valid a concept in politics as in economics; it refers to the debts which a politician must often incur in order to secure support for his policy, through such ways as supporting other persons' policies in exchange or of modifying his original aims to suit their wishes or of forfeiting some of his influence or "credibility" among those who dislike the policy in question. Of course there is a major difference—money can be measured and influence cannot.[15]

Yet if the economists can calculate predictively and thus clarify choices, the political aspects cannot be wished away simply because they lack precision. Political analysis needs the economists to structure and explain and predict those elements of decision making which are tied to resource management. An attempt to link different forms of financial sponsorship to the behavior of universities may be found in Gareth Williams's essay (chap. 3, below). He demonstrates well how the organizational structures and behaviors described by Clark (chap. 4, below) can be linked both to the kind of behavior analyzed through economics and to the processes and policy outcomes that are the business of political science. Such formulations may lead to a much needed synopsis of the calculable and the less calculable.

There is, again, the issue of economics as a determinant, taken up by Premfors. "How can variation in policy contents, operationalized as expenditure levels, be accounted for? Are political or socio-economic variables most important in determining outputs?"[16] Premfors records that we seem

[15]This section leans heavily on Self, *Econocrats and the Policy Process*, esp. Part II, "Political and Economic Choice," p. 104.

[16]Premfors, *Politics of Higher Education*, p. 3.

to be far removed from clarity when describing the relative importance of politics and economics. Output studies show that political variables have relatively less direct and independent impact than socioeconomic variables, but economics does not account for much either. And, in higher education, "all things considered, the analysis of financial constraints does not seem to contribute to the explanation of policy developments."

Enough has been said to expound upon the dependence on and complementarity to the political and to the other social science perspectives of higher education. It is now time to illustrate some of the issues in more detail.

ISSUES AND PERSPECTIVES AT THREE LEVELS

Which issues should a fully developed political science of higher education tackle? We may group the issues in either of two ways: by themes that emerge at all or at most points in the political system, or by levels of the system. Since the texture of the politics of higher education changes markedly as we move from one level to another, I take the analysis through three levels: the intrainstitutional; the relationship between institutions and the larger polity; and politics at the center. General points are illuminated by reference to the situation in the United Kingdom.

The Institution as a Political System

At the institutional level Baldridge's political model may be taken as the major descriptive datum. Largely one of a self-governing collegium, the depicted system is affected by the routines imposed on it by its own needs for self-maintenance and by the changes incurred through its connection with external environments.

Although students have often acquired a powerful position in the past,[17] the modern university has essentially been a guild of professors. The recent "triumph of participation" means that a client group, the students, has broken into the guild government of the university. The students themselves, having modified or even broken some institutions, institutionalize their positions and modes of action through unionization, a process apparently now encountering some student resistance in Sweden. Junior academics have also acquired a larger place. There is, too, wider access to policymaking, both informal and formal, for the academic trade unions. There has also been a breakup of "pure" academic criteria for the admission of students, often urged prescriptively rather than argued analytically,[18] so

---

[17]Ashby and Anderson, *Rise of the Student Estate in Britain.*
[18]For example, Berube, *Urban University in America.*

that academic norms have been compelled to defend themselves against desiderata forced on the academy by external interest groups. Higher education has also become "legalized" through the introduction of appeal procedures and rights of appeal to due process which have turned some universities into veritable forensic play schools, as professors sit on appeal panels and measure their judgments against what might come to court.

All these changes may be thought of as responses to exogenous influences which have sometimes become internalized and perhaps made stronger by the hospitality shown to them by the university. Together, they have moved institutions away from the predominant style of organized anarchy toward new kinds of interplay in which the academy tries to pull itself together to face statutorily armed power blocs. Academic ritual is joined by newly prescribed rituals which are the legitimation of new forms of due process.

These changes in the environment carry with them changes in internal patterns of governance. Faculties gained power until the 1960s, which was commensurate with the expectations placed upon higher education by the society that succored it. In the United States, however,[19] the power held by presidents of institutions of higher education seems to have been reduced in the face of increasing control by sponsors. It is argued later in this paper that the authority of vice-chancellors in Britain, where the recent government-induced contraction has been drastic, has been enhanced, although at what cost we do not as yet know. At the same time faculty power has now everywhere been reduced commensurately with the growth of the authority of sponsors outside the institutions and with the growth within institutions of administrative technocracy. The shift of power to administrators and deans, not a traditional feature of academe,[20] is partly a result of the need to manage resources that come from more diffuse sources, and partly because academic individuality has to be enjoyed within more accountable procedures and forensically defensible processes.

Individual and group behavior within institutions has been changed by the need to defer increasingly to outside markets. Once expansion was forced to give way to steady state and then to positive contraction, hitherto containable tensions emerged. Those institutions whose goal was individual excellence, or perhaps those that believed they could afford to sit tight, felt able to disagree more openly with others that saw the need to go to the market and to meet the wishes of sponsoring authorities. Individual academic behavior surely came to be far more sensitive to norms being set by outsiders. In some countries, as in Britain, there is, indeed, a conflict of messages reaching the academy. Decisions, recently made, are said to have taken into account both the norms of academic excellence and the needs of Britain's faltering economy and society at one and the same time.

[19]Baldridge et al., *Policy Making and Effective Leadership.*
[20]Premfors, *Politics of Higher Education.*

The different kinds of pressures from outside call for explanation or at least more detailed analysis. Both the rates of change and, by inference, the causes of it, differ from country to country. One reason is tautological: that institutions are subjected to different degrees of control. Those degrees of control vary over time, but there seem to be different political cultures affecting the relationships between the state and its freestanding universities. In both the United Kingdom and the United States, universities are certainly affected by the demands of their sponsors, and these have become intense in Britain in the last few years. Nevertheless, the internal governance of the institution and such key controls as the selection of types of students remain an academic prerogative. In Sweden, in spite of recent moves toward decentralization, state management has been far stronger than in Britain and the United States. Indeed, in promoting decentralization, the Swedish central authorities have imposed certain principles such as "co-determination," allowing external lay groups far more say over the educational life of institutions, as well as about decisions regarding the types of students from which universities may choose.

Working within the environments set up by sponsoring bodies—analogous relationships between state authorities and the trustees of private institutions in the United States might also be described—there are interchanges within the institution itself. Key managerial authority rests with the formal management of institutions. Presidents or vice-chancellors may not be able to appoint staff of their own choice but are always present at the key appointments, and they usually have a veto power. That power is rarely used in overt form but most academics would recognize that the heads of an institution make judgments that are not to be ignored. In many systems the rewards allowed to academics are determined by these individuals. When tenured staff resign from an institution, the head of it has an opportunity to influence changes in the orientation of that part of the institution. Institutional resources—money, buildings, and staff—are again strongly conditioned in their distribution by managerial structures.

At the same time, however, there is the power of the collegia. With them rest the primary academic judgments to which resource decisions must be related. They are, indeed, the key institutional resource, for without active academics securing the reputation of the institution the managers would have nothing worthwhile to manage. There is, therefore, a process of exchange between those who manage and those who provide the main academic outputs of the institutions. They provide the expertise upon which the institution thrives or fails. The institution provides the resources enabling them to perform their academic tasks. Among the academics, acting in collegial forms, negotiation and exchange also occur when they reach collective decisions upon how the management might be advised to distribute its resources. Here, certainly, we may rely upon fictional as well as academic literature for our accounts of exchange, negotiation, and manipulation: C. P. Snow, Malcolm Bradbury, and many others come to our aid. In these exchanges, no doubt, the discussions are not simply about strictly academic issues. The demands for external markets and sponsors, the rewards that they can offer the whole institution, the maintenance of existing systems, and sectional interests are all part of the terms of trade.

If, then, relationships among external sponsorship, internal management, and collegial controls form one web of analysis, a further strain derives from classic normative political theory. What authority does a president or a vice-chancellor have when such varied and subtle conditions of consent hedge it around? At what point are diffused power and influence converted into authority? The concept of participation, too, is given a good run for its money when the concept is urged, and resisted within very different units of government—students vis-à-vis staff, vis-à-vis senior staff, teaching staff vis-à-vis the administration and sponsors.

The generalizations stated above apply to the British experience. The culture of government has, until recently, enabled higher education institutions in Britain to make their own way, once established, on the basis of quinquennial grants, a system that lasted for more than a quarter of a century. British institutions are relatively small. The collegium is more often able to have a stronger purchase on them. The model of the Oxbridge College powerfully pervades the consciousness of those in other institutions and, probably, in Whitehall itself. Until recently, the environment of sponsorship ensured that while government intervention could certainly be decisive, academic continuities were largely protected from it. But as central government has decided on a radical contraction of higher education, to be imposed within a very short period of time, the universities and other institutions have been, willy-nilly, burdened with some of the harshest tasks of managerialism. Councils, the largely lay bodies, and vice-chancellors have been required to enforce drastic reductions, and senates, consisting largely of academics, have been required to join the dialogue of reduction.

Recent changes in higher education policy in Britain give political scientists wide scope for analysis of the internal dynamics of institutions. We have already mentioned the changing patterns of interaction among academics. A second line of analysis is the relationship between vice-chancellors and teaching staff within the institutions.

Vice-chancellors have always had a Janus-like role.[21] They are chief executives formulating and handing out allocative and other decisions, while at the same time, as heads of senates, they are the conveners of collegia. Now they are required to impose cuts, with virtually no option as to the timetable or the scale, and with restricted options of the areas to be selected for cutting or preservation. These central directions impose sub-

---

[21]Moodie and Eustace, *Power and Authority in British Universities.*

stantial changes in the patterns of negotiation and decision making among vice-chancellors, university councils, university senates, heads of departments, and trade unions. Legally, councils can act only after consultation with senates in the establishment or disestablishment of posts. Accordingly, vice-chancellors are required to persuade senates to come into line and accept determinations of which cuts should be made and where, before councils make the final decisions. For the most part, senates, with more or less reluctant acceptance by vice-chancellors, have agreed to "lose" staff by voluntary severances. At the same time the Committee of Vice-Chancellors and Principals and the Association of University Teachers have engaged in negotiations about the amounts of money and the conditions needed to allow for voluntary early retirements or severances. But it is only now, as this account is being written, that the first groups of residual compulsory retirements and redundancies are likely to come before senates and councils; and the collegial mode of senate and vice-chancellor, and of relationships between heads of departments and vice-chancellors, may well be broken by the first hard case.

We might begin by asking what is, in any event, the nature of the authority and power relationships between the vice-chancellor and academics on tenure? They lack many, but not all, of the ordinary sanctions of the manager. And they are often dealing with colleagues (may they also be considered subordinates?) who have substantial power lines outside the institution itself. But once tenurial relationships are broken, new kinds of exchanges begin to take place between vice-chancellors and heads of departments, among the heads of departments themselves, and between heads of departments and tenured members of their departments. There is surely a move away from the organized-anarchy garbage-can models of internal governance toward more deterministic institutional planning, as vice-chancellors and other seniors take stock of what they believe must at all costs be preserved, of what they could reluctantly lose, and what they would be delighted to let go.

Moreover, the cycles of power and authority within an institution begin to move more frenetically. Vice-chancellors have had to gain a surge of authority at a time of cuts, which places them in a contracollegial stance. But presumably all institutions, or at least those that survive, will settle back to a steady state. If so, it may be predicted that collegial patterns will begin to reassert themselves. Equally, heads of departments have had degrees of authority, if in limited terms, vis-à-vis members of their departments.[22] Now, for the first time, they have taken on a classic dimension of management, namely the ability to initiate removal from a post. With all these changes, too, the notion of "sanctuary,"[23] or "privacy,"[24]—the

---

[22]Startup, "Role of the Department Head."
[23]Levy, *Universities and Governance.*
[24]Trow, "Public and Private Lives of Higher Education."

ultimate impermeability of academic institutions from their sponsors—has been broken. From negotiated sponsorship and freedom within that negotiation a more managerial and assertive pattern of authority and power has emerged.

The Institution and the State

The next level of analysis concerns the relationship between the internal running of institutions and the politics of the environment to which they respond. For purposes of discussion we may artificially separate these relationships from the issue of the structure of politics of central authorities and the groups that press upon them.

The main actors include the central authorities; the system through which the central authorities co-opt members of the academic collegium to help them with allocations; the specialized and other interest groups placing demands upon both central and institutional authorities; and the official authorities of the institutions themselves.

The conceptual issues arising from the politics of central-institutional relations are manifold. One version of the relationship, from which I dissent, would place higher education institutions into the role of a subsystem that has purposive linkages of authority and of norm setting with the total system of government. Such a construct might be true in some instances but it has no logical inevitability and it preempts the issue of how far higher education institutions are licensed to be free to set their own norms, or even to be in conflict or tension with the society that sponsors them to be its antibodies.

A second conceptual issue concerns the nature of the macro and micro systems. The normative modes of the different levels are different.[25] So are the patterns of political behavior. At the institutional level academic self-satisfaction is supposed to be all, but it is tempered by the needs and demands of the social and economic market. At the central governmental level, social and economic desiderata dominate policy. The extent to which institutional and central norms are in conflict or are in accord varies with the beliefs of politicians of the time and of the academics whom they sponsor. Politicians have, in the best years of higher education, assumed that the advancement of reflective thought and knowledge also advances social ends. They can equally well take a contrary view. By the same token, if there is normative differentiation, then political behavior also differs at different levels. At the institutional level decision making is primarily negotiative but in uncertain juxtaposition with management. At the center there is more determinedly a hierarchy of objectives and authority to stipulate them. The texture of politics changes at the different levels because the norms are different.

---

[25]Becher and Kogan, *Process and Structure in Higher Education*.

Finally, the organizational issues, taken up by Burton R. Clark (in chap. 4, below) and in many monographs,[26] concern the ways in which coordination is achieved throughout the whole higher education enterprise. Clark has noted the curious alliances between relatively oligarchic professoriats and central authorities and the modes of academic coordination. Robert O. Berdahl,[27] in a pioneering discussion of British universities and the state, depicted both the process of academic co-optation and the essentially hygienic approach to the politics of education entailed traditionally in the workings of British ministries, the University Grants Committee (UGC), and universities. More recently, Premfors, in analyzing the politics of higher education in France, Sweden, and the United Kingdom,[28] has shown how both the French and Swedish systems were among the most centralized in western Europe with the most reputable professors co-opted to the policymaking function of the center. Just at the point in time when the British institutions were becoming more susceptible to central authority, the French reforms of 1968 and the flow of public policies in Sweden in the 1960s and 1970s pushed toward greater decentralization.

Higher education institutions, however, are in a cat's cradle of conflicting pulls and pressures. Paradoxes abound. The Swedish state used central power to simultaneously enforce decentralization and codetermination on higher education, although the degrees of that movement might be open to dispute. This action by the government was regarded by many professors as a way of insinuating trade-union influence at the local level and, with it, participation by nonacademics and students in decision making which would reduce the powers of the professors.

The analyst of authority and power might indeed ask whether a reduction of power at the center, particularly when the state itself is the prime actor in that reduction, necessarily means a reduction of authority and power over the basic units and individuals in higher education. Studies testing whether there is a finite quantum of authority, and whether it simply shifts from one level to another and never quite goes away, would be useful here.

Is there, indeed, a zero-sum game being played out? Some would argue that as more groups have entered the higher education battlefield, and as more of them have achieved the right to participate in decision making, so the amount of authority and power to be distributed increases. In one sense this argument must be valid if one takes the right to be involved in politics to be a substantive benefit per se. From another point of view, however, there is only a certain amount of authority to go around because, in the end, increasing participation does not increase the resources about which con-

---

[26]Clark, *Academic Coordination*; Clark, *Higher Education System*.
[27]Berdahl, *British Universities and the State*.
[28]Premfors, *Politics of Higher Education*.

flict may take place. It must follow, therefore, that if students and non-teaching staff have a bigger say over the distribution of the same resources, academic staff will have a smaller say.

At the higher education level, and referring back to Clark's modes of academic coordination, there is the theme of the co-opted academic (to which more detailed reference is made later). The academic advises governments and shares their decision making concerning the destinies of individual institutions and departments. The notion of co-optation, developed by Philip Selznick,[29] allows for "the process of absorbing new elements into the leadership or policy-determining structure of an organization as a means of averting threats to its stability or existence." Formal co-optation applies when there is a need to establish the legitimacy of authority or the administrative accessibility of the relevant public; informal co-optation occurs when there is a need of adjustments to the pressures of specific centers of power within the community. The conditions under which co-optation arises occur when formal authority fails to reflect the true balance of power within the community. Selznick further hypothesizes that "co-optation which results in an actual sharing of power will tend to operate informally, and . . . co-optation oriented towards legitimization or accessibility will tend to be effected through formal devices." In Britain, as we will see, the most potent forms of co-optation have operated informally, in line with Selznick's hypothesis.

If, then, there is no certainty about the relationships between institutions and the center we may look to some general constructs with which to describe them more acutely. Archer's "unslavish" application of systems theory[30] describes how action may take place through different forms of negotiation applying at different levels. In her view, all such processes involve the exchange and use of resources. Institutions, and their inhabitants, have been able thus far to put a desired expertise into the exchange relationship. If they can no longer negotiate so confidently for resources, statements, or even permanency of tenure, it is because their services are now less valued by their political and financial sponsors.

Other descriptions, including those of co-optation, take up the sense of recent writing about corporatism and networking. They represent government less as an authoritative mechanism than as one in which several groups— including those that receive the impact of decisions—are involved partly to secure legitimacy for what the authorities wish to do, and partly because, without their support, implementation will not take effect.

The British case.—We turn again now to the United Kingdom to consider changes between the center and the institutions. Britain has several distinctive characteristics. Universities are legally private, either existing on

---

[29]Selznick, *TVA and the Grass Roots*, p. 13.
[30]Archer, "Educational Politics."

historic trusts or on a royal charter. Until the late 1960s they received grants that were not completely "free" but were hedged around by a minimum of planning indication. Until the late 1970s universities were still allowed to conduct forward planning within broad guidelines set down on behalf of the central government by the UGC. There has now been a radical change in both policies and in structural relationships. The government has moved away from the Robbins Committee recommendation[31] that all qualified students find a place in higher education. This drift of policy has caused the UGC, at the behest of the Department of Education and Science (DES), to cut drastically both the money and the student planning figures in universities.

We must first ask whether political science can explain the radical break away from "demand-led" to controlled and "expenditure-led" higher education, and with these, the resulting changes in relationships between the center and the institutions. But we are frustrated by the lack of data. It may be assumed that there has been a change in public support for education and with it a reversal of the "expansionist ideology." But it is not clear to which constituency education ministers and the Treasury thought they were responding. The political scientist might spend time analyzing what, if anything, substantiated the ideology of reduction.

A second decision was to redistribute and slightly increase the number of students reading for degrees in some of the hard sciences, engineering, and business studies and, correspondingly, to reduce arts and social sciences. It is not clear whether this decision was determined by rationalistic manpower planning at the center or by ministers' and officials' intuitive assumptions about what society wanted. Certainly, however, some move from rationalistic planning toward heroic ministerial decision making may be inferred.

Other important, but not well-documented, features of the British case are the role of co-optation and the operation of academic elites. The University Grants Committee was required to convert government decisions into allocations to institutions which were then required to make decisions about departments and individual teachers. By acting through the UGC, the government was, in effect, co-opting academics to help with allocative decisions. Academics were required to do two things. First, they were asked to help the national authorities, through the UGC, to make academic decisions that ranked institutions according to academic excellence. This procedure takes place in all academic systems and has done so for a long time. But, second, some academics co-opted to the national authorities, or co-opted more informally, not only ranked institutions in order of merit but also were consulted about the government and the

---

[31]Report of the Committee Appointed by the Prime Minister under the Chairmanship of Lord Robbins, 1961–1963, *Higher Education*, Cmnd. 2154.

UGC's policy decisions. So the UGC consulted the five research councils and such learned groups as the Royal Society. The Royal Society overtly supported the UGC's decision to sustain centers of scientific excellence at the expense of some of the newer and less prestigious and more applied centers of engineering and science. This sponsoring of "best science" and "excellence" by the "best" scientists could be taken, skeptically, to be interest groups protecting their own interests. Heads of research councils, too, were directly consulted regarding which institutions were to be reduced, which were to be left alone, and the criteria to be applied to them. It is, perhaps, difficult to say at what point the co-opted academic ceases to help administer the total system by the application of academic norms and at what point he becomes involved in reductions that are imposed on criteria other than academic. On the face of it, the mode of decision was contra-academic because the criteria being adopted were kept hidden. Academics often have to make allocative and other decisions in secret. It would seem, at the least, that the criteria are expected to be open to challenge and scrutiny. At one time Berdahl[32] could accurately describe British higher education as being both secretive and apolitical, as working in a context when it was thought seemly to leave politics out of it. The process of policymaking was thus made indeterminate. It is still true that the internal but higher politics of higher education in Britain are secretive. But an elite at work has taken co-optation further than ever before.

The British case is thus indicative of the familiar phenomenon of co-optation, even if the procedures displayed paid increasing attention to the state's criteria. It is also an example of the academic elite at work.

In applying a theory of elites or of pluralism to higher education we must take into account its eccentric nature. Higher education embraces institutions and individuals with highly specialized functions which are, themselves, concerned with substantiating elites. It acts in an elite sense in the selection, rejection, confirmation, and extension of knowledge and in determining the access and selection and appointment of academic staff, the stratification of institutions, staff, and students. These functions are predicated on notions of individual excellence and of the collective endorsement by an elite of excellence. Elites are institutionalized through making academic authority routine and conferring it upon a minority of academic leaders. In principle, collegiality might mean that many and even most academics are members of the invisible colleges and serve on allocative committees, appointment boards, research councils, the referee systems of learned journals, and so on. But in all higher education systems the elite transmutes itself from a collegial manifestation to be part of the allocative system of governments.

---

[32]Berdahl, *British Universities and the State.*

One explanation of the working of the elite cannot be sustained. A Marxist interpretation would link the working of the elite to the needs of capital. Industrial leaders, however, protested against the policies of Conservative ministers, policies that would reduce some of the newer universities. Indeed, the word "political" has become too easily expropriated—the vocabulary is easily caught from the main culprits—by those who wish to advance a particular view of recent political and social history. Recent attempts to write theories of the state identify education as an agent of the capitalist beast to which all state activity is devoted.[33]

Politics at the Center

Finally, we come to the nature of national politics of higher education. Here we are concerned with the black box of government—the government as a sponsor, as a legitimizer, along with the interest groups pressing on it—and with other influences upon it such as the press and the individual colleges of practitioners. Relevant phenomena also include markets and unorganized constituencies which, in contrast with interest groups, operate indirectly and more ambiguously as "interests" and "forces" to be interpreted by government.

There is first the question of issue emergence, of how higher education interlocks with the larger political system. We have already rejected the view that it is necessarily a subsystem of the larger political system. There are inputs and outputs between higher education and its sponsoring environments. But the larger system hardly looks to higher education to maintain support for it. The striking degree of autonomy achieved by higher education in most political systems hardly suggests that it is one of the interests that is reduced before allocations are made to it. The autonomy of higher education is supported by beneficial myths that also surround the medical profession: that it is to the social and individual good if institutions are allowed, on the whole, to go their own ways.

We again rely on Premfors for recent discussion on the subject. He found, at the level of central politics, that many commentators have exaggerated the extent to which higher education has become an issue in national politics. In Sweden and France, differences between potential majority coalitions were wider than in Britain (he was writing before the recent cuts). And I might add that there is no stated evidence that party political differences were effective in postwar American history of higher education until the election of a radical conservative government analogous to the one that made the changes, from 1979, in the United Kingdom. In

---

[33]Tapper and Salter, *Education and the Political Order* (their view is somewhat modified and elaborated in *Education, Politics and the State*); Centre for Contemporary Social Studies, *Unpopular Education*.

other words, there is no intrinsic logic that converts higher education into a subset of the larger political system.

As far as interest groups are concerned, the major "corporativist" interest organizations of labor and capital were significantly more involved in the politics of higher education in Sweden than in France or the United Kingdom or in the United States. The politicians and bureaucrats, as well as the interest groups, had more influence, and the place of academics has been significantly weakened in national policymaking. In all countries, and perhaps self-evidently, individual major politicians make a difference: Edgar Faure and de Gaulle on the formulation of the 1968 *loi d'orientation* in France; Harold Wilson and Jennie Lee on the Open University in Great Britain; Olaf Palme on the new student-aid system in Sweden; and Ronald Reagan on reducing federal subsidies to state and private higher education institutions in the United States.

In general terms, Premfors summarizes evidence that policy content significantly shapes implementation. What is at issue defines the area, the principal actors, their principal tools, and their available resources. In higher education, however, he says that "the freedom for action for elites, and even individuals, seems relatively greater than in areas of political salience." In Britain, the expansion seemed to have come out of a quite small group of decision makers. DES officials were long concerned about the pressure building up in the schools, as they qualified more potential students for higher education places. Liberal and expansionist conservative ministers picked up the issue. The trade unions gave only generalized support for the expansion of higher education but made no particularly large issue of it. In Sweden, a powerful coalition of interests, well institutionalized through commissions and the like, saw the new policy in. Even so, we cannot say that higher education is an issue with votes or even constituencies.

If, then, political science continues to struggle with what are the determinants of policy, what constitutes "issueness," and what affects the nature of the impacts of different policies, we are at least left with vocabulary and preliminary concepts with which to make order of our main cases.

The British case.—To complete this descriptive stratification of the issues for the United Kingdom, it is clear that interest groups are not strong. As noted earlier, the institutionalized groups that mediate their influence through the DES impinged on Conservative ministers early in the 1960s and advanced the argument for expansion. The issue was not presented politically and was never contested but was simply installed after a process of legitimation which included the appointment, by the prime minister, of the Robbins Committee and the instant acceptance of its expansionist recommendations.

This brings us to the question of what constitutes political science evidence. We can search for the main agents of educational expansion in

Britain. We know how ministers became convinced, in the early 1960s, that pressure from the schools created irresistible demands on higher education which should be met. The minister of the time, Sir David Eccles, made this very point in a debate in 1961 in the House of Commons. We know that such pressures were being enunciated through the Secondary School Examinations Council as it criticized the universities' requirements for students seeking admission. We know that economists were putting their analytic force behind the arguments for expansion, particularly in the format of labor-market economics. It is noteworthy, too, that two of the most active promoters of educational expansion, Geoffrey Crowther and Lionel Robbins, both of whom headed key government commissions reporting, respectively, in 1959 and 1963, were leading economists. We may infer that the cloudburst of consumer demand and of demand for access to the skills training that would enhance life earnings was an important contextual factor underlying expansion. So were the two kinds of educational demographic change: that induced by increases in the birthrate and that induced by educational policy which either required or encouraged longer periods of exposure to education. Yet the precise mechanisms linking these expressions of the expansionist ideology and policy-making are lacking.

We cannot identify presentation of wants by client groups, stakeholders, or the development of constituencies in this period, other than those of the schools wanting more places for their pupils, persons wanting to be employed by higher education, and towns that wanted to have their own universities. The most important trends of the time were, apart from the growth of the power of the state, the increased power of an academic elite and the admission to decision making of members of academe, junior teachers, and students. The professoriat certainly yielded some ground to nonprofessorial teaching staff. Also the eliteness of British higher education was reduced by the decision of government to provide competition from a large publicly maintained sector.

Yet throughout this period of expansion many of the structural relationships remained intact. It has been remarked that because of the relatively collegial relationships enjoyed with students, revolutionary attitudes were softened, and in the end concessions to student activism could be milder than in some of the European counterparts. Although charters approved by the Privy Council made provision for councils with considerable power, with a majority of lay members, the power of the departments and of the academic staff remained largely untouched either by lay intervention, or by the state, or by internal bureaucracies until the early 1980s.

When the government inaugurated a policy of sharp reduction in 1981, higher education found no constituents who would bring pressure upon the wider political system. It could not depend upon its distinctive and professional contributions to knowledge and learning to safeguard resources and autonomy. At this distance, it is impossible to know whether changes in macropolicies, and the resulting uncertainties, will affect the resilience of the basic units and the academic profession.

CONCLUSION

In examining the experience of the United Kingdom, with references to the United States and to Sweden, I have attempted to demonstrate distinctive political aspects of the higher education system. The university and other higher education institutions are indeed intensely politically complex units in which lines of authority cross with lines of influence, but which, none-theless, produce decision-making structures and formalized relationships which then go on, in their turn, to affect interactions. Those interplays and structures may be analyzed as reflecting the changing ideologies of the larger society, the changing pressures of sponsorship and government, and the more continuous academic norms that emphasize the individual need for intellectual self-satisfaction and creative work.

If we look for key areas for future research we must begin with higher education as a laboratory for developments in normative political theory. Composites of modified authority, of the relationship between authority and consent, and of multiple concepts of participation leap from the case studies. Clark has already clarified concepts of academic power[34] but that power is now shifting and needs conceptual monitoring. It is perhaps in this zone that political science moves from modalities to substantives. Normative theory is primarily concerned with the substantives of relationships. To assess how those relationships and their conceptualizations change as the environment presses on institutions and causes change in their political working is a prime task. In undertaking this task for higher education, the formulations of new political linkages, co-optations and conflicts, and their legitimation are key empirical starting points.

The next level of much needed analysis should be the relationship between institutions and their constituencies and stakeholders. We do not yet know, but some are trying to learn,[35] how the expectations of particular groups, such as employers, affect the normative development of academic subjects and how the institutions themselves, through their decision-making mechanisms, determine relationships with outside groups. A wide variability over time and among countries is demonstrated on the extent to which coalitions of interest sought to expand higher education or sought its contraction.

---

[34]Clark, *Academic Coordination*.

[35]A research team in the Department of Government at Brunel University is studying the expectations of higher education of employers, providing data for institutions and students.

At a further level of analysis, there is the classic zone of the relationship between the state and the institutions dependent on it for resources and legitimacy. Here there are many areas for research. There are questions of the coalitions of interests which are or are not operating at the national level. There is the phenomenon of the co-opted academic, the elite that has taken on a particular role during a period of contraction. There are the concepts of academic coordination so well developed by Clark.[36] The political scientist cannot easily conceptualize the heroic minister except to notice the impact that he makes on norm setting within institutions, on rates of access, and on the political effects of changing the rates of access.

Finally, there are studies of implementation and impact. Questions of reduced or changed access are economic and sociological but also strike hard at degrees of institutional freedom, at distributions of power both intrainstitutional and in the larger society. In policy studies, such issues as the boundaries of rationality, the modes of pluralism and participation, help to clarify both process and outcome.[37]

Political science can, therefore, illuminate historical developments in higher education. It has no predictive models of why particular issues emerge within particular political cultures. It falls short of explaining fully the "why" but it can structure the "how"—the modalities of change and policy outcome. It can contrast the likely force of ideology and of processual factors against economic and broader social factors in creating changes in policy. If issue determination is a weak art, that is because it requires the summation and analysis of complex historical states which must, however, be attempted.

The points suggested in these concluding paragraphs are surely a sufficient and wholesome agenda for the thinking social scientist.

---

[36]Clark, *Academic Coordination*.

[37]A recent example of attempts to codify policy studies is Carley, *National Techniques in Policy Analysis*. Rune Premfors, on whose work this paper is strongly dependent, has drawn my attention recently to the appendix to Hines and Martmark, *Politics of Higher Education*, entitled "Conceptual and Methodological Issues for Research."

BIBLIOGRAPHY

Archer, Margaret S. *Social Origins of Educational Systems*. London: Sage Publications, 1979.

————. "Educational Politics: A Model for Their Analysis." In *Politics and Educational Change*, ed. Patricia Broadfoot, Colin Brock, and Witold Tulasiewicz. London: Croom Helm, 1981.

Ashby, Eric, and Mary Anderson. *The Rise of the Student Estate in Britain*. Cambridge: Harvard University Press, 1970.

Baldridge, J. Victor. *Power and Conflict in the University*. New York: Wiley, 1971.

Baldridge, J. Victor, David V. Curtis, George Ecker, and Gary L. Riley. *Policy Making and Effective Leadership*. San Francisco: Jossey-Bass, 1978.

Becher, Tony, and Maurice Kogan. *Process and Structure in Higher Education*. London: Heinemann, 1980.

Berdahl, Robert O. *British Universities and the State*. Berkeley and Los Angeles: University of California Press, 1959.

Berube, Maurice R. *The Urban University in America*. Westport, Connecticut: Greenwood Press, 1978.

Carley, Michael. *National Techniques in Policy Analysis*. London: Heinemann, 1980.

Centre for Contemporary Social Studies. *Unpopular Education: Schooling and Social Democracy in England since 1944*. London: Hutchinson, 1981.

Clark, Burton R. *Academic Coordination*. Higher Education Research Group Working Paper no. 24, 1978. New Haven: Yale University, 1979.

————. *The Higher Education System: Academic Organization in Cross-National Perspective*. Berkeley, Los Angeles, London: University of California Press, 1983.

Fielden, John, and Geoffrey Lockwood. *Planning and Management in Universities: A Study of British Universities*. London: Chatto and Windus, 1973.

Gove, Samuel K., and Carol E. Floyd. "Research on Higher Education Administration and Policy: An Uneven Report." *In* Leonard Goodall, ed., *State Politics and Higher Education*. Dearborn, Michigan: LMG Associates, 1976.

Harman, Grant. *Politics of Education: A Bibliographical Guide*. New York: Crane-Russak, 1974.

————. *Research in the Politics of Education, 1973–1978: An International Review and Bibliography*. Canberra: Research School of Social Sciences, Australian National University, 1979.

Hastings, Anne H. *The Study of Politics and Education: A Bibliographic Guide to the Research Literature*. Eugene, Oregon: ERIC Clearinghouse on Educational Management, April 1980.

Hines, Edward R., and Leifs Martmark. *Politics of Higher Education*. ERIC/Higher Education Research Report no. 7, 1980. Washington, D.C.: American Association for Higher Education, 1980.

Kogan, Maurice. *The Politics of Educational Change*. New York: Fontana Books; Manchester: Manchester University Press, 1978.

Levy, Daniel C. *Universities and Governance: The Comparative Politics of Higher Education. A Review Essay*. Higher Education Research Group Working Paper no. 31. New Haven: Yale University, 1978.

Mackenzie, William J. *Politics and Social Science*. London: Penguin Books, 1977.

Moodie, Graeme C., and Rowland Eustace. *Power and Authority in British Universities*. Montreal: McGill-Queen's University Press, 1974.

Premfors, Rune. *The Politics of Higher Education in a Comparative Perspective: France, Sweden, United Kingdom*. Studies in Politics, 15. Stockholm: University of Stockholm, 1980.

Robbins Committee on Higher Education. *Report*. London: HMSO, Cmnd. 2154, October 1963.

Self, Peter. *Econocrats and the Policy Process: The Politics and Philosophy of Cost-Benefit Analysis*. New York: Macmillan, 1975.

Selznick, Philip. *TVA and the Grass Roots*. New York: Harper and Row, 1966.

Startup, Richard. "The Role of the Department Head." *Studies in Higher Education* 1, no. 2 (1976):233–243.

Tapper, Ted, and Brian Salter. *Education and the Political Order: Changing Patterns of Class Control*. New York: Macmillan, 1978.

―――. *Education, Politics and the State: The Theory and Practice of Educational Change*. London: Grant McIntyre, 1981.

Trow, Martin. "The Public and Private Lives of Higher Education." *Daedalus* (Winter 1975):115–127.

Trow, Martin, ed. *Teachers and Students: Aspects of American Higher Education*. New York: McGraw-Hill, 1975.

Whitaker, Tim. *School Governing Bodies and the Politico-Administrative System*. Uxbridge, Middlesex: Department of Government, Brunel University, 1982.

3. THE ECONOMIC APPROACH*

Gareth
Williams

Adam Smith offered two penetrating insights into the behavior of systems of higher education. The first is macroeconomic and has become an established part of the literature on labor economics during the past quarter century. The theory of human capital offers a convincing explanation of changes in the demand for higher education. Although much detailed empirical testing—in particular, distinguishing the extent to which higher education creates human capital as opposed to identifying potential productive capacity—remains to be done, however, the theory appears unlikely to regain the intellectual preeminence and political influence it enjoyed during the 1960s.

Adam Smith's second insight was microeconomic and has been little remarked in the literature. The mechanisms by which universities and other higher education institutions receive their financing can exert a powerful influence on their organizational behavior. There are three main ways in which universities receive funds: financial control by external political or bureaucratic agencies; by academics who supply educational services; or from students and others who consume the services. Economic explanations of the institutional behavior of universities are a useful complement to those of sociologists and organizational theorists, particularly in predicting how institutions are likely to react to financial stringency.

THE RISE AND FALL OF HUMAN CAPITAL THEORY

Human capital theory, which has dominated the economics of higher education for two decades, can be traced to a well-known passage of Adam Smith's:

When any expensive machine is erected, the extraordinary work to be performed by it before it is worn out, it must be expected, will replace the capital laid out upon it, with at least the ordinary profits. A man educated at the expense of much labour and time to any of those employments which require extraordinary dexterity and skill

*I am pleased to acknowledge helpful suggestions made by participants at the UCLA seminar and, in particular, the useful commentaries by Professors Lewis Solmon and Ulrich Teichler.

may be compared to one of those expensive machines. The work which he learns to perform, it must be expected, over and above the usual wages of common labour, will replace to him the whole expense of his education, with at least the ordinary profits of an equally valuable capital. It must do this, too, in a reasonable time, regard being had to the very uncertain duration of human life, in the same manner as to the more certain duration of the machine. . . .

. . . Education in the ingenious arts and in the liberal professions is still more tedious and expensive. The pecuniary recompense, therefore, of painters and sculpters, of lawyers and physicians, ought to be much more liberal: and it is so accordingly.[1]

Modern human capital theory, however, is usually considered to have originated in Chicago in the early 1960s with Theodore Schultz's presidential address to the American Economics Association on "Investment in Human Capital," and with publication of Becker's *Human Capital* in 1964.

At the heart of empirical human capital economics is an analysis of differences in earnings of workers with different levels and types of education. Typically, after allowing for a number of background variables such as sex and race, the average lifetime earnings of individuals are positively correlated with their levels of education. Earnings differences are so large that even when the private costs of education are taken into account, there is a positive financial return to individuals who invest in their own higher education. These private returns tended to diminish in many countries in the early 1970s, but they remain substantial.[2]

Analysis of private rates of return is a potentially powerful instrument for explaining and predicting changes in the overall levels and patterns of demand for higher education. Until the late 1970s, however, there was little research interest in the positive economic implications of this private rate of return. Instead, the earnings differences were interpreted as showing a "social" rate of return with the help of the assumption that earnings reflect the marginal productivities of individual workers. The reason for the emphasis on social rates of return was both theoretical and practical. Theoretically, the assumptions about earnings and productivity enabled the economics of human capital to bring together in a single explanatory framework the returns to labor and the returns to capital. Thus there is no real difference between owning a machine and possessing productive skills. Economic men will, in the long run, switch from one to the other form of capital according to the relative rates of return.

The practical reason for the interest in social rates of return arose from the rapid growth of public expenditure on higher education during the 1960s. The proper allocation of resources between higher education and alternative uses became a major policy issue. The concept of a social rate of

---

[1]Smith, *Wealth of Nations*, Book V, p. 90.

[2]The earnings differential in favor of graduates apparently started to widen again in the late 1970s. See Lindley, *Higher Education and the Labour Market*.

return offered an apparently objective and unambiguous criterion: public authorities should go on investing in higher education or in specified higher education activities until the net social rate of return on the human capital embodied in each type of graduate is equal to the return on investment in other long-term investment projects.[3]

From the outset the economics of education has been closely associated with policy. Politicians and administrators with only a hazy knowledge of the assumptions and evidence of the human capital model justified expansion of higher education partly because the social returns of such an investment were higher than the average returns on other long-term investments. The evidence of the economics of education in the 1960s supported the political priorities that were popular at the time.

The great expansion of higher education in most countries in the 1960s was followed in the 1970s by lower rates of economic growth; and the lifetime earnings of graduates, at least in Europe, North America, and Australia, declined relative to those of other groups of workers. This decline cast doubts in the minds of politicians and potential students about the investment value of higher education.

At the same time the theory of human capital began to meet an intellectual challenge originating in the sociology of education. This hypothesis implied that earnings differences between graduates and nongraduates may be attributed not to the creation of capital through the process of higher education, but to the role of higher education in selecting individuals with attributes, such as intellectual ability, high motivation, and willingness to work hard, which are also likely to prove useful in employment.[4]

There are many loose versions of the "screening," or "credentialist," hypothesis which do not stand up to rigorous empirical investigation. For example, the decline in relative earnings in the 1970s may be attributed to a declining marginal productivity of human capital resulting from an oversupply of graduates, after the expansion of the 1960s, relative to the demand. Credentialism, in most of its versions, would predict a maintenance of differentials in such circumstances, since the larger number of graduates forced nongraduates to a lower rung on the job hierarchy. Advocates of credentialist theories have been strongly influenced by the apparent inflation of educational qualifications of new entrants to jobs, without looking at the price offered for these qualifications in terms of relative earnings of people with different educational qualifications, and without "committing themselves to a decisive prediction that might falsify it."[5] Some authors doubt that a convincing test is possible. As Layard and

---

[3]Blaug, "Empirical Status of Human Capital Theory."

[4]Arrow, "Higher Education as a Filter," pp. 51–76; Berg, *Education and Jobs*; Dore, *Diploma Disease*; Thurow, "Education and Economic Equality."

[5]Blaug, "Empirical Status of Human Capital Theory," p. 848.

Psacharopoulos point out, no simple market test is likely to discriminate between human capital and screening explanations because the question is not whether schooling explains earnings differences but why it does.[6]

Whatever their implications for social rates of return, credentialist theories and the screening hypothesis leave the concept of private rates of return of investment in higher education untouched. For individuals, unlike governments, it does not matter why a university education leads to increased earnings; it is the fact that it does which is significant. If individuals take an investment view of their higher education, their demands for it will be influenced by expectations of future earnings, whether these earnings are a result of attributes acquired during the process of higher education, or whether the credential is simply believed by employers to be a guarantee of authenticity of attributes that were already there.

The implications for the public financing of higher education resulting from the outcome of the debate between human capital theory and the screening hypothesis are considerable. If credentialism comes to offer a satisfactory explanation of the economic function of higher education, both the "efficiency" and the "equity" cases for public subsidy will disappear. On efficiency grounds, the argument for subsidy is that without it there would be underinvestment in higher education because of capital market imperfections and the uncertainty of the returns for any individual. If, however, as credentialists claim, higher education results in no net gains in national income, there can be no underinvestment, but merely different distributions of the same income. On equity grounds, if the effect of public subsidy is to allow some individuals to obtain a redistribution of income in their favor, it is unfair to subsidize these distributional advantages. Indeed, it can be argued that equity might demand that graduates pay a tax surcharge over and above the full cost of their higher education to compensate the rest of society for the unjustified advantages they obtained.

There has been some shift in recent years away from the apparently intractable problems arising from the normative concept of a social rate of return toward an interest in private rates of return, as a way of explaining changes in the private demand for higher education. In the United States, Richard Freeman has been prominent, and in Europe, Dolphin, Pissarides, Williams and Gordon, and Psacharopoulos have contributed evidence.[7]

The value of the economic model of private demand for higher education

[6]Layard and Psacharopoulos, "Screening Hypothesis."

[7]Freeman, "Response to Change in the United States," pp. 86–119; Dolphin, "Demand for Higher Education"; Pissarides, "From School to University"; Williams and Gordon, "16 and 18 Year Olds' Attitudes to Education"; Psacharopoulos and Soumelis, "Quantitative Analysis of the Demand for Higher Education."

is its contribution to an explanation of changes in demand over time.[8] There are always some individuals who will go to the university under almost any circumstances. There are others who are equally certain not to do so. Between these extremes lies a spectrum of individuals more or less likely to go, depending on circumstances. The economic model claims that over parts of this spectrum, expectations of economic return are a factor influencing the decisions of some individuals. This range does not have to be very broad to explain the kinds of changes in demand for higher education which have been experienced in Europe and North America during the past twenty years. I have shown elsewhere that at the point of leaving compulsory education, about 30 percent of those who do so in Britain are undecided about whether or not to continue their studies on tracks leading to higher education.[9]

It is unlikely that human capital theory will regain the intellectual preeminence and political popularity it enjoyed in the 1960s. The interest of economists in higher education is, however, likely to remain strong. The relationship between private returns to higher education and the demand for it by individual students in conditions of uncertainty and imperfect information remains to be properly explored.

THE FINANCE OF HIGHER EDUCATION

An area where economists may be able to contribute new insights is the study of financing mechanisms which may offer further insights into the models of institutional behavior developed by sociologists and organizational theorists. Burton R. Clark,[10] for example, identifies four possible "pathways of academic coordination: bureaucracy, profession, politics and the market."

A recent study by Garvin[11] offers useful empirical evidence on how American universities operate as economic organizations. Earlier economists have written on the subject of higher education finance; but, attracted

---

[8]An analogy is the depth of the sea along a coastline. Obviously, the fundamental explanatory factor is the contours of the coastline, and for them we must look to geography and geology. If, however, we are concerned with why at a particular point the sea is sometimes six centimeters and sometimes six meters deep, we must look elsewhere, to the tides and the effect on them of the position of the moon and the sun. If we are concerned with smaller (but for many practical purposes, much more important) fluctuations of the waves, we must consider the winds and the laws of motion of liquids.

[9]Williams and Gordon, "16 and 18 Year Olds' Attitudes to Education."

[10]Clark, "Many Pathways of Academic Coordination"; Clark, *Higher Education System*.

[11]Garvin, *Economics of University Behavior*.

by pressures similar to those that oriented human capital theory in the direction of direct policy advice, they have tended to focus on the normative concept of efficiency in resource utilization, rather than explore the behavioral implications of different ways of allocating finance to and within universities and colleges.

Adam Smith presaged the study of the financing mechanisms of higher education in a durable essay, "The Education and Instruction of Youth," in Book V of *The Wealth of Nations*. In the remainder of this paper I explore the implications for university behavior of the three main sources of finance identified by Smith: the state, the university, and the student.

The thesis is that not only does he who pays the piper call the tune, but also the way payment is made determines how the tune is played. Mechanisms of finance have a significant influence on the behavior of institutions of higher education and the principal actors within them. There is, obviously, a problem of identification of cause and effect. The way any particular university is financed is largely a result of political attitudes about the social function of higher education at critical stages of the history of the university. Because of the vested interests it creates, however, a system of finance, once established, is hard to replace except by one that is more favorable to a majority of the interests concerned. We might expect the financial procedures of a higher education institution or system of interacting institutions to reflect the period in which its main features were established. Mechanisms of finance evolve as particular arrangements show themselves inadequate or inappropriate for changing circumstances; but these changes are normally the result of benefit maximization or, in bad times, coping strategies by existing interests that control the financing mechanism.

There are four fundamental resource allocation decisions in higher education: the total resources to be devoted to the sector as a whole, the allocation of these resources among institutions, their distribution among the operational activities within each institution, and their allotment to individual academics. These correspond to the four levels of authority identified by Becher and Kogan;[12] the central authority, the institutions, the basic units, and the individual academics. This chapter is concerned primarily with the effects on their organizational behavior of the ways in which resources are allocated to institutions. A similar analysis is possible for each of the other three levels.

Resource-allocation decisions at each level may be taken in three broad ways, depending on whether the priorities of interest groups at a higher level, the same level, or a lower level are dominant. Finance represents a significant part of the total resources at an institution's disposal, and we can

---

[12]Becher and Kogan, *Process and Structure in Higher Education*.

devise three basic models of university behavior according to which of these three levels of interest controls its allocation.

In the first situation financial decisions are made by a body external to the institution—for example, by central government—and resources are allocated to institutions according to specified distributional rules. Power is in the hands of the political authorities and of the administrators who translate political priorities into operational rules for distributing funds. Political and bureaucratic pathways of coordination are dominant.

In the second situation, the institutions have access to independent sources of income. The classic form is ownership of land, property, or endowments. Control over the use of finance is internal to the institution, and such control encourages self-regulation of an essentially professional or collegial nature.

Third, universities may obtain their income by selling services, principally teaching, but also research and consultancy. Financial power is now with numerous individual customers. This corresponds to Clark's market model. It is important to distinguish sources of finance from the mechanisms by which resource is allocated. In particular, governments may choose to adopt all or any of the three financial mechanisms for channeling public funds into universities. The accompanying figure gives a broad indication of the relative magnitude of the main financial channels for British universities as a whole and suggests which form of institutional behavior we may expect to be stimulated by each mechanism.

No real system of higher education is financed as a pure bureaucratic, a pure collegial, or a pure market model. Furthermore, it is quite possible for decisions at some levels to be made bureaucratically, whereas at other levels they are made according to other criteria. For example, central government may allocate resources to institutions according to certain fixed allocation rules, and the institutions may allow the departments to compete for them. Alternatively, departments may sell their services, but only according to rules determined by the institutions or by government. Again, government may provide finance but channel it through subsidies to students, so that the institutions and their operating departments find themselves in a market competing to provide services for subsidized students. Nevertheless, as an analytical tool, the concept of three distinct models of higher education finance offers a number of insights into university behavior; and, in broad terms, they may be likened to several aspects of actual national systems.

Financing under Bureaucratic Control

Bureaucratic financial procedures have their advantages. National priorities for higher education agreed upon through political processes can be implemented directly and quickly by allocating resources in accordance with them. Bureaucracy is probably the only effective way of implementing higher education policies based on estimates of long-term national needs for qualified manpower. If the state decides that more electrical engineers and fewer sociologists will be needed in the 1990s, it is possible to allocate more resources to departments of electrical engineering and to specify the ways in which these resources should be used, while withdrawing resources from departments of sociology.

Bureaucratic allocation procedures can also protect the quality of higher education by ensuring that adequate resources are made available for the tasks that universities are asked to perform. The central authorities can ensure uniformity of standards across the system by withholding resources from activities that appear incapable of meeting required standards or strengthening those whose weakness is owing to lack of resources. Such a policy can put institutions in a strong bargaining position: if they are required to perform certain tasks, they can demand adequate resources to perform them. Examples may be found in the activities of the Council for National Academic Awards (CNAA) in public sector higher education in Britain. When the CNAA has criticized courses on the grounds that the resources are inadequate to maintain standards, local education authorities have sometimes increased resource provision for their polytechnics.

There are also disadvantages. Many academics claim that the most fundamental of these is the threat to academic freedom. A procedure in which resources are allocated down through a hierarchy with each lower level subject to conditions imposed by the level above it clearly impinges on the freedom of action of those lower in the hierarchy. Either formally established rules must be followed, or special permission must be sought for authorization to use resources in ways not sanctioned by the rules. Of course, when the issue is control over resources, truth is many-sided; and some of the claims made on behalf of academic freedom bear a resemblance to protection of vested interests.

Bureaucratic resource allocation procedures are not necessarily the same as political control of higher education. Although it is hard to conceive of a situation in a publicly financed system of higher education where decisions about overall resources for higher education are not influenced by government policy, most of the intermediate decisions that affect the day-to-day life of academics in which freedom actually operates may be reached under a variety of administrative arrangements. The four different types of machinery which can be envisaged are found in one form or another in higher education systems around the world.

One is a pure bureaucracy, in which funds are allocated by administrators with accountability to a single central authority. All resource decisions are refinements of the basic decisions taken by the central authority. Sometimes universities are run as civil service departments.

Another bureaucratic form gives some measure of discretion and political accountability lower down on the resource allocation hierarchies. The

RELATIONSHIPS BETWEEN METHODS OF FINANCING UNIVERSITIES AND THEIR ORGANIZATIONAL BEHAVIOR

Source of finance	Approximate percentage of U.K. university income received by each route	Method in which finance is received by institution	Form of university behavior predicted
Government	0	Earmarked (categorical) - - grants	Bureaucracy
	60%	Single (block) - - - - - grants	College
	0	Formulas based on student numbers	Market
	10%	Sale of academic services	Market
Households	20%	Fees - - - - - - - - - -	Market
Firms	5%	Sale of academic services	Market
Property of higher education institutions	5%	Property income - - -	College

administrators at intermediate levels work within less rigid rules, but they are accountable for their decisions to external agencies other than the central government. Public sector higher education in Australia and in England is at present financed in this way. Most of the funds derive ultimately from central government, but the institutions are administered by other politically controlled bodies that operate within a framework of laws and guidelines laid down by central government. These arrangements soften many of the harsher features of pure bureaucracy, but only at the expense of a considerable amount of "buck passing." Each level of political authority is anxious to ensure that it gain the credit for popular decisions, letting the obloquy for unpopular ones devolve upon the other.

A third "bureaucratic" model, centralized professional control, is a form of state syndicalism. The central government relinquishes detailed control of resource allocation to committees of professionals drawn from all the institutions and activities that expect to be ultimate users of the resources. There are two versions of this bureaucratic form: (1) a group of professionals appointed on the basis of their individual expertise; (2) a group that is intended to be representative of the various vested interests in the user agencies. Both arrangements have in common the fact that accountability is partly to the central authority making the initial resource allocation and partly to their colleagues at the same level in the hierarchy. The two forms differ in that the committee of professional experts owes its ultimate allegiance to some concept of the standards of the profession, whereas the committee of representatives must seek some sort of compromise among the various vested interests or constituencies they represent. Research councils in Britain and in several other countries, which distribute funds for specific research activities, are examples of the former: their accountability is to "science" and often to particular "disciplines." Strictly representative bodies for allocating public funds are not common. Unless resources are very plentiful, they are likely to be in a state of permanent deadlock; and if they are able to operate by consensus, governments are likely to see them as potentially too powerful a vested interest of users as opposed to suppliers of funds.

In general the freedom of individual academics, operating units, and institutions is undoubtedly less under bureaucratic allocation procedures than in other resource allocation models. Some, however, are less rigid than others; and some forms of outside control may be seen as less burdensome, in that they are operated by peer groups or they offer opportunities for individual maneuver.

A charge against bureaucratic mechanisms is that they are inefficient and cumbersome. Recipients of finance seek to further their own priorities within the constraints of any effectively policed regulations. If monitoring of actual resource use is inadequate, funds made available for one purpose may be put to entirely different uses. If monitoring is adequate, it is likely to be oppressive. When a new discrepancy is identified, the higher authority makes additional rules. The difficulty of measuring the outputs of higher education means that it is often the activities of academic staff which must be monitored, rather than their outcomes. This is always an irksome task.

The problem has not changed very much in the past two centuries. Adam Smith was aware of the difficulty:

> If the authority to which he [the university teacher] is subject resides . . . in some other extraneous persons, in the bishop of the diocese for example, in the governor of the province, or perhaps in some minister of state, . . . all that such superiors can force him to do, is to attend upon his pupils a certain number of hours, that is, to give a certain number of lectures in the week, or in the year. What these lectures shall be, must still depend upon the diligence of the teacher; and that diligence is likely to be proportioned to the motives which he has for exerting it. An extraneous jurisdiction of this kind, besides, is liable to be exercised both ignorantly and capriciously. In its nature it is arbitrary and discretionary; and the persons who exercise it, neither attending upon the lectures of the teachers themselves, nor perhaps understanding the science which it is his business to teach, are seldom capable of exercising it with judgement. . . . Whoever has attended for any considerable time to the administration of a French university must have had occasion to remark the effects which naturally result from an arbitrary and extraneous jurisdiction of this kind.[13]

Rules and monitoring procedures tend to increase as resource users exploit loopholes. Some of these stratagems are well known: for example, the end-of-the-budget-year spending spree, and the insistence that only the highest-quality equipment may be used for particular tasks. The difficulty of identifying and measuring output in higher education makes such dysfunctions particularly likely. It is difficult to quantify the extra benefits students receive from having access to a particular computer rather than to one costing half as much. When preparing budgets, the only real indication the allocating bodies often have of what users need is what they spent last year, which ensures that all budgets are fully spent whether or not what they purchase is really necessary.

University teachers are inevitably highly qualified professional workers with abilities that would ensure independent, professional, or managerial status in many other areas of employment.[14] Academic employment subject to bureaucratic procedures is likely to be unattractive to faculty unless their conditions of service allow them to devote a substantial part of their time to independent professional work or to other suitably rewarding activity. This situation is perhaps one of the reasons for the high proportion of part-time staff in French universities and for the small number of hours senior staff are actually required to be at the university.[15]

---

[13]Smith, *Wealth of Nations*, Book V, chap. i, p. 247.

[14]Perkin, *Key Profession*.

[15]Cerych and Neave, "Structure, Promotion and Appointment."

Forms of finance conducive to collegial and market forms of coordination could not keep pace with the rapid expansion of the 1960s. Endowments and property incomes could not expand fast enough to keep pace with rates of expansion which were demanded politically.

The increase in the proportion of higher education income derived from public funds was accompanied by an increase in bureaucratic public control, as public authorities sought, quite understandably, to ensure a use of funds that was "efficient" in relation to national political priorities. Institutions traded off some of their previous independence for the increased income from government sources.

The increase in bureaucratic control was not always perceived in the initial phases. Rapid expansion of resources meant that considerable central influence on university behavior could be secured through control of incremental resources, and any university always felt it was in a position to reject incremental resources or accept them on its own terms.

Financing under Collegial Controls

The collegial idea of a university derives from the substantial endowments made to English universities during the sixteenth century, after the expropriation of the Church's wealth by the monarchy and its supporters. Many of the colleges at Oxford and Cambridge became wealthy corporations whose fellows could afford to provide tutoring and other educational services on their own terms. The essential financial characteristic of the collegial model is that institutions have an independent source of income sufficient to cover a substantial part of their total costs. Thus they enjoy financial freedom from dependence on student fees on the one hand and from an interfering government bureaucracy on the other. The contemporary mythology in Britain about academic freedom, and the need for academic staff to have lifetime tenure to protect it, derive ultimately from the financial independence enjoyed by the corporations of fellows of Oxford and Cambridge colleges from the mid-sixteenth century onward.[16] In contrast with the academic employees of a bureaucracy, the members of a college make their own decisions about the management of their wealth and how to use the income it generates. In Oxford and Cambridge colleges, the bursar, who has charge of college investments, is often one of the most prestigious members of the college.[17]

---

[16]Although the details of the present arrangements whereby nearly all teaching staff in British universities have tenured appointments are the result of half a century of bargaining by the Association of University Teachers, the arrangements were facilitated ultimately by the need of universities to attract large numbers of staff during the rapid expansion of the 1960s. See Perkin, *Key Profession*.

[17]It is well known that John Maynard Keynes put his economic theory to good practical use and increased the value of the investment of Kings College, Cambridge, very considerably (see

The effects of academic freedom supported by such financial independence are by no means always beneficial. Adam Smith, who was at Oxford in the 1740s, was shocked at what he found:

> If the authority to which he [the college fellow] is subject resides in the body corporate, the college or university, of which he himself is a member, and in which the greater part of the other members are, like himself, persons who are or ought to be teachers, they are likely to make common cause, to be all very indulgent to one another, and every man to consent that his neighbour may neglect his duty provided he himself is allowed to neglect his own. . . . In the University of Oxford, the greater part of the public professors have, for these many years, given up altogether even the pretence of teaching. . . . The discipline of colleges and universities is in general contrived, not for the benefit of students but for the interest, or more properly speaking, the ease of the masters. Its object is, in all cases, to maintain the authority of the master, and whether he neglects or performs his duty, to oblige the students in all cases to behave to him as if he performed it with the greatest diligence and ability.[18]

Of course, Smith's strictures may have been tinged with envy. In Edinburgh and in Glasgow, Smith, like the other Scottish professors, was expected to earn his keep by attracting student fees.

The short length of student terms at Oxford and Cambridge—less than half the year—may derive in part from the organization of these universities to serve "the ease of the masters" rather than to provide the best learning conditions for students. We may even speculate that the much esteemed tutorial system, in which students read an essay once a week to their tutors, evolved as a means of relieving the masters of the burden of preparing lectures.[19]

Despite Adam Smith and the concern that has led to the setting up of numerous royal commissions of inquiry into the universities of Oxford and Cambridge, the collegial model of university finance has proved very durable. Some of the great private universities of the United States have modeled themselves in part on Oxford and Cambridge. Most of the countries of the former British Empire have universities whose financial

---

Harrod, pp. 386–390). He was succeeded by Kenneth Berrill who subsequently became chairman of the University Grants Committee and head of the government's Central Policy Review Staff.

[18] Smith, *Wealth of Nations*, Book V, chap. i, p. 248.

[19] Adam Smith indulged in similar speculation: "The lecturer, instead of explaining to the pupils himself the science which he proposes to instruct them, may read some books upon it . . . or, what would give him less trouble, by making them interpret it to him, and by now and then making an occasional remark upon it, he may flatter himself that he is giving a lecture" (Smith, Book V, chap. i, p. 249). Sheldon Rothblatt, in commenting on a first draft of this paper, pointed out to me that the tutorial as we know it was not one of the teaching techniques used at eighteenth-century Oxford. As the tutorial evolved throughout the nineteenth century, it may have been accepted as an adaptation of a teaching method that the dons had come to know and love.

arrangements owe something to what were believed to be the virtues of the traditional English university.

In Britain, central government began to be heavily involved in providing financing for universities after World War I, but their financial autonomy was considered paramount. The quasi-autonomous University Grants Committee established in 1919 arranged to transfer funds to universities by means of quinquennial block grants which were, in effect, deficiency grants to offset financial losses in institutions whose main income was assumed to have been derived from other sources. Between 1919 and the mid-1970s, when the quinquennial grant system collapsed under the pressures of inflation and stagnating student demand, the system developed into an arrangement whereby central government provided about 80 percent of the expenditures of universities, while at the same time preserving the collegial principle that universities had full legal autonomy over their expenditures.[20] The new plan was widely praised and only rarely criticized adversely (one example is Morris, 1974). It was directly copied in Australia, Bangladesh, India, Israel, New Zealand, and Nigeria, and it was partly adapted in many other countries.

The main features of UGC financing arrangements as they developed up to the mid-1970s were:

1) The committee itself consisted almost entirely of academics.
2) At five-year intervals the government made firm commitments to the committee concerning the amount of real resources that would be available for universities during the following five-year period.
3) Within very broad limits a grant was unconditional, though increasingly during the 1960s the government issued general guidelines about the future development of the universities.
4) The committee allocated funds in the form of five-year block grants to individual universities on the basis of submissions setting out their intentions for the following five years.
5) The grants to universities were unconditional except that the UGC offered an increasing amount of academic advice to individual universities as the size of the grants became larger and larger. The advice was sometimes followed, sometimes not. It is not possible to be more precise about the extent to which UGC advice was followed, as there was little formal monitoring of the relationship between proposed expenditures by universities and their actual expenditures. Indeed,

---

[20]Central government provided more than 95 percent of university income, as the other two major components, research grants and student fees, were both very heavily subsidized. These sources of income, however, were conditional upon providing the service demanded by students and the sponsors of research and may therefore be considered to represent a market mechanism.

even when the comptroller and the auditor general were given authority, stemming from a report issued by the House of Commons Public Accounts Committee, to audit the accounts of universities, they did not concern themselves with comparisons of the stated expenditure intentions of universities and their actual expenditure patterns other than to ensure that no laws were being broken.[21]

6) In making its allocations to universities, the UGC specified only in very general terms the assumptions about each university's pattern of expenditure on which the level of a grant was based.

7) During the 1960s the UGC did come to exercise detailed control over capital expenditures. Any large capital expenditure had to be authorized specifically, and it was subject to costing norms specified by the UGC according to government guidelines.

All these arrangements are consistent with the collegial principle. The UGC itself, with its specialist subject subcommittees, is essentially a collegial organization. Its members are appointed on the basis of individual merit and not as representatives of their own institutions. Their prime concern has been to defend the essential characteristics of the universities as institutions, rather than to consider whether the needs of society as a whole, or those of individual students, require universities to be fundamentally different institutions. It is significant that the two most important innovations in British higher education during the past twenty years, the establishment of the polytechnics and the creation of the Open University, both occurred outside the ambit of the UGC. Both may be considered as implied criticisms of the role of the UGC in protecting the status quo in existing universities.

The quinquennial block grant system amounted to an arrangement whereby government underwrote the collegial model by giving universities five-year unconditional endowments. Since the period from 1920 to 1980 was one of expanding governmental financial support, the universities came to treat the quinquennial grant as if it were permanent endowment income. For example, they appointed staff to permanent tenured posts up to the limit of their grant in each quinquennium, a practice that in retrospect seems irresponsible now that government expenditure is contracting.[22] It was, however, a legitimate application of the collegial principle on the basis of what, at the time, appeared to be permanent income.

The secrecy surrounding the precise assumptions underlying the allocation of grants to individual universities is intended to enhance the capability

---

[21]For an excellent account of the debate that led up to this development, see Kogan, "Audit, Control and Freedom."

[22]In 1970, 74 percent of British academic staff had permanent tenured contracts of employment (Williams et al., *Academic Labour Market*). It is almost certainly considerably higher now.

of universities to make their own financial decisions. Were the UGC to indicate the basis on which the grants are made, the committee, it is felt, would be exerting undue influence on the internal resource allocation procedures of individual universities.

At first sight the arrangements for funding capital expenditures seem to be based on a different principle, because these grants are authorized on a project basis and expenditure limits are tightly controlled. However, they, too, can be readily comprehended within the collegial model. Just as the quinquennial grant is similar in many respects to an unearmarked endowment, so capital grants correspond to private gifts for capital projects whose nature is specified by the donor. The essential features are that the initiative in seeking the new capital items originates in the universities and that the facilities created are available for use at the discretion of the university.[23] Hence, the acceptance of the gift by the university, whether it be from the government or from a private donor, forms part of the expanded "college" whose interests the university serves in the future. Any university is free to accept or reject such capital "gifts." Whether the facilities created for specific purposes under UGC project funding have always continued, in the long run, to be used for their intended purpose, is another topic about which nothing can be said, as no monitoring takes place.

Increasing demands in Britain for greater university accountability suggest that the potential disadvantages of "collegial" arrangements for the financing of universities have not changed significantly since Adam Smith's day. There are also, however, advantages. One is academic freedom as an end in itself. Many academics claim that only by having full control over their own resources can they pursue and disseminate truth; and it is this unfettered concern with truth which is the real contribution higher education makes to society. This view of academic behavior is clearly different from that held by Adam Smith.

Instrumental advantages arise because waste of resources is likely to be minimized if the individuals who make decisions about resource allocation are the same as the ultimate users. A fundamental truth of economics is that resources used for one purpose cannot simultaneously be used for other purposes. This truth, however, is apparent only to those who have full control over their own resources. If the income of the college is put to a certain use, another possible use must be foregone. Members of the college will seek to achieve their aims in the most efficient way, since this procedure will allow the maximum number of objectives to be successfully pursued. The inefficiencies of the bureaucratic model are avoided. Nevertheless,

---

[23]The facilities are not technically university property, as any proceeds from the sale of the asset would revert to Her Majesty's Treasury. In all other respects, however, the capital asset belongs to the university.

maximizing the welfare of members of the college may not be the best use of those resources as viewed by the wider society or by individual students.

The Market Model

All financing mechanisms have market elements. The behavior of an organization is largely determined by its incentive structure, which means mainly the way resources are allocated to it and within it. If research is rewarded more highly than teaching, university teachers will maximize the amount of time and effort they devote to research, subject to the constraint of not appearing to neglect their teaching to a larger extent than is prescribed by the rules or the ethos of their particular institution. If bureaucratic rules require that financial reserves cannot be carried forward, annual budgets will be exactly spent; if, as in Britain, generous financial support is available for students enrolled in full-time degree courses, and grants are almost impossible to obtain for students in other kinds of courses, higher education will come to be dominated by full-time degree courses; if universities have financially independent subject departments, interdisciplinary research and teaching will be difficult to establish.

Although there are such quasi-market mechanisms in all but the most rigidly bureaucratic forms of organization, a market model of university finance usually refers to arrangements in which the continued existence of the institution is directly dependent on the sale of academic services. Universities sell teaching services and students buy them. They sell research services and governments and economic enterprises buy them. Power over resource allocation decisions, and hence ultimately over the determination of priorities, rests with large numbers of individual students and purchasers of research services.

The main advantage of the market is the incentives it provides for universities and colleges to respond to changing economic and social circumstances. An institution that fails to attract students or research grants finds its income reduced. During the 1970s, 144 colleges in the United States had to close, mainly because of insufficient enrollments. The total number of institutions continued to increase, however, as about 260 new institutions were established.[24]

If they must meet the full cost of their higher education, many people are unable to attend college or enter a university because they lack adequate financial resources. This criticism of a market orientation is easily dealt with by the economist: there is no evidence that any other form of higher education system results in a socially equitable distribution of higher

---

[24]Freeman, "Response to Change in the United States," pp. 86–119.

education. The aggregate effect of subsidizing higher education by providing free facilities is often to transfer resources from relatively poorer families to richer families. Rate-of-return studies have shown that the effect of higher education subsidy has been to make investment in higher education more profitable privately than socially. The rest of society thus contributes toward the advancement of some individuals, without an equivalent recompense to the rest of society. The claim that a fully market-based higher education system would be less equitable than other models is not justified; and in the light of the private investment benefits, there is a growing body of economic opinion supporting the view that a market-based system with subsidy directed at students who need it is likely to be more equitable than many currently in existence.[25]

Another response to the alleged inequities of a market system is that students who wish to invest in their own future can do what other investors do if they have potentially profitable projects they are unable to finance from their own resources: they can borrow. There is a considerable economic literature on student loan schemes, and during the past fifteen years many countries, including the United States but not Britain, have followed the example of several Scandinavian countries and have started subsidizing part of the costs incurred by students by means of repayable loans. Woodhall has surveyed loan arrangements in Canada, Sweden, and the United States.[26]

Higher education as an investment has several characteristics that distinguish it from most other forms of investment: the investment takes a long time to complete, the returns are long-term, and, for any individual, they are very uncertain. So individual investors cannot afford to make mistakes; but at the same time they are not well informed about the implications of different decisions, and most of them are not in a position to make this investment decision more than once. Most successful loan schemes skirt these difficulties by having some form of income-contingent repayment arrangement: the amount a graduate repays in any year depends on his current income.[27] Thus students need not be deterred from borrowing to finance their studies by the fear that their personal investment will be one of the unsuccessful ones. Put another way, an element of insurance is built into the loan schemes.

Other weaknesses of pure market financing arrangements are more difficult to overcome. The market is likely to generate a less than optimal investment in basic research. The benefits of basic research, like those of teaching, are long-term and uncertain. But unlike the human capital

[25]OECD, "Intergovernmental Conference on Policies for Higher Education."
[26]Woodhall, *Student Loans.*
[27]Ibid.

embodied in graduates, much basic research cannot be appropriated by any particular economic enterprise.

The main weakness of the market model results from its possible effects on the supply of educational services. In some respects it is an alternative interpretation of the social responsiveness already claimed as an advantage of markets. Unrestrained competition can lead to reductions in quality as institutions indulge in price competition and hard-selling tactics. Freeman has described some recent trends in American higher education, as reductions in federal and state funds have increased the competition for students among institutions:

Various . . . recruiting techniques were resorted to. Testing organizations, such as the College Entrance Examination Board, have sold names and addresses to college administrators who used them to solicit applicants. The Riverside campus of the University of California sent out 12,000 oversized decks of playing cards carrying campus facts on the back. Some colleges pressure prospective students with the type of hard sell once associated only with profit-making proprietary schools or business colleges—mailing out slick brochures, conducting telephone canvasses, and giving out such gimmicks as free T-shirts, bumper stickers, and so on. In some cases, public relations firms have been hired to take over the whole admissions operation, receiving substantial fees for recruiting. While apparently still rare, the tactic of bounty hunting—for which proprietary schools have earned much opprobrium— has appeared, with recruiters paid on the basis of the number of students "delivered." The job of admissions officers, particularly at weaker institutions, is no longer to weed out unsuitable applicants but to find warm bodies.

. . . newspaper stories indicate that market efforts have if anything been expanded, referring to the torrent of direct-mail advertising, marketing and recruiting in college admissions. Among recent efforts are:
—preparation of elaborate filmstrips and television tapes;
—college fairs, which function like trade shows;
—ads in newspapers and on radio;
—direct mailing, with the college board selling names at 12 cents a name plus a $100 fixed fee.
Indicative of the pattern, a new quarterly magazine, *The Higher Education Marketing Journal*, was instituted to provide information on how best to expand the market.[28]

Martin Trow has drawn attention to the dangers of recruiting inadequately informed students who are being competed for by institutions whose survival depends on success in the market:

. . . Take, for example, the elaborate, indeed sometimes desperate, efforts of many, especially weaker, institutions to recruit students, whether for their tuition fees or for the enrollment-driven formulas by which most public institutions are funded. Most institutions do not confront the question of whether the strenuous recruitment

---

[28]Freeman, "Response to Change in the United States."

of some of these students serves the interests of the students as well as those of the institution. Sometimes the justification for these activities draws on the widespread American belief (only now beginning to be questioned) that on the whole people ought to get as much formal education as you can persuade them to sit still for; sometimes this is combined with the market's classic disclaimer of moral responsibility—*caveat emptor*. But whether the market is for warm bodies to meet budgets, or for black or brown bodies to meet affirmative action targets, it is clear that there is not a perfect correspondence between the interests of the recruiting college or university, and the recruited student. Important moral issues arise in this area. One can question the institution's responsibility in recruitment for what might be called "consumer protection," or, after students have been admitted, for providing counselling and other support services. The "revolving door" has moral dimensions, as well as academic and financial implications for colleges and universities. Grade inflation and the lowering of demands and standards to attract students are among the other pathologies of colleges and departments that are acutely threatened by the decline of enrollments and the fear of administrative action or budget cuts. There are similar dangers on the research side.[29]

Selling services is likely to affect the internal resource allocation procedures of institutions. When universities and colleges depend on consumers for their income, they have an incentive to meet the preferences of their students and to reward the operating units according to the extent to which they gratify these preferences and generate income for the institution. Resources, and the influence associated with them, flow upward from the successful operating units to the central administrative and policy-making bodies, instead of downward in accordance with central administrative decisions. The structure of power in the institution is the opposite of that under bureaucratic allocation arrangements.

All the difficult problems of values, of judgment, of the measurement and aggregation of different inputs and outputs are swept away. Consumers' preferences, expressed through and mediated by available technology, decide. Nevertheless, there is a considerable element of judgment involved in adopting this position. Consumer's preferences are an amalgam of a great many individual preferences; and it is not clear why the satisfaction of possibly uninformed consumers' preferences in an activity such as higher education should be considered any more deserving than the satisfaction of preferences of expert producers or democratically elected governments.

Nevertheless, a market encourages somebody to maximize something. The rules of the particular market determine who and what. The income of departments and of individual academics may be linked to their success in attracting students or research grants. Maynard has suggested that the incomes of individual academics may be related to their academic performances. Salary structures could "give a basic salary with an incremental

---

[29]Trow, "Comparative Perspectives on Access," pp. 115–116.

and decremental system of payments related to the performance of the academic in relation to agreed criteria of performance." The creation of a market in tutorials is suggested, whereby students are given tokens to "spend" on the tutorial of their choice, and tutors are able to cash these tokens.[30]

Another possibility would be to use cash incentives, not to influence individual incomes but to determine the disposable income of departments. Departments might be rewarded by being paid according to the number of students registered for their courses. The income of the department would determine the academic standard of living of its members. Members of successful departments would be able to attend conferences, have good library and research facilities, offer hospitality to their academic visitors, and so on.

There might also be a market for the central services of the university: lecture rooms, library facilities, and so on. The rate of utilization of many university facilities is low. Lecture rooms in British universities are empty for at least 75 percent of the time they could conceivably be used. Many of the books in a university library have been borrowed only once, if at all. Equipment of considerable value lies idle for much of the time in science and technology laboratories. If a market for such facilities were to be created, and lecture theaters could be hired at weekends or in the evenings for a fraction of their cost at prime time in midweek and mornings, departments would be less reluctant to teach at what are currently seen as unsocial hours. If some of the financial benefits were passed on to students in the form of lower fees, or better-prepared lectures, or teaching materials to accompany the lectures, there would be less reluctance to attend such lectures. Similarly, if departmental book allowances were related to the number of times books were borrowed in the department's teaching section, there would be less incentive to order books unrelated to teaching and more incentive to order multiple copies of those used intensively by students.

Of course, all such arrangements create inequalities within the university between successful and less successful departments and individuals. Activities that are "efficient," in the sense that they provide what consumers want, expand at the expense of activities that are in less demand. Thus, the pattern of provision within the institution responds to changing economic and social circumstances. For this reason such proposals are not popular with academics who have grown used to collegial methods of financing in which all members of the college are treated more or less equally. A proposal made in 1968 by the National Board for Prices and Incomes in Britain, that a small part of the incomes of lecturers might be determined on

---

[30]Maynard, "Privatisation and the Market Mechanism."

the basis of assessed teaching performance, was utterly rejected by university teachers as being completely out of touch with the British university tradition.[31] A similar outcry has followed attempts by the UGC, in the face of massive government cuts in expenditure on higher education, to apportion the cuts selectively on the basis of various indicators of performance by universities and departments within them.

Possible Empirical Research

Each of the different financial mechanisms outlined above is likely to stimulate different organizational behavior in the institutions receiving the finance:

Have . . . public endowments contributed in general to promote the end of their institution? Have they contributed to encourage the diligence and to improve the abilities of their teachers? Have they directed the course of education towards objectives more useful, both to the individual and to the public, than those which would naturally have gone of its own accord? It should not seem very difficult to give at least a probable answer to each of these questions.[32]

In order to begin to turn Smith's speculative probabilities into testable hypotheses, in this section I indicate the types of prediction which are susceptible to empirical investigation.

In a system where finance originates in the center and is distributed according to certain fixed rules, we would expect the relationship between users and providers of finance at each level to be one of conflict. Users would seek to manipulate the rules to their advantage, and providers would make new rules to close what were seen as loopholes. In such a system any expenditure would be subject to detailed administrative checks, and academics would complain that initiative was stultified.

Bureaucracies resist change until the pressure becomes irresistible, because change requires rewriting the rules. Change would be infrequent, but when it did occur it would be externally generated, substantial, and nonincremental.

Academic staff would adopt the attitudes of employees of the bureaucracy who are paid to perform specific tasks. They would have the same security of tenure as other government employees, as well as prescribed hours of work and clearly specified responsibilities and conditions of service. They would probably be willing to adopt methods of industrial confrontation in the furtherance of disputes. Staff and students would have a common interest in extracting more resources from administrators.

When ultimate financial power rests in the corporate body, there are no explicit outside pressures that can force the members of the college to make

---

[31]National Board for Prices and Incomes (NBPI), *Pay of University Teachers, First Report.*
[32]Smith, *Wealth of Nations*, Book V, chap. i, p. 246.

changes against the interests of its members. So here, too, change would be infrequent and nonincremental. Occasionally there may be a sufficient shift in collegiate opinion to bring about discrete reforms;[33] more rarely, outside forces may build up sufficient power to bring about sharp changes.

In most other respects the college would differ from the bureaucratic university. There would be differences of opinion among members of the college, with no joint community of academic interest to confront external purveyors of funds. Without bureaucratic rules or market mechanisms to allocate funds, shifting coalitions and unstable alliances would determine resource distribution. Power struggles between ambitious members of the college would be common, and there would be little impediment to those who wished to use the security of college membership either as the basis of a quiet life or as a springboard for other income-generating activities, such as industrial consultancy or writing novels. "If he is naturally active and a lover of labour, it is his interest to employ that activity in any way from which he can derive some advantage, rather than in the performance of his duty, from which he can derive none."[34]

Members of the college would grant themselves security of tenure and would have an interest in limiting their numbers. They would enforce a lengthy period of probation on novitiates, partly to limit numbers and partly to ensure conformity with the college ethos. Students, too, would be limited in number to those the college felt it could deal with readily within the available resources. Increased demand by students would merely increase the competition for entry. Students who were admitted would tend to have attributes of which members of the college approved. Staff-student relations would be easygoing and informal, with students feeling privileged to be admitted and sharing common values with their teachers. Members of the college would see no reason to inform outsiders of their affairs and the college would be something of a mystery to those outside it.

In the university that depends for its income on the sale of services, evolutionary change in response to the changing external environment

---

[33]The point is well made in the following anecdote related by Liam Hudson: "I was, for a short while, a fellow of a Cambridge college deeply and historically dedicated to the exclusion of women. A small group of us on the college council, married and insensitive to history, urged two things: the admission of women to meals, and the curtailment of some of the more gluttonous excesses of the college's feasts. We urged and urged; and the college's stalwarts resisted and resisted. The going at times became troubled; I remember that we were once stigmatized collectively as 'young fellows hastening home to their impatient wives.' I remember, too, a member of the college's old guard, shedding tears as he stood before us in his sandals, reminding us that while none of us particularly enjoyed feasting, it was our duty to the college servants to leave traditional practices unaltered. The upshot was that we lost, comprehensively. As a concession, women were allowed in for two nights a week to the High Table, as long as they did not retire to take port afterwards, where they might cause offence to the unmarried fellows. And yet, and yet. . . . Within a few months, a number of us had gone off to jobs elsewhere. And within a few months more, the whole college had gone totally co-ed, and, it seems, with little more than a murmer" ("Eureka Syndrome," p. 8).

[34]Smith, *Wealth of Nations*, Book V, chap. i, p. 297.

would be continuous and incremental. There might be demands from time to time for changes in the rules regulating market conduct: for example, accreditation agencies might be asked to protect consumers from exploitation by ruthless marketing methods. There would not, however, be external pressures for major reforms of institutions. Institutions would provide outsiders with an abundance of information about themselves, possibly not always strictly accurate. Within universities there might be demands from those engaged in less successful activities for protection from market forces in the form of special subsidies because of academic merit, or claims of unfair competition.

There would be considerable debate about the best balance between short-term and long-term income maximization. Some within the university enterprise would press for maximization of current sales by admitting as many students as possible and adapting course provision to client demands. They would claim that the best provision for the future is to have the largest possible market share. Others would draw attention to the long-term security of an up-market brand image. Arguments about prestige and status are, in many respects, arguments about preserving long-term market advantages. High-prestige institutions would endeavor to ensure that their product was perceived as one of high quality, and thus they would seek to limit sales as a way of enhancing that prestige. Special discounts in the form of scholarships would be offered to high-ability students likely to add to the institution's rating by the market.

Tenure of members of the academic staff would be largely dependent on their success in obtaining funds, and most tenure contracts would contain a clause making inadequate resources a sufficient reason for dismissal. A few luminaries, outstanding scholars useful for promotional purposes in attracting students or getting research grants, would be offered particularly attractive financial terms in the form of more secure tenure or higher salary.

Subject to the constraints of long-run marketing strategy, institutions would seek to admit as many students as possible, and buyer-seller relations between staff and students would be usual. Staff would be aware of the costs of the time devoted to students; and students would expect to have the right to certain amounts of staff time and interest, and they might seek redress if they felt they were not getting value for money. They would adopt consumerist behavior and would make arrangements for their own evaluations of courses and academic services.

FINANCE, POLICY, AND CHANGE

Governments can influence the behavior of higher education systems and institutions by altering the terms on which financial resources are made available. They can encourage or discourage activities by making it easier or more difficult to earn income by undertaking them. When a government is not the main provider of finance, it can usually influence financial mechanisms more readily than it can make legal and administrative regulations that will have the desired effect. Direct regulation is cumbersome and ineffective. Discrepancies between policy intentions and policy outcomes often arise because systems of financial incentive do not correspond to the legal regulations through which government tries to implement its policy. Vested interests find loopholes and exploit them.

Governments that concentrate on financial mechanisms as a way of implementing higher education policy do not have to be particularly concerned about the intractable problem of measuring outputs in order to evaluate the efficiency with which funds are being used. In a sense, resources are always used efficiently. The individuals or groups who control their use pursue their own priorities. It may well be that having a comfortable life has a high priority, or that priorities are based on misconceptions. The task of government is to manipulate the regulations governing flows of finance so that the priorities of other groups and individuals will have more influence.

It is not claimed that financial incentives are the only factors that influence the authority structure and behavior of universities. Financial flows can be manipulated, however, whereas such intangible sources of power as charisma, tradition, contractual rights, experience, prestige, and expertise cannot.[35] Governments normally wish to modify the behavior of universities at the margin. It can be argued that government support in Britain for the collegial tradition, by means of the University Grants Committee, has given too much influence to the suppliers of academic services and too little independence to the users of the services or that the support has not worked for the collective good of society. If so, what is required is not a revolutionary change that would take power completely away from the professional staff of universities, but a marginal shift of emphasis which would make the institutions more responsive to changing social and economic needs. For such changes, financial instruments are particularly well suited. Financial incentives operate at the margin, and it is at the margin that change occurs.

---

[35]Cf. Clark, *Higher Education System.*

BIBLIOGRAPHY

Arrow, Kenneth S. "Higher Education as a Filter." In *Efficiency in Universities*, ed. R. Attiyeh and K. G. Lumsden. New York: Elsevier, 1974.

Attiyeh, Richard. "Survey of the Issues." In *Efficiency in Universities*, ed. R. Attiyeh and K. G. Lumsden. New York: Elsevier, 1974.

Becher, Tony, and Maurice Kogan. *Process and Structure in Higher Education*. London: Heinemann, 1980.

Becker, Gary S. *Human Capital: A Theoretical and Empirical Analysis with Special Reference to Education*. Princeton: Princeton University Press, 1964.

Berg, Ivar. *Education and Jobs: The Great Training Robbery*. Harmondsworth, Middlesex: Penguin Books, 1970.

Blaug, Mark. "Approaches to Educational Planning." *Economic Journal* 77, no. 1 (1967):48–65.

———. "The Empirical Status of Human Capital Theory: A Slightly Jaundiced View." *Journal of Economic Literature* 14 (1976):51–76.

Cerych, Ladislav, and Guy Neave. "Structure, Promotion and Appointment of Academic Staff in Four Countries." Paris: European Institute of Education, 1981. Mimeo.

Clark, Burton R. "The Many Pathways of Academic Coordination." *Higher Education* 8 (1979):251–267.

———. *The Higher Education System: Academic Organization in Cross-National Perspective*. Berkeley, Los Angeles, London: University of California Press, 1983.

Dolphin, Anthony M. "The Demand for Higher Education." *Employment Gazette* (U.K.) (July 1981), pp. 134–136.

Dore, Ronald A. *The Diploma Disease: Education, Qualifications and Development*. London: Allen and Unwin, 1976.

Freeman, Richard B. "Response to Change in the United States." In *Higher Education and the Labour Market*, ed. Robert M. Lindley. Guildford, England: Society for Research into Higher Education, 1982.

Garvin, David A. *The Economics of University Behavior*. New York: Academic Press, 1981.

Hansen, W. Lee, and Burton Weisbrod. "The Distribution of Costs and Direct Benefits of Public Higher Education." *Journal of Human Resources* 14 (1969): 176–191.

Harrod, Roy F. *The Life of John Maynard Keynes*. London: Macmillan, 1951.

Hudson, Liam. "The Eureka Syndrome." *The Times Higher Education Supplement* (November 6, 1982), p. 8.

Kogan, Maurice. "Audit, Control and Freedom." *Higher Education Bulletin* 1 (1969): 16–27.

Layard, Richard G., and George S. Psacharopoulos. "The Screening Hypothesis and the Returns to Education." *Journal of Political Economy* 82 (1974):985–998.

Lindley, Robert M., ed. *Higher Education and the Labour Market*. Guildford, England: Society for Research into Higher Education, 1982.

Maynard, Alan. "Privatisation and the Market Mechanism in Higher Education:

Some Myths and a Little Reality." In *Resource Allocation in Higher Education*, ed. Alfred Morris and John Sizer. Guildford, England: Society for Research into Higher Education, 1982.

Morris, Alfred. "The Quinquennial Settlement: A Commentary." *Higher Education Review* 5 (1973):26−51.

———. "Changing the Ways of Allocating Resources to Universities." *Higher Education Review* 6 (1974):8−36.

———. "Separate Funding of University Teaching and Research." *Higher Education Review* 7 (1975):42−58.

National Board for Prices and Incomes (NBPI). *Standing Reference on the Pay of University Teachers in Great Britain. First Report*. Report no. 98. London: HMSO, Cmnd. 3866, 1968.

———. *Standing Reference on the Pay of University Teachers in Great Britain. Second Report*. Report no. 145. London: HMSO, Cmnd. 4334, 1970.

Organisation for Economic Co-operation and Development (OECD). "Intergovernmental Conference on Policies for Higher Education in the Eighties: Conclusions." Paris: OECD, ref. SME/ET/81.3, 1981. Mimeo.

Perkin, Harold. *Key Profession: The History of the Association of University Teachers*. London: Routledge and Kegan Paul, 1969.

Pissarides, C. A. "From School to University: The Demand for Post Compulsory Education in Britain." *Economic Journal* 92 (September 1982): 654−667.

Psacharopoulos, George, and Bikas Sanyal. "Student Expectations and Labour Market Performance: The Case of the Philippines." *Higher Education* 10 (1981): 449−472.

———. "Student Expectations and Graduate Market Performance in Egypt." *Higher Education* 11 (1982):27−50.

Psacharopoulos, George, and Costas Soumelis. "A Quantitative Analysis of the Demand for Higher Education." *Higher Education* 8 (1979):159−178.

Schultz, Theodore W. "Investment in Human Capital." *American Economic Review* 51 (1961):1−17.

Smith, Adam. *The Wealth of Nations*. 1776. Repr. London: Everyman's Library, 1971.

Thurow, Lester C. "Education and Economic Equality." *Public Interest* 28 (1972): 66−81.

Trow, Martin. "Comparative Perspectives on Access." In *Access to Higher Education*, ed. Oliver Fulton. Guildford, England: Society for Research into Higher Education, 1981.

Williams, Gareth L., Tessa A. Blackstone, and David H. Metcalf. *The Academic Labour Market*. New York: Elsevier, 1974.

Williams, Gareth L., and Alan G. Gordon. "16 and 18 Year Olds' Attitudes to Education." *Higher Education Bulletin* 4, no. 1 (1975):23−38.

———. "Perceived Earnings Functions and *Ex Ante* Rates of Return to Post-Compulsory Education in England." *Higher Education* 10 (1981):199−227.

Woodhall, Maureen. *Student Loans: Lessons from Recent International Experiences*. London: Policy Studies Institute, 1982.

4. THE ORGANIZATIONAL CONCEPTION

Burton R. Clark

An organizational perspective on higher education commonly takes analysts inside the system. It sends researchers in search of what academics actually do. With a little imagination it allows observers to see the system from the bottom up, looking out from the positions and perspectives of faculty, students, and local administrators, as well as from the top down, where analysis flows toward the problems and orientations of central officials, national legislators, and those who advise and influence them. In either event, this approach allows us to see the world through the eyes of the main actors and hence to portray the relations of the system to the environment from the inside out. When this perspective is at the top of its form, it becomes a way to give the system its due. The higher education system is taken seriously when observers focus on how it initiates and responds, how it maintains stability and induces change, as well as how it follows paths that are determined by others.

When we take an internal approach to the shaping of action and policy we are able to resist the temptation to say that "society" or "social forces" determine higher education. By emphasizing immediate contexts, we start close in; then, as need be, analysis moves outward to larger settings. This tactic is parsimonious, since we take up proximate causes first and clarify the local contexts that mediate the effects of larger ones. It is also increasingly necessary. As in other major spheres of society, sectorial hegemony develops when bureaucrats and professionals occupy key internal sites in ever more complicated webs of work and authority. Modern systems of higher education develop massive structures and elaborate procedures that strengthen internal control over operations and provide defense in depth against environmental turbulence. Analysts of diverse conviction have argued the need to go inside "the black box" of organized higher education. The organizational approach does so, joined increasingly by investigators converging on internal features as they pursue specific historical developments, political dimensions of the system, the economic behavior of universities, the determinants of access and achievement—in short, those applying other perspectives presented in this volume. A focus on organizational dimensions assists these other ways of viewing higher education by helping to establish which internal characteristics are important, pulling together in integrative frameworks the crucial features of organizations that otherwise would be treated in a fragmented fashion.

The view from the inside also emphasizes institutional response. Identifying such external "demands" as more consumers or more available jobs is only the beginning of analysis. We need further to ask: What is the response to a particular change in external conditions? Or, as a "demand" flows into the system, who supports it, who resists it, and how is it organizationally implemented and thereby shaped? How much did the system determine the demand in the first place, as, for example, when decades of enforcing high standards in the educational system convince the overwhelming majority of young people that higher education is not for them?

An internalist perspective leads researchers to search for the ways in which the higher education system, moving by its own internal logics and its forms of response, will shape other institutions and society in general. This point hardly needs any further initial support than to emphasize the obvious effects of scientific research being carried out in academic systems, particularly in the international centers of learning, but also flowing out from them to other systems to make them dynamic too. We are near the end of a half century in which academic physicists have harnessed atomic energy, academic biologists have made revolutionary advances in genetic engineering, and academic mathematicians and engineers have helped develop the computer. And since academics prepare nearly all the professional cadres of society, as well as those persons who engage in research and development elsewhere, it is appropriate to view the academic system as the home of the key profession, the one that trains all the others.[1] With so many major avenues of influence there is growing reason to pursue the question of how higher education shapes society.

After the comparative research of the past decade, it is possible to offer a major first cut in what can be seen when we approach higher education as an organized system. First, knowledge is the common substance involved in the activities of the system: research creates it; scholarship preserves, refines, and modifies it; teaching and service disseminate it.[2] The handling of advanced bodies of knowledge has been central to higher education since its beginning and remains common ground across varied national systems. When we look to "the factory floor" of higher education, what we see are clusters of professionals tending various bundles of knowledge. They are the "subjects" or "subject matters," and it is around them that organization takes place. Hence, the concentration on knowledge is what academics have most in common. But what they have least in common is common knowledge, since the bundles they tend are specialized and separated one from another.

---

[1] Perkin, *Key Profession*.
[2] Clark, *Higher Education System*, chap. 1, "Knowledge."

To start with subjects as substance is to steer analysis toward actual operations and away from the stated goals and purposes of higher education. For several decades, organizational analysts have been conscious of the distinction between nominal and operative ends. Sophisticated administrators in higher education, as well as elsewhere in society, surely have long been aware of the difference. The analysis of proclaimed ends of universities and higher education soon degenerates into a largely empty exercise of determining who proclaims which clichés, focusing on the broad statements that tell little about what is being done or what will occur. The "purposes" of any major sector of society are increasingly stated in general terms, as activities within the sector become more numerous, complex, and ambiguous. Stated purposes then become wide philosophies that leave the determination of action and policy largely to interest-group struggles and operational mandates. It matters not whether we study small or large systems, in the West or in the Communist bloc. Swedish statements of purpose in higher education, for example, "democracy, personality development, social change," tell us no more than American statements, such as research, teaching, and service. Official declarations in Communist nations, such as those in Poland—"education for self-fulfillment" and "instruction of qualified personnel for all jobs in the economy, culture, and all sectors of social life requiring credentials of higher education"—are hardly an improvement.[3] In contrast, to pick up on the many bundles of knowledge which are the substances of the system is to steer attention to the operating levels where specific groups have specific operative goals: the improvement of research in physics; the teaching of history to undergraduates; the provision of outpatient medical services in an urban neighborhood.

The organization of the system around subjects has its first important dimension in a structure of work.[4] It is inescapable that research, teaching, and other academic activities are heavily conditioned by how tasks are apportioned to academic groups within and among academic enterprises. There is a highly structured division of labor, a finely tuned specialization, and the specific location of academics in that structure becomes the prime determinant of their more material interests. For example, physicists behave like physicists, not like professors of Greek literature. Further, physicists in community colleges, or in other short-cycle units where they teach introductory materials many hours a week to large numbers of first-year students, and do virtually only that, cannot possibly think and act like physicists in research universities.

The higher education system as a whole portions its personnel along at least four different horizontal and vertical dimensions: sectors, hierarchies,

---

[3]Kerr et al., *12 Systems of Higher Education*.
[4]Clark, *Higher Education System*, chap. 2, "Work."

sections, and tiers. The sectors are different types of universities and colleges, including those that many countries prefer to categorize as further, or postsecondary, rather than higher education. Academics also find places in an institutional hierarchy, since the sectors, and enterprises within them, become arranged everywhere to some degree in functional and status ranks. Attached to positions in the hierarchy are different sets of tasks and duties, privileges and punishments. Then, within the individual academic enterprise, similar horizontal and vertical assignments take place: to sections, that is, departments, chairs, and institutes; and to tiers, essentially to a graduate or professional specialized higher tier or to the less specialized work of the undergraduate segment. In all its many divisions, the structure of work everywhere becomes a primary element.[5]

It is also inescapable that activities and outcomes, indeed the nature of knowledge itself, are conditioned by the orientations that academics absorb from their disciplines, universities and colleges, the academic profession overall, and even their national system at large.[6] There are "thought styles" rooted in "thought collectives";[7] there is a symbolic side of academic life, a "culture" as well as a social structure. In a section of society which traffics in ideas, many types of symbols, with related meanings, loom large. Quiet fanaticism may even be characteristic, since academics seem inclined to view their own disciplines and subspecialties as superior to all others. Academic subcultures are frequently in conflict: among students, for example, and between them and the faculty; or between those of the faculty and those of the administrators grouped in institutional and national offices. Notable is the ascendance of disciplinary cultures and subcultures, now catching the attention of researchers internationally, as reported in chapter 6 by Tony Becher on the cultural view and suggested in chapter 7 by Simon Schwartzman on scientific activity.[8] In all its many divisions, the belief or cultural side of academic organization everywhere becomes a second primary element.

Third, as elsewhere, organization is authority, a way of concentrating and diffusing legitimate power.[9] As work and belief are joined together in amalgams of material and subjective interest around particular subjects— the location of some physicists in a university department together with the

---

[5]For some of the better descriptive materials on the structure of higher education in various countries, see Ben-David, *Centers of Learning*; Blau, *Organization of Academic Work*; Clark, *Academic Power in Italy*; Halsey and Trow, *British Academics*; Van de Graaff et al., *Academic Power*; Becher and Kogan, *Process and Structure in Higher Education*; Premfors, *Politics of Higher Education*; Geiger, *Private Sectors in Higher Education*; Levy, *The State and Higher Education in Latin America*.

[6]Clark, *Higher Education System*, chap. 3, "Belief."

[7]Fleck, *Genesis and Development of a Scientific Fact*, passim.

[8]See also Becher, "Towards a Definition of Disciplinary Cultures"; Dill, "Management of Academic Culture."

[9]Clark, *Higher Education System*, chap. 4, "Authority."

beliefs they have absorbed from the culture of physics—then the many academic groups thereby solidified in the understructure seek influence that will aid their efforts and protect their positions. They particularly develop professional or guild forms of authority at the local level—some personal, some collegial—and try to extend them upward to control or influence action at the higher levels, including the national center. At the institutional level there are independent bases of influence in many countries in the form of trustee control and institutional bureaucracy. At the system level we often find an administrative class of civil servants occupying roles in which they are responsible for systemwide allocation and order. There, legitimately, they are joined by some legislators, some other public executives, and, increasingly, by judges. Outside interest groups seek and often gain systematic representation, leading toward corporatist or semicorporatist patterns of influence. Again, the divisions are many and the picture is increasingly complex. But the structure of authority is without doubt a primary component. From the bottom to the top, the many groups that wish to steer the course of events will seek to lay hands on some levers of control.[10]

To focus on these three broad elements is to see the higher education system itself as a principal determinant of the behavior of academics, even of the behavior of the flow-through clientele we call students. The participants take up shared positions, or roles, in the system, which come equipped with duties and responsibilities, incentives and sanctions. They learn from vicarious and personal experiences in the system, experiences of those who have gone before and of their contemporary peers as well as their own, what they can and cannot accomplish, what is worth doing, what effort and achievement will cost. From the broadest roles of administrator, faculty, and student and the more specific ones, such as registrar, professor of chemistry, or art student, come conceptions of necessity and possibility. Differentially integrated in the set of roles are three faces of power: power to prevail in overt conflict over explicit issues, power to keep issues off the agendas of action, and power to shape conceptions of what can and ought to be done.

Considerable advance has been made during the 1960s and 1970s in grasping these elements and understanding how they vary within and among systems. We have learned how to compare universities and colleges, within and across countries, in the horizontal arrangements of academic tasks and groups. For example, cross-national research has isolated the chair, the department, and the interdisciplinary college or program as the

---

[10]In addition to the references specified in note 5 above, most of which deal with power and politics, see Moodie and Eustace, *Power and Authority in British Universities*; Levy, *University and Government in Mexico*; Clark and Youn, *Academic Power in the United States*; van den Berghe, *Power and Privilege at an African University*; Epstein, *Governing the University*; Berdahl, *British Universities and the State*.

three primary ways of organizing at the operating level and has provided some footing for estimating the advantages and disadvantages of each. As the rigidities of the chair in the systems of continental Europe, as well as the excesses of personal influence it permits, have become more apparent, they have generated reforms that move toward broader operating units as supports for fields of study growing in size and complexity. We have also observed that national systems vary significantly in how they vertically organize elementary and advanced work, with related rungs of certification and exit, and again can point to broad effects. As an example, the two-tier structure of undergraduate and graduate levels in the American university clearly separates and supports the most advanced research and training in a way not possible in universities of many other countries where specialization became rooted in the first tier, with less deliberate structure above that level. Those universities then have to contend with the access and selection problems of the lower rungs of mass higher education.

In the pursuit of beliefs, we are now more aware than we were two decades ago about how national systems vary in supporting disciplinary cultures and institutional identities. Some turn the disciplines loose to fragment as they please, as in the United States; others rein them in, as in Italy. Some leave institutions to form character individually, as in Great Britain; others try to render them interchangeable parts of a larger collectivity, as in France traditionally. And we clearly have learned much about the exercise of legitimate academic power at several levels, with many possible combinations of such basic forms as the personal, collegial, bureaucratic, and political thinning down empirically into several modes. We can specify a traditional European mode that combined central bureaucracy with local and national academic oligarchy, and compare it with a traditional American mode of weak central staff, trustee and bureaucratic strength at the institutional level, and faculty influence at the local level which has not become, to the same extent as in Europe, a basis for national control. On all these topics, cross-national comparison has broadened research horizons and widened conceptions of the possible, including many unanticipated ways of lessening the effectiveness of higher education.

Perhaps the most significant awareness that has come from cross-national organizational analysis is the sense that modern national systems contain an ever expanding, inordinate complexity of tasks and relationships. We find Islamic poetry and biometeorology, forestry and international studies, French literature and econometrics—and on and on, virtually without end. We are not very surprised when the proliferation of subjects moves on to auto repairing, hair styling, and belly dancing. If the core faculty of the university will not permit certain subjects, then the Extension Division or evening college will. If the university as a whole will not, then other colleges take up the new subjects. General nomenclature shifts to widen the boundaries, from "higher education" to "postsecondary." The boundaries are stretched, even under strongly centralized and concentrated rule; some Communist nations, such as Poland, count colleges of sport and tourism as part of postsecondary education.[11] In short, the modern university is in itself a relatively open system. When various nonuniversity sectors and specific specialized schools develop, the openness is greatly extended and boundaries become virtually impossible to define. In their willingness and capacity to take on new subjects as additional tasks, we are increasingly confronted by systems of ever expanding scope. Modern higher education becomes an almost limitless system.

To seek the more important joints of this complex system, we may pursue three questions: What is central in the way that so many fields of study coexist and relate? What then follows for the operation of the system as a system? What follows for changes the system undergoes? In short, we may pursue composition, coordination, and change. Composition has pride of place, since it comes first in the logic of the system.

THE MASTER MATRIX

Academics have a host of memberships that bring them under various influences. They often belong to a specific subspecialty within a discipline while belonging to the discipline as a whole. They often belong to a discipline and a multidisciplinary unit: an undergraduate college such as a residential college at Oxford or Cambridge; a multidisciplinary professional school such as medicine or education; an area studies program such as Latin American or African studies; a problem-centered unit such as urban or environmental studies. Academics belong to a discipline and to the academic profession at large. They belong to a particular university or college and to the entire national system, the latter turned into a potent membership in nationalized systems by means of civil service rank and salary and other systemwide categories. Academics are caught up in various matrices,[12] with multiple memberships that shape their work, call upon their loyalties, and apportion their authority. Central among the matrices is the most common fact of academic work: the academic belongs simultaneously to a discipline, a field of study, and an enterprise, a specific university or college.

These two primary modes of organization crisscross each other. The individual university or college collects in one place some members of the disciplines, putting some physicists, economists, and historians together. It thereby links together small segments of the separate disciplines but also fragments each discipline, scattering physicists, for example, among a host

<hr />

[11]Szczepanski, *Systems of Higher Education: Poland*; Matejko, "Planning and Tradition."
[12]On the concept of matrix in organizational thought, see Sayles, "Matrix Organization"; Mintzberg, *Structuring of Organizations*, pp. 168–175.

of sites and thereby turning them all into local operators. The enterprise mode of organization clearly cuts sharply across the lines of the disciplines. In turn, the discipline is a point of common commitment and identification along precise lines of specialization. But it is also comprehensive in that it pulls together a craftlike community of interest which reaches across large territories, nationally and, usually, internationally. We may see its members as specialists who are "assigned" to the enterprises. The discipline links parts of one enterprise with similar parts in others but it also thereby fragments each institution. As has been widely noted, locals are made into cosmopolitans, reducing local identification while orienting academics to the far-flung norms and interests of national and international cohorts of colleagues. As a result, a national system of higher education may be and often is as much a set of disciplines and professions as it is a set of universities and colleges.

The crossing of these two lines of membership provides the master matrix of the higher education system. Therein lies much of the underlying uniqueness of higher education, since the discipline-enterprise matrix is not found elsewhere in anything like the same scope and intensity. Nearest to it is the independent research institute and the research and development (R&D) laboratory in business and industry, each of which is staffed with university-trained experts concentrating on their specific subjects. In this regard higher education diverges sharply from elementary and secondary education. The lower levels lack the disciplinary commitments, and related rewards, which in higher education so strongly slash across institutions and national systems. They are more bounded by local structure and national culture.

This master matrix of higher education is not the same everywhere. The relative weight of the discipline and the enterprise varies across and within national systems. The primary source of variation is the importance given to research rather than teaching. The dominance of research in the German system since the early part of the nineteenth century means that modern German universities "emphasize disciplinary criteria almost to the exclusion of collegiate ones."[13] In partial contrast, British universities, influenced by the Oxford-Cambridge pattern of primary membership in interdisciplinary colleges and the concentration on teaching undergraduates, ensnare their academic staff in a stronger set of institutional commitments and values. In sharp contrast with the German model, universities in many developing countries, for example, Nigeria,[14] with little money for research, have weak rewards for disciplinary competence and strong incentives for pleasing those who control the institution from within and without.

---

[13]Turner, "Growth of Professorial Research in Prussia," p. 159.
[14]Van den Berghe, *Power and Privilege at an African University*.

Within the American system the research university gives substantial weight to the specialty and to recognized performance in it. It becomes discipline-centered and relatively professor-driven. In contrast, the community college emphasizes teaching to the exclusion of research and weakens the bonds of specialty. The instructor may teach all of sociology rather than a segment of it and then also teach anthropology and psychology. The enterprise becomes more administrator-driven and student-driven.

At bottom, higher education needs disciplines to concentrate on research and scholarship and it needs universities and colleges to concentrate on teaching and dissemination. If teaching were not necessary higher education could and probably would dismantle its enterprises and concentrate each discipline in a lesser number of major clusters, as happens in part whenever research is divorced from the university and given over to a set of institutes, as in the French structure of research academies. It is teaching that insists on wider dispersal of specialists, moving the disciplinarians to where the students are. If research were not necessary, higher education could and probably would have fewer disciplines, and more general major ones, as happens in part in the teaching-centered sectors in differentiated systems.

Another source of variation is the importance given to general or liberal education compared with specialized education. For example, the independent liberal arts college in the United States, in comparison with the university, reduces the weight of the discipline and makes professors more enterprise-centered. Within the American research university, the undergraduate level is more enterprise-centered than the graduate level. Notably, selection of undergraduate students is carried out by offices and committees of the whole, whereas selection at the graduate level is primarily made by the individual departments and professional schools. The packaging of larger bundles of knowledge pulls specialized personnel together, thereby changing their mix of commitments toward a more holistic view at the local level.

But amid such differences we discern a basic trend: as bundles of high knowledge multiply and knowledge-bearing groups proliferate, the higher levels of education take the form of this master matrix. Disciplines ascend, as they have been doing in the leading systems for a century and a half, with disciplines and enterprises then crosscutting one another in ever more complicated arrangements. To analyze matrix organization is then to cut analytically at the joints of the confusing complicated structures of modern higher education. And to emphasize the matrix concept is to insist that analysis pursues the disciplines as concerns that have their own peculiar nature, individually and collectively. As Norton Long wrote some thirty years ago,[15] "The organization of a science is interesting for a student of

---

[15]Long, "Power and Administration," p. 262.

administration because it suggests a basis of cooperation in which the problem and the subject matter . . . control the behavior of those embarked in the enterprise. Thus physics and chemistry are disciplines, but they are not organized to carry out the will of legitimate superiors. They are going concerns with problems and procedures that have taken form through generations of effort and have emerged into highly conscious goal-oriented activities." These going concerns go far in determining the nature of academic work. We may even view them as institutional instruments of fundamental importance in efficiently serving certain values and achieving certain outcomes. R. Steven Turner has noted "that universal character-istic of the modern professoriate which underlies its unparalleled efficiency as an instrument of science and scholarship: appointive procedures which subordinate institutional to disciplinary values."[16]

Since the discipline and the enterprise converge and commingle in the operating units of universities and colleges, a department or a chair is simultaneously an arm of a discipline and a part of an enterprise and draws strength from the combination. Thus there is an organic base for the impressive primacy of these units which has been widely noted in the research literature.[17] Bottom-heavy organization, we may call it, with each disciplinary (or interdisciplinary) unit within the enterprise having self-evident and acclaimed primacy in a front-line task. Special status accrues to each unit as it becomes authoritative, within the organization, in its "own" field of learning. The degree of authoritativeness naturally varies: across national systems, higher in the more advanced; across sectors within dif-ferentiated systems, higher in those concentrating on higher levels of expertise; and across subjects within the university or college, higher where knowledge is the most plentiful, structured, and arcane. But overall it is in the individual and combined strength of these authoritative units that we find the first reason that universities and colleges are something other than unitary organizations, that the considerable exercise of personal and col-legial forms of authority is not a mere historical survival, and that an unusual vocabulary of craft and guild, federation and conglomerate, is required to tease out the realities of academic organization which remain hidden when approached by the standard terminologies of organizational life.

BUREAUCRACY AND ITS ALTERNATIVES

How are disciplines and enterprises and their many members concerted, linked together in larger systems of state, region, and nation? Clearly not in

---

[16]Turner, "Growth of Professorial Research in Prussia," p. 159.

[17]See Moodie and Eustace, *Power and Authority in British Universities*, p. 61; Berg and Östergren, *Innovations and Innovation Processes in Higher Education*, p. 102; Becher and Kogan, *Process and Structure in Higher Education*, chap. 6, "Basic Units."

neat patterns, not anywhere. The master matrix ensures confusing complexity, for if a larger system is a set of disciplines as well as a set of enterprises, operating on different axes, then who can be clearly in charge? The concept of loose coupling which has been creatively applied to higher education at the institutional level[18] has to be applied in the large, so broadly, in fact, that we shift from organizational imagery as normally understood. Here analysis is aided by the body of thought developed in political economy which centers on politics and markets,[19] a literature that explores the pros and cons of state authority and market linkages in coordinating the efforts of large numbers of people.

As elsewhere, state authority in higher education divides into political and bureaucratic forms. In turn, the market form is found everywhere in national systems of higher education but in varying strength in such subtypes as the consumer market, the internal labor market, and the institutional market in which institutions voluntarily compete, cooperate, and imitate more on the basis of reputation than of monetary exchange.[20] It is then also necessary to add professional oligarchy as a basic form of national integration, since research has revealed in one country after another, from Italy to Sweden, from Mexico to Japan, that professors are a major and often dominant force at national as well as local levels, using mechanisms of influence they have constructed over a long period of time.[21] Coordination can now be seen as vastly more complicated than depicted when the eyes of coordinators and planners fix only on the formal channels of state allocation and supervision. The concerting of action proceeds along varied, intermingled channels. The four general types of coordination labeled as political, bureaucratic, professional, and market offer only the beginning of a useful analytical grasp.

All these major means of linking actors and actions seem to have expanded in recent decades. The bureaucratic tools are clearly more noticeable than those of a quarter century ago, in small as well as in large systems. Bureaucratic staffs have been strengthened; the jurisdictions of educational bureaus have been enlarged; administrative layers have been added, at national, regional, and local levels; bureaucratic rules have become far more numerous; administrators have specialized more and have become more professional in many matters of allocation and supervision. Bureaucracy becomes more assertive and seemingly more dominant. Yet, at the same time, the political modes of coordination have been strengthened. The use of higher education as a political issue has expanded con-

---

[18]See Cohen and March, *Leadership and Ambiguity*; March and Olsen, *Ambiguity and Choice in Organizations*; Baldridge et al., *Policy Making and Effective Leadership*.

[19]Lindblom, *Politics and Markets*.

[20]Clark, *Higher Education System*, chap. 5, "Integration."

[21]Clark, *Academic Power in Italy*; Premfors and Östergren, *Systems of Higher Education: Sweden*; Levy, *University and Government in Mexico*; Cummings et al., *Changes in the Japanese University*; Van de Graaff et al., *Academic Power*.

siderably, first increased by the dramatic events of student discontent in the 1960s but held to a higher level of attention over the long run by the much higher cost of expanded and enriched systems and the stronger popular concern and interest that are entailed in more accessible higher education. The regular political channels of legislative committees, top officials in the executive branch, the courts, and the political parties are now more involved in higher education than they were earlier. Internal interest groups have multiplied and hardened their own organizations and representation, as when faculty move into collective bargaining or establish lobbying consortia. External interest groups pay more attention, given the higher stakes and more numerous payoffs, moving toward corporatist patterns of formal participation in governmental decision making in higher education.

Then, too, professors are not pushed aside in national coordination or in local control. Subject expertise everywhere pushes for home rule on the part of the many local groups. These groups carry their influence up the dual lines of discipline and enterprise, and thus a basic source of influence grows in importance. With it, there is a long-run expansion of collegial, if oligarchical, bodies of academics which have jurisdictions at higher levels: research councils are the most obvious, moving along disciplinary lines; national bodies of rectors, vice-chancellors, and presidents develop as representatives of the local enterprises; the headquarters of the associations of the individual disciplines shift from amateur operation toward professional and bureaucratic expertise in representation. Although senior professors visibly lost power in many countries during the 1960s and 1970s, the professoriat as a whole continued to deepen and widen its involvement in the integration of national systems. The increased influence of the bureaucratic and political channels steadily stimulates a reaction by professors and related staff, with the always powerful leverage of expertise. Knowledge is power, more here than elsewhere.

Finally, analysis has begun to grasp the many ways that marketlike exchanges concert national systems, whether small or large, centralized or decentralized, expanding their role as members increase and tasks multiply. Consumer markets are everywhere at work: there is some consumer choice, some voting with one's feet, in even the most state-driven systems, and of course there are many such choices, among courses, departments, disciplines, enterprises, and even national systems, when state constraints are light. And everywhere there is a powerful latent consumer market in the basing of budgets on enrollments. This common practice institutionalizes an enrollment economy that sharply limits the discretion of politicians, administrators, and professors. The budgeting problem then becomes "one of finding a set of allocations that produces an educational program that attracts enough enrollment to provide the allocations."[22] This latent depen-

---

[22]Cohen and March, *Leadership and Ambiguity*, p. 102. On the concept of the enrollment economy, see Clark, *Adult Education in Transition*, pp. 61–63.

dence on customers becomes sharply manifest when institutions, individually or collectively, face a dwindling number of students. Then everything may be up for grabs, including academic tenure, as changes in the enrollment base produce "financial exigencies" that change some of the fundamental rules of the game. In any event, consumer markets, in various forms, coorder academic structures and practices, shuffling allocations, changing personnel assignments, and altering the respective places of whole enterprises.

Internal labor markets are also everywhere at work, ever more sharply differentiated by discipline and even by precise specialties within disciplines and professional fields; universities go looking not for an academic person but for a physicist or a historian and then for a particular kind of physicist or historian who may even serve locally as one of a kind. And from the side of labor there is always some choice, for nowhere is the state allocation of persons to academic posts so complete as to eliminate choice by faculty and administrators. But there are very large differences in degree and range of choice, and hence in the contribution of the labor market itself to coordination. This market form of linkage may be steered or strongly constrained by a host of conditions: primarily firm regime control (e.g., in the Soviet Union), but also including strong inhibition on the flow of academic labor by uniform national rules and norms (e.g., France), strong control by senior academics over junior staff and advanced students (e.g., Italy), and cultural traditions of lifelong employment in particular institutions (e.g., Japan). A modest amount of mobility is found in such systems as those of the United Kingdom, Canada, and Australia in which institutions hire personnel on their own and stress individual achievement as the basis for the aggregate prestige of the whole. Among the national systems that have mostly full-time personnel, the United States remains the extreme example of academic labor mobility, even when economic depression and/or an "oversupply" of academics seriously dampens the job market for young recruits.

Such functions as high-quality research may heavily depend on the way this type of market operates. The most powerful hypothesis in the comparative sociology of science remains the one advanced by Joseph Ben-David and Abraham Zloczower in 1962: major national systems that are decentralized and competitive are more conducive to scientific progress than are centralized and noncompetitive ones, in large part because of the opportunities thereby given to talented academics, especially younger ones, to move from less to more attractive settings for the development of their ideas.[23]

Institutional markets consist of the interactions of whole enterprises with one another. Reputation seems to be the main commodity of exchange;

---

[23]Ben-David and Zloczower, "Universities and Academic Systems in Modern Societies."

relative prestige not only affects the judgments of consumers and workers but also guides the actions of institutions. Highly valued institutions may sit astride the whole structure. As they do so, they commonly generate strong tides of academic drift, with other enterprises imitating and attempting to converge upon their ways. In the more competitive systems institutions also try to carve out a protected niche in the consumer market, against others, to ensure a favorable enrollment economy.

Notably, we may now observe whole sectors of institutions emerging and developing in response to "market failure" or "state failure." State-financed sectors have often been encouraged by the "failures" of private sectors to provide sufficient access, low-cost education, and secular education. In turn, private sectors are encouraged by the "failures" of public sectors to provide high-quality education or better access or religious education. Latin America is now a laboratory of public-private experiments, with important private sectors emerging as academically superior in some instances, as mass service in others, as religious, and often as escape from politicization.[24] The idea occurs that as national systems continue to come under pressure for "more and better" higher education, a differentiation is likely to occur in the simply structured state systems in which there will be a major residual market, of tasks, for private sectors. If public institutions are providing "the better," they become stubborn about the more, and much of the expansion is likely to go into that residual market. If public enterprises carry "the more," the residual institutional market echoes with demands for the better. And when the public sector is providing neither the more nor the better, government officials as well as multitudes of consumers and workers are likely to tilt toward those institutions, new and old, which compete in that residual market. The interplay among sectors as well as among particular institutions, actions constituting an institutional market, is then an important dynamic driving the interior differentiation of modern systems.

These several major forms of market coordination express a bias that is fundamentally different from political and bureaucratic forms. When an activity is transferred from market contexts to state control, it comes under a bias for aggregation.[25] Things are to be added up. The expectation grows within and outside the government that someone will deliberately pull things together and otherwise systematize. When an activity remains under market conditions or creeps away from state regulation to a more marketlike context, it comes under a bias for disaggregation. Things are not to be

---

[24]Levy, *The State and Higher Education.* On the interaction of private and public sectors in western Europe, the United States, Japan, and the Philippines, see Geiger, *Private Sectors in Higher Education.*

[25]Windham, *Economic Dimensions of Education.*

added up in one heap, in one place: they are to be in a piecemeal state. "System" is then a different matter, but it is still a system.

* * * *

The coordination and integration of national systems become ever more entangled. The nearest to a root cause within the system is the growing complexity of tasks and related groups. Central to that complexity is the matrix of disciplines and enterprises. As disciplines subdivide and proliferate, they stretch one axis of complexity. As additional institutions emerge, they stretch the second dimension. Since the two intersect, parts and relationships are created at a rapid rate. Five disciplines in five institutions produce twenty-five intersects. The addition of five of each—making ten disciplines in ten institutions—produces a hundred intersects. Even allowing for a partial allocation of disciplines among types of institutions, the master matrix leads toward exponential expansion in the structures of work, belief, and authority which support the tasks and technologies of higher education.

CHANGE: THE MOVING MATRIX

Change remains the most recalcitrant subject in the social sciences. The term is used to refer to alterations that vary from simple reproduction, more units of the same kind, to revolution and radical transformation. Those who seek the causes of changes in different institutions bog down in the complexities of history, perplexed by unique conditions and trends that seemingly converge and part in accidental and hence unpredictable ways. As Harold Perkin points out (chap. 1, above), historical analysis is weak in "covering laws," weak in systematically grasping linkages. Yet historians, like other social scientists, want to go beyond facts and particulars to explanations. All are interested in some degree of determinism, some lawlike statements. If to understand the past is to help us understand the present, and the past and present give us some guide to the future, then we mean there are regularities, recurrent phenomena, and constraints at time one that delimit, even decide, events at time two. In one sense, organizational analysts are deeply involved in such searches, fixing on the more firmly built structures that we call organizations with the strong belief that these structures make a difference, over time as well as in contemporary events. Yet organizational analysis has been history poor, rarely engaged in systematic study of development over an extended period of time.

In considering how the analysis of change might be positioned and strengthened within the organizational analysis of higher education, it helps to distinguish between the emergence of a system of higher education as an obviously major form of change and the alteration of a system already in place and structured.[26] In the first, the system itself has little or no structure and culture, generic to it, to guide interaction and change. Bits and pieces are brought in, even impressed upon it, from other segments of society. But as the system develops it builds its own sources of continuity and change.[27] It usually grows larger and definitely becomes much more complex. It acquires the structures, discussed above, of work, belief, and authority. Institutions and subsectors thereby become rooted, turned into centers of interest and influence which have their own traditions and rationales. Budgets become entrenched, personnel remain fixed in categories, and costly physical plants turn into sunk costs. Sectorial hegemony develops, as pointed out at the beginning of this chapter, as inside professionals and bureaucrats occupy key sites and expand their influence.

Thus we progress in studying change in systems of higher education by pursuing the question as to how their structures and beliefs—their many parts individually and collectively—constrain and induce changes. As simply put by Margaret Archer, "once a given form of education exists it exerts an influence on future educational change."[28] This internalist logic has thus far divided into two analytical approaches: (1) to seek historical explanation of contemporary forms and (2) to try to link change to existing properties of the system.

To explain contemporary forms it is possible simply to walk back through time in search of critical periods and conditions. Thus, one study of the character of three leading liberal arts colleges in the United States at the end of the 1950s placed the crucial period of character definition, in one instance, as occurring in the earliest years, and hence effected under the conditions of new organization so many innovators desire, but in the other two instances as taking place much later in the life of the college, when transforming leaders worked under different sets of evolutionary and revolutionary conditions.[29] The accounts were historically specific in considerable detail, but the analyst used them to identify common and unique developments and outcomes, highlighting their commonality in having sturdy self-belief, a self-love worked up over time which amounted to an "organizational saga." Ethnographic in nature, this approach is heavily inductive.

Another analysis has shown that the development of a large institutional sector in higher education may be explained by deducing from theory what

---

[26]This is the primary distinction in Margaret Archer's mammoth historical and comparative analysis of change in educational systems, reflected in the division of her volume into a first part devoted to the "emergence of state education systems" and a second part centered on "educational systems in action" (Archer, *Social Origins of Educational Systems*).

[27]Clark, *Higher Education System*, chap. 6, "Change."

[28]Archer, *Social Origins of Educational Systems*, p. 3.

[29]Clark, *Distinctive College*.

could happen and then determining what actually took place and what institutional responses did not occur. Studying the expansion of California higher education in the 1950s and 1960s, Neil Smelser hypothesized six types of structural adaptation which could have been made, noting that several occurred while others did not, and then used certain "missing" responses as explanations of discontent and conflict.[30] This systematic approach to change is particularly beneficial in its emphasis on institutional responses. Even though the context was severely constraining, the analyst posed alternatives that were to some degree open for consideration.

For analysis over a long time span, a powerful argument is presented by Arthur L. Stinchcombe on the persistence of types of organization.[31] Why does a particular mosaic of organizational types exist in a sector of society at the present time, with the parts "deposited" into the present out of different periods in the past? Persistence may come from effectiveness, from doing better than competing alternatives; or from location in a niche that protects against competition; or from the phenomena of institutionalization which turn a form into an end in itself and a center of group interest and legitimating ideology. The third possibility may readily dominate the other two, particularly in public sectors and especially in such normative organizations as schools and colleges. In academic systems, forms are in perpetuity as they become centers of vested interest located in protective noncompetitive niches.

As we pursue the persistence of organizational types and forms from the past to the present we are led on to probe how forms established early conditioned those that came later, as seen in the overwhelming influence of Oxford and Cambridge, with a six-hundred-year head start, on the styles of all the other sectors that have emerged in Britain since the mid-nineteenth century, or in the similarly strong influence of the University of Tokyo on everything else that was to follow in the modernization of Japanese higher education. In the American system, one can find in the successive emergence of major sectors the transference of beliefs and forms from the earlier to the later. The tradition of the liberal arts college, two hundred years old before the birth of the American university, in effect dictated that the university would have an undergraduate level of somewhat general or liberal education, with European-style specialization then added on in a second, graduate tier; the trustee form of control flowed from the college to the university and from the private market-oriented sectors into the public state-budget-oriented ones. Explaining types of institutions, their practices and beliefs, by referring to their predecessors is a fairly precise way of engaging in historical analysis within an organizational perspective.

---

[30]Smelser, "Growth, Structural Change, and Conflict."
[31]Stinchcombe, "Social Structure and Organizations."

The above approaches to the development of contemporary forms have centered almost entirely on institutions and sectors. Another angle of vision applies particularly well to the emergence and institutionalization of disciplines. This is the sociological approach to the ever expanding division of labor and the dynamics that drive it. Emile Durkheim placed high among the causes of social differentiation the mutual interests that existing and emerging groups have in protecting themselves.[32] Specialization pulls apart groups that otherwise may have to fight it out or share meager resources. This peace-from-conflict perspective may readily be applied to higher education. Sociologists and anthropologists did not have to fight over common turf when they gave up joint departments and went their separate ways, one to "structure" and the other to "culture." Historians of science and medicine reduce conflict with historians and those who populate medical schools, and gain in claims on resources, as they pull away in new departments. Cell splitting occurs within academic departments as subgroups use their specialization to protect themselves against domination by others and to reduce conflict over unified courses of action. Important dynamics of academic differentiation are thus to be found in interest-group struggles. The motor power is found in the interests of specific academic groups and their resulting interactions.

The second major stream of thought in pursuing the organizational determination of change is less historical, concentrating instead on linking current change or lack thereof, in a general or specific way, to current properties of the system. Various recent analysts have concluded their studies of innovation and change on the theme of the importance of the system's own composition and dynamics. After an extensive review of the literature on innovation in United States higher education, and intensive analysis of a major reform effort at the Buffalo campus of the State University of New York, Arthur Levine pointed to "the centrality of organizational facts of life in shaping change."[33] After conducting a systematic study of the entire British system, Tony Becher and Maurice Kogan concluded that "the main constraints on change are social, not psychological: they depend more on the way the system operates than on the particular stand that its individual members choose to take."[34] The broad dictum of the approach that builds on such findings is to put change in context by linking it to immediate structures and procedures, then, as need be, working out from there to increase the power and fullness of explanation. The existing forms have predispositions, we might say, tendencies that when identified inform us not only about systematic resistance to change but also about

---

[32]Durkheim, *Division of Labor in Society.*
[33]Levine, *Why Innovation Fails,* p. 43.
[34]Becher and Kogan, *Process and Structure in Higher Education,* p. 147.

imperatives for change, as in the huge commitment to the production of new knowledge, hence to innovation, found in the research imperatives of most fields of knowledge in the advanced national systems. We may look for the way change is conditioned by "the way the system operates"—at many levels, in many ways.

Finally, if we sum up my earlier discussion about the matrix composition of higher education, we are confronted by a system of concerted activity which tends to have the following characteristics: it is relatively bottom-heavy, since large numbers of thought groups take up authoritative location at the operating level; it is multicoordinated, as the many groups found at administrative as well as operating levels use different forms of authority and as integrating actions range from political dictates to market involvements; the system is ambiguously bounded and virtually limitless in absorption of knowledge tasks; and the backbone of the structure is a grand matrix of disciplines and enterprises. Such properties encourage changes of the following types.

Grass-roots innovation.—Invention and diffusion of thought styles and specific ideas, with related practices, are institutionalized in the work of departments and schools that embody the disciplines and professions. Academic enterprises move ahead in a somewhat self-propelled, or at least internally guided, fashion in the areas of new thought which academics perceive to be acceptable within general conceptions of academic knowledge: biochemistry becomes more readily established than ethnic studies, computer science than urban affairs. This basic form of change is widely overlooked. It is typically not announced in ministerial bulletins or master plans as an item of reform. It is not introduced on a global scale and it is not taken as changing a structural feature of the whole system. But in a bottom-heavy matrix of disciplines and enterprises, grass-roots innovation is a crucial form of change.

Innovation by persuasion.—More than elsewhere, changes initiated at the top commonly need the support of interests residing at lower levels. With the characteristic diffusion of types and amounts of authority, and the lower placement of authoritativeness, those at the top generally have to "carry the field" rather than command it, negotiating with equals and building internal coalitions in order to implement their own desires, even their own "orders." The thought groups located at the grass-roots level become key participants in implementing policies and reforms.

Incremental change.—Since tasks and powers are so extensively divided, global changes are ordinarily very difficult to effect. The more advanced the system, the more true it is that "anything that requires a coordinated effort of the organization in order to start is unlikely to be started. Anything that requires a coordinated effort of the organization in order to be stopped is unlikely to be stopped,"[35] despite the growth of managerial tools and

---

[35] Cohen and March, *Leadership and Ambiguity*, p. 206.

theories. The leading false expectation in academic reform, especially in democracies, is that large results can be obtained by systemwide plan and central edict. Such major reforms are occasionally initiated and a few even succeed, but the more characteristic flow of change is that small alterations in small parts follow from a mélange of confusing actions. There are diverse and contradictory efforts at the top, in the middle, and especially at the bottom which entail false starts, wrong experiments, and zigzag adjustments, as in the "reform" of the history curriculum, for example, in most nations over a period of several decades. And, as indicated at the outset, dramatic examples of such change are to be found in the evolutionary buildup of knowledge in the twentieth century in the physical and biological sciences, flows that have been accompanied by increased dominance of those fields within universities and national systems. Of course, in systems under authoritarian or totalitarian rule, the centralization of authority and the central concentration of administration allow more manipulation from above and on a large scale. But even in the more top-influenced systems, with such controls as those found in the Soviet Union, observers report that adaptation characteristically takes place "by small steps instead of far-reaching reform."[36] Small steps come with the territory. Incremental adjustment is the pervasive form of change.

We may suggest that inertia increases with scale. A university is more difficult to change than a department. A national system is more difficult to change than a university. We face then a central dilemma of planning. In the name of change, planners make systems. They thereby produce more inertia, large batches of rigidities that reduce the capacity for flexible response by institutions and departments.

Boundary-leaking change.—The master matrix ensures that boundary-spanning roles are diffused throughout the operating levels of the individual university or college. Boundary roles in organizations are normally viewed as limited to offices that specialize in contact with the environment, such as the admissions office, the public relations bureau, and the grants and contracts office in the university. But boundary roles spread through the operating structure as those in the basic disciplines and the professional schools reach to their counterparts within and outside the larger system. Professors scan and monitor events in their own fields which are external to their local enterprise; they engage in information gatekeeping; they transact with other groups; they link and coordinate between the inside and the outside.[37] Thus the bridges to the outside are numerous, structurally dispersed, and unsupervised by hierarchical superiors. Changes creep across those bridges quietly and with little notice.

---

[36]Glowka, "Soviet Higher Education between Government Policy and Self-Determination," p. 182.

[37]For criteria used in the definition of boundary roles, see Miles, *Macro Organizational Behavior*, chap. 11.

Invisible change.—Knowledge is relatively invisible as a material, a product, and especially as a process. Developing thoughts, as in research; transmitting thoughts, as in teaching; absorbing thoughts, as in learning— all are difficult to see and evaluate directly at the time they occur. Of course professors and administrators track these activities or give them external markers as best they can: reports on research show what came out of research activities; textbooks, examinations, and course grades, even certificates, represent tangibly what is happening in teaching and learning. But much is intangible or beyond measurable touch. Then, too, since the basic academic operations are diverse, arcane, and increasingly shielded by layers of organization, they are particularly opaque. It is difficult to perceive from on high or from the outside, or indeed from within, what is constant and especially what is changing. The relative invisibility of the main substance of work may be at the core of the difficulty in sensing what occurs in academic systems.

And thus the matrix moves: with much grass-roots initiative; with persuasion and voluntary initiative rather than command; incrementally rather than grandly; with changes flowing quietly over institutional boundaries; and often in highly intangible ways. These tendencies are rooted in the received, enduring structures of work, belief, and authority, in the basic composing of the system around disciplines and institutions, and the coordinating of the systems by multifarious means. To the extent they differ from patterns of change in other sectors of society, these tendencies testify to and help illuminate the underlying unique features of higher education. When the underlying internal structure is well explicated, then what we see largely determines what we get and reveals much about how altered states come about.

THE NECESSITY OF AN ORGANIZATIONAL APPROACH

A robust organizational perspective leaps over the fences of the social sciences. It is no accident that organizational theory is written by sociologists, political scientists, economists, psychologists, and anthropologists, as well as by analysts in business management and public administration, and that even historians pursue the development of specific organizations and sectors thereof. All are looking at the major tools of modern social action, the key collective actors who bind and divide. As a general approach, the organizational perspective is thus in luck, at once particular and even idiosyncratic but also flowing readily into wider streams of thought. There is some arcane language and even an emerging subculture, but its carriers penetrate a number of disciplines and therein have to make their peace. The particular organizational approaches to higher education emphasized here flow naturally toward the other perspectives presented in this volume, which center on historical, political, economic, status, scientific, cultural, and policy dimensions. There is also often the touchstone of application to practical affairs, in the service of improvement, and thereby the need to interact with common sense.

Organizational analysis of postsecondary education cuts a large cloth. It needs to cover levels of activity from "the factory floor" of classroom and laboratory to the national ministry and legislature, relating parts, suggesting causes, and indicating effects. It needs to span large sectors of universities and colleges which together stretch across nearly all advanced knowledge and, increasingly, do not know where to stop. It must track disciplines as well as enterprises, thereby following lines of functional connection which leap across institutional, regional, and national boundaries and turn pursuit into an international chase. Included in the tapestry of analysis is the flow of academic forms and ideas from one country to another, making central the problems of the new hosts accepting transplants voluntarily or under imposition and, in either event, adapting them to fit different contexts.

From an organizational perspective we may claim that higher education has an essential nature. That nature begins with high knowledge cast in the form of specialized bundles that have been awarded legitimacy by academic groups and are carried by them over time and space. Around those bundles there develop characteristic compounds of forms of work, belief, and authority, with each of these elements having its own peculiar configuration. To be organized around multifarious subjects is to have a particular structure of work which is found in only a weak degree in other sectors of society. The discipline is the touchstone. In turn, to emphasize disciplinary points of view and such doctrines of the academic profession as freedom of research and freedom of teaching is to have a configuration of core beliefs which is characteristic of the system and reflected only lightly elsewhere. Group autonomy and individual choice are magnified. To put much authority on a personal and collegial footing, combining the two in a guild or craft type of authority, and then to interweave that type with bureaucratic and political forms of control is to produce unique configurations of authority which occur elsewhere only to the extent that "noneducational" sectors engage in high-level educational work and behave, in part, like universities and colleges. Much guild organization in the understructure is characteristic.

As these three elements, with local and national variation, combine in national systems, all else about those systems is heavily conditioned. If it is not to be out of phase with the underlying organic reality, the superstructure of higher echelons must adjust to and extensively reflect the organization of work around subjects, the cultural life of the disciplines and the professional fields, and the legitimated powers of individuals and groups in many specialties. Changes are strongly guided by the underlying internal features and the beliefs of internal groups which help mold responses to external pressures. The streams of diverse incremental changes that follow at the operating level from the internal logics of the individual disciplines are missed or poorly grasped by those who fix their sights on higher levels in the search for holistic change. But many flows of change are brought within our analytical imagination when we pursue the underlying structures of work, belief, and authority and seek the actions that thereby follow.

At the organizational heart of higher education is the crisscrossing matrix of disciplines and enterprises which turns larger systems into thousands of linked intersects occupied by autonomy-seeking groups of thinkers upholding specific styles of thought. It is at those intersects that the work gets done; within them the productive powers of disciplines and enterprises converge. It is upon them that we may fruitfully center much future research.

At the end of the twentieth century, the need to grasp the central place of organizational elements is no different from the same need eight centuries ago at the beginning of the Western university. Then, too, in simpler ways, sustained intellectual commitment required appropriate organization. A. B. Cobban has brilliantly analyzed the earliest efforts to construct universities in medieval Europe, facing the central question of why Bologna and its imitators in northern Italy survived to become a strong influence on higher education in the Western world, while an earlier promising effort in Salerno died out. "The central weakness of Salerno," he notes, "was its failure to develop a protective and cohesive organization to sustain its intellectual advance." Cobban concludes from the fate of Salerno and the history of medieval universities in the large that "institutional response must follow quickly upon academic achievement if the intellectual moment is not to be dissipated. The absence of regular organization may initially provide a fillup for free-ranging inquiry, but perpetuation and controlled development can only be gained through an institutional framework."[38] Then and now, it is regular organization that supports and perpetuates intellectual advance and indeed helps to create the intellectual moment.

---

[38]Cobban, *Medieval Universities*, pp. 47, 38.

BIBLIOGRAPHY

Archer, Margaret S. *Social Origins of Educational Systems*. London: Sage Publications, 1979.

Baldridge, J. Victor, David V. Curtis, George Ecker, and Gary L. Riley. *Policy Making and Effective Leadership*. San Francisco: Jossey-Bass, 1978.

Becher, Tony. "Towards a Definition of Disciplinary Cultures." *Studies in Higher Education* 6 (September 1981):109–122.

Becher, Tony, and Maurice Kogan. *Process and Structure in Higher Education*. London: Heinemann, 1980.

Ben-David, Joseph. *Centers of Learning: Britain, France, Germany, United States*. New York: McGraw-Hill, 1977.

Ben-David, Joseph, and Abraham Zloczower. "Universities and Academic Systems in Modern Societies." *European Journal of Sociology* 3 (1962):45–84.

Berdahl, Robert O. *British Universities and the State*. Berkeley and Los Angeles: University of California Press, 1959.

Berg, Barbro, and Bertil Östergren. *Innovations and Innovation Processes in Higher Education*. Stockholm: National Board of Universities and Colleges, 1977.

Blau, Peter M. *The Organization of Academic Work*. New York: Wiley, 1973.

Clark, Burton R. *Adult Education in Transition: A Study of Institutional Insecurity* (1956). Repr. New York: Arno Press, 1980.

———. *The Distinctive College: Antioch, Reed, Swarthmore*. Chicago: Aldine, 1970.

———. *Academic Power in Italy: Bureaucracy and Oligarchy in a National University System*. Chicago: University of Chicago Press, 1977.

———. *The Higher Education System: Academic Organization in Cross-National Perspective*. Berkeley, Los Angeles, London: University of California Press, 1983.

Clark, Burton R., and Ted I. K. Youn. *Academic Power in the United States: Comparative, Historical, and Structural Perspectives*. ERIC/Higher Education Research Report no. 3, 1976. Washington, D.C.: American Association for Higher Education, 1976.

Cobban, A. B. *The Medieval Universities: Their Development and Organization*. London: Methuen, 1975.

Cohen, Michael D., and James G. March. *Leadership and Ambiguity: The American College President*. New York: McGraw-Hill, 1974.

Cummings, William K., Ikuo Amano, and Kazuyuki Kitamura, eds. *Changes in the Japanese University: A Comparative Perspective*. New York: Praeger, 1979.

Dill, David D. "The Management of Academic Culture: Notes on the Management of Meaning and Social Integration." *Higher Education* 11 (1982):303–320.

Durkheim, Emile. *The Division of Labor in Society*. New York: Free Press, 1947.

Epstein, Leon D. *Governing the University*. San Francisco: Jossey-Bass, 1974.

Fleck, Ludwik. *Genesis and Development of a Scientific Fact*. Chicago: University of Chicago Press, 1979.

Geiger, Roger L. *Private Sectors in Higher Education: Structure, Function, and Change in Eight Countries*. Forthcoming.

Glowka, Detlef. "Soviet Higher Education between Government Policy and Self-

Determination: A German View." In *Higher Education in a Changing World*. World Year Book of Education 1971—72, pp. 175—185. London: Evans Brothers, 1971.

Halsey, A. H., and M. A. Trow. *The British Academics*. Cambridge: Harvard University Press, 1971.

Kerr, Clark, John Millett, Burton R. Clark, Brian MacArthur, and Howard Bowen. *12 Systems of Higher Education: 6 Decisive Issues*. New York: International Council for Educational Development, 1978.

Levine, Arthur. *Why Innovation Fails*. Albany: State University of New York Press, 1980.

Levy, Daniel C. *University and Government in Mexico: Autonomy in an Authoritarian System*. New York: Praeger, 1980.

———. *The State and Higher Education in Latin America: Private-Public Patterns*. Forthcoming.

Lindblom, Charles E. *Politics and Markets: The World's Political-Economic Systems*. New York: Basic Books, 1977.

Long, Norton E. "Power and Administration." *Public Administration Review* 9 (1949):257—264.

March, James G., and Johan P. Olsen. *Ambiguity and Choice in Organizations*. Bergen, Norway: Universitetsforlaget, 1976.

Matejko, Alexsander. "Planning and Tradition in Polish Higher Education." *Minerva* 7 (1969):621—648.

Miles, Robert H. *Macro Organizational Behavior*. Santa Monica, California: Goodyear, 1980.

Mintzberg, Henry. *The Structuring of Organizations*. Englewood Cliffs, N.J.: Prentice-Hall, 1979.

Moodie, Graeme C., and Rowland Eustace. *Power and Authority in British Universities*. Montreal: McGill-Queens University Press, 1974.

Perkin, Harold. *Key Profession: The History of the Association of University Teachers*. London: Routledge and Kegan Paul, 1969.

Premfors, Rune. *The Politics of Higher Education in a Comparative Perspective: France, Sweden, United Kingdom*. Studies in Politics, 15. Stockholm: University of Stockholm, 1980.

Premfors, Rune, and Bertil Östergren. *Systems of Higher Education: Sweden*. New York: International Council for Educational Development, 1978.

Sayles, L. R. "Matrix Organization: The Structure with a Future." *Organizational Dynamics* (Autumn 1976):2—17.

Smelser, Neil. "Growth, Structural Change, and Conflict in California Public Higher Education, 1950—1970." In *Public Higher Education in California*, ed. Neil Smelser and Gabriel Almond. Berkeley, Los Angeles, London: University of California Press, 1974.

Stinchcombe, Arthur L. "Social Structure and Organizations." In *Handbook of Organizations*, ed. James G. March. Chicago: Rand McNally, 1965.

Szczepanski, Jan. *Systems of Higher Education: Poland*. New York: International Council for Educational Development, 1978.

Turner, R. Steven. "The Growth of Professorial Research in Prussia, 1818 to 1848: Causes and Context." In *Historical Studies in the Physical Sciences*, ed. Russell McCormmach. Philadelphia: University of Pennsylvania Press, 1971. Vol. 3, pp. 137—182.

Van de Graaff, John H., Burton R. Clark, Dorotea Furth, Dietrich Goldschmidt, and Donald F. Wheeler. *Academic Power: Patterns of Authority in Seven National Systems of Higher Education*. New York: Praeger, 1978.

Van den Berghe, Pierre L. *Power and Privilege at an African University*. Cambridge, Mass.: Schenkman, 1973.

Windham, Douglas M. *Economic Dimensions of Education*. Washington, D.C.: National Academy of Education, 1979.

5. THE ANALYSIS
OF STATUS*

Martin A. Trow

The study of the stratification of higher education is not a discipline, but a perspective, more like the study of size and the implications of scale than like the economics or sociology of higher education. It is, moreover, a perspective by which all disciplines may address the universal phenomenon of the ordering or ranking of institutions and sectors of higher education by prestige, wealth, power, or some combination of these or other measures of status. And like all perspectives, it omits and distorts even as it illuminates.

The perspective is most useful, not as a set of descriptive categories, but as a way of looking at change, the physiology rather than the anatomy of education. This may seem paradoxical, given the remarkable stability of status rankings of institutions and sectors of higher education through time and around the world. But that stability is itself the outcome of a set of active forces and processes in society and education which the study of stratification may illuminate.

The effort to make statements about the stratification of higher education across national boundaries requires one to take a bird's-eye view of broad trends and patterns within and across national systems. But such a perspective tends to slight the unique qualities of national systems and sectors and such internal variations of ranking as are the outcome of unique historical events or circumstances.

We ordinarily think of the relative prestige of universities and colleges in relation to the social stratification of the societies in which they exist, as institutions that play a large part in determining the social placement of at least a fraction (and an especially important fraction) of the members of that society. But I would like, in this essay, to focus not on the role of higher education in social stratification, but higher education itself as a stratified system of institutions, graded formally or informally in status and prestige, in wealth, power, and influence of various kinds.

In every country we find variations in the status of colleges and universi-

*My thanks to the participants in the Los Angeles Summer Conference who commented on an early draft of this paper, and to Janet Ruyle for her close critical reading of the final draft.

ties; some have achieved world renown and some are scarcely known beyond the commuting range of their students. The shape of these hierarchical systems varies. One extreme example is the steep pyramid in Japan with Tokyo as the highest peak, Kyoto, Nagoya, and some of the older private universities and the remaining national universities as lower peaks, down to the large mass of local public and modest private institutions below. Japan's system is in contrast with the relatively flat university hierarchy of West Germany, which has no single institution preeminent in all fields but has a second tier of *Fachhochschulen*.

The perspective of stratification allows us to raise such questions as these:

1. Why are institutional rankings so stable across time and in different countries? What are some of the mechanisms that account for this relative stability of ranking of institutions in systems of higher education?
2. What are the links, if any, between the status of institutions of higher education and their social and educational functions?
3. What are the effects of rapid growth, of relatively stable conditions, and of the contraction and decline of resources on the mobility of institutions?
4. Do the growing egalitarian pressures in Western democracies reflect themselves in more equality among institutions of higher education, or do those pressures paradoxically increase and stabilize existing inequalities among institutions?
5. What are some of the forms and consequences of stratification within institutions of higher education, among departments, categories of staff, and the like?
6. How do public policies with respect to higher education affect the shape and character of its stratification system? What policies should governments pursue, and by what criteria should those policies be shaped or chosen?
7. Do the organization of higher education and the character of its stratification system affect the character and quality of the teaching and research that go on within it? For example, what difference does it make to engineering studies in polytechnics if they do or do not exchange students and staff with universities?

As we see, although we start with the question of prestige rankings, which might be dismissed as mere status snobbery, the perspective of stratification in higher education brings us very quickly to more substantial issues, such as the organization of higher education systems, the relation of status to function, the academic division of labor, institutional autonomy, faculty power and authority, and the quality of teaching and research within institutions of various kinds and ranks.

DIMENSIONS OF INSTITUTIONAL STATUS

The status of institutions has an objective and a subjective dimension. Some institutions or categories of institutions are defined by the state as "superior" to others: they have formal rights and privileges that others do not have, ordinarily including more institutional autonomy, control over their own budgets, and the right to award certain degrees and certificates; they have larger resources and more material support than other institutions and segments; their standards for student entry and requirements for the earned degree are also usually higher.

These are all matters of law and regulation but not necessarily of reputation. In California, the university has a monopoly among publicly supported institutions on state-supported research and on the awarding of doctoral and higher professional degrees; in Britain, the universities have had a high measure of autonomy as compared with the polytechnics, and a near monopoly on basic research and advance degrees; in Japan, the federal universities have marked formal advantages over all other kinds of publicly supported institutions; in France, the advantages of the *grandes écoles* in per capita expenditure and in their high selectivity for admission, coupled with their elaborate links to the civil service and to big business and industry, make them clearly the elite sector of the French system of higher education. In some countries government has attempted to narrow the status gap between the elite sector and other sectors of higher education. For example, Sweden's regional policy after the U68 study has reduced the formal advantages of the country's six universities over its professional and technical schools, in per capita support, in criteria for student admissions, institutional autonomy, and the like.[1] But the survival of the research function and of the higher graduate degrees in Swedish universities still gives them a status position superior to that of other sectors.

The objective dimension of institutional status is largely a function of formal law and state policy; it is that kind of formal regulation which defines the boundaries between different sectors of higher education, rather than those between institutions within a single sector. The subjective dimension of status, marked by distinctions in reputation and prestige, is largely a matter of the differentiation of institutions within segments, and also, in the United States, of the ranking of private institutions whose status position is not determined by state government.

The American interest in, indeed almost an obsession with, relative prestige rankings among universities arises out of the unique importance of private universities in the United States. Other countries, notably Japan and Brazil, also have large private sectors, and even a few quite distinguished private universities. But in the United States, by contrast with

---

[1]Lane, "Higher Education in Scandinavia."

both of those countries, the large majority of the more prestigious universities are private institutions, as is also true of four-year colleges. In the remarkably stable league standing of American universities, a stability that deserves further discussion later in this paper, eight of the top ten universities are private institutions, and of the top twenty, perhaps fifteen are private. The intense interest of the leading American universities in these league standings reflects the competitiveness among American research universities, arising out of the very large role of the leading private universities and colleges, and their dependence upon, indeed their vulnerability to, judgments of the several markets in which they compete for high-quality students, for distinguished teachers and researchers, for research support, and for scholarly and research publications and honors.[2] And these universities, their academics and administrators alike, believe that their success in those markets will be affected by their academic status, that is, their perceived standings in the league tables. But if their comparative reputations affect their success in those markets in the short run, it is equally true (or believed, which amounts to the same thing) that over the long run their reputational standing will be determined by their success in those markets, and particularly in the market for distinguished professors and academic distinctions. So reputation and prestige are thus a kind of reservoir or bank of accumulated successes in all these markets, but most especially in the competitive pursuit of scholarly and scientific honors, for which the acquisition of topflight students, staff, and financial support is seen as the means. Many of the policies and academic decisions of American universities are oriented toward maintaining or improving their comparative standing in the ranks of universities, and the competition includes those public universities that are at or near the top.[3]

When we speak of the ranking of a college or a university, we ordinarily mean its prestige status based on its perceived quality and distinction as an academic institution. We can distinguish between its status in the eyes of academics, the scholars and scientists who presumably are qualified to judge academic status, and whose judgments incidentally affect whether or not they will, if given the opportunity, move from their present institution to another, and its status in the eyes of legislators or governing bodies who fund it or of the students who attend it. The rankings of the several

[2]Trow, "Elite Higher Education." The status of the leading four-year colleges in the United States is not based on research or graduate training. In respect to their national reputations as academic institutions, they are very much like the leading *lycées* and *gymnasiums* in western European countries and the best public schools and maintained schools in Britain. While not themselves universities, they are part of the elite university system: their staffs are graduates of the best universities, many with research experience; their students are drawn from the social and intellectual elites and are destined for entry into the research university and then on into leadership roles in all institutions of society.

[3]Berelson, *Graduate Education in the United States*.

recurrent American studies are based on the judgments of supposedly knowledgeable populations—department heads, distinguished senior scholars, and well-informed junior scholars—supplemented by such "objective" measures of quality as the research productivity of its staff and the quality of its faculty and students as measured by the number who have been awarded fellowships or have won other academic awards and honors. We might add such additional indicators of academic quality as the size of the institution's library and of its budget or, for private institutions, its endowment per capita and its support from external sources for research. There may be some discrepancies in these rankings in specific instances, but the leading universities that rank high on one indicator of quality usually rank high on others, yet another example of Paul Lazarsfeld's dictum of the interchangeability of indices.[4] Institutions that show discrepancies in their ratings on different indicators of status often are mobile, up or down. For example, a number of major universities located in the American Sun Belt have over the past several decades made efforts, more or less successfully, to move upward in the prestige rankings, largely by using their comparative wealth to buy distinguished scholars and sometimes whole departments from other leading universities, and by backing that policy up with generous salaries, research facilities, library acquisitions, graduate student support, and the like. The universities of Texas and Houston, and other institutions that have pursued that policy, have in fact improved their comparative status through those tactics, though they have not yet moved into the first rank of research universities. Other universities may show a discrepancy between their current high prestige ranking and the hard facts of declining support levels for salaries, research, and the like; here one anticipates, over a decade or two, a decline in an institution's overall prestige ranking, reflecting its inability to attract or retain its share of the finest scholars in the various subjects. Columbia University is an unfortunate example of this process of downward mobility, a fate that also threatens the University of Michigan and some other northern universities

---

[4]Lazarsfeld and Rosenberg, eds., *The Language of Social Research*, pp. 15–108. Subjective assessments of the quality of graduate education in American universities have been carried out periodically since 1924, when Raymond Hughes rated twenty graduate departments in each of the leading thirty-eight American research universities, based on a summary of the views of national scholars in those fields of study. See also American Council on Education, *Report of the Committee on Graduate Instruction*; Keniston, *Graduate Study . . . at the University of Pennsylvania*; Cartter, *Assessment of Quality in Graduate Education*, esp. pp. 1–9. See also *Chronicle of Higher Education*, September 29, 1982, pp. 8–10, and November 10, 1982, pp. 4–6, for preliminary reports of the most recent nationwide study of graduate departments and programs in the leading research universities. To take just two disciplines as examples: of the sixteen highest-rated English departments in 1982, eleven were included in the sixteen top departments in 1925; of the top ten departments in 1982, seven were among the top ten in the 1925 study. Of the leading fifteen physics departments in 1982, ten were on the 1925 list of top fourteen departments in American universities.

that are hard hit by declines in the economies of their states and thus by the decreasing ability of those states to support their universities at the level required for maintenance of status in the first rank.

The presence, indeed the predominance, of private institutions at the top of the status ladder of American universities is of enormous importance for the autonomy of the public universities and, more broadly, for their relations with their public funding authorities. The reason is that the intense competitiveness of American universities allows the public institutions to demand of their state governments the same or comparable levels of support and degrees of freedom as are enjoyed by the leading private institutions. The great public universities do not always get quite what they ask, and in recent years there has been a pattern of declining resources for public higher education, along with a steady encroachment of state authority on the autonomy of the leading public universities, paralleling what is happening almost everywhere else in the world. But this tendency is growing much more slowly and has progressed much less far than it would have were it not constrained by the exemplary models of Harvard and Stanford, Chicago and Princeton, Yale and the Massachusetts Institute of Technology.

Stratification of Higher Educational Systems

The importance of private institutions, of the market principle, and of institutional competitiveness makes the comparative prestige and reputation of colleges and universities in the United States of central importance in the life of all American institutions of higher education, a force guiding and shaping many of their policies. But the stratification of higher education may also be seen in the large majority of countries whose institutions are, with few exceptions, supported wholly by state funds, and whose systems of higher education have, especially over the past decades, been the object of public law and policy.

In all societies the stratification of higher education takes several forms: (1) the stratification of sectors of higher education; (2) the stratification of institutions within sectors; (3) the stratification of units and departments within institutions. Let us consider first the situation of the new institutions created by almost every advanced industrial society during the 1960s and 1970s in response to the very rapid growth of enrollments and costs of higher education. As we know, the tremendous expansion of those two decades was absorbed for the most part in the traditional university systems, in part through a growth in the existing universities, and in part through the creation of new universities. In almost every western European nation, however, the government also created or markedly expanded one or more new kinds of institutions within its system of higher education, such as the *Fachhochschulen* in Germany, the *instituts universitaires de technologie*

(IUT) in France, the polytechnics in England, the colleges of advanced education in Australia, the regional colleges in Norway. So in each country there now are at least three different kinds of institutions: (1) the prewar universities, (2) the "new" postwar universities, and (3) the nonuniversity institutions of higher education. And of course there may be several varieties of the latter category. The first two categories are, in each country, within the same segment of higher education; nowhere is a formal distinction made by government between new and old universities. Nevertheless, on the whole, the old universities tend to have a higher academic status than the new ones, despite the fact that the broad policy of governments everywhere (except in the United States) is to treat all universities alike with respect to support, autonomy and governance, standards for student entry, staff salaries, and the like. The other "nonuniversity" sector is sometimes divided into a number of different subsegments: polytechnics, colleges of advanced education, teachers colleges, technical and professional schools, and regional colleges by one name or another.

The American counterparts to these are the postwar "state universities." In contrast with the older generation of state universities—land-grant institutions created in many states in the second half of the nineteenth century as centers for technical and agricultural study, and the even older state universities whose pre−Civil War models were the elite private universities of the eastern seaboard—these post−World War II state universities developed through a strategy of institutional mobility, starting out as the normal schools of the nineteenth century, becoming colleges of education in the early part of the twentieth century, state colleges in the 1930s, 1940s, and 1950s, and then campuses of a "state university" in the sixties and seventies. Changes in name only partly reflect changes in character and function; they reflect at least as much a hope, a status claim, an effort to make a self-fulfilling prophecy. For example, the nineteen California state colleges have now become campuses of the recently renamed California State University, all universities without significant research capacity or the power to award doctoral degrees.[5] In this respect they are more like the nonuniversity sectors of higher education in European countries than like the new universities created in those countries after World War II.

The new postwar nonuniversity institutions, whatever other differences they may reveal from one country to another, generally have a status below

---

[5]The leaders of the California State University, however, would argue that in order to gain those rights and functions in the future, and the resources to sustain them, it is necessary first to become "a university," and the legislature apparently finds it relatively inexpensive to give the name if not the substance of full university status to nineteen more public California institutions. Incidentally, the University of California did not protest this nominal upgrading of the state colleges, though it surely would resist strenuously the diversion of resources which would necessarily accompany the development of significant research activity and doctoral instruction on those campuses.

that of both the old and the new postwar universities, so that the new sectorial ranking becomes (1) old prewar universities, (2) the new universities, and (3) new nonuniversity forms of higher education.

This ordering may seem to be natural and obvious, but it may be worth pausing for a moment to ask why the same thing has happened everywhere, a question that may shed light on the unfulfilled hopes of expansionists and egalitarians in many countries for new institutions of higher education which would break the monopoly of the old elite institutions on access to the leading roles in the economy and in government.

Expansion, Steady State, Contraction, and Institutional Mobility

The 1950s and 1960s and the first half of the 1970s were a period of very rapid expansion of higher education in all industrial nations. Enrollments grew by three or four or five times in a period of fifteen to twenty years. Many new universities were created, and alongside the universities, new sectors of higher education were also introduced or upgraded. National expenditures increased even faster than enrollments. Under the impact of growth, student pressure, and political ideologies, new structures of organization, governance, and finance were formed to deal with the new systems of higher education. What did all that growth and ferment do to the stratification of higher education in the countries that experienced it?

Surprisingly little. Everywhere the institutions that were preeminent in 1950 are still preeminent, still the institutions to which others look as models and exemplars. In most places these are the universities and, within the university sector, the older universities; in France, as always, almost untouched by reform, is the elite sector of the *grandes écoles*.

The new European institutions—IUTs, *Fachhochschulen*, and others—and the new state and community colleges in the United States were created or expanded for a variety of purposes: to reduce enrollment pressures on the universities; to increase access to higher education in regions where there were no universities; to expand and improve the status of existing short-cycle and vocational institutions; to provide alternative forms of instruction, freed from the constraints of the university chair and faculty system, with more scope for systematic instruction and interdisciplinary work; and often, though not always explicitly, to create a set of institutions free from historical links to the upper classes, closer to the world of work, and thus with an intellectual climate more attractive to working-class students.[6]

Whatever the motives, the new systems of nonuniversity higher education have, on the whole, had only a qualified success, both in their numerical growth and in their status rankings. In most countries, with the United

---

[6]Boudon, "The French University since 1968," pp. 171–202.

States and Japan as conspicuous exceptions, the bulk of the growth in enrollments after World War II was absorbed by the universities; the new sectors enrolled, at the best, only 10 to 20 percent of the students in higher education. But while these new sectors could not and did not seriously challenge the status preeminence of the universities, the concern for the status of the new sectors ironically has reduced their popularity with students. In the United Kingdom, the famous speech by Anthony Crosland at Woolwich Polytechnic in April 1965, announcing the formation of a "binary system," insisted on an equality of status though a differentiation of function between polytechnic and university. To ensure status equality the polytechnics were given the right to award degrees, though only in courses approved by a central accrediting body largely composed of university professors and lecturers, thus mandating the presence of university standards in the polytechnics. In other respects, the polytechnics were given resources comparable to those of the universities; although their pay scales are set through a different procedure, salaries have been close to those of university staff, and sometimes higher. Broadly, and research aside, per capita student costs have been similar, as have been student entrance requirements, student grants, and the like. Nevertheless, the polytechnics have not been highly successful in attracting students who could gain entry to a university; they still serve largely to take the overflow of university applicants who cannot obtain admission to the institution of their choice but can meet the slightly lower admissions standards of the polytechnics. The polytechnics also have not been highly successful in maintaining their own academic identity; through the processes of emulation and "drift" they have moved closer to the curriculum of the universities, sloughing off their nondegree work while admitting large numbers in the social sciences, social science—based semiprofessions, and the arts, rather than the sciences and technologies for which they were primarily designed. The polytechnics, like other new institutions of higher education, suffer severe disabilities in their quest for academic status, not least of which are the relative absence of basic research and their inability to award higher degrees. The significance of research for academic status is crucial for institutions that aspire to university status.

Although the limited appeal of the polytechnics is understandable, the inability of the IUTs in France to achieve a higher status and wider appeal is less clear. On the whole, other things being equal, the more selective an institution in student admissions, the higher its status. In Britain both universities and polytechnics are highly selective, though the polytechnics' standards are a little lower than those of the universities. In France, by contrast, a central problem for the universities has been their open access to all who earn the *baccalauréat*. The IUTs are moderately selective, though not as highly selective through competitive examination as the *grandes écoles*. Boudon estimates that the overall rate of acceptance is "not above 50 percent" of those who apply.[7] Moreover, the course of study at the IUTs lasts two years, as compared with the three to six in a university. The work is not done in large anonymous lectures, but in small groups, with a more carefully designed and planned curriculum, determined less by the traditional academic disciplines than by the needs of the regional or national economy. Moreover, scholarships are more generously awarded to IUT than to university students. And at least by early experience, the IUT graduates get jobs comparable to those of students who have completed three, four, or five years in the university and have received the *licence*.[8]

By several criteria, then, the IUTs should have become at least as attractive to students as the universities, and perhaps more prestigious within the academic community. Boudon and others[9] develop a rather strict "rate of return" explanation. Even if, on average, a student can get as good a job by attending an IUT for two years as by attending a university for three or four or five years, they argue, students know (or believe) that the very best jobs go to university graduates, and, like gamblers, they take the chance at the university where risks and investments may be higher but where, for a small minority, the return in both salary and career prospects may be better than for IUT graduates.

That argument seems to me a bit mechanical and rationalistic; it ignores the actual character of the two types of institutions and the kinds of experience they provide. The IUTs, besides not offering the *licence*, also require students to have a clearer idea of the vocation or profession they want to enter, and students must be prepared to accept a severely regulated course of study including required courses and compulsory attendance. The French universities, with their open access and relaxed disciplines, attract many students who do not have clear goals or who are unwilling to work very hard. Moreover, increasing numbers of them are able to work part-time, further reflecting a tendency to withdraw their energies from their university studies.

The status of French universities is made more precarious by the existence of a truly elite system above them providing recruits to the top levels of government and the economy; by the location of much research work outside the university in centers and institutes; by open access; by little internal organization of the curriculum; by the handicaps of cumbersome participatory governance machinery and the politicization of academic appointments and promotions; and by the proximity of a moderately selective and more "relevant" IUT sector.

Moreover, in France, Sweden, and some other countries the worldwide recession and widespread unemployment have led to a decline in the

---

[7]Ibid., p. 177.
[8]Ibid., p. 178.
[9]Ibid., pp. 178–179.

prestige of institutions based on their academic values and standing and a rise in the importance for an institution's reputation in the eyes of the general public (and of potential students) of the employability of its graduates.[10] In the past these sources of prestige have tended to converge; currently they tend to diverge, generating changes in the status order of institutions and sectors.

French universities have responded to these forces by a dramatic increase in the degree of diversity among them. Using the increased (if still limited) autonomy they gained under the reform law of 1968, they have pursued different policies, especially with respect to the curriculum, modes of instruction, and forms of governance and participation. Some are now mass universities, highly politicized, with open access, lower standards, and lower standing. Others, sharply restricting access to their high-status disciplines and professional schools, have become almost like *grandes écoles* in their forms of elite recruitment, high standards, and intensive teaching.

In addition, declining resources have led French universities to be more oriented to the markets for students, research grants, and graduate employment than ever before. And some of them have been much more successful in this competition than others. The market competition so familiar to American universities has now been brought inside the centrally controlled French university system.

These developments have led, in France and elsewhere, to a blurring of status between what were formerly "noble" and "nonnoble" sectors of higher education, together with an increase in the status differentiation within sectors. Nevertheless, the formal differences in governmental policy between sectors, in their degree-granting powers, autonomy, funding patterns, and forms of governance, keep competition internal within each sector and prevent the sectors from becoming one single large unified system, internally stratified through the play of market forces and institutional leadership.

In state-supported and -governed systems, the state is the major determinant of the life chances of an institution or a sector. It is, as we have noted, not the only determinant, and, as we see in the United Kingdom, the state cannot command an equality of status between sectors when the institutional qualities and characteristics that earn prestige are not present. Nevertheless, governments since World War II have intervened directly in higher education systems to democratize access and governance, to increase the relevance of studies for the economy and careers, and, perhaps above all, to increase their own influence over the size, shape, costs, and future direction of the higher education system.

---

[10]I am indebted here to the comments of Dorotea Furth and Ladislav Cerych on the draft of this paper presented to the Los Angeles conference. The paper by Furth, "New Hierarchies in Higher Education," which appeared after this paper had been completed, develops these ideas more fully.

On the whole, the aims of central governments have led them to attempt to reduce the height of the stratification system, rather than to create conditions for mobility and the change of status rankings, either of institutions or of sectors. The latter, whatever the state did, would ultimately depend on the play of competitive forces in markets for distinguished professors and the most competent young teachers, for research support, for able students and graduate students, and so on. And states on the whole do not like the market principle: its results are unpredictable; it gives power to institutions and their members, or to students and their parents, rather than to society and state officials. A system oriented to these markets, and thus to competition, is likely to be disorganized, hard to govern and administer, and often seemingly inefficient, as institutions make decisions in response to market forces that central government may think unwise or too costly, for example, creating departments and programs that appear to duplicate offerings elsewhere.

These are indeed among the effects of academic competition, as we can see in the United States, or in Ben-David's account of nineteenth-century German universities.[11] Competition under close constraints does operate in European systems of higher education, more within segments than between them, under conditions that give status advantage to those universities that already have certain advantages—location, wealth, libraries, buildings, the prestige of ancient foundation, and marginal resources from their own endowments—or are already strong in high-status fields of study.

Competition in higher education paradoxically leads to both more diversity and more homogeneity. It leads to wider diversity as the outcome of differing degrees of success which institutions within a given sector have in their market competition, and of the "marginal differentiation" employed by lower-status institutions and sectors in their efforts to gain an advantage in the market when competing with others. But competition and the accompanying emulation of high-status exemplars by lower-status institutions tend to make for a leveling upward of the whole system, toward the characteristics and styles of the leaders; competition accounts for the "drift," noted everywhere, of second- and third-rank institutions and of new institutions and sectors toward the academic forms and styles, the curriculum and standards, of elite institutions. Governments generally do not like the tendency of modest or new institutions to emulate the styles and pretensions of the old elite ones. What they want is more diversity in the national higher education system, more vocationally relevant studies, new and more efficient modes of instruction, new and more democratic governance arrangements, new channels of access. The last thing they want is a bigger and bigger university system, with all the new colleges and technical schools aping the universities, taking on more arts programs, and demand-

---

[11]Ben-David and Zloczower, "Universities and Academic Systems in Modern Societies."

ing the rights and privileges of the universities, their research and graduate work along with their autonomy and self-governance.

If competition in higher education leads toward a leveling upward, though countered and resisted by the enormous advantages of the top institutions, governmental intervention has tended toward a leveling of national systems downward, toward the development of a large comprehensive unitary system marked by the characteristics of mass higher education, with certain small and selective elite "centers of excellence," chiefly in the leading institutions dedicated to scientific and medical research and graduate or professional training.

TRENDS IN GOVERNMENT-UNIVERSITY RELATIONS: THE AUSTRALIAN CASE[12]

The taming of an elite university system, the process of transforming it into what is increasingly a sector of a unitary system of higher education managed and controlled by state authorities, is clearly seen in the postwar history of Australian higher education. I suggest that the events there are a paradigm for the growth of state power over the universities and the rationalizing of systems of higher education elsewhere, though the precise steps and the exact sequence are surely different in Sweden or Denmark or the United Kingdom.

Australia came out of World War II with a few universities,

. . . small, rather ineffectual institutions, almost solely concerned with providing for the professions and some higher clerical positions. Fees were charged in all universities except the University of Western Australia, so that students were invariably drawn from the homes of parents who could afford the fees, although there was a very limited scheme of scholarships. Even without fees the universities would have been out of the reach of most students, because only a small minority went on to the higher levels of the secondary school.

Society demanded little of the universities. They were so remote from the ordinary man it was difficult for him to comprehend their relevance, and the universities were happy for that situation to continue. This isolation from society indirectly safeguarded the autonomy of the universities from the State governments which created and financed them.[13]

These "small, . . . ineffectual" universities were governed by the states and supported by annual state grants, student fees, and gifts and endowments. The effects of World War II changed that. Like universities elsewhere, those in Australia were called on to meet new demands from society and the economy for skilled manpower and for growing student enroll-

---

[12]I am grateful to Grant Harman for his comments on a draft of this section.
[13]Bessant, "Erosion of University Autonomy in Australia," p. 27.

ments, responding to economic, political, and cultural changes in the society. Responses by the Commonwealth (federal) government to this growth and change were inexorable:

In 1946 a constitutional amendment proposed by the Commonwealth government and allowing it to give financial support to students was passed by referendum.

In 1950 legislation was passed providing federal funds to the states to expand the activities of their universities.

In 1957 an important report to the Commonwealth government asserting an "irrefutable need for the development of a national policy for Australian universities to prevent unnecessary duplication and wastage of resources"[14] was published.

In response, the Commonwealth began to share the funding of universities with the states, on an agreed formula, providing half of capital expenditures and about a third of recurrent funds, an arrangement that lasted for seventeen years. Then in 1974 the Commonwealth assumed all regular recurrent and capital costs of all universities within the states, leaving nominal responsibility for their government and direction in the hands of the states. In 1974, at the insistence of the Commonwealth government, student fees were completely abolished.

Meanwhile, the 1960s saw the emergence of a sector of "colleges of advanced education" (CAEs) emerging out of former technical, agricultural, and other special colleges, plus some new foundations. These colleges initially offered diplomas and associate diplomas, but from the early 1970s degree courses became increasingly common, in the familiar pattern of academic drift. Teacher education courses were initially excluded from this sector, but in 1969 the Commonwealth agreed to fund teacher education courses in six colleges, and in 1973 thirty-two teachers colleges were absorbed into the CAE sector. In 1963 another advisory body was appointed to give the central government advice on this sector. In the mid-1970s a third sector, comprising colleges of technical and further education (TAFEs), short-cycle institutions that did not grant degrees, received recognition and regular Commonwealth funding, and it soon had its own committee (and then statutory commission) advising the central government. In 1977 the three advisory commissions for the three sectors were replaced by the Tertiary Education Commission (TEC), with a council for each sector. The TEC itself is composed of a chairman, the chairmen of the three councils, and five nonacademic public members.[15]

In 1979 the principle of block grants by the Commonwealth to the universities was further eroded and tied (earmarked) funds were substituted. At the same time the Commonwealth government (with or without

---

[14]Williams, "Governance and Universities since 1959," p. 3.
[15]Fensham, "Some Reflections . . . as a Member of the Universities Council," pp. 27–47.

the advice of the TEC) was empowered to make decisions on specific programs that were either to be supported by or cut out of federal grants.[16]

In 1981 the TEC recommended, but the government has not yet accepted, the principle that programs of instruction not approved by the commission would not only not get federal funds, but could not be funded from sources other than Commonwealth grants. The logic of this sweeping recommendation is that if the Commonwealth government is to have full control it cannot allow new teaching developments or programs to arise and be supported from sources not under its own control. In addition, the Commonwealth government has specifically ordered the closing of certain university programs and the amalgamation of certain colleges of advanced education with one another, or with nearby universities. These are indeed "very serious developments" for university autonomy,[17] very substantial steps toward a unitary system that includes a measure of internal differentiation of function but is managed and governed even in the details of teaching and research by central governmental bodies: the TEC, the Ministry of Education, and the cabinet itself.

This account reveals social mobility downward of the Australian universities, toward membership in a mass and managed unitary system with markedly constrained internal freedom to set its own academic and research programs. The decline has not yet reached that point, and much freedom for Australian universities still remains. Although the direction of movement seems clear, the possibility of a reversal, in the form of a shift back to state authority and perhaps even back to shared funding, still exists; as elsewhere, movements toward decentralization and regionalization present clear alternatives to increasing central governmental control of higher education.[18]

Something like this story could be told about most west European countries, though the process has been slowed and complicated by the enormously greater power and prestige of the elite university systems of Europe at the beginning. Matters could move so swiftly in Australia precisely because, at the beginning, the universities there were small and relatively weak, with a status borrowed from the universities of the United Kingdom. The postwar decade saw them grow in size and quality. But as they grew, simultaneously grew the power of the Commonwealth over

---

[16]Harman, "Defining the Issues in University-Government Relations"; Harman, " 'Razor Gang' Decisions."

[17]Williams, "Governance and Universities since 1959," p. 11.

[18]Beswick, "Current Issues in Australia," p. 38. Beswick suggests that Australian states are exercising more authority in the field of tertiary education than they were ten years ago. "Whether this means that the States are moving into a position where they might reclaim their historic constitutional functions in higher education is a question of great importance for the institutions and the community. . . . The diversity of the funding base, especially since the abolition of fees for tuition, must remain an attractive aspect of any shift towards State responsibility."

them. And events that seemed to academics, at the time, as supportive of the growth and development of the universities, such as the rationalization of their funding by the Commonwealth government, at least initially on a more generous basis, their apparent liberation from the uncertainties of the market for student fees and from the constraints of their own state governments all in the end proved to have consequences quite different from those originally anticipated. What we see is the centralization, rationalization, and bureaucratization of Australian higher education. That will surely have consequences for the shape of its internal stratification which, through a leveling downward, will seem to be increasingly egalitarian as it becomes more subject to state control.

ELITE HIGHER EDUCATION AND THE MATTHEW EFFECT

The past three decades have seen a number of developments that have threatened the primacy of the elite sector of higher education in most Western countries. The growth of enrollments has markedly increased the size of the universities, bringing into them students of lower social origins, reducing the value of their degrees, often diluting the quality of their traditional forms of instruction, and, in many countries, overloading their facilities and reducing the quality of their instructional staff. During the decades of most rapid growth many instructors and lecturers were hired with qualifications that would not have earned them appointment to a university post either before the buildup or after it leveled off, and these people have remained on university faculties.

Moreover, as they grew, many universities took on more of the characteristics of mass institutions; for example, they diversified their curricula, introducing more training for new and emerging semiprofessions, such as social administration, applied psychology, and business administration. These developments have all helped to change the image of the university in the eyes of decision makers in government as well as of the public at large.

Alongside the expanding universities, new institutions were created, often with encouragement in generous state funding, at least initially. At the same time, and increasingly after 1968, central governments encroached on the traditional freedoms of the university, both because of the rising overall costs of higher education and in response to increased political pressures for public control in the democratization of governance, greater responsiveness to societal needs, and broader access.

All these trends and forces, and others, including the financial constraints of the late 1970s and early 1980s, have threatened the status position of universities, both absolutely in terms of the respect accorded them by society at large and relatively in relation to other forms of higher education. But, although firm and comparable measures of these aspects of status are hard to come by, especially over time, the evidence suggests that the most distinguished, prestigious universities have in most countries retained a position of preeminence as well as their special privileges and freedoms. The reason is that the tremendous expansion of the university sectors in all industrial societies after World War II led their governments to become increasingly reluctant to grant to all universities the privileges and autonomies accorded in the past to the leading ones. And this growing reluctance leads to differential policies as between the more and the less prestigious universities. Academics on the whole resist this tendency, partly out of guild loyalty, partly out of an uneasiness about where governments will draw the line. It is one thing to draw the line between sectors, as, for example, between all polytechnics and all universities, but quite another to draw it within sectors, between Brunel and Oxford, for example. So difficulties arise when governments try not so much to abolish the privileges of the university sector as to reduce its scope after deciding that this protected "autonomous" sector of higher education has grown too powerful. Part of it, in this view, the less prestigious part, must be made more accountable to the public interest, while the leading universities, or departments, or faculties, or "centers of excellence" continue to be accorded the privileges and autonomies now formally granted to the whole sector. In most places these new policies are not fully formalized and institutionalized and may never be, so that, formally, all universities will continue to be equal, but some will be more equal than others. Whether that is a wise policy for higher education is another question, but it is one that is emerging in parts of the United States, in European nations, and in Australia.

The tendency toward more state intervention in the affairs of higher education is not consistent at all levels. For example, the academic upgrading of the second tier of institutions in various countries over the past decade—British polytechnics, Australian CAEs, Norwegian regional colleges, French IUTs, and German *Fachhochschulen*—has been accompanied by a loosening of state controls over their budgets and programs. The result is that they have gained more of the freedoms traditionally associated with universities as their first degree programs have become increasingly similar to those offered by the universities. This tendency has further narrowed the gap of status and function between these second-tier institutions and the less prestigious universities in their own countries.

Given the marked growth of higher education since World War II, and the substantial changes in its character and in its relations with the state, what perhaps needs explaining is not why there has been a decline in the status of the leading universities but why there has been so little change in the stratification of higher education systems at the very top. The answer seems to be a variant of what Robert K. Merton has called "the Matthew Effect," which is translated roughly in American idiom as "them that has gets."[19] Put slightly differently, the advantages of elite institutions are so overwhelming that they create what is for them (but perhaps not for the rest of higher education or the larger society) a kind of "virtuous circle" in which advantage begets advantage, while the resources and activities that mark high-status institutions gravitate toward those same institutions, which already have the most of them. But the tendency of like to beget like seems to be strong enough, with a few exceptions, to sustain elite higher education against the strains of rapid growth, democratization, bureaucratization, and governmental regulation.

Most of the mechanisms of the Matthew Effect in higher education are familiar to members of the elite universities, but they are worth brief mention here if only to clarify the problem for any public policy intended to modify the hierarchy of institutions or reform the system in other ways.

• Universities almost everywhere have a monopoly on research-based postgraduate degrees and, in many countries, a near monopoly on basic research. This is perhaps the greatest advantage the universities possess; the creation of knowledge, especially scientific knowledge, is (or is believed to be) of so much importance to economic development or national prestige that it commands substantial public support even from unfriendly governments and even in times of fiscal stringency. In addition, research and its facilities attract the ablest, most productive, and best-known scholars and scientists, and the leading institutions borrow the prestige of the distinguished academics they recruit. There are many mediocre scholars and scientists in universities, alongside the best; there are very few distinguished scholars and scientists at nonelite institutions. And by a familiar self-reinforcing process, leading universities recruit staff from their own and other leading graduate schools; they provide a climate and facilities for high scholarship and research, they borrow status from their own most distinguished research faculty, and then, by being prestigious themselves, they also confer status on their staff, thus making recruiting easier and also enhancing their ability to attract research funds and the academic honors and distinctions that accrue to research.

• There are two distinctive characteristics of institutions that carry on advanced instruction and research. First, the teachers and researchers they employ are the highest authorities on their own subjects; there is no one, in government or out, who can tell them what to teach or how, or how to conduct research and on what problems. Second, their activities are not "programmable"; the universities must have the freedom to act spontaneously in response to discoveries and research opportunities and findings.

---

[19]St. Matthew put it this way, "For unto every one that hath shall be given, and he shall have abundance: but from him that hath not shall be taken away even that which he hath." Merton, "Matthew Effect in Science," pp. 439–459.

This freedom is seen most clearly in the high physical and natural sciences, but it is present at the frontiers of all disciplines that borrow the prestige and the claims to freedom of the sciences. These two characteristics, the academics' monopoly on expertise and the necessity for internal freedom to direct their own advanced instruction and research, place limits respectively on governmental control over the curriculum and on the bureaucratization of university work. The climate of professional control over teaching and research, over the use, by academics, of their own time and space, is in sharp contrast with the more highly managed, externally monitored, activities of nonuniversity educational institutions. One may cite the example of Sweden, where the major rationalizing "reform" of U68 excluded graduate education and research but transformed undergraduate education into a number of vocationally linked lines of study, largely taught by a nonresearch-oriented teaching staff with titles that sharply distinguish them from the research faculty. The parallel public state colleges in the United States also have far less autonomy in relation to public authorities, as in California, where their "line-item" budgets specify each staff position and activity, by contrast with the block grants given by the state to the university. Another parallel is the polytechnics in Britain, sharply distinguished as "the public sector" from the "autonomous" universities and more closely managed by the local authorities and the central Department of Education and Science, with their course offerings approved by an external agency, the Council for National Academic Awards. The academic climate of these nonuniversity institutions reflects the closer control and management by external governmental agencies: they are and are intended to be instruments of public purpose rather than institutions whose value, at least in part, is intrinsic, independent of government purpose or political ends. And this climate in the nonelite sectors cannot attract either the most creative scholars and scientists or the best students, though, of course, there are exceptions. Without the most distinguished academics, the nonelite sectors can claim neither the expertise nor the autonomy that the elite universities can.

• In order to provide an environment for advanced teaching and research, the universities must have the resources required for research: the great libraries and laboratories where knowledge is created. Moreover, by and large, the more distinguished the institution, the larger are these facilities, though the costs of both libraries and laboratories are rising so rapidly as to force new schemes for sharing them with other universities. The facilities themselves bring prestige and distinction to the institutions that house them and attract the best research scientists, as mentioned earlier.

• The combination of autonomy over expenditures and research grants and contracts provides universities with discretionary funds, "slack" or uncommitted funds available for spontaneous application to promising programs either of instruction or research. The importance of slack funds at the discretion of university staff and administrators, and the bearing this privilege has on the climate of innovation and creativity, can hardly be exaggerated; indeed, the drying up of slack funds in universities under the pressure of declining resources overall may be a more severe threat to their academic quality and intellectual creativity than the closing out of whole departments or the redundancy of a fraction of the teaching staff. But nonuniversity institutions have little if any unplanned or unbudgeted resources, and this lack, as both fact and symptom, sharply distinguishes their academic climates from those in universities.

• One aspect of slack resources is that they allow universities to invite visiting scholars to teach or to lecture. Indeed, one of the mechanisms of the "virtuous circle" is the steady flow of visitors to and from the leading universities.[20] They come because the leading universities have the marginal resources, the research centers, the distinguished scholars, and the scientists whom visitors want to see and spend time with. And they have the status that makes them an attractive place for scholars and scientists to visit. The visitors are of all kinds: senior scholars who come to teach a course and spend a semester or a year; junior scholars and scientists coming to a research center as research associates; scholars and scientists from overseas, often supported by their home countries and institutions, to upgrade their own scientific knowledge and to bring back to their institutions the ideas and currents of work which are present on the frontier of the leading research universities.

But all these visitors give to the leading research universities at least as much as they take from it. They bring their own ideas and perspectives, often representing currents of thought and work which are not strongly represented in the institutions they are visiting. Thus the cosmopolitan university becomes even more cosmopolitan; it does not have to contain within its own faculty all the currents of work in every discipline but can count on visitors to continually bring to the attention of its departmental staff and graduate students the newest ideas in subdisciplines that are not represented, or only weakly represented, in the host research university.

The visiting scholar or scientist brings something perhaps even more valuable than his expertise and specialized knowledge, and that is his freedom from the research conventions and subdisciplinary assumptions that are institutionalized in the research university. The visitor has a freedom from the boundaries of "turf" which the local does not share. Academic departments have rather clear notions of who is competent to

---

[20]For example, in recent years the University of California, Berkeley, has employed more than 100 visiting scholars each year to teach regularly scheduled courses at the university, and another thirty or forty each year to carry on research. During 1981–82 more than 1,300 foreign scholars visited the university for one purpose or another, and that number includes only those who came to the attention of the university's Foreign Scholars' Office.

deal with what subject, and these often determine the distribution of research funds and the training of graduate students. Colleagues in departments sometimes do collaborative work, and in the research centers and institutes of the university they do cross-disciplinary and interdisciplinary work as well. But a visitor has the freedom to ignore subdisciplinary boundaries and the conventional definitions of courses and subjects by virtue of the fact that he is there only temporarily, and that whatever he does is not necessarily setting a precedent for a department or its definition of the appropriate division of academic labor and subdisciplinary boundaries. A visitor can thus offer a course more easily across disciplinary and subdisciplinary boundaries than locals can. Much of the teaching time of the permanent staff is committed to providing the courses and sequences that undergraduates need for their majors and graduate students need to fulfill their requirements. The visitor is often free from these constraints and can offer courses and seminars of his own choosing; indeed he may be invited precisely in order to hold seminars in the subjects of his own research specialty.

The point is that the leading research universities attract visitors in a way that second- and third-rank universities do not and cannot. On the other side of the coin, elite university teachers frequently visit other top universities, a form of elite "in-service training" for them, thus enhancing the reputation of their home universities elsewhere. But lesser universities are largely (and nonelite sectors almost completely) excluded from this flow of leading scholars and scientists among top universities around the world. Entertaining prominent scholars is a significant instrument by which the leading institutions maintain their comparative advantage over second- and third-ranking institutions. And it is one of the ways in which an institution of the second or third rank which has money and ambition seeks to move up the ladder into a higher-status ranking, that is, by translating its funds into visiting appointments on advantageous terms. People who take those appointments may or may not be the leading scholars in their respective fields, but at least they do contribute to the general cosmopolitan atmosphere of the heretofore provincial institution and help in the long, slow process of modifying its general status and reputation in the scholarly world.

Some universities, both in the United States and in western Europe, which cannot sustain teaching and research of the highest quality across the board employ the strategy of putting very substantial resources into one, two, three, or four departments, making them at least the peers of the very best. Once they have achieved first rank in some fields and are thus able to attract outstanding scholars to those fields, it becomes possible for them to try to expand the number and range of their departments of distinction, if in fact they have such ambitions and the necessary resources to implement them.

• Basic research and graduate teaching require and provide a special climate for intellectual life, a higher measure of autonomy, discretionary resources, visitors, and other advantages associated with research, all central to the prestige of universities everywhere. But the cost of all these advantages and privileges makes governments extremely reluctant to extend them to the new nonuniversity institutions or even to lower-status universities. Colleges and their spokesmen and staffs are constantly pressing governments to give them research facilities and support, and with research, the accompanying graduate education and higher degrees. Many of the teachers in nonuniversity institutions were trained in the universities, and they want to continue the research work for which they were trained; they want also the freer and livelier intellectual climates of the university, linked, as I suggest above, to the requirements of graduate education and research and carrying the prestige that attaches to those activities. In short, they know that upward mobility for their own institutions requires the acquisition of universitylike characteristics and, most particularly, of the capacity and freedom to do research. This mechanism is behind the emulative drift that governmental spokesmen everywhere decry.

In some countries the spokesmen for the new nonelite sectors of higher education appeal to the principle of equality, making the point that these institutions, designed in part for more relevant studies and more democratic access, deserve the same treatment as the long-favored elite institutions. But while governments, and especially socialist governments, have given the new institutions parity with the old in whatever areas they could, as, for example, in staff salaries, staff/student ratios, per capita costs of instruction, and sometimes also in student admissions and standards, stipends, and other amenities, they draw the line at research and higher degrees, both because of the heavy costs of research and also because such a policy would effectively subvert the aims of vocational training and regional and class access for which the new institutions were created. Thus real "equity" between sectors is effectively prevented and the continuing status primacy of the old universities is guaranteed.

Nevertheless, outside the United States the gestures that governments have made to the principle of equality of sectors, especially in respect to salaries and standards, while not sufficient to achieve true parity for nonuniversity institutions, have been enough in most countries to discourage the expansion of the nonuniversity sector. The new institutions, as I noted earlier, have not been attractive enough to compete effectively with the universities for enrollments, and they are too expensive, too near the elite universities in their costs and standards, to serve as large low-cost sectors (like the American community colleges) which would encourage broad access to lower- and working-class students. Governments have thus responded to the dilemma of standards versus access, of excellence versus equality, by creating sectors that could neither challenge the traditional status hierarchies of higher education nor provide effectively for mass higher education.

• The universities, and especially the leading research universities, retain an advantage in their modes of governance, an advantage growing out of the traditional collegiality of the professoriat and its extension in recent decades to junior staff. As Smelser observes, the "academic profession retains to a remarkable degree the fundamental nature of a 'calling,' which rests on a kind of value-commitment around which the motivation and energy of men and women are organized."[21] But the strength of that calling, as compared with economic incentives or bureaucratic authority and power as mechanisms of social control, varies in different kinds of institutions, and it is typically stronger in the leading research universities:

In four year colleges and in junior colleges, where there is usually less commitment to a calling based on the core value of cognitive rationality, the tendency is to rely more upon bureaucratic controls, such as the authority of chairmen, deans, and presidents, and to treat the occupational role more in the nature of a job rather than a calling.[22]

When internal professional controls, institutionalized as faculty senates and other forms of collegial self-government, are weak, the management and control from outside are stronger. Typically, governments have imposed forms of participatory governance on the new nonelite sectors more successfully than on the universities. For example,

New principles of governance oriented toward replacing professionalism with representation have been implemented in the Finnish system, in the first place in the new units created in the sixties and in the seventies. Whereas the University of Helsinki, the institutes of technology at Helsingfors and Uleåborg University are still governed by internal participation and professionalism, the new units . . . are run by means of representation.[23]

It is, however, a matter of degree. Determined governments have also changed the governance structures of universities in Germany, France, the Netherlands, and elsewhere in western Europe, aiming toward a broader, "more democratic" form of participation. Indeed, in many countries—perhaps Britain is the only exception in western Europe—there has been a broad shift in the basis of university governance away from academic expertise and toward the principle of representation of estates—senior faculty, junior faculty, administrative staff and clerks, and students—on various levels of university government from the department, or its equivalent, up. But the academic staff, especially full professors, have retained a

---

[21]Smelser, "Social Structural Dimensions of Higher Education," p. 402.
[22]Ibid., p. 403.
[23]Lane, "Higher Education in Scandinavia," p. 16.

larger influence in the old elite universities, an influence and an authority based on their continued control over research and higher degrees.

Broad democratic participation in academic governance invites politicization, and the politicization of academic life, especially in the appointment and promotion of academic staff, inevitably leads to a degradation of its intellectual quality and, over time, of its academic status. Raymond Boudon describes the process of politicization in French universities:

The effort of the 1968 reformers to stimulate higher levels of student participation in the universities was naturally linked to their desire to democratize the system. It was necessary first to encourage the admission of students from modest backgrounds and, second, to involve students in the making of decisions concerning them. . . . [But] students have little interest in university governance. Thus, the reformers who initiated the mechanisms of participation forced politicization at the expense of participation. As soon as nominations for offices were subject to elections, a process of politicization was inevitable. . . .

Politicization naturally spreads to the faculty. Union organizations can occasionally intervene decisively to further the careers of junior faculty members; these unions enjoy success similar to that of "voluntary" organizations capable of offering their members collective benefits. . . . But university unions also benefitted from the 1968 reforms. By officially politicizing the university, the reforms paved the way for the emergence of political groups. The formation of these groups reinforced, by a sort of multiplier effect, the unions, which are traditionally associated with them.

Politicization, an outgrowth of this institutional system, not only governs elective offices in university government, but often leads to basing decisions on appointments of professorial or more junior positions on political criteria, and only secondarily, on scientific criteria. . . . It is certainly not an exaggeration to say that, as a consequence of the institutional procedures now in operation, many members of higher education institutions devote considerable energy to such issues as avoiding or insuring that a certain party might receive or lose a single post in a given institution.[24]

One wonders whether the defense of academic norms and values in French universities would have been stronger if there were not an elite sector of higher education "above" the universities, and if it were not also possible for the leading scholars and scientists in the university to do much of their research outside the university. In any event, the process Boudon describes may be seen in operation elsewhere but, on the whole, more strongly and with less resistance in nonelite sectors. In the United States, for example, "faculty unionization—and, along with it, arrangements for collective bargaining over remuneration and conditions of work—bureaucratize the academic organization further. Unions being defensive and protective of their membership, insist on formal safeguards relating to the

---

[24]Boudon, "The French University since 1968," pp. 187–189.

conditions of work."[25] Their stance leads to standardized regulation of the work role, substitutes blanket job security and promotion by seniority for earned and competitive tenure and promotion by merit, and further undercuts collegiality in governance. In Smelser's view, this situation helps explain differential trends toward unionization in American higher education, where even now no leading research university faculty body has accepted union representation. As the lower-status institutions are more highly bureaucratized, resulting, in part, from the weakness of the academic profession in those institutions, "the unionization of college and junior college teachers has proceeded more rapidly and further than that of university faculties, largely because unionization is a collective response to bureaucratic discipline and control."[26] And where it is introduced, unionization contributes to the very bureaucratization and politicization to which it is a response; it is the mirror image of the bureaucratization of the university.

Matters may differ in some European countries, where staff unions have long existed side by side with a measure of collegial organization and self-governance. But in most countries unions of academics play a different and more active role in nonelite sectors and in the less distinguished universities. For example, in Britain the response of the union of academics to the recent severe budget cuts has been to discourage its members from playing their traditional role as part of university governance in helping to allocate the cuts; the union has defined its members as employees whose jobs have to be defended however possible without regard to the situation of the university or its budget. The union has been more successful in this effort in the less distinguished universities.

To sum up, the more thorough bureaucratization of the nonelite sectors and the stronger role of unions in them and in some of the universities threaten that package of "calling," collegial governance, and academic freedom which has traditionally underpinned the pursuit of excellence in scholarship and research. When those characteristics have been pursued by lower-status institutions, in the process of emulation and drift, faculty members have successfully improved their status and the quality of their academic work as well, as in the long march of the normal school to state university in the United States.[27] But there and elsewhere bureaucratic

---

[25]Smelser, "Social Structural Dimensions of Higher Education," p. 403.

[26]Ibid., p. 404.

[27]Many, perhaps most, of the teachers in the nonelite sectors of higher education are in fact trained and educated in the universities, where they acquire the values and attitudes of the universities both as undergraduates and, for a significant fraction, as graduate students in pursuit of research degrees. So the staffs of the second and third sectors of higher education are, on the whole, downwardly mobile, as compared with their classmates who went on to a career in the universities or research institutes. The fact that so many teachers in the new nonuniversity sectors were trained in the universities explains the tendency of those institutions to "drift" toward the forms and functions of the universities and especially of research; it

controls, both from within and outside the institution, the more active role of unions, and politicization all tend to impede the efforts of nonelite institutions and sectors to improve their status and help preserve the advantage of the research universities, at least so long as they can also resist those tendencies toward bureaucratization and politicization.

ATTITUDES TOWARD THE STRATIFICATION OF HIGHER EDUCATION

Debates about the policies governments should pursue with respect to higher education have, since World War II, centered on the issues of expansion and democratization, that is, on the size and shape of the higher education system and of its several sectors. In various countries there seem to be four recognizably distinct positions on this question which may be defined by a typology, the dimensions of which are "pluralists" versus "unitarians" on one dimension and "meritocrats" versus "egalitarians" on the other (see accompanying table).

ATTITUDES TOWARD THE ORGANIZATION OF
HIGHER EDUCATIONAL SYSTEMS

	Unitarians	Pluralists
Meritocrats	I	II
Egalitarians	III	IV

In Category I we have the "meritocratic unitarians," the orthodox or traditional elitists who really do not approve of any other forms of higher education which grant degrees or are in any way comparable with or competitive with universities. People with these views, however, are not necessarily unsympathetic to nondegree forms of adult education as, for example, workers' education or higher vocational studies. People in this category have largely been overtaken by events as new sectors of higher education have been added in almost all countries. But their views are represented not only in universities but also in many conservative govern-

---

also helps explain the widespread disappointment, dissatisfaction, and alienation experienced by so many teachers in the nonuniversity sector. The real issue is whether the nonuniversity sector is able to create for itself a distinctive identity and mission, separate from that of the universities and acceptable to its staff as an alternative to a position in the university. This seems more feasible the further the sector is from university status. For example, my impression is that morale based on a sense of a distinctive institutional mission is much higher among teachers in American community colleges than in the public four-year colleges that offer master's degrees and recruit staff, complete with doctorates, directly from the big research university graduate departments.

ments which, while not abolishing the new sectors, can effectively restrain their development and discourage their growth.

The "meritocratic pluralists" in Category II support the coexistence of various sectors of higher education; they are the true binarians, trinitarians, and so forth. They accept a status hierarchy with the universities at the top, and therefore a measure of differential support and other inequalities between the sectors as, for example, in their staff salaries, standards for admission, and the awarding of degrees. Some holding these views, especially in the United States, also support a measure of mobility by students and staff between segments, but on a meritocratic and competitive basis.

In Category III are the "egalitarian unitarians," by and large radical equalizers, who are hostile to the elite sector of higher education on political and social grounds and who favor a full integration of all forms of higher education in the service of "the people." Those holding these views are not only commited to full equality among different kinds of institutions but are offended by the autonomy of the elite sectors, and they see in full "comprehensivization" the achievement of equality and social (i.e., state) control over all sectors and forms of higher education, to bring them into the service of the whole society.

Category IV comprises "egalitarian pluralists," people who accept the de facto existence of multiple sectors of higher education, recognizing that the nonuniversity sectors do not (as yet) have the resources to do research or graduate instruction. But these people support measures to "reduce the gap" in such ways as lowering entry requirements to the universities, gradually bringing them to the same level as all other sectors of higher education. These people also support equality of salaries and of other resources between sectors. Some hope that "sooner or later" the system will be made unitary and comprehensive, with all the segments folded into one, with one governing board and one budget. Those who have considered the costs of research and graduate instruction realize that that event must be long delayed, but this position allows them to reconcile their realistic commitment to the continued existence of an elite sector of higher education with their egalitarian principles.

Others do not see consolidation as an interim solution but believe in the continued existence of separate sectors, different in character, function, and mission but of equal prestige. These people would argue for equality in all those aspects of higher education which do not involve the loss of an institution's distinctive functions; thus, they would support the existence of a nonuniversity sector that does less or different research, or is more clearly linked to the local economy, with more technical and vocational studies, than are most universities.

In the United States there are almost no egalitarian unitarians; since so much of the best of higher education is in the private sector, no serious proposals to do away with private higher education altogether have been put forward. On the other extreme there are few meritocratic unitarians, since a pluralistic system is already in place and no one proposes to strip the existing nonelite institutions of their powers to grant degrees and even occasionally to do research. The main arguments, such as they are in the United States, are between those in Categories II and IV, and their differences really boil down to whether they want to maintain or gradually reduce the differences in character and support among different kinds of institutions within the broad pluralistic American system. In European countries all four positions are represented both in the universities and colleges and in government agencies that make decisions about higher education.

The meritocratic unitarians are, strictly speaking, reactionaries, since every major industrial society has created one or more nonuniversity sectors of higher education. Those who still hold these views, both in the universities and in government, can use the current recession and budget cutting to attack the new nontraditional sectors. In Germany, for example, senior academics have boldly suggested the closing down of the *Gesamthochschulen*. Although these efforts have not been successful, the resistance of people with such views, both in the universities and in the *Länder* governments, have prevented the growth and development of these comprehensive universities.[28] And the closing of a good many training colleges in the United Kingdom during the 1970s, rather than their conversion into colleges of advanced education, reflected, at least in part, the view that the nonuniversity sector of higher education, if it cannot be suppressed entirely, should not be allowed to grow and drain resources from the universities.

Meritocratic pluralism, the support of several sectors formally differing in their functions and status, is the dominant philosophy of public higher education in the United States. In other countries, where equality is embedded in ideology rather than in culture, it is difficult to sustain this position without qualification. In another culturally egalitarian society, the three sectors in Australia seem to resemble closely the public sectors in California and other states, for there, too, the universities have a near monopoly on research and higher degrees. There are differences between the two systems. Although Australian colleges of advanced education (CAEs) have a rough equality with the universities in student entry requirements, formal degree requirements, and academic staff salaries,[29] their courses are primarily vocational, and the "process of accrediting college courses or programs for degrees or diplomas has relied a great deal

---

[28]Cerych et al., *Student Flows and Expenditure in Higher Education.*
[29]Beswick, "Current Issues in Australia," pp. 17, 34.

more upon external review than is the case with the universities."[30] In this respect they resemble the British polytechnics. The CAEs differ from the polytechnics in offering more subdegree teaching, but paradoxically they overlap with the Australian universities in the hierarchy of prestige.[31] The Australian institutions of technical further education (TAFEs) resemble American community colleges (except that they offer work at the secondary level) and would more closely resemble British colleges of further education if the latter were organized as a system and treated as a sector of higher or postsecondary education.

Whatever the differences, these systems reflect the views of meritocratic pluralists, certainly in the formal assignment of different functions and necessarily therefore, to some extent, of resources. Even with overlap at the margins, then, status distinctions between the sectors are created despite the egalitarian rhetoric that attended the creation of those sectors and continues to press for parity in more respects with the universities. Everywhere, distinctions between sectors come under attack from egalitarians, not least because the lower-status institutions have a higher proportion of working-class and lower middle-class students. The argument there is that, if you finally recruit students from groups historically disadvantaged, you do not put them into second-class institutions: for them, especially, "nothing if not the best." The introduction of the issue of differential class recruitment to second-tier institutions makes the issue of what is the "best" in higher education of high symbolic importance to progressives concerned with equality of access.

The egalitarian position takes two forms: those who press to reduce existing status distinctions between sectors but would not abolish the sectors are the egalitarian pluralists; and those who press for the abolition of sectors and their replacement by comprehensive universities are the egalitarian unitarians. The first group accepts the idea that there might be an argument for different kinds of institutions and sectors but wishes that they had absolute equality of prestige and status. People with these views are consistent in pressing for equality between sectors in resources, salaries, staff stipends, staff/student ratios, and also in academic standards for the earned degree. All these desiderata have been largely achieved by the new nonuniversity sectors outside the United States. But many are also consistent in pressing for research and graduate training in these sectors, though, as I have noted earlier, governments have generally drawn the line there. On the whole, the pressure for equality across sectors has constrained growth, through the cost of the new sectors and the deterrent of high academic standards. The determination of egalitarians in the new

[30]Ibid., p. 34.
[31]Ibid., p. 7.

sectors to match the older sectors in academic standards and status, in order to provide the very best for their lower-class clientele, has surely inhibited the growth of mass higher education throughout western Europe.[32]

The second group, the egalitarian unitarians, mistrusts different sectors of higher education as inherently hierarchical, arguing for "comprehensive universities" combining university and nonuniversity work in the same institution as a solution to the problem. As Burton R. Clark observes, "The search for fair shares on the part of institutions and staffs, and for equality of treatment and outcomes for students, pushes systems to be rid of binary, tripartite, and other multiple-sector arrangements. Thus national systems still actively seek a way to *de*-differentiate."[33] Clark goes on to say that the "modern comprehensive university in some countries is an effort to have it both ways, to allow for differentiation of major parts, while assigning a formal equality that hopefully will keep down invidious distinctions." It is true for some countries, as Clark notes, that this form seems to be unstable, "as the more prestigious parts resist the lumping of everyone together and as attentive publics as well as insiders perceive real differences and attach different values to the parts." And pointing to the failure of the German *Gesamthochschulen*, and to the idea of a comprehensive university in Sweden as well, Clark draws the conclusion that "explicit sectors thus seem to be the chief answer to the macro-organization of an evermore extended division of academic labor."[34]

Separate sectors and comprehensive universities are not necessarily alternative solutions to this problem, but they may be complementary, as the big public research universities in the United States show. Berkeley and UCLA, Michigan and Wisconsin, are genuinely comprehensive universities, overlapping with all other sectors (including community colleges) in their formal and informal functions. They manage their internal diversity and hierarchy of activity in the face of egalitarian pressures, in part by not making those differences explicit, that is, by obscuring them, in part by making movement from the internal sectors of mass education to the elite forms and activities relatively easy and largely meritocratic, thus legitimating them. The entry from the undergraduate to the graduate colleges and professional schools in such universities is a case in point.[35]

Yet to argue that the comprehensive university can survive in the United States and manage its complex internal tensions successfully is not to deny the vulnerability of its counterparts elsewhere, whether they arise out of an enormous expansion of the old elite sector, as in Italy, or are invented as a

---

[32]Trow, "Comparative Perspectives on Access," pp. 89–121.
[33]Clark, *Higher Education System*, p. 194.
[34]Ibid., p. 195.
[35]Trow, "Elite Higher Education."

new form, as in West Germany. But those failures should not obscure the peculiar advantages of comprehensive universities for reconciling the dilemmas of excellence and equality, if such comprehensive universities are part of a diversified system and not a substitute for one.

CONCLUSION

The stratification of institutions of higher education in Western industrial democracies shows two rather different principles of hierarchy in operation. One is based on the pursuit by individual institutions of competitive advantage in the market for the factors that make for academic prestige: scholarly honors, distinguished professors, research funds, endowments, and the like. In this status system the determination of prestige and institutional life chances is a function of success in these markets, and that in turn is heavily determined in any given moment by past success.

In the other status system, rank is determined by the allocation of functions, rights, privileges, and resources by governments to specific institutions and to sectors. Those allocations reflect the policies and other mechanisms by which governments manage the academic status and life chances of the institutions they fund and control.

By and large, European institutions are creatures of the state, which determines their membership in a given sector and the relative status of the sectors. But the status of any specific institution is conditioned by its historical status, by inherited resources such as libraries, buildings, and geographical location, and by its success in the competition for scholars, students, and resources. In the United States the status of private universities is largely determined by the first of those processes. The status of public universities in the United States and other advanced societies is governed by a complex mixture of competitive success in various academic markets and governmental policies.

A natural sequel of this analysis is the question of what bearing the stratification of academic institutions has on the quality and quantity of higher education and university-based research in a given country. Do the size and shape of the system have much bearing on how "good" the higher educational system is, by whatever criteria one wants to judge it? These questions lead more or less naturally to issues of public policy toward higher education. But the policies of industrial nations toward their higher educational systems in recent decades have not been adopted chiefly for their effects on the quality or character of higher learning in those societies. On the whole, those policies have been shaped by social, economic, and political forces and ideas, and they are likely to be modified by similar forces in the future.

BIBLIOGRAPHY

American Council on Education. *Report of the Committee on Graduate Instruction.* Washington, D.C.: ACE, April 1934.

Ben-David, Joseph, and Abraham Zloczower. "Universities and Academic Systems in Modern Societies." *European Journal of Sociology* 3 (1962):45–84.

Berelson, Bernard. *Graduate Education in the United States.* New York: McGraw-Hill, 1960.

Bessant, B. "The Erosion of University Autonomy in Australia." *Vestes* 25, no. 1 (1982):26–33.

Beswick, David. "Current Issues in Australia, 1981: An Introduction to the Australian Higher Education System, with Particular Attention to Federal-State Relationships." Unpublished paper, presented at UCLA seminar, November 1981.

Boudon, Raymond. "The French University since 1968." In *French Sociology*, ed. Charles C. Lemert. New York: Columbia University Press, 1981.

Cartter, Allan. *An Assessment of Quality in Graduate Education.* Washington, D.C.: American Council on Education, 1966.

Cerych, Ladislav, Sarah Coulton, and Jean-Pierre Jollade. *Student Flows and Expenditure in Higher Education, 1965–1979.* Amsterdam: European Cultural Foundation, 1981.

Chronicle of Higher Education, September 29, 1982, pp. 8–10; November 10, 1982, pp. 4–6.

Clark, Burton R. *The Higher Education System: Academic Organization in Cross-National Perspective.* Berkeley, Los Angeles, London: University of California Press, 1983.

Fensham, P. J. "Some Reflections on Four Years as a Member of the Universities Council." In *A Time of Troubles*, ed. John E. Anwyl and Grant S. Harman. Centre for the Study of Higher Education. Melbourne, Australia: University of Melbourne, 1981.

Furth, Dorotea. "New Hierarchies in Higher Education." *European Journal of Education* 17, no. 2 (1982):145–151.

Harman, Grant. "The 'Razor Gang' Decisions, the Guidelines to the Commonwealth Education Commissions, and Australian Education Policy." Centre for the Study of Higher Education. Research Working Paper no. 81. Melbourne, Australia: University of Melbourne, July 1981.

———. "Defining the Issues in University-Government Relations: Mapping the Shifting Loci of Effective Power." Conference paper of Australian Vice-Chancellors' Committee Conference of University Governing Bodies. Melbourne, Australia: University of Melbourne, August 1982.

Keniston, Hayward. *Graduate Study in the Arts and Sciences at the University of Pennsylvania.* Philadelphia: University of Pennsylvania Press, 1959.

Lane, Jan-Erik. "Higher Education in Scandinavia in a Comparative Perspective." In *Enzyklopädie Erziehungswissenschaft*, ed. L. Huber. Forthcoming (in German).

Lazarsfeld, P. F., and Morris Rosenberg, eds. *The Language of Social Research.* Glencoe, Ill.: Free Press, 1955.

Merton, Robert K. "The Matthew Effect in Science." In *The Sociology of Science*. Chicago: University of Chicago Press, 1973.

Smelser, Neil. "Social Structural Dimensions of Higher Education." *In* Talcott Parsons and Gerald Platt, *The American University*. Cambridge: Harvard University Press, 1973.

Trow, Martin. "Elite Higher Education: An Endangered Species?" *Minerva* 14 (Autumn 1976):355–376.

————. "Comparative Perspectives on Access." In *Access to Higher Education*, ed. Oliver Fulton. Guildford, England: Society for Research into Higher Education, 1981.

Williams, Bruce. "Governance and Universities since 1959." *Vestes* 25, no. 1 (1982):2–11.

6. THE CULTURAL VIEW*

Tony Becher

An autobiographical note offers the simplest way of identifying the central theme of this paper and of explaining my approach to it. When I graduated in philosophy from the University of Cambridge, the first job that came my way—alongside some part-time undergraduate teaching—was as an academic editor at Cambridge University Press. Apart from commissioning, receiving, and evaluating new titles, preparing texts for the printer, and keeping a general oversight on their progress—a job shared with other colleagues—it fell to me, as the most junior member of the staff, to see to the dozen or so endowed university lectures which custom or statute required to be formally published by the University Press.

In general, the print runs for these slim volumes varied from 750 (for a very specialized topic) to 2,000 or even 2,500 (for a "big name" or a newsworthy theme). When I had some five years of publishing experience behind me, one of these lectures, which I thought rather poor, came to my desk. I sent it off to press with an order for a thousand copies. That decision finally convinced me that I lacked the market instincts of a true publisher; I was too much guided by my own judgment of intellectual worth. A year or so afterward I took up another post. The lecture in question was the annual Rede Lecture for 1959, whose eventual sales were above 50,000. It was delivered by C. P. Snow, and its title was *The Two Cultures and the Scientific Revolution.*

This episode was not my only source of concern to gain a better understanding of academic cultures. It was my conviction at the time, however, and has been ever since, that Snow's sharp division between the worlds of science and the humanities was both damaging and misleading. I have to admit to myself a long-standing, if not altogether laudable, desire to vindicate my dismissive decision about his Rede Lecture. I have a vested interest in proving that there are many more cultural boundaries than he allows for within both the scientific and the nonscientific disciplines, and

*I am indebted to a number of critical friends and friendly critics for comments on an earlier draft of this chapter. In particular, those whose suggestions led to significant changes for the better, or so I believe, include Philip Altbach, Stephen Ball, Dorothy Jerrome, Maurice Kogan, Trevor Pateman, Gary Rhoades, and Sheldon Rothblatt.

many unacknowledged bridges across what he depicts as a grand canyon of the intellect.

Although the twenty years and more that have passed since this event have nurtured my interest in academic cultures, I have only recently sought a way of giving that interest a direct expression. If I owe the late C. P. Snow the debt of making me think about the question, I owe to the distinguished anthropologist, Clifford Geertz, perhaps more than to anyone else, the inspiration of how to set about tackling it in a systematic way. It was his unpublished paper, "Towards an Ethnography of the Disciplines," which set me off on the investigation described below.

There are three main implications to be drawn from this brief apologia for the discussion that follows. First, it is colored by the mental habits of a philosopher, the culture in which I was myself reared; second, that approach is moderated by the practical precepts of anthropology; and third, its main emphasis is on disciplinary boundaries, as against other cultural distinctions.

The structure of the argument as a whole is straightforward. It begins with a brief exploration of the concept of culture and its applicability to academic life. Three relevant fields of investigation—institutions, roles and functions, and intellectual arenas—are then examined in turn. Against this background the discussion focuses on the particular empirical study mentioned above and draws out its implications, particularly in terms of how far the cultural features of disciplines are related to social and environmental factors and how far they derive from epistemological considerations. In the final section, returning to a more general level of discourse, I attempt to assess the potential of the cultural study of higher education and to place it in the context of some of the other approaches discussed in this book.

THE NOTION OF CULTURE

If there were any word to serve the purpose as well, I would unhesitatingly use it in preference to one that seems at times downright slippery and at other times impossibly vague and all-embracing. But although "culture" has uncomfortably many denotations, it is the only term that seems satisfactorily to combine the notions, central to the theme of this argument, of a shared way of thinking and a collective way of behaving. The weaving together of philosophical analysis with phenomenological inquiry might be argued to be particularly important when dealing with tribal groupings that owe their very existence to a common form of intellectual pursuit, and for which—as I hope to show—epistemological considerations play their part alongside environmental ones.

At the outset, however, it may be well to note some of the main components in the concept of culture. Snow, who seems on this occasion to have been much taken with the number two, distinguishes, in his "second look" at the two cultures argument, between two meanings: "the dictionary definition, 'intellectual development, development of the mind' "; and the term "as used by anthropologists to denote a group of persons living in the same environment, linked by common habits, common assumptions, a common way of life."[1]

I shall return to elaborate in a moment, but it is worth remarking here that Snow has omitted an important, and in my view more basic, meaning that serves to unite the two. The term "culture" is also used as closely cognate to "cultivation," denoting nurture, growth, and production; hence, among other derivatives we have agriculture, cultured pearls, and bacterial cultures (as organisms maintained in a bounded environment—the culture medium—within which new growth can take place).

It is by extension of this idea that the notion of the product of sound breeding is derived: the cultivated or cultured man, embodying a knowledge of all that is best in the artistic and literary tradition of his country, the finest flower of civilized upbringing and a gentlemanly education. Such was the refined man of culture defended by Matthew Arnold against the barbarians in his *Culture and Anarchy*, and nowadays perhaps most commonly extolled by certain schools of literary criticism. The links with Snow's first definition are obvious enough.

But another extension of the same basic meaning takes us in the direction of the process of upbringing and the forms in which social beings are nurtured. Here we move into the territory marked by Snow's second definition, namely the set of values, beliefs, and symbols that govern the behavior of a society or a social group. To the anthropologist, culture is a fundamental concept: it embodies the traditional and social heritage of a people; their customs and practices; their transmitted knowledge, beliefs, law, and morals; their linguistic and symbolic forms of communication, and the meanings they share. (The status differences, relationships, and boundaries that can be identified within a society tend to be distinguished as part of its structure, and thus to be contrasted with its culture as strictly defined.)

Perhaps this rich anthropological notion has to be weakened into metaphor when the subject of study is not the complete way of life of a relatively isolated tribe, but rather one part of the way of life of a group of twentieth-century academics. Nonetheless, the broad concept of culture as developed in social anthropology does, I suggest, have considerable relevance to the exploration of culture in higher education.

Any such claim has, of course, to be assessed against the actuality that, amid the large corpus of literature on the subject, only a relatively insignificant portion is devoted to the cultural aspects of higher education, in the

---

[1]Snow, *Two Cultures: And a Second Look*, pp. 62, 64.

sense outlined. An attempt is made in the concluding section of this chapter to explore the reasons for this relative neglect. Here it may be more useful to concentrate on mapping the type of work in question and contrasting it with other types of study which bear some superficial resemblance to it.

An inquiry that starts by viewing higher education, or some component of it, as a cultural system must, at the very least, seek to single out the underlying pattern of concepts, values, and activities that give it a coherent identity. It may well go beyond this goal to portray, and perhaps even to offer some explanation for, the relationships among such concepts, values, and activities. Both the more modest, descriptive, requirement and the more ambitious, analytic, one call for a certain sense of distance—the ability to stand back and recognize the obvious, taken-for-granted assumptions that, by not being taken for granted, often provide important starting points for understanding.

The requirement for psychological disengagement from one's subject matter gives rise to familiar dilemma. Traditionally the anthropologist has always been an outsider, viewing the subject culture at second hand. How could it have been otherwise? No one among the Nuer, or the Trobriand Islanders, or the Cherokee, possessed the appropriate training and qualifications to attempt a rival insider's account. But once the scene of action moved closer to home, there was no such shortage of contenders for the insider's role. The argument emerged quite sharply in the early 1970s in the context of the sociology of science,[2] where the relative merits of sociologists turned quasi-scientist and of scientists turned quasi-sociologist were the subject of much debate. The pros and cons of each position are evident enough and need not be labored here. What is essentially at stake is the coming together of a set of skills and a set of understandings: whichever of these one happens already to possess, the other takes time and intellectual effort to acquire.

The context of theory within which a cultural analysis is carried out may or may not be ambitious. Some researchers impose little in the way of framework on their portrayals; others import not only existing concepts but ready-made explanations. All would, however, expect to base their results on some form of systematic observation, linked wherever possible to some strategy for cross-checking their findings. It is principally this feature that differentiates them from various other groups whose members study and write about higher education as a cultural phenomenon.

The four main areas of activity bordering on the territory with which this paper is concerned need to be distinguished from it if confusion is to be avoided. The first comprises fictional studies of academic life. Perhaps the

---

[2]See, for example, Merton, "The Perspectives of Insiders and Outsiders," in *Sociology of Science*; Rose and Rose, "Do Not Adjust Your Mind."

currently best-known work in this genre is Malcolm Bradbury's *History Man*, though a significant number of other novelists have ventured into the field. But however soundly based on experience and observation, such works cannot offer more than indirect and unsubstantiated visions of reality. They may embody rich insights and suggest fruitful areas for empirical inquiry, but they are not in the required sense systematic and capable of validation.

The second area consists of history and memoirs. Again, these fields offer valid raw material for cultural analysis, but they do not themselves constitute it. Memoirs, by their very nature, emphasize individual rather than collective experience. The historical study of higher education is, except for rare instances,[3] concerned less with exploring the values and practices that go to make up the characteristic cultures of university life than with cataloging the minutiae of everyday academic affairs or with charting the broad sweep of intellectual reform.

A third group of studies is characterized by its prescriptive emphasis. It sets out with a deliberate mission: to argue the case for a particular school of thought or a particular group of institutions. It is, by definition, partisan, polemic, and political. Again, the evidence provided by such writings may well be relevant to the type of inquiry with which we are here concerned, but the writings themselves lack the critical distance that would qualify them as acceptable accounts of cultural phenomena.

Finally, a sizable category of writings sets out to introduce and explain contemporary higher education to the intelligent public, whether former or current students, would-be students or their parents, or those individuals who would have liked to participate, but did not, and who retain a lively interest in academic affairs. Accounts of this kind are usually presented by insiders, and they rest heavily on personal experience.[4] As tourist guides to the groves of academe, they tend both to partiality and to prejudice. They seldom meet the requirement of systematic observation, and they are understandably lacking in any theoretical content.

A Primitive Taxonomy of Cultural Systems

In attempting to sketch a taxonomic framework for the comparatively sparse and scattered literature on the cultural aspects of higher education, I find it useful to start from three main categories, albeit ones that overlap one another, are not sharply defined, and are subject to further internal differ-

---

[3] Notable exceptions include Rothblatt, *Tradition and Change in English Liberal Education*, and Church, "Disciplinary Dynamics."

[4] A classic in the genre is Truscot, *Redbrick University*. A more modern counterpart is Rose and Ziman, *Camford Observed*.

entiation. These are institutionally based studies, portrayals of actors and their roles, and studies of intellectual arenas.[5] The categories are illustrated by particularly interesting and important examples, which, for that reason, are likely to be widely known and generally recognizable.

Institutionally based studies—The wider the scope of institutional study, the less easy it becomes to view the domain as comprising a single identifiable culture; thus, understandably, there are very few studies that tackle a complete national system of higher education from a cultural standpoint. The more common approaches tend to be descriptive rather than analytic and to adopt either a historical or a managerial stance.[6] There are, however, a few striking instances that view a country's higher education from a cultural standpoint. If Halsey and Trow's *The British Academics* fails to qualify, it is only because of its greater preoccupation with academics than with academies (see below). However, the study by Talcott Parsons and Gerald Platt, *The American University*, offers at least a plausible candidate in this category.

As the field narrows to particular types of institutions, appropriate examples are relatively easier to find. One clear case in point is the study, by Burton R. Clark, of the private liberal arts college, as particularized in Antioch, Reed, and Swarthmore.[7] Aspects of *The American College* also quite clearly fall under this heading, notably the chapter by David Riesman and Christopher Jencks on "The Viability of the American College."[8] A later study of experimental colleges, by Riesman in association with Gerald Grant, adopts a comparable approach, with general argument loosely woven round a series of ethnographies of selected institutions.[9]

It is at the level of the individual university or college that the most obvious dividing line can be drawn between a particular cultural climate and the wider environment outside. One much quoted study in this genre is Benson R. Snyder's devastating analysis of intellectual and social life at the Massachusetts Institute of Technology, *The Hidden Curriculum*. More recent work in the same general style has been carried out by Malcolm R. Parlett in a number of private American colleges.[10]

Parlett has also written about cultures at the subinstitutional level. His

---

[5]Clark, in his masterly analysis of the field (see *Higher Education System*, chap. 3), uses a different, but recognizably related, form of classification, giving stronger emphasis to the culture of educational systems as a whole.

[6]A range of examples is to be found in the accounts of twelve national systems of higher education sponsored by the International Council for Educational Development in the late 1970s and summarized in Eurich, *Systems of Higher Education in Twelve Countries*.

[7]Clark, *Distinctive College*.

[8]Sanford, ed., *American College*, chap. 3.

[9]Grant and Riesman, *Perpetual Dream*.

[10]See, for example, "The Wellesley Milieu" in Parlett and Dearden, eds., *Introduction to Illuminative Evaluation*.

analysis of the "department as a learning milieu"[11] is one of relatively few studies at this degree of specificity, perhaps because anthropological penetration into a single cell of the higher education honeycomb is likely to be thought both obtrusive and threatening to those whose rightful territory it is. Another reason may be that most investigators with such a starting point develop an interest in the relevant disciplinary culture rather than in the way of life of the particular department.

Portrayals of actors and their roles.—It is intriguing, but readily understandable, that the academic world is identified as consisting of two simple categories: the teachers and the taught. The fact that every university has a significant share of nontenured, nonteaching researchers, a sizable cadre of administrators, and a substantial payroll of ancillary, secretarial, and technical staff is not commonly acknowledged in any cultural analysis of the inhabitants of higher education. But leaving aside those who form the supporting cast, the two main actors are certainly not wanting in attention.

By far, the most impressive study of university faculty to date, both in its range of coverage and in its depth of analysis, is Halsey and Trow's *The British Academics*. Although it offers an account of academic man in one particular national system at a point in time when that and other systems were in the process of expansion, the fundamental characteristics of the portrayal remain valid in the very different context of the present. Other writings, though they are on a more limited scale, offer supplementary or confirmatory evidence about the culture of academics at large. A useful overview of the main dimensions of faculty culture is given in Burton R. Clark's study[12] which predates Halsey and Trow and is focused mainly on North American material. A more recent investigation by Richard Startup[13] concentrates on academic roles, relationships, and rewards, based on material collected within a single British university. It edges toward a study of departmental and disciplinary subcultures, in that particular emphasis is given to the similarities and differences of the practices of four departments: classics, pure mathematics, civil engineering, and psychology.

There is also a subset of such writings which concentrates on the political aspects of the academic's life. One distinguished precursor of such studies, though not itself in the empirical tradition of contemporary writings, was Francis Cornford's well-known satire, *Microcosmographia Academica*. An anthropological study by F. G. Bailey (otherwise known for his studies of Mediterranean cultures) explores "the folk lore of academic politics."[14] In contrast, Cohen and March adopt an approach based primarily on policy

---

[11]Parlett, "Department as a Learning Milieu."
[12]Clark, "Faculty Cultures."
[13]Startup, *University Teacher and His World.*
[14]Bailey, *Morality and Expediency.*

studies and organization theory, with a central emphasis on the ambiguities in the role of the American college president.[15]

The cultures of university and college students are also well served by research. One of the outstanding contributors to this field is Howard Becker, a sociologist whose style is predominantly anthropological. *Making the Grade* is a masterly examination of "the academic side of college life"; the earlier *Boys in White* focuses more specifically on life in a medical school, but it offers an equally penetrating analysis of the social and cultural pressures that impinge on the students who share that way of life. On the other side of the Atlantic, the only study on any sizable scale is by Peter Marris.[16] Its method is very different, because it substitutes questionnaires and structured interviews for participant observation; and it pays considerable attention to campus residence, now largely an outdated issue. Nonetheless, both Becker and Marris identify assessment as a crucial issue in student culture, a theme subsequently taken up by Miller and Parlett[17] in their detailed examination of examinations as seen from the learner's standpoint. Mention may also be made, among other specific studies of student cultures, of a relatively recent exploration by Bliss and Ogborn in *Students' Reactions to Undergraduate Science.* As a contribution to the sociology of science this study could perhaps equally well have been considered under the next category.

Studies of intellectual arenas.—A number of inquiries focus on the content of intellectual life rather than on its context; their prime concern is neither with institutions nor with particular academic roles, but rather with one or more of the constituent territories on the map of knowledge. A distinction needs to be drawn here between the types of cultural analysis which form the subject of the present paper and the often more theoretically oriented studies which are properly labeled as contributions to the sociology of knowledge. The latter study, as I see it, takes knowledge to be a commodity whose transactions are largely or wholly determined by abiding social mechanisms and whose value is largely or wholly established by deep-seated social pressures. The main goal of inquiry is to reveal these mechanisms and pressures and to explain their interaction. In contrast, the cultural analysis of intellectual arenas has less to do with knowledge as such than with the mores and the life-styles of those who seek it. Its concern is to understand the interrelationship between the beliefs and the practices of academics and to discover how these affect and are affected by the nature of the particular inquiries they happen to pursue.

Again, within this genre, the approach may be a broad or a narrow one. I

[15]Cohen and March, *Leadership and Ambiguity.*
[16]Marris, *Experience of Higher Education.*
[17]Miller and Parlett, *Up to the Mark.*

have already argued that C. P. Snow's attempt to divide the whole world of learning into two constituent cultures is unacceptably simplistic. A somewhat more refined set of cultural categories—humanities, social science, natural science, and professional studies—formed the basis of an investigation, related to the problems of introducing interdisciplinary degree programs, by Gaff and Wilson.[18] They concluded that "there are significant differences between faculty members in different fields of study on such aspects of culture as educational values, teaching orientation, and lifestyle. These differences seem sufficiently great to regard the four divisions as distinct faculty cultures. . . . This is not to say that these cultures are discrete; indeed there are areas of overlap on every item and every scale."

When the focus is narrowed to particular disciplines or groups of disciplines, it becomes immediately obvious that one domain, the natural sciences, has been very thoroughly studied at the expense of the rest. Why the cultural analysis of science should have attracted so much attention, and the cultural analysis of history, philosophy, or economics so little, is a question that seems to deserve more attention than it has been given. Is it, one might ask, a matter of the sociology of knowledge? Are more incentives offered by society, or by grant-giving bodies, for looking at what scientists are up to, as against the behavior of academics in other fields? Or is it, instead, a product of the sociology of sociology where, within the culture of that discipline, better pickings are earned by looking at the well-organized, relatively stable, and fairly public (or at least intersubjective) practices of the scientists than by attempting to pin down the elusive and semiprivate activities that characterize many nonscientific fields of inquiry?

Whatever the answer to these speculations might be, the sociology of science is undoubtedly an oasis of exploration in what otherwise remains largely desert territory. One of the most often quoted individuals is Thomas Kuhn, whose *Structure of Scientific Revolutions* appeared in 1962. This work, by questioning the orthodox view of scientific progress as rational and evolutionary, has had a major impact both on the philosophy of science and on sociological thinking. In a very different intellectual style, Robert Merton must also be regarded as one of the founding fathers of the sociology of science movement.[19] Michael Mulkay's analysis in *The Social Process of Innovation* is one of many studies that adopt a similar approach.

Broadly speaking, the characteristics of the Merton school include a predisposition toward the "hard" empirical sciences (physics, as against meteorology; genetics, as against ecology); a tendency to lump all scientific disciplines together, rather than to take account of internal differences; and an emphasis on certain salient features of a scientist's way of life, such as the

---

[18]Gaff and Wilson, "Faculty Cultures and Interdisciplinary Studies."
[19]His major writings are brought together in Merton, *Sociology of Science*.

attribution of excellence, the nature of discovery, and the problems associated with establishing priority. Hagstrom[20] avoids at least one of these limitations because he consciously differentiates among the practices of different scientific disciplines; and Whitley and others, in *Social Processes of Scientific Development*, are emphatic about "the need for comparative studies of the development of different sciences" and "the move away from regarding cognitive structures in each science as monistic and fully integrated."[21]

In contrast with this wealth of research[22] the depictions of other intellectual cultures are disappointingly sparse. In the social sciences, there is what Clifford Geertz describes as a kind of proto-ethnography of British psychology, the cult of the fact.[23] There are some sociological writings about sociology, not least among them Jennifer Platt's *Realities in Social Research*. But I know of no substantial studies across the wide range of the humanities or the professions. This apparent dearth of investigation[24] has lent added stimulus to the inquiry that forms the subject of the next section.

A DISCIPLINE-BASED APPROACH TO ACADEMIC CULTURES

This point in the argument marks a change in gear. Thus far my concern has been with delineating the overall context in which research into higher education as a cultural system has been carried out. I now turn from the general to the particular, concentrating on the explication of a piece of work in progress. In this section I outline the nature and scope of the investigation so far and then go on to identify what seems to me to be a key methodological issue, namely, the question of intrinsic and extrinsic characteristics of inquiry. This done, I then go on to outline three broad groups of findings.

The study with which I am currently concerned owes its origins—as noted earlier—to a profound dissatisfaction with C. P. Snow's argument in *Two Cultures*, together with a means of testing out that dissatisfaction as suggested by Clifford Geertz. My initial concern was to explore the similarities and differences of a variety of intellectual cultures on an empirical basis

---

[20]Hagstrom, *Scientific Community*.

[21]Whitley, ed., *Social Processes of Scientific Development*, p. 3.

[22]A comprehensive review of the relevant literature is provided by Mulkay, "Sociology of the Scientific Research Community."

[23]Geertz, "Toward an Ethnography of the Disciplines," in which he draws upon the work of Hudson, *Cult of the Fact*.

[24]The picture is not quite so bleak as I have represented it to be. A significant number of historicocultural studies of the professions and semiprofessions (including engineering, social work, and nursing) are currently in progress in Sweden, sponsored by the National Board of Universities and Colleges. In Britain there is a steadily growing literature on the impact on secondary schools of disciplinary traditions in the humanities. Two examples are Ball, "Competition and Conflict in the Teaching of English," and Goodson, "Defending the Subject."

and at a level of analysis considerably more subtle than that achieved by Snow. To this end, I chose as a starting point six disciplines that promised to provide usefully contrasting case studies: biology, engineering, history, law, physics, and sociology. Quite early in the day, it became apparent that the first two were likely to prove unmanageably broad, which led me to narrow them respectively to botany and zoology and to mechanical engineering.

The plan, which by and large I adhered to, was to interview at least twenty academics in each discipline, at various levels of seniority from doctoral student to departmental chairman. Each sample was drawn from two or three reasonably representative and well-regarded departments in England[25] and, by way of a modest transatlantic contrast, the counterpart department at the University of California, Berkeley.

The interviews were unstructured; they lasted from forty minutes to over two hours, with the average about an hour and a quarter. Overall, though not necessarily in each interview, I sought the views of respondents in each discipline under five main categories. The first concerned the characteristics of the discipline: its overall nature and content; its internal and external boundaries; its degree of unity across subspecialties; its nearest intellectual neighbors; the extent to which its nature varied from one country to another, and so on. The second group concerned epistemological issues: the role of theory; the importance of specialized techniques; the extent of quantification and modeling; the degree to which findings could be generalized; the way conclusions were established; terms of approval and criticism, and the like. The third explored questions about professional practice, such as the nature of communication patterns; forms and rates of publication; the structure of personal networks; competition and priority; plagiarism and sharp practice; grantsmanship and fashion; the extent of teamwork; and the incidence of jargon. The fourth category concerned career patterns, including questions about the recruitment of new members and their induction into the discipline; how their specialisms were chosen; how they established independence and gained tenure; how reputations were earned; how much mobility was possible between specialties; and whether it was common to experience a "midcareer crisis" in one's research. Finally, a further set of questions sought, without intruding too far into respondents' private lives, to explore the extent of their involvement in their work; the aspects of their jobs which they considered particularly rewarding or unrewarding; the degree to which, as professionals, they were concerned with contemporary social and environmental issues; the wider

[25]For botany and zoology, I visited Bristol and Reading; for history, Exeter and University College London; for law, Kent, the London School of Economics, and Southampton; for mechanical engineering, Birmingham and Imperial College London; for physics, Bristol and Imperial College London; and for sociology, Essex, Kent, and the London School of Economics.

benefits of their academic training; their stereotypes of fellow practitioners; and their stereotypes of practitioners in the other five disciplines investigated in the study.

As a first stage in analyzing the substantial quantities of data arising from more than 120 interviews, I set out to produce for each discipline a detailed ethnographic account; I then sought the reactions to the account of the twenty or so informants who had contributed to it. This exercise was useful both in correcting minor errors of interpretation and in confirming that, by and large, the portraits were readily recognizable by their subjects. It was, however, only a first step toward my main goal, which was to explore some of the important commonalities and contrasts among disciplines.

My first published attempt at a comparative analysis along these lines[26] merely looked at cultural similarities and differences without questioning why they occur. But it did establish that the tendency, mentioned earlier, of some sociologists of science to treat (for example) physics, biology, and mechanical engineering as closely comparable is a gross distortion of the characteristics of those three disciplines; and that C. P. Snow was as mistaken as I had originally suspected in his implication that history, sociology, and academic law are natural bedfellows. Indeed, in some important respects the two most closely comparable disciplines among the six chosen for my initial study are biology (or, strictly, botany and zoology) and history.

Three points arising from my earlier paper are relevant to the present argument. First, the value of the basic data is obviously limited in a number of respects. A population of between twenty and twenty-four practitioners in any given discipline might well yield a somewhat partial and misleading portrayal of the culture of that discipline. Ideally, the findings would need to be cross-checked against those derived from a further set of respondents, preferably from departments other than the ones already sampled. In any event, the method used in the inquiry, in relying entirely on verbal testimony rather than on the full-fledged anthropological techniques of participant or nonparticipant observation, restricts its validity to the perceptions, as opposed to the practices, of those within the culture.

Nevertheless, at the general level at which comparisons can be drawn between one discipline and another, it is possible to acquire some useful insights into cultural activities as well as cultural values by attending to what people say and noting what words they use in describing good practice and bad practice. To take just one example, the contrast between physicists and mechanical engineers, a typical term of praise for the former is "elegant," whereas the latter more often tend to extol what is "concise" or "clear-cut." Physicists are apt to describe themselves as arrogant and elitist; engineers see themselves as pragmatic and conservative. Those physicists

---

[26]Becher, "Towards a Definition of Disciplinary Cultures."

who spoke of their spare-time interests referred most frequently to the theater, art, and music; the engineers typically resorted to aviation, deep-sea diving, and "messing about in boats." Of course, one may reasonably object that these polarities are oversimplified. Still, they serve to convey a consistent set of personal and intellectual differences which are likely to be echoed in any other systematic attempt to match these two paticular disciplinary cultures.

The third comment leads me directly into the arguments advanced later in this paper. In the process of attempting to define and contrast disciplinary cultures, I found myself drawn inexorably into a recognition of various subcultures within each discipline, and even into a separate classification of those subcultures which cut across disciplinary boundaries. At the outset I attempted to do no more than characterize the main elements of this classification as "urban" and "rural" research styles: a distinction that was, I hoped, evocative, but that made no pretense to be explanatory.

What is now called for is not further description and classification of the material I have so far assembled (nor even at this point an extension of it), but rather an attempt, however sketchy it may have to be, to generate an explanatory framework that has something to say about causes and effects. Before this endeavor is possible, however, there must be a preliminary clearing of the ground.

INTRINSIC AND EXTRINSIC DETERMINANTS OF CULTURE

A number of the sociologists I interviewed spoke of their shared sense of possessing a powerful mode of explanation for human behavior, which was, they felt, far more potent and effective than that offered by the psychologists. As evident from the review of various approaches to the study of academic cultures above, sociologically oriented contributions have been more numerous, and on the whole more influential, than those from any other disciplinary perspective.

It is a common temptation for those who have a good hand to overplay it, and I want at this point to argue that this is what a number of sociologists (particularly sociologists of science and sociologists of knowledge) have done. In advancing such a claim, I do not want to make the same mistake of overplaying my own hand. Let me therefore begin by acknowledging that many of the cultural phenomena associated with particular forms of scholarly inquiry may indeed be more credibly explained in terms of underlying social mechanisms than through any other modes of explanation.

To make this statement, however, is not necessarily to commit oneself to the thesis that any other form of explanation of academic culture must be, in principle, unacceptable. Nor is it necessarily to consider that every aspect of intellectual life—indeed, more generally, every aspect of social behavior—is ultimately reducible to sociological considerations. Any such extreme form of intellectual imperialism seems open to question, especially when, as is often true, it goes hand in hand with an uncompromisingly relativist world view. To illustrate the point, Edmund Leach, in an interesting paper entitled "Culture and Social Cohesion,"[27] argues that "science and the products of science . . . exist only because they are given names and uses by the members of society"; that "we become slaves to science because we begin to think of science as a reality existing outside ourselves"; and furthermore that "cultural behaviour derives its meaning from the social matrix; it has no autonomy." On the contrary, some aspects of disciplinary cultures do have autonomy, and in some respects we have to see them as "existing outside ourselves" if we are to make any sense of them, or of their impact upon us.

Such an approach is also illustrated by a recent study of the process of discovery in science.[28] By carefully attending to the social context in which certain claims are recognized and labeled as discoveries, the author, Augustine Brannigan, argues that "discovery is an attribution of a social status conferred according to certain criteria of intelligibility which operate collectively as a method of interpretation used by members of society to organize the world of scientific achievements"; and again that "discoveries *per se*, and all the associated characteristics which they have for members of society, are socially constructed by the endogenous operation of the interpretative practices of members of the culture." But if questions of truth and falsity owe nothing to phenomena outside the socially constructed interpretations of members of the culture, it would seem no more than a matter of arbitrary consensus that Newton's laws of motion were held to be valid, or that the periodic table of elements happened to be adopted. Again, any apparent sense of progress, any claim that our understanding of the natural world has advanced over time, must presumably be attributed to no more than an intersubjective strengthening of confidence in our criteria of intelligibility. To go along with such a view, to imply that what is scientifically acceptable is somehow independent of empirical evidence, except insofar as that evidence is itself a cultural artifact, is surely to make scientific inquiry less, rather than more, comprehensible.[29]

In saying what is amiss in the argument, a useful prior question may be to ask why discovery is important in some fields of inquiry and unimportant, or perhaps important in a different way, in others. For instance, in funda-

---

[27]Leach, "Culture and Social Cohesion," pp. 30, 37.

[28]Brannigan, *Social Basis of Scientific Discoveries*, p. 167.

[29]Perhaps this judgment is not entirely fair to Brannigan, in that at one point (p. 79) he distinguishes between what he calls "the methodological relativism of the sociology of knowledge, and the ontological relativism typically attributed to it by its critics." His account of discovery "merely puts its social features into vivid relief for social analysis." But he seems altogether to forget this disclaimer as he proceeds with his argument.

mental-particle physics, solid-state physics, and molecular biology, discovery is a central notion. It is less obviously so in taxonomic studies of plant and animal life, whereas in mechanical engineering the concept is largely replaced by that of invention. Moving further afield, the term seems out of place in academic law; and in history, the discovery of new primary material, though it may be important when it occurs, is by no means crucial to the historian's task. These differences do not, I suggest, lie merely in the differing social norms that mark off the members of one academic culture from another; they derive in part at least from the epistemological characteristics of the types of enterprise on which the academics in question are engaged.

Later, in focusing on the evidence from my current research which relates directly to the intrinsic properties of different modes of inquiry, as opposed to those extrinsic features that may reasonably be attributed to the action of social forces, or those mixed characteristics which seem to derive partly from each, I return to this hypothesis. But having contested the excessive claims made by some of those adopting a sociological approach to the analysis of disciplinary cultures, let me begin by acknowledging the extent to which their contribution seems fruitful and illuminating.

Some Environmental Aspects of Academic Cultures

Some general ways in which an academic discipline may be said to reflect its environment are obvious. One is at the level of conformity with broad national stereotypes. For example, biological research was portrayed by one respondent as "a bit plodding" in Germany, and French biologists were seen by another as "autocratic, and convinced of their intellectual superiority." Other contrasts are a consequence of economic resources: thus, physics and engineering are inevitably different in Bangladesh from what they are in Britain, because the costs of laboratory equipment serve to rule out whole areas of investigation. Again, differences of content and emphasis may spring, in such disciplines as history and law, directly from considerations of national relevance.

At a somewhat more specific level, the intellectual traditions of a particular society clearly have some impact on the attitudes and values within its higher education system. The German concept of *Wissenschaft*, to take one notable example, has given legitimacy to a very different relationship from that celebrated by C. P. Snow, between the natural sciences on the one hand and such subject areas as history, linguistics, and sociology on the other. So, too, the importance attached in the German university world to the symbolic notion of kinship between professor and protégé has had a noticeable effect on the demography of academic disciplines. The French sponsorship, in the Napoleonic tradition, of high technology as an elite pursuit through the agency of the *grandes écoles* has had its predictable consequences in the downgrading of university instructions, a set of problems compounded by according academic staff the status of civil servants.

Some of the clearest and most specific variations among national academic cultures are exemplified in the contrasting structures of British and American higher education. This is not to say that all disciplines are very different in the two systems; in most respects, they seem remarkably similar. But differences in both the granting of tenure and in the expectations for outside funding in the two countries were cited by respondents, in various disciplines, as a basis for significant discrepancies in value and practice. Controversy and competition tend to be sharper in the United States, even within the gentlemanly traditions of history, and certainly in physics and mechanical engineering, than they are in the United Kingdom. People are generally more on their toes: they do not have "long, leisurely lunch hours." The broader pattern of undergraduate degrees in American universities may also yield useful dividends. American historians are admitted by some of their British counterparts to be methodologically more versatile, because of their exposure to other disciplinary approaches. In a similar way, differences in the pattern of legal education give rise to a significant contrast in the profile of academic law in the two countries. Because American law schools are entirely postgraduate institutions, they are able to encompass a wider and intellectually more sophisticated range of issues than do their opposite numbers in Britain, where it is uncommon to go beyond a narrow, "black-letter" approach to legal scholarship. (Law graduates in the United States, incidentally, enjoy a far wider range of vocational choice in commerce, industry, and public service, than their transatlantic counterparts; whether this is a cause, an effect, or merely a concomitant of the distinction already remarked remains to be established.)

One structural feature, fundamental to all advanced higher education, accounts for a potential limitation and also for a potential benefit in the pursuit of academic goals. With the exception of schools of advanced study and research centers, the constituent elements in universities are expected to provide undergraduate alongside postgraduate teaching, as well as to engage in scholarly pursuits. They must therefore recruit staff across a broad enough spectrum of specialties to maintain an acceptably wide-ranging undergraduate program. Unless a department in a given discipline is very large, consisting of, say, thirty or forty faculty members, it is unlikely that more than two or three people at most will share sufficiently similar academic interests to make collaborative teamwork a realistic possibility. In those fields where teamwork is important, collaboration may have to take place across institutional boundaries, with possible losses in both effectiveness and efficiency. But the sacrifice of research ideals to teaching demands is not entirely negative. As many respondents commented, the need to teach elementary courses outside one's specialty may help to counteract stagnation and promote research mobility by opening up new areas of intellectual interest. At the very least, it encourages one to read more widely than one might otherwise do, and to keep abreast of general developments in the discipline.

Group self-images and the impressions of how outsiders view the group are not altogether negligible elements in the delineation of a culture. As noted earlier, physicists tend to see themselves as arrogant and elitist. It would appear that practitioners of other disciplines see physicists differently: as clever but incomprehensible and alien, technocratic and narrowminded, introverted, paranoic, and defensive. Such a confluence of judgments could hardly do more than reinforce them in their isolation. In a similar way sociologists are prone to a collective sense of persecution and a suspicion that they are intellectually undervalued; this view is not exactly undermined by the contention, from fellow academics, that they are woolly thinkers, prone to overgeneralize, jargon-laden, and inarticulate.

Such examples, though apparently disparate, have one feature in common. Each illustrates how the way in which a particular discipline (or group of disciplines) is characterized may be affected by considerations that are irrelevant to the epistemological makeup of that discipline. Disciplinary cultures may be shaped by environmental forces, whether these be in terms of their national or institutional contexts, their organizational settings, or their mutually reinforcing stereotypes. There remains, I suspect, a large and fruitful area of investigation here; but rather than attempt to pursue it further I want now to turn to a group of phenomena that seem to be grounded in neither purely extrinsic nor purely intrinsic origins, but in a mixture of the two.

Hybrid Influences on Disciplinary Ways of Life

Some fields of intellectual inquiry appear more open than others to the influence of ideology and to discussions about values. To equate this difference to the difference between disciplines concerned with things and disciplines concerned with people is clearly to oversimplify. In a sense, engineering is concerned with both, but engineers as a group tend to portray their work as value-free and apolitical. Nonetheless, few physicists could identify any aspect of their practice as subject to external doctrine, except in the very general sense that someone's philosophy of life might affect his views about the discipline and so might influence his professional judgment; hypotheses are one thing, but demonstration is quite another. And even though Hilary and Steven Rose[30] argue convincingly against the supposed neutrality of science, it is perhaps significant that they choose neurobiology as their field and show its rival approaches to reflect particular views about human beings.

---

[30]Rose and Rose, "Do Not Adjust Your Mind."

History, par excellence, is a discipline in which each practitioner's value position is covertly or overtly manifested in his work, so much so that it is extremely unusual for anyone far left of center to choose to study military history or for anyone far right of center to specialize as a labor historian. Historians, in common with sociologists, would seldom contemplate using "biased" as a term of criticism, because "it is taken for granted that every historian is biased in one way or another." The position in law is less straightforward, in that any overt expression of personal commitment is frowned upon. There is (as a respondent remarked) "a craft tradition of constructing arguments from different sets of values," in a profession in which a well-formulated legal argument is considered independent of the side of the case it takes.

Those areas that are themselves value-laden appear hospitable, not surprisingly, to imported values and ideologies; they allow their practitioners room for self-expression. But areas that seemingly remain value-neutral, while leaving their practitioners, as one respondent claimed, "not educated towards feelings," may put a higher premium on intellectual precision to compensate for this lack. The picture is complicated here, as elsewhere, by the fact that a particular discipline may have both patterns coexisting within it (botany alongside human physiology, paleography alongside the history of modern Europe).

The ideological content of a discipline is one thing, but its political context is quite another. Certainly, many physicists, while maintaining that their profession is devoid of value considerations, are ready to take an active stance on issues in which science impinges on society. Some respondents attributed this readiness to "a sense of tribal guilt, arising from the atomic bomb and other misapplications of science." Other explanations included the contention that physicists are able to transfer their skills at problem solving and are confident of getting the right answers, and the more cynical suggestion that the social responsibility in science movement "offers a high status slot for those who are played out—it lets them indulge their social consciences and excuses them from doing real science." Engineers are as heavily implicated as physicists in the current controversy about nuclear power. Insofar as they take a more cautious, less politically committed stance, that is in keeping with their pragmatic traditions, their natural line of argument being that if it works, it must be good. Interestingly, biologists in Britain tend to steer clear of the politics of protest, not only because ecological and other pressure groups are too time consuming and because they tend to take a simplistic view of difficult issues, but also because such activity "adds nothing to your professional prestige." On the other side of the Atlantic, respondents commented on a growing interest in matters of social moment, but even in the United States "there are still plenty of biologists who don't give a damn." Historians also have a strong tendency, despite the value-laden nature of their enterprise, to avoid relating their scholarly concerns to contemporary affairs, on the ground that generalization from one context to another is highly suspect. Sociologists, in contrast, have few inhibitions in connecting their academic values with their attitudes toward wider political issues. Because of the differences already noted, academic lawyers in the United States are likely to take a more cosmopolitan attitude toward public affairs than are academic lawyers in Britain. The pattern of academics' wider political involvement is thus a complex one, stemming in part from characteristics inherent in their discipline, but also in comparably large part from extraneous considerations.

A further set of influences derives from what might be called the topology of academic subjects: the degree to which their external frontiers are permeable and the extent to which they overlap with those of other disciplines; and the nature of their internal boundaries, and the discontinuities, if any, to which these demarcations give rise. History provides a striking example of a discipline that is open to outside ideas and techniques and readily able to assimilate them. In recent years it has incorporated ideas from political theory, sociology, and anthropology, as exemplified in the work of the French *Annales* school. At the same time it has managed to maintain a strong sense of internal coherence. (This is not necessarily the result of a widely shared intellectual paradigm; the evidence tends rather to suggest that it is the consequence of a vague and open-ended definition that allows the subject to be all things to all men.) Patterns of emigration and immigration offer another useful indicator: biology, for example, has in the postwar generation been hospitable to émigrés from the physical sciences; physics, on the other hand, seems to have been a net exporter not only to such other pure sciences as chemistry and biology, but also to engineering.

The unity of a discipline is important not merely in intellectual terms, but in terms of institutional credibility and status. It is perhaps for this reason that physicists protest their sense of oneness, their overriding feeling of kinship, their shared intellectual style and mutuality of interests, despite the fact that there is little intercommunication among different specialties, and the scholarly community is becoming increasingly fragmented as knowledge advances. To invoke a different, but now notorious, example, the internecine battle within the Cambridge English faculty between the structuralists and the traditionalists has done little to enhance either the public image or the domestic standing of English literature as an academic pursuit.

Internal divisions do not necessarily imply schisms or sources of dissent. Nonetheless, tightly knit intellectual groups clustered around a particular subspecialty often assume the characteristics of a clique. If their field of inquiry becomes fashionable, they may easily succumb to the temptation of "freezing out" potential interlopers, not only in terms of refusing to issue invitations to conferences but also through a reluctance to publish the papers they submit to the relevant specialist journal. The accepted way around this blockade is to approach a leading member of the clique for advice on a suitable research topic and thus help to secure acceptance of a research paper. The initiation rite is then completed by invited participation in one of the group's conferences.

Another significant consideration, in addition to questions of ideological content and political context, and alongside internal and external boundary conditions, is the degree to which knowledge in a given discipline is accessible outside the specialized community for which it is the prime concern. The existence of an amateur tradition—for example, in astronomy, descriptive biology, and history—marks an important dividing line in this respect between one group of disciplines and another. Where amateurism is strong, the discipline in question (and this is certainly true of the examples given) places a premium on lucid prose and clear communication. Where amateurism is weak or nonexistent there is sometimes a tendency (as in architecture or mathematics) to attribute competence to the possession of some special, presumably innate, talent. Forms of inquiry which exclude amateurism often do so because of the complex techniques and apparatus they demand (the use of the electron microscope, for example, marks off many of the areas of the biological sciences which are not accessible to the lay public). The existence of a particular set of concepts and an accompanying battery of technical terms operates as another type of barrier between amateur and professional, a form of mystification which hedges around much of the potentially accessible territory of the sociologist. Once an intellectual domain is annexed in this way, it imposes the need for new entrants to acquire the proper credentials before they are given license to trespass on it and to adopt the language and the way of life of its rightful inhabitants.

Obviously, the less publicly accessible a field of inquiry becomes in terms of its conceptual structure, its methodological techniques, and its accompanying instrumentation, the larger the amounts of time and effort an individual will need to invest in qualifying as a specialist in that field. The larger the investment, the stronger the need fully to capitalize on it, and hence, the more powerful the reluctance to forgo the possible dividends by reinvesting in a new intellectual enterprise.

One familiar outcome is a high level of career stability among those who might be classified as heavy investors. For example, biologists who have painstakingly acquired the techniques of electron microscopy tend, understandably enough, to seek research problems amenable to that approach. Medical sociologists who have had to become conversant with the specialized language, concepts, and practices of the world of medicine are often predictably hesitant to move into a completely different domain of sociological inquiry. The consequent reduction in intellectual mobility is reinforced by the reluctance of many mid-career researchers to abandon their existing tools in favor of new ones, such as computing skills, which are not immediately easy to master, even though this avoidance may remove them from the mainstream of intellectual development in their discipline. Indeed, the failure to acknowledge that one's approach has become dated, coupled with the psychological reluctance as a fairly senior member of one's profession to resume student status and start to learn something new from scratch, was advanced by a number of respondents as an explanation for the phenomenon of "burnout," the gradual extinction in middle life of youthful research promise. As in other contexts, it is the adaptable who survive.

Conservatism and the closed nature of ideas are also manifested in some disciplines by the initial reactions to a new theory that challenges established assumptions; by and large, people have an investment in the status quo, in the ways of thought with which they feel comfortable. As one physicist remarked, "you have to be open to the unexpected; but all the same, people don't like their existing ideas unsettled"; and as another commented, "recognition of a new finding can sometimes be delayed, because it takes time to realize the importance of new ideas." But this is perhaps no more than a particular instance of a very general property of cultural life. Edmund Leach observes that

the process of sect formation is dynamic; sect and countersect proliferate through dialectical disputes over points of dogma, but there is also a deep-rooted conservatism with which each particular sectarian group seeks to preserve the special tenets of its doctrine in unsullied purity from generation to generation. All culture has this dual characteristic: culture develops through the dialectical reinterpretation of symbol categories, yet at the same time the established culture of any group operates as an active force which seeks to impose on all new recruits the life-ways of existing members.[31]

THE NATURE OF KNOWLEDGE AND ITS IMPACT ON ACADEMIC CULTURES

Some examples have been offered to show how disciplinary cultures may be affected by extrinsic considerations and also by factors that are neither purely extrinsic nor purely intrinsic. I want now to argue that certain important aspects of academic culture cannot be explained in terms of social or environmental factors. Instead, their explanation seems to stem from a direct relationship between the epistemological characteristics of a particular type of inquiry and the mode of intellectual life associated with that inquiry.

To prepare the way for the argument it may be useful to make two points. First, in coming down to what must necessarily be a more detailed and specific level, I found myself forced to abandon the academic discipline as

---

[31]Leach, "Culture and Social Cohesion," p. 33.

the unit of analysis. When one begins to look closely into the epistemological structures of disciplines, it is apparent that most of them embrace a wide range of subspecialties, some with one set of features and others with different ones. That is to say, there is no single method of inquiry, no single verification procedure, no single set of values or purposes, which characterizes any one discipline. It is, in the end, more meaningful to talk about the identifiable and coherent properties of particular areas of inquiry within one discipline or another. Once this change of emphasis is adopted, it becomes possible to see patterns of similarity and difference among subspecialties that cut right across disciplinary boundaries. The implication is, of course, that while history, or physics, or law may offer a perfectly adequate basis for cultural analysis at one level of generality, there is also a point at which it ceases to serve as a viable framework for such an analysis, and the boundaries have to be drawn along different lines.

The second point of clarification concerns my own philosophical position. The account I offer here of knowledge and its properties is not dependent on an objectivist world view. I do not wish to suggest that truth is somehow "out there." But if, as Wittgenstein remarks, "the limits of my language mean the limits of my world,"[32] a change in these limits may stem, I would argue, either from a development in language ("form of life")[33] or from a development in understanding of the world, or from the interaction of the two. Nor would I want to contend that the characteristics of knowledge are immutable; it must be allowed that people look at the same phenomenon in different ways at different times and, more generally, that the nature of a field of inquiry may change as our apprehension of it increases. Once such a field becomes invested with a certain character, however, once it is defined, for example, as dealing in generalities rather than particularities, a whole set of properties inherent in that definition come into play. Such properties may profoundly affect the way of life of those engaged in the exploration of the field. The cultural consequences in these instances have to be seen as directly derived from epistemological considerations.

Two aspects of knowledge serve my present purposes. First I explore the consequences, for academic culture, of what might be called the focus of knowledge, and then I go on to consider the structure of knowledge. In each instance I draw on a number of examples from the current research reported above.

The Focus of Knowledge

There is an important set of contrasts between activities that seek to establish general propositions and those that have to do with particularities,

---

[32]Wittgenstein, *Tractatus Logico-Philosophicus*, p. 146, par. 5.6.
[33]Wittgenstein, *Philosophical Investigations*, esp. Part I, p. 88e, par. 241.

although it would be excesssive to claim that the distinction runs across the whole domain of intellectual inquiry. Thus a cosmologist, even though concerned with a single event—the origin of the universe—seeks to explain it in terms consistent with the established general laws of nature; a theologian, when dealing with the same event, offers an account that rests on a cause defined to be unique. A different but closely related opposition is between those who seek simplicity and those who embrace complexity. To illustrate the point, among the mainstream physicists I interviewed, most were ready to assent to the proposition that everything is basically simple; the problem is to show how simple it is. Most historians, on the other hand, shared the world view that things are always more complex than they seem. The intellectual worlds inhabited by some academics, to point up yet another polarity, are characterized by their uniformity; one's task is to find recurrent patterns and to explain their interconnection in terms of demonstrable laws. For others, the world of intellectual exploration is characterized by its diversity; its phenomena are not in their nature subject to direct and repetitive causal connections of any such kind.[34]

With these differences in the properties attributed to knowledge are differences in techniques of inquiry and methods of analyzing and handling data. Processes that are replicable lend themselves to a different kind of investigation from those that are unique. (They also, as we shall see shortly, lead to a different kind of relationship between their investigators.) It is possible to think of deliberately generating evidence when sufficiently identical situations can be made to recur. The domain of inquiry becomes subject to manipulation, in a way it cannot easily be when what is in view is a set of circumstances unlikely to be, or incapable of being, repeated. The individual instance is not amenable to experiment; the evidence must be carefully assembled, but it cannot be created de novo. To pursue the point, it is first and foremost those domains of research which concern repetitive, manipulable phenomena (e.g., low-temperature physics) which lend themselves neatly to quantification. Statistical or mathematical regularities are not even in question when a historically unique event (such as the siege of Lucknow in the Indian Mutiny) is the focus of attention. In the latter instance, qualitative judgment substitutes for quantitative demonstration. Whereas the first type of pursuit may sensibly seek laws, equations, or models, the second has to build up an explanatory argument by analogy from related cases.

Although this set of contrasts does not embrace all types of intellectual activity, it is clearly discernible as a dividing line within the sciences as well as within the humanities, rather than as one that distinguishes between

---

[34]This distinction is closely analogous to but not, I think, identical with the contrast between "restricted" and "unrestricted" sciences marked by Pantin, *Relations between the Sciences*, and subsequently developed (in a direction highly relevant to the present argument) by Whitley, ed., *Sociology of Scientific Work*.

them. Thus there are elements in historical data which lend themselves to analysis in economic terms, constituting the quantitative end of the subject labeled economic history. But there are also elements in biological research, especially within such areas as taxonomy and ecology, where the distrust of overgeneralization is as sharply marked as that of the middle-of-the-road historian. Indeed, many botanists and zoologists, while firmly identifying themselves as scientists, regard variation within a particular species as more significant than uniformity; along with the historians, they see themselves as being in the trade of unraveling complexities rather than identifying commonalities. As one respondent neatly put it, "some biological scientists look for a simple idea to explain a complex system; others try instead to find out what makes the system complex."

It must be acknowledged that the distinctions drawn thus far have tended toward oversimplification in a concern to bring out salient epistemological features and to point up cultural connections. For example, the distinction between the general and the particular is not absolute. Electromagnetic phenomena and gravitation are general and pervasive features of the physical world; the Seven Years' War is a unique and unrepeatable series of events. But what is one to say of the zoologist encountered in my series of interviews who was working on the optical system of the tadpole? Clearly, there are plenty of tadpoles, and there seems likely to be a general explanation of how their eyes work. Intuitively, however, one is inclined to place this theme toward the end of the spectrum dealing with particularities, since the researcher in question had little expectation that what he discovered would be readily applicable to the optical systems of other species.

Given that the analysis needs to be taken further, it may be said with some confidence that those who deal in generalization and simplification have a different professional relationship one with another from those who pursue the particular and seek to unfold its complexities. The quest for universal explanations is public in the sense that its processes of investigation are not normally dependent on a single source of data (the evidence can be generated anew). The quest for particular understandings, on the other hand, is more private, for there is not to the same degree a common framework of assumptions. Even if two or more individuals happen to hit on the same theme and work from the same source of data, they are likely to be operating in a relatively closed context of knowledge and understanding. They will have few colleagues to talk to who appreciate, at first hand, the intricacies of their particular research.

The distinction may be usefully illustrated by a familiar contrast within the biological sciences between those interested in mechanisms and systems and those concerned with whole organisms. As one botanist put it, "you might work on the responses of plants to drought stress, without being particularly concerned at which plants occupy your attention; or concentrate on classifying buttercups in all their varieties across the world." In the former case it is generalities that matter; in the latter it is particularities. And it is noticeably the systems-based biologists who find value in comparing notes, keeping in touch, and attending conferences with like-minded colleagues. Their whole-organism-based counterparts tend to be more isolated and to have a smaller and more scattered group of professional contacts.

Accordingly, a generalizer's "invisible college"—his circle of scholarly acquaintances—may be quite large, of the order, sometimes, of a couple of hundred people working on the same or a closely related problem. A particularizer, on the other hand, may not have more than half a dozen colleagues in various parts of the world with whom he finds it useful from time to time to exchange ideas.[35] With this difference goes an important difference in the degree to which experience, understanding, and data are shared. Whenever a group of specialists in fluid mechanics are gathered together, its members confess to an automatic tendency to talk shop. In contrast, reliable informants claim that a comparable group of English historians of the Tudor period would resort only to academic gossip. Lacking the specialized knowledge of detail which could enable them adequately to discuss a colleague's research, they can share experience only at the general level of exchanging notes about sources, library collections, and the like. In the first case professional societies are strong; in the second, weak.

The differential ratio of people to problems—with more people tending to cluster around general, replicable research issues than around particular, unique themes of inquiry—brings other differences in its train. The larger the number of people who are trying at any given time to find the answer to a problem, the more intense the competition becomes, particularly as there is an expectation, in a field dealing with general propositions, that a unique solution can be found and that the winner is the individual who first finds and establishes it. What might be called the "double-helix syndrome" is particularly evident in areas involving a high degree of generalization. Biochemistry and fundamental-particle research are obvious examples. In contrast, when the norm is for less than a handful of individuals to be involved in some topic, and when in any event each will be likely to offer an individual interpretation of it, competitiveness manifests itself in a general concern with building up one's professional reputation rather than in a straightforward race for the finishing post. To underline the point, a number of the mechanical engineers interviewed in my study commented on the relative unimportance, for them, of priority as such: "It's usually wise to wait for your work to mature, to be sure you've got it right and

---

[35]Crane, in *Invisible Colleges*, which is again limited solely to the natural sciences, records this diversity in size without drawing any conclusions from it, or even apparently taking it to be significant in any way.

followed up the main implications before you send off the final typescript"; "It isn't usually a rat race to get your paper published before anyone else's"; "For my part, I think it's more important to be right than to be first."

The extent of possible plagiarism, and the incidence of other types of professional sharp practice, are again likely to be much greater among generalizers than among particularizers. Examples were cited by respondents in physics departments of the bright ideas of doctoral students being taken over by supervisors without acknowledgment, and of papers turned down for publication and then reappearing in a new guise under another name. No such phenomena were recorded by historians, and indeed it is difficult, given the nature of the enterprise, to imagine sharp practice taking this form, as against the single quoted case of a researcher who deliberately misplaced a whole set of material in an archive to do down a rival.

Generalizers are also more prone to get caught up in a careerist rat race, and to become so heavily involved in their work that they find it hard to unwind and spare much energy for other things in life. The time element becomes crucial, in a way it seldom is for those working steadily away on complex and relatively self-contained investigations of their own. This contrast is reflected, among other things, in the differential patterns of publication of research findings. The publication lag quoted by historians for journal articles ranged between a year and three years. In contrast, in some areas of physics the delay of the three months necessary to have one's discoveries announced in *Physical Review Letters* is considered excessive; and there is also recourse to the immediate circulation of preprints of papers. Much communication takes place "on the grapevine" in a variety of ways: conferences, laboratory visits, staff exchanges, summer schools and workshops, seminars and colloquiums; through group newsletters, personal correspondence, and long-distance phone calls. In short, the different foci of knowledge would seem to give rise on the one hand to a predominantly written, and on the other to a predominantly oral, culture.

The Structure of Knowledge

The distinctions I want now to emphasize can perhaps best be put across by the use of analogies. One might portray some sectors of knowledge as growing like a tree, with each new branch in its turn sending out fresh shoots, and other sectors as flowing like a river, fluid in texture and fickle in direction. Or one might talk of knowledge with a hard, crystalline structure, as against knowledge with a soft, cellular structure. These offer alternative ways of coming at the distinction between what might be called areas of contextual imperative and areas of contextual association. The former present closely patterned sequences of explanation, with each new finding fitting neatly into place as the whole picture is steadily pieced together. The latter offer loosely knit clusters of ideas, with no clearly articulated framework of development.

These epistemological differences are matched by cultural contrasts of a fairly obvious and familiar kind. Where the structure of knowledge is crystalline, it is usually possible to divide the domain into a series of discrete, easily manageable problems, and to distribute these in a rough-and-ready way among those working on the problem area in question. Thus it is that some subdisciplinary domains are characterized by research teams of varying sizes, while others—the areas of contextual association—are made up mainly of individual researchers. In history, for example, there is only a very limited number of specialties in which research teams appear to serve a useful function ("team" meaning something more than the distinguished researcher with his or her single research assistant engaged to do the routine chores). Historical demography is one such area. But for anything involving complex interpretation, "what is needed is a single intellect to turn over the material. . . . at the end of the road, only one person—or two at the most—can write an effective book." For the main part, "the historian is an individual, lonely scholar."

Contextually imperative fields are also typified by the fact that doctoral students are likely to be assigned a research topic by their supervisors (on the grounds that they are not in a position to know the context well enough to make their own choice) and that any papers they produce will normally carry their supervisor's name as coauthor (on the grounds that the supervisor must take credit for identifying the problem and overseeing its solution as a component in his own wider research program). Both these practices are commonplace in chemistry, for example, but are rarely found in sociology.

The time span of inquiry is often quite brief in fields governed by a contextual imperative, in that, as already noted, problems may conveniently be divided into short, relatively straightforward stages. In contrast, many problems in areas of contextual association, being large and less readily divisible, may occupy a solitary worker for years rather than months. The distinction here, as elsewhere, may cut across a single discipline. In such contextually imperative subdisciplines as solid-state physics, it is possible for an entrepreneurial researcher to move into a new area of inquiry, pick out one or two important but rapidly soluble problems and then move elsewhere to "skim the cream" (in physicists' slang) once again. But when it comes to studying the physics of thunderstorms, the area (like its subject matter) lacks clear internal divisions or sharply defined external boundaries, and there is no cream to skim. One of my informants had been grappling with this topic for nearly a decade.

It is an obvious corollary of this difference in scale of problem that publication rates are liable to differ substantially from hard, atomistic areas to soft, holistic ones. Biochemists, for instance, who may use a single technique to produce a series of results, might publish a couple of dozen short papers a year. In many other biological specialties, especially where findings depend on field observation during a particular season, the average annual output is one or two longer papers. Indeed, an analysis of publication rates (if it could somehow accommodate disciplines such as history, where writing books tends to take precedence over journal publication) could itself provide a useful guide to areas within a discipline which are cumulative and those that are not.

The purposes of citation differ too. In biochemistry, on the one hand, references are given mainly to set the context for the current findings, to demonstrate that the author has an up-to-date knowledge of the field, and to underline the extent to which the new material is a cumulative addition to what has gone before. In statute law, on the other hand, reference to secondary sources (as opposed to the primary data, legislative documents) commonly has the function of adducing confirmatory opinion, dismissing contrary opinion, and emphasizing the extent to which the new material offers a reappraisal of what has previously been asserted.

It is possible, when knowledge has a sequential development, to speak of "productive research" in the sense of a piece of work which opens up a novel line of investigation and so offers gainful employment to a new generation of researchers. It is also, as implied above, relatively easy to predict which problems will be most worth investigating and which approach will be most worth adopting at any given time. Such bounty is seldom afforded where the division of knowledge is based on a loose association of themes. There is little likelihood of opening up a tract of territory for collective exploration; there is also as much luck as judgment involved in achieving an important breakthrough. Accordingly, a relatively unknown researcher may have a better chance of making his or her name in such a loosely knit area: "It's anybody's guess who will be next to hit the jackpot."

Perhaps related to this conjecture is that only in areas of contextual imperative does any very clear hierarchy of prestige emerge in particular subdisciplines. In sociology, for example, no respondent felt able to relate the academic standing of his or her own specialty to that of other parts of the discipline; there seemed to be no established pecking order to which to refer. But many physicists put the main branches of the subject in rank order with little hesitation (and a good deal of common agreement); not surprisingly, it was the most fundamental and the purest aspects of the subject which ranked highest.

Cumulative areas also give rise to pacesetters and opinion leaders in a way that associative areas do not. For such people, gifts of personality are at least as important as intellectual prowess. It was remarked of one leading particle physicist, "He's not that smart, but he's very tough and good at promoting himself." Once a leadership position is established it tends to be reinforced in a variety of ways: refereeing papers, being invited to talk at conferences, being co-opted onto research committees, being elected to elite groups, and the like. Such opportunities of high visibility and influence over fellow professionals are relatively rare for those who choose to work in the less tightly structured specialties within any given discipline.

Intellectual fashion, too, takes a different form in the two areas. Cumulative knowledge may build up to a point of reaching a dead end, where the area of inquiry in question seems to lack any real connection with other current developments, and little more remains to be said or done. But this characteristic of unfashionable areas of inquiry clearly does not hold for associative knowledge, where new approaches to, and interpretations of, familiar problems are a means of reinvigorating any field and preventing it from becoming arid after it has been harvested. Fashion in this instance tends to reflect a collective judgment that a particular theme is unexciting, or has been done to death, a judgment that may often be based on extrinsic considerations rather than on those deriving from the intrinsic characteristics of knowledge.

Epistemological Characteristics: Some Reflections

The two sets of considerations which have been explored, relating respectively to the structure and to the form of knowledge, are meant to be no more than illustrative of the connections between epistemological properties and academic subcultures. Much work still remains to be done in clarifying these issues. The small-scale study from which this analysis stems needs to be extended, not only by enlarging and diversifying the sample of academics from each of the six disciplines so far investigated, but also by undertaking a more comprehensive search of the relevant source material and possibly by widening the range of disciplines under review. But other, complementary studies would also be of value in enlarging a neglected but potentially rich field of inquiry. Three examples of the type of question which demands further research suggest themselves.

First, the categories of form and structure may need to be augmented by others, or even superseded altogether as more subtle analysis is brought to bear on more extensive data. Even if not, the relationship between the two categories needs further investigation. My hunch is that they are not entirely congruent, even though much quantitative knowledge is also cumulative and much qualitative knowledge noncumulative (some apparent exceptions are in areas of engineering, quantitative/noncumulative, and case law, qualitative/cumulative).

Second, academic migration patterns between disciplines may well be illuminated in terms of continuities or discontinuities in epistemological characteristics. Even in my own small sample of 120 or so, there were some ten respondents who had changed disciplines during their academic careers, not enough to allow generalization, but enough to inspire some hypothesizing. For example, a fairly common pattern seems to be a move from quantitative/cumulative to nonquantitative/noncumulative areas. Movement takes place less often in the opposite direction, or even from like to like. (The individual's status seems also to be a factor, with most moves being made by the less successful or the highly successful, rather than those in the middle ranks of their original specialty.)

Again, migration within a discipline from one area to another—or indeed the initial choice of a particular area—gives rise to a further set of intriguing questions. Given that most disciplines seem to span the range from generality to particularity and from hard knowledge to soft, most academics ought, in principle, to be able to find a niche that fits their particular personal makeups. The evidence of my study on this point, though indirect, is generally confirmatory. But is it indeed true (as Martin Trow has suggested to me in discussion) that noncognitive characteristics crystallize around cognitive differences and that those who recoil from feeling are attracted by hard knowledge areas, while those with gentler temperaments gravitate to soft areas? And where does this leave the nature/nurture debate?

Having devoted so much space to questioning the notion of disciplines as a unit of analysis, it is perhaps only proper for me to wind up this part of the argument by setting my own findings in perspective. Nearly every country has a variety of geographical features—highlands, plains, areas of scattered population, and densely populated conurbations—with each feature affecting the ways of life of those whose environment it is. So, analogously, each discipline has a variety of epistemological features in common with other disciplines (though not in exactly the same configuration) which condition the intellectual cultures of those who work in any given context. But such commonalities, like those between hill folk, plain folk, rural folk, or city folk in different countries, do not override, but merely supplement, the cultural distinctions among different primary groups. Nations remain nations, and disciplines survive as disciplines because their bonds are powerful enough to encompass considerable internal diversity. A proper cultural analysis should allow for both the unity and the variation.

THE SCOPE AND LIMITS OF A CULTURAL APPROACH

The exploration of disciplinary cultures and their associated epistemological subcultures is, of course, only one aspect of a much wider issue. It is clear from the existing literature that other profitable and relatively underresearched areas exist in the study of the distinctive way of life of teachers and learners, the ethnography of individual institutions, and the cultural characteristics of particular sectors in the system, or even of the system as a whole, in one or more national settings.

It seems likely that major gains in our understanding of higher education as a whole would accrue from a wider analysis than has so far been attempted of the similarities and differences between forms of academic life in advanced and developing nations. The historical dimension, in its turn, may prove to be as fruitful as the geographical one, highlighting crucial stages in the development of the various cultural categories discussed earlier. The cultures of nonelite institutions are an almost totally neglected area, though a potentially important one, since they promise a very different perspective on the findings derived from elite cultures. So, too, do the cultures of other sectors, and especially those of secondary and further education.

The relationship between higher education and the outside world is a significant topic. Cultural studies could well help to clarify the role that academics play when co-opted into national policy-making agencies (see chap. 2) as well as the way in which external pressures are mediated by internal value systems.

The advantages of such research seem to be various. First, unless one is prepared altogether to dismiss the pursuit of knowledge for its own sake, ethnographically or anthropologically based studies are an effective means of enhancing our understanding of the different values and practices that hold sway in different parts of the complex structure of the academic world, and also of the phenomena of power and prestige in intellectual life. Further, this understanding may help to bridge the evident cultural divisions within academia. To quote Clifford Geertz again,

The problem of the integration of cultural life becomes one of making it possible for people inhabiting different sorts of worlds to have a genuine, and reciprocal, impact upon one another. . . . the first step is surely to accept the depth of the differences, the second to understand just what they are, and the third to construct some sort of vocabulary in which they can be publicly formulated.[36]

Finally, research along these lines may help to create, among politicians and administrators, a more sophisticated awareness of the different varieties of academic enterprise and their associated functions of teaching and research.

To take this last point further, major advances in the study of higher education policy might accrue from a closer marriage of organizational analysis (as outlined by Burton R. Clark in chap. 4) with cultural studies of the type examined here. The articulation between structures and cultures seems likely to prove a key issue in the understanding not only of how any given system functions but also of how far a particular policy initiative is destined to be effectively implemented within that system.

The limitations of the approach are perhaps more obvious than the advantages. The provenance of inquiries into academic cultures is by definition sectional and localized; their impact on the system as a whole is muted at best. They lack the obvious relevance, the broad and authoritative sweep, of organizational, political, or policy-centered research. Dealing as they do with the mundane and everyday—the plain tales of average aca-

---

[36]Geertz, "Toward an Ethnography of the Disciplines."

demics—they are low on glamour and high in hard grind. It is scarcely plausible to sit at one's desk and produce a cultural study by a priori reasoning, since such a study calls for fieldwork of a demanding and time-consuming variety. So research along such lines may seem unattractive to many students of higher education, as well as unpromising in its contribution to career advancement.

Nonetheless, the prospects for development seem more optimistic than this forecast suggests. Whereas the 1940s and 1950s saw the heyday of psychology among the social sciences, and the sixties and seventies gave pride of place to sociology, there are signs that the wheel of fashion has begun to favor anthropology as the new promise in our shared concern to make better sense of human behavior. If this diagnosis is correct, the funding agencies, being sensitive barometers of the intellectual climate, will doubtless begin to promote further research into the cultural aspects of higher education. But even if the diagnosis is mistaken, cultural studies will by no means stand alone in offering the kind of intellectual rewards for which only dedicated enthusiasts need have reason to apply.

BIBLIOGRAPHY

Arnold, Matthew. *Culture and Anarchy*. London: Smith, Elder, 1894.

Bailey, Frederick G. *Morality and Expediency*. Oxford: Blackwell, 1977.

Ball, Stephen J. "Competition and Conflict in the Teaching of English," *Journal of Curriculum Studies* 14, no. 1 (1982):1–28.

Becher, Tony. "Towards a Definition of Disciplinary Cultures." *Studies in Higher Education* 6 (September 1981):109–122.

Becker, Howard S., Blanche Geer, and Everett C. Hughes. *Making the Grade: The Academic Side of College Life*. New York: John Wiley, 1968.

Becker, Howard S., Blanche Geer, Everett C. Hughes, and Anselm Strauss. *Boys in White: Student Culture in Medical School*. Chicago: University of Chicago Press, 1961.

Bliss, Joan, and Jon Ogborn. *Students' Reactions to Undergraduate Science*. London: Heinemann Educational, 1977.

Blume, Stuart S., ed. *Perspectives in the Sociology of Science*. New York: John Wiley, 1977.

Bradbury, Malcolm. *The History Man*. London: Secker and Warburg, 1975.

Brannigan, Augustine. *The Social Basis of Scientific Discoveries*. Cambridge: Cambridge University Press, 1981.

Church, Clive H. "Disciplinary Dynamics." *Studies in Higher Education* 1 (October 1976):101–118.

Clark, Burton R. "Faculty Cultures." In *The Study of Campus Cultures*, ed. Terry F. Lunsford. Berkeley: Western Interstate Commission and Center for the Study of Higher Education, University of California, 1962.

———. *The Distinctive College: Antioch, Reed, Swarthmore*. Chicago: Aldine, 1970.

———. *The Higher Education System: Academic Organization in Cross-National Perspective*. Berkeley, Los Angeles, London: University of California Press, 1983.

Cohen, Michael D., and James G. March. *Leadership and Ambiguity: The American College President*. New York: McGraw-Hill, 1974.

Cornford, Francis M. *Microcosmographia Academica*. Cambridge: Bowes and Bowes, 1908.

Crane, Diana. *Invisible Colleges: Diffusion of Knowledge in Scientific Communities*. Chicago: University of Chicago Press, 1972.

Eurich, Nell P. *Systems of Higher Education in Twelve Countries: A Comparative View*. New York: Praeger, 1981.

Gaff, Jerry G., and Robert C. Wilson. "Faculty Cultures and Interdisciplinary Studies." *Journal of Higher Education* 42, no. 3 (1971):186–201.

Geertz, Clifford. "Towards an Ethnography of the Disciplines." Mimeo. 1976.

Goodson, Ivor. "Defending the Subject: the Case of Geography." In *The Sociology of Curriculum Practice*, ed. Martyn Hammersley and Andy Hargreaves. Brighton: Falmer Press, 1962.

Grant, Gerald, and David Riesman. *The Perpetual Dream*. Chicago: University of Chicago Press, 1978.

Hagstrom, Warren O. *The Scientific Community*. New York: Basic Books, 1965.

Halsey, A. H., and Martin A. Trow. *The British Academics*. London: Faber and Faber, 1971.

Hudson, Liam. *The Cult of the Fact*. London: Jonathan Cape, 1972.

Kuhn, Thomas S. *The Structure of Scientific Revolutions*. Chicago: University of Chicago Press, 1962. 2d ed. (with postscript). 1970.

Leach, Edmund R. "Culture and Social Cohesion." *Daedalus (Science and Culture)* 94 (Winter 1965):24–38.

Marris, Peter. *The Experience of Higher Education*. London: Routledge and Kegan Paul, 1964.

Merton, Robert K. *The Sociology of Science*. Chicago: University of Chicago Press, 1973.

Miller, Carolyn M., and Malcolm R. Parlett. *Up to the Mark*. London: Society for Research into Higher Education, 1974.

Mulkay, Michael J. *The Social Process of Innovation*. London: Macmillan, 1972.

———. "Sociology of the Scientific Research Community." In *Science, Technology and Society*, ed. Ina Spiegel-Rösing and Derek de Solla Price. London: Sage, 1977.

Pantin, Carl F. A. *On Relations between the Sciences*. Cambridge: Cambridge University Press, 1968.

Parlett, Malcolm R. "The Department as a Learning Milieu." *Studies in Higher Education* 2 (October 1977):173–181.

Parlett, Malcolm R., and Garry J. Dearden, eds., *Introduction to Illuminative Evaluation*. San Diego: Pacific Soundings Press, 1977.

Parsons, Talcott, and Gerald M. Platt. *The American University*. Cambridge: Harvard University Press, 1973.

Platt, Jennifer. *Realities in Social Research*. Brighton: Sussex University Press, 1976.

Rose, H., and S. Rose. "Do Not Adjust Your Mind, There Is a Fault in Reality." In *Social Processes of Scientific Development*, ed. R. Whitley. London: Routledge and Kegan Paul, 1974.

Rose, Jasper A., and John M. Ziman. *Camford Observed*. London: Gollancz, 1964.

Rothblatt, S. *Tradition and Change in English Liberal Education*. London: Faber and Faber, 1976.

Sanford, Nevitt, ed. *The American College*, New York: John Wiley, 1962.

Snow, Charles P. *The Two Cultures and the Scientific Revolution*. Cambridge: Cambridge University Press, 1959.

———. *The Two Cultures: And a Second Look*. Cambridge: Cambridge University Press, 1964.

Snyder, Benson R. *The Hidden Curriculum*. New York: Knopf, 1971.

Startup, Richard. *The University Teacher and His World*. Farnborough: Saxon House, 1979.

Truscot, Bruce [pseud.] *Redbrick University*. London: Faber and Faber, 1943.

Whitley, Richard D., ed. *Social Processes of Scientific Development*. London: Routledge and Kegan Paul, 1974.

———. "The Sociology of Scientific Work and the History of Scientific Developments." In *Perspectives in the Sociology of Science*, ed. Stuart S. Blume. New York: John Wiley, 1977.

Wittgenstein, Ludwig. *Tractatus Logico-Philosophicus*. London: Routledge and Kegan Paul, 1922.

———. *Philosophical Investigations*. Basil Blackwell, 1953.

7. THE FOCUS ON SCIENTIFIC ACTIVITY*

Simon
Schwartzman

The idea that scientific research and higher education are necessarily linked together is widespread. The relationship is seen as basic in the formation of educational policies in many countries. A classical version of this idea has been stated by Talcott Parsons, who believes that the modern scientist has a social place similar in many ways to the position of the humanistic scholar in the early universities. For Parsons, the scholar was "the precursor of the scientist and is of course today his colleague in the most highly educated sector of the population." Both embody a common tradition of scholarship and respect for impartial objectivity and evidence, a tradition that is characteristic of Western culture. "In the most modern era, this cultural tradition has above all become embodied in the university as its principal institutionalized frame."[1]

A more modern version of this linkage places the university fully within the technological revolution of our times. "Throughout the period of emerging industrialism in Europe and America," states A. H. Halsey,

the principal function of the universities has been that of status differentiation of elites with some assimilation of students from the lower strata. But the progressive secularization of higher learning since medieval times has increased the potential of the universities as sources of technological and therefore of social change until now they are beginning to occupy a place as part of the economic foundation of a new type of society. . . . Both as research organizations and training establishments, the institutions of higher education in this period have been drawn more closely to the economy either directly or through the state. . . . The exchange of ideas, people and contracts between university departments and research institutes and their counterparts in private industry and government agencies is such as to merge these organizations and to assimilate the life styles of their staff.[2]

This marriage, however, not at all well established, has a clouded past. "Far from being a natural match," observes Joseph Ben-David, "research and teaching can be organized within a single framework only under

---

*I am grateful to Roger Geiger, Morikazu Ushiogi, Edmundo Campos, and Burton R. Clark for their comments and criticism, some of which I was able to incorporate.
[1]Parsons, "The Institutionalization of Scientific Investigation," from *Social System*, 1951, in Barber and Hirsch, *Sociology of Science*, pp. 12, 13.
[2]Halsey, "Changing Functions of Universities," pp. 460–463.

specific circumstances."[3] Historically, this unification of science and the university found its best example in Germany, specifically in the University of Berlin in the nineteenth century; today, it is best represented by the leading universities in the United States.

The vitality of these systems of higher education made them models to be followed and imitated internationally; and the notion that the universities are the natural setting for research follows naturally. The reverse, however, is not nearly so clear. The volume that brings together the classic papers of Robert K. Merton on the sociology of science contains references to universities on only seven of its 600 pages.[4] A more recent book, *Science, Technology and Society*, does not fare much better: it has about twenty scattered references to universities within its 600 pages. None of these references make any mention of systems of higher education in a broader sense.[5]

If the marriage has so many problems, why insist on it? It would be very easy to show that the overlap between the systems of science production and those of higher education has not been significant in the past and to muster good reasons for keeping them apart in the future. There is, however, an obvious gap between this empirical reality and the strong convictions about the linkages between science and higher education; this fact is significant in itself and should be examined with care. Let us first examine the evidence, and then try to understand the tensions and difficulties that are involved.

SCIENCE AND HIGHER EDUCATION: PAST AND PRESENT

With reference to the past, let it be understood that we are not dealing here with two well-identified social realities, but rather with several highly changing aspects of social phenomena which often come together under the same names.[6] "Higher education" in contemporary systems, bringing together thousands of teachers and millions of students, is very different from the type of advanced learning which took place in the old and exclusive European universities of past centuries. Aside from the obvious differences in structure and size, the systems of higher education have traditionally performed (and still do) at least three quite different but not necessarily convergent functions. First, there was the traditional role of training for the

---

[3]Ben-David, *Centers of Learning*, p. 94.
[4]Merton, *Sociology of Science*.
[5]Spiegel-Rösing and Price, eds., *Science, Technology and Society*.
[6]This stability of names for changing realities is central to Harold Perkin's analysis of higher education as a historical system (see chap. 1, above). See also his overview of the development of modern universities from its medieval origins and the impact of the nineteenth-century German model in other countries.

scholarly professions, law, medicine, and theology. This function was later expanded to include the new technology-oriented engineering careers. Second, the function of general education, first serving as propaedeutics for the professions, gradually evolved as a cultural and intellectual function on its own. Third, the function of generating new knowledge is, in modern times, associated with the idea of "science."

"Science" has different meanings, and sociologists of science often give to it a narrow definition which makes it only one among several forms of advanced knowledge. In this specific sense, scientific knowledge is based on empirical observation, in contrast with classical knowledge based on hermeneutics and rational speculation; it tends to be systematized and geared toward explanation, in contrast with practical, applied knowledge; it is produced by a community of freethinking scholars, in opposition to all forms of authoritative systems of thought and belief.

Science as technological knowledge is very old, and all forms of higher education have always implied, if not the production, at least the systematization and transmission of highly developed knowledge.[7] Historians of science narrowly tend to link its emergence to the European Renaissance, as part of the general breakdown of medieval order and the assertion of individualism in its different cultural, intellectual, and economic forms. The institutional history of European science up to the beginning of the nineteenth century is a tale of its gradual conquest of a central position in the culture and international outlook of Western societies. Experimental science, as it is also called, evolved basically outside and in opposition to the traditional universities. Only in the nineteenth century did they establish the intimacy that today is often taken for granted.[8]

The starting point of this long process is probably best dramatized by Galileo Galilei's plight, but less because of his specific proposition that the earth revolves around the sun than because of the way the truth is to be established, be it through the authority of "classical" works endorsed by the Church or through empirical observations and rational persuasion.[9] Galileo's prosecution was one of the last attempts of the religious establishment of his time to keep the findings of empirical observation of the physical world subordinated to its dogmas and institutional authority. From that time on, and in line with the individualist ethics of emerging capitalism and

---

[7] About non-Western forms of scientific knowledge in a broader sense, see Needham, *The Grand Titration*.

[8] For this history see Ben-David, *Scientist's Role in Society*.

[9] Galileo's telescope "did not prove the validity of Copernicus' conceptual system. But it did provide an immensely effective weapon for the battle. It was not proof, but it was propaganda." After Galileo's observations "Copernicanism could not be dismissed as a mere mathematical device, useful but without physical support." This explains in part the strong opposition it aroused. (See Kuhn, *Copernican Revolution*; I am grateful to Sheldon Rothblatt for calling my attention to this point.)

Protestantism, empirical science has flourished, moving from its main cradle, Italy, to the much more fertile soils of France, England, and, later, Germany. In the nineteenth century, with Darwin's evolutionism, the biological sciences took their turn in establishing their autonomy while confronting the religious dogmas of the time.

This new and increasingly prestigious type of knowledge did not easily become a part of the university. The universities in Paris, Oxford, and Cambridge were older centers of classical learning and as such paid no more than secondary attention to the empirical sciences. In England, however, scientists of the new type met at the Royal Society, founded in 1660. Its aim, according to its founders, was eminently practical and technical: ". . . to improve the knowledge of natural things, and all useful Arts, Manufactures, Mechanick practices, Engynes, and Inventions by Experiments (not meddling with Divinity, Morals, Politicks, Rhetoric or Logick)."[10]

This definition of purposes did not correspond to the full truth, since many of the leading figures of the Royal Society (Robert Boyle, John Wilkins, and several other members of the "Philosophical College" that gave birth to the Royal Society) were strongly identified with Puritanism and parliamentarism. The practical purposes of the society tended to make room for a much more ambitious view of the new science, as the foundation of a new philosophy. If in its first years the practical influence of Francis Bacon was very strong; it "declined during the 1670's and. . . was supplanted by a 'Galileian' trend as manifest above all in the work of Newton who became a fellow of the Society in 1671."[11]

A similar practical aim preceded the establishment of the French Academy of Sciences in 1666. Contrary to its English counterpart, it was not a voluntary association, but a government-sponsored institution organized with the explicit aim of helping the expansion of French commerce and industry. Nevertheless, the scientific success of the French Academy seems to have been inversely proportional to its devotion to practical tasks.

In both England and France the establishment of scientific societies played a dual role. On the one hand, practical and useful purposes were served which benefited only the economic and political elites of that time. On the other, groups of distinguished scientists launched a protracted assault on the traditional culture and philosophy, whose strongholds were the traditional universities. This new science was, in other words, the foundation of a new world vision—some authors have called it a "scientistic ideology"—linked to the emergence of new social groups who benefited from the social, political, and economic changes brought about by the industrial revolution they engendered. The climax of this process was the publication of Isaac Newton's *Philosophiae Naturalis Principia Matematica*,

[10]Quoted by Mason, *History of the Sciences*, p. 259.
[11]Ibid., p. 260.

the mathematical foundation of natural philosophy. The title was a clear indication of the immensity of Newton's undertaking, which went far beyond a simple and utilitarian determination of empirical phenomena. What Newton achieved was a new understanding of the universe, where reason combined gracefully with empirical observation. Modern science, with the Newtonian synthesis, finally reached its dominant position in relation to the old scholastic culture, by means of its own language and style. There was an obvious analogy between the harmony of Newton's universe and the ideal of social harmony which was to be created by the advance of individual freedom and rationality.[12]

While Newton provided the empirical sciences with the necessary respectability to challenge the old scholarship entrenched in the universities, the modernization of the professions gradually forced open other gates. In the eighteenth century some institutions began to provide a much more technical and specialized type of education than that found in traditional universities—medicine in the Scottish universities and engineering in the École Normale des Ponts et Chaussés in France and in the Gergakademie in Freiberg were among the best known. Very often the new professional training was provided outside the university, and the tendency around 1800 seemed to suggest that education for the "learned professions" provided by the traditional universities was about to disappear, taking with it the whole system of professional privileges it entailed.[13] The new trend was related to two pressures: the need to bring to the old professions the new knowledge being produced by the experimental sciences; and the need to break the privileges of the old professions and their corporations so as to allow for the emergence of new professions, new schools, new methods of teaching and learning, and the final substitution of one intellectual elite for another.

In no country was this substitution more dramatic than in France. According to Ben-David,

the new system that began to emerge in 1794 consisted of a series of professional schools for teachers, doctors, and engineers needed by the state. Scientific studies and scientistic philosophy were to inherit the central place that had been occupied by the classics in both secondary and higher education. Eventually, under Napoleon, the scientific orientation was weakened, the emphasis on the new scientific philosophy was completely abolished, and classical learning was restored to its former importance in secondary schooling. But higher education remained identified with specialized education for various professions.[14]

Gradually the old privileges were replaced by new ones. The *grandes écoles* created by the Napoleonic system to form the technical cadres for the state

---

[12]See Crosland, ed., *Emergence of Science in Western Europe*; Merton, *Science, Technology and Society in Seventeenth Century England*; Bernal, *Science in History*.

[13]Ben-David, *Centers of Learning*, p. 36.

[14]Ibid., pp. 15–16.

became centers for training the new French intellectual leadership. While these schools provided a high-level education for the elite, a second tier of higher education was created for the larger population, eventually incorporating some of the institutional elements of the old universities. The *grandes écoles* performed, in practice, a subversion of the old notion that general education should precede and provide the foundation for professional training. In the new system, specialized education was perceived as the best way to intellectual development, and those who passed through these schools were considered men of a new type of culture.[15] Scientific research was never a central activity in this system; it was tangentially taught by some scientists, who did most of their work in separate institutions.

Changes in Britain were more complex and less dramatic. The old, traditional universities never abandoned their role of training the country's aristocracy, but they gradually included in their programs the specialized studies of modern science, while insisting, according to Ben-David, that "the purpose of specialized study was not necessarily the acquisition of practical skills, but that it was the best way to the education of the mind and was an end in itself."[16] At the same time other institutions of higher learning, more directly geared toward professional education, started to appear. Ultimately, professional training became the main aim of the country's higher education system, but the emphasis on scholarship and general education provided fertile ground for scientific research in the leading universities.

The most widespread revolution, which would become the model for other countries in the late nineteenth century, was the one that began at the University of Berlin. The more general social context seems to have been provided by the emergence of an educated middle class which lacked the alternatives of economic and social participation existing in England and France at the time, and which placed all the pressures for mobility on the state and on the educational system. The university became one of the few channels of social mobility available to this emerging group, and its social role was perceived as much more than a simple ground for professional training. The philosophical meaning of the new knowledge developed at German universities tended to be emphasized by the preeminence given to the German philosophers (beginning with Kant, who sought to provide the philosophical foundation for modern science) and by the development of *Naturphilosophie*, a much more humanistic and romantic vision of the world than the Cartesianism and positivism that had spread to the rest of Europe from France. The strength and vitality of the German scientific community

[15]Gilpin, *France in the Age of the Scientific State.*
[16]Ben-David, *Centers of Learning*, p. 75.

is expressed by the establishment, in 1822, of the Deutsche Naturforscher Versammlung, an association of German-speaking scientists and doctors which preceded the political unification of Germany by several decades.[17]

It was in this context that an effective integration between teaching and research was achieved for the first time. It occurred early in the fields of chemistry, pharmacy, and physiology, disciplines that were systematized enough to allow for coherent and integrated teaching with an experimental content. More important than the content, however, was the fact that a large educational system was being created in German-speaking countries and scientific production became a decisive factor in the competition for prestigious positions in that system. The universities, to enhance their reputation, searched for researchers, while they, in turn, demanded laboratories and other research facilities. Students who wished to enter university careers were obliged to follow the path of their masters, and physicians, chemists, and pharmacists had the opportunity to obtain scientific training in their schools. From the beginning this university system benefited from the strong ties it established with the emerging German chemical and pharmaceutical industries.

The notion that teaching and research should necessarily be joined arose from this context and became the model in spite of obvious difficulties.[18] Scientific research tends to absorb resources and time, which is often a liability and a problem for institutions geared to professional training. Also, the qualifications needed for a scientific education are often superior and much more specialized than those required for the competent exercise of the professions. These difficulties have been overcome in some places and times; in Germany they led to the creation of a differentiated system of scientific research, the Kaiser Wilhelm Gesellschaft (today the Max-Planck Institutes). The American system, when it later revived the linkage between teaching and research, did so through an absolute innovation: the establishment of scientific careers in graduate schools side by side with education for the classic professions. A doctoral degree in this new system became an alternative to a professional title. In the European system, in contrast, the degree is mostly a preparation for advancement in a teaching career within the university. In other words, scientific research in the American model is not a propaedeutic activity in the teaching process but a goal of its own, with its own requirements, resources, and dedication. This system, though not enough to bring all research into the universities, provided science with much more room than it ever had in other countries and places.

---

[17]Mason, *History of the Sciences*, pp. 578 ff.

[18]It has been noted that the German *Wissenschaft* is much broader than the English "science," since it includes a component of scholarship which is not necessarily part of its Anglo-Saxon meaning. Cf. Mayr, "Science-Technology Relationship."

This historical overview confirms the lopsidedness of the relationship between science and higher education. From the standpoint of science, systems of higher education are not necessarily very important. For those who think of science in Mertonian terms—as the work of a community of scholars engaged in the search for truth—what is paramount is the absence of social and political pressures that might challenge the scientist's commitment to the norms of the scientific ethos. The university can provide a favorable environment for scientists, but it can also threaten them with the imposition of external criteria and demands on their work.[19] For those who think of science and technology as an integrated component of modern industrial societies, the emphasis is much more on the linkages between science and economy than on those between science and the educational system.[20] With this perspective, as exemplified by Halsey's comment at the beginning of this chapter, university research is nothing but one sector of a large research and development establishment, and the educational process is identical wth manpower training.

The picture is not the same from the point of view of the higher education system. Here, the notion that the university is basically a community of scholars engaged in the pursuit of knowledge plays a highly significant role in the legitimation of its demands for social recognition, autonomy, resources, and prestige. This role is no doubt more strongly stressed in countries where other functions of higher education—professional training, general education—are still not well established. It is certainly not by chance that, in a country such as Brazil, the expressions "higher education system" and "university" are used almost interchangeably, so that the aura of prestige usually associated with the latter is extended to the former. This legitimation function explains, according to Joseph Ben-David, the resistance of most university systems to accepting the differentiation of their functions. For Ben-David, "this combination of advanced research and study has been realized only in small parts of the university, but those parts, in which teachers and students use their freedom for its original purpose of research and study, have legitimated the turning of freedom by others who do not do research or study into unjustified privilege."[21]

Systems of higher education in general, then, need science more than the scientific systems need them. For this reason the notion that science finds its "natural" place in the university seems to be self-evident (when seen from

---

[19]See Merton, "Science and the Social Order," in *Sociology of Science*, p. 256, for the plight of scientific research in German universities during the Nazi regime.

[20]For an overview, see Böhme, "Models for the Development of Science," pp. 319–354.

[21]Ben-David, *Centers of Learning*, p. 166. A recent publication from the Organisation for Economic Cooperation and Development lists four arguments against the differentiation of careers for researchers and teachers in the universities of the OECD countries. They are, first, the creation of a stratification between them with first- and second-class citizens; second, the loss of quality of teaching; third, the creation of an institutional split between teaching and

the latter's standpoint) and is so even in societies where linkages between the two are rather weak. If this is true, one might expect that systems of higher education would commonly reserve a special place for scientific research. In fact, they very often do, but the coexistence of scientific research with other explicit and implicit functions of the educational systems is not always pacific.

In short, the study of higher education systems from the perspective of their relationships with scientific research calls attention to some paradoxes that, if properly understood, lead to a better understanding of the systems' mechanisms of social legitimation. The basic paradox is that there is a large gap between the ideology of the centrality of scientific research in the higher educational systems and the historical fact that the overlap between the two is problematical and often reduced to a small number of elite universities. If the empirical and historical analysis is not done properly, there is the danger of taking ideology for reality and of overlooking the other functions performed by systems of higher education as well as the different institutional settings where scientific research tends to base itself. When properly understood, however, the analysis illuminates some basic inner tensions and conflicts frequently observed in higher education systems which are often ignored when they are seen only from a strictly educational or functional point of view.

SCIENCE IN LATIN AMERICA

Latin America is a living laboratory, a privileged ground in which to examine the interplay among scientific research, scientistic ideologies, and the realities of higher education systems. The Latin American educational institutions have always been part of Western culture, but they very often are superimposed upon a completely different society. This duality sometimes has been interpreted as a contradiction between the "ideal" and the "real" Latin American societies, leading to the notion that the "ideal," or "European," parts are false and alienated and should be replaced by the "real" ones. In fact, this contradiction is part of the reality itself, and this is probably one of the reasons why ideologies play so important a role in these societies. Science, as the ideal of Western rationality, is an obvious candidate for ideologies that affect educational systems most directly.[22]

---

research institutions; and fourth, the instability of the research institutions themselves because of their dependency on the countries' R&D changing budgets and policies. While acknowledging all the difficulties of the relationships between research and teaching at the universities, the OECD concludes that new organizational forms should be tried to reestablish the old belief in the indivisibility between them. (OECD, *L'Avenir de la Recherche Universitaire*, pp. 49–50, 86.)

[22]For an earlier version of the problems discussed in the following section, see Silvert, ed., *Social Reality of Scientific Myth*.

The Iberic Heritage

Spain, from the early sixteenth century, brought its university system to Latin America, but Portugal did not.[23] At the time of independence, in the early nineteenth century, there were universities in Mexico, Peru, Cuba, Guatemala, Chile, and Argentina, among other countries. In Brazil, under Portuguese influence, the first schools of higher education were established no earlier than 1808, and only in 1920 was the first university created in Rio de Janeiro. The ties with Spain were severed during the wars of independence, and the old, church-controlled universities were transformed according to the French Napoleonic professional model: different schools, or "faculties," for each profession, and official licenses for professional practice granted by the government to students upon graduation. In Brazil, where there was more continuity with Portugal, a few technical schools and institutions were established by an exiled Portuguese king in the first decades of the nineteenth century: a botanic garden, a library, a naval and military school, two schools of medicine, two schools of law, a museum of natural history.[24] Eventually, the Brazilian system also developed in the direction of the Napoleonic model, and the universities and professional schools became a necessary step for access to bureaucratic and political positions by the children of the elites.

Without trying to cover the wide variety of experiences throughout the continent, it is safe to say that the professional schools did not emphasize technical training and, even less, scientific research. Medicine and engineering are supposedly technical professions and, therefore, should command some measure of technical expertise. But the requirements for professional licensing tended to be formal and bureaucratic, rather than substantive and technical, and the professional schools tended, as a rule, to expel or push to the margin those who tried to bring them closer to the European standards of proficiency.

Scientific research was typically brought to Latin American countries in the late nineteenth and early twentieth centuries by foreign immigrants who worked in government research institutions outside the university systems: astronomic observatories, geographic and geologic institutes, botanic gardens, museums of natural history, and, later, institutions for public health and disease control. There, the newcomers eventually trained

---

[23]The following analysis is based in part on Schwartzman, "Universidade, Ciência e Subdesenvolvimento," which is published also in Lavados Montes, ed., *Universidad Contemporanea*, pp. 57–78.

[24]For the contrast between Portuguese and Spanish educational practices in their colonies, see Carvalho, "Political Elites and State Building." For a detailed history of Brazilian developments in science and professional education, see Schwartzman, *Formação da Comunidade Científica no Brasil*. For specific information on different scientific traditions, see Azevedo, ed., *As Ciências no Brasil*. For an overview of Argentina's experience, see Babini, *La Evolución del Pensamiento Científico en la Argentina* and *Las Ciencias en Argentina*.

their own disciples and sometimes taught at the engineering and medical schools and at the universities. They usually tried to expand research beyond their institutional charters, and sometimes they were successful, as in the case of the Manguinhos Institute of Bacteriology in Rio de Janeiro.[25] In general, however, they could not expand or institutionalize their work as part of a long-lasting scientific tradition; the impact of their work, if it was transmitted, was mainly perceived in Europe.

By the time of World War II research in science had already made significant inroads in the university systems of some of the largest Latin American countries, and the notion that these universities could become the preferred place for the scientific development of these countries did make some sense. A few centers of medical and biological research attained high standards of scientific work, among them the Instituto de Fisiologia of the Universidad de Buenos Aires, under Bernardo A. Houssay (Nobel prize in physiology and medicine, 1947), and later the Instituto de Biofísica of the Universidade do Rio de Janeiro, under Carlos Chagas Filho.

Advances in medical and biological research tended to have a limited impact on the higher education system as a whole, as they were largely restricted to the medical schools and related institutes. The introduction of modern mathematics and physics, on the other hand, was usually coupled with projects for comprehensive reforms of the universities and of the educational system in general. These projects were often inspired by some version of the nineteenth-century German model of integration of science and teaching, even when the most apparent influence was French, as in the case of the Brazilian initiatives in the 1930s. (The old Escola de Medicina, however, incorporated in the Universidade de São Paulo in 1934, was already receiving support from the Rockefeller Foundation and established full-time teaching and research in the decade 1910–1920.)[26]

The Introduction of Science and the Search for a New University

The most comprehensive attempt to launch science within a new university in Brazil was the establishment of the Universidade de São Paulo and its Faculdade de Filosofia, Ciências e Letras in 1934. This university was created during a period of intense mobilization by the state of São Paulo's economic and intellectual elite in the wake of their defeat in the conflict with the Vargas regime. The state of São Paulo was already the country's economic leader, thanks to the coffee plantations and to an emerging

[25]Stepan, *Beginnings of Brazilian Science*; Fonseca Filho, "A Escola de Manguinhos."

[26]See Schwartzman, *Formação da Comunidade Científica no Brasil*, chap. 7, for the creation of the University of São Paulo, and chap. 8, pp. 242–249, for the presence of the Rockefeller Foundation in Brazil. For an overview, see Schwartzman, "Struggling To Be Born," pp. 545–580.

industrial complex that had started to grow in association with it, benefiting from a large mass of European immigrants. A new university, structured around a school of sciences, was thought to be a long-range project that could give the state the leadership position its elite desired. At the same time it could provide the state with the intellectual, technical, and professional cadres needed in a rapidly modernizing economy. All members of the new Faculdade were recruited in Europe. German chemists and biologists, Italian physicists and mathematicians, French historians and anthropologists, all came with different motivations and for different periods. Some remained throughout the years of World War II and afterward.

Thanks to the quality of some of the new professors and students, to the autonomy granted the university in its first years (which contrasted sharply with the growing centralization that was the landmark of the Vargas regime), and to the resources that a growing state economy provided, the Universidade de São Paulo became the most important teaching and research establishment in the country. As a center for scientific and technological research, however, it was limited by the initial constraints of the Faculdade de Filosofia as well as by established interests in professional careers.

A similar, if less successful, attempt was made a few years later in Rio de Janeiro by Brazil's Ministry of Education. In 1937 most of the city's higher education institutions were brought together under a newly created Universidade do Brasil, which was supposed to be the model for all institutions of higher education in the country. According to its plan (which became law in 1937), the university had to establish courses and research facilities in all areas, and a new Faculdade de Filosofia, Ciências e Letras was to be created, also staffed with foreign scholars. This project was less successful than the earlier one in São Paulo for several reasons, one of which was the authoritarian climate that prevailed in the Brazilian national government from 1937 to 1945. The new school never attained São Paulo's quality, and it had little influence over the older parts of the university. The notion that a single model could be established for the whole country, however, together with the idea that all higher education should be buttressed by scientific research, became an undisputed assumption for Brazil's education policy in the years that followed.[27]

Postwar Optimism: University Science and Technology for Development

Optimism was high in the first years after World War II regarding the positive role science and technology might play in raising the levels of social and economic development in Latin American countries. The war, having shown the awesome destructive power of science and technology, led to the

---

[27]See Schwartzman, "A Universidade de Padrão."

hope that if oriented constructively these forces would have a positive impact upon society. The wave of technological change which swept the industrial and agricultural sectors in those years seemed only to confirm this idea.[28]

In Chile, the formation of the National Council for Scientific and Technological Research was suggested in the early 1950s by the dean of the Facultad de Ciencias Fisicas y Matematicas of the Universidad de Chile. He believed research, government, teaching, and economic development in Chile, and in South America in general, should be joined: ". . .development agencies, linked closely with the universities, must necessarily influence the orientation and priority given to large-scale national-level research in areas relating to these countries' natural resources and their improved exploitation. We also believe that technological research should be closely related to high-level scientific training, and through this medium to scientific research and teaching."[29]

This idea was implemented with relative success during the tenure of Juan Gomes Millas as rector of the Universidad de Chile (1953–1958). A law in 1954 created the Fund for University Construction and Research, which specified that plants, laboratories, experimental stations, and research institutes be created and oriented "toward cooperation with the Corporation for the Development of Production, with state technical organs, and with private entities and firms. A council, made up of the Rectors of all the universities in the country, headed by the Rector of the Universidad de Chile, was to prepare annual plans for coordinating all the technological research which the universities carried out."[30]

The view that science at the universities could play a central role in socioeconomic development was part of a "developmentalist" ideology that emanated from the United Nations' Economic Commission for Latin America (ECLA). In a document published in 1970, Raul Prebisch emphasized the need for the adaptation and recombination of international technological knowledge to meet the specific conditions of Latin America. He pointed out that priorities should be established from an economic planning

---

[28]The idea that scientific research should be brought to bear upon a central role in national planning was first put forward by the Soviet Union, was adopted by the French in the years of the Front Populaire (which led to the creation of the Centre Nationale de la Recherche Scientifique), and was supported very strongly in England by the group of Marxist scientists led by J. D. Bernal. In the United States it was adopted during World War II by the Organization for Scientific Research and Development, which, under Vannevar Bush, had direct access to President Franklin Roosevelt. See, among others, Graham, "Formation of Soviet Research Institutes"; Bernal, *Social Function of Science*; Gilpin, *France in the Age of the Scientific State*; McGucken, "Scientific and Technological Advice in the United Kingdom during the Second World War."

[29]Quoted by Fuenzalida, "Institutionalization of Research," p. 12. The following presentation of the Chilean experience is based on Fuenzalida's paper.

[30]Ibid., p. 19.

point of view, and that research programs should be organized to respond to these priorities. "All this has a close relationship with education. It will be necessary to promote educational programs that, besides the diffusion of technologies, should have as one of their main purposes, the stimulation of the creative capacity in this field."[31]

While agreeing with Prebisch that the educational system could do little by itself without an overall policy of socioeconomic development, Jorge Graciarena, a sociologist who also belonged to ECLA, believed that "until now, the Latin American university has remained at the margin of the problems of underdevelopment because of its little or no capacity to identify and solve them. . . . Today, however, it is difficult to conceive future solutions for the basic problems of development without a more active and large participation of the university," which had two strategic roles to play: to train manpower and to produce knowledge—not any knowledge, however, but knowledge that would be relevant to local conditions. Thus there was need for a "national, scientific ideology" and even a Latin American ideology, which in fact was present in the frustrated attempt to organize a continentwide system of graduate courses in the social sciences.[32]

This idea also found support in the United States and was a significant part of the Alliance for Progress program during John Kennedy's tenure, both directly through the United States Agency for International Development and indirectly via several private foundations which increased their activities in South America during the 1960s. Chile was a privileged recipient of this type of international support. In 1965, after a long internal discussion, the Facultad de Ciencias was established at the Universidad de Chile. Its creation coincided with an ambitious *convenio* between the University of Chile and the University of California, with support from the Ford Foundation; the agreement specified reciprocal acknowledgment of courses of study and degrees between the two institutions and several cooperative programs. During the 1965–1978 period, 323 Chileans and 287 Californians took part in the program: "127 Chileans obtained degrees from the University of California; 42 in Agriculture and Veterinary Medicine; 4 in Arts and Literature; 6 in the Library Development Program; 63 in Natural Sciences and Engineering; 12 in Social Science. Close to 1,000 books, articles in journals, papers presented to conferences and meetings, dissertations, theses, audio recordings, films, paintings, resulted from re-

---

[31]Prebisch, *Transformación y Desarollo*, quoted by Graciarena, *Formación de postgrado en ciencias sociales en America Latina*, p. 32. For an overall view of Prebisch's role and ideas, see Love, "Centro-Periferia e Troca Desigual." See also Balán, "Social Sciences in the Periphery."

[32]Graciarena, *Formación de postgrado en ciencias sociales en America Latina*, pp. 33–34 (my translation). This project was nursed for several years by the Latin American Council of Social Sciences, and had it succeeded, it could have counted on the support of the United Nations Development Program.

search projects supported directly or indirectly by Convenio funds during the period 1964–78."[33]

A similar, optimistic view preceded the creation of the Universidade de Brasilia in the early 1960s under the inspiration of Darcy Ribeiro. For him, "the mastery and cultivation of science—as the language of the emerging civilization—can be fruitfully achieved only within the universities, especially in underdeveloped countries. Isolated institutes tend to become wasteful institutions of low scientific creativity, with almost no contribution in terms of technological research and nothing whatsoever regarding the education of highly qualified personnel. The university, on the contrary, as it performs its role as a teaching institution at the graduate level, can and must not only contribute to the understanding of man and nature but must also develop, as a by-product of its day-to-day activities, the multipliers of research that could lead to the development of science, self-awareness of the national reality, and the search for solutions of its problems."[34] This was not to be a university simply for professors and scientists; it was to be for intellectuals, "each of whom would project his own field through a personal and sometimes dramatic experience of the Brazilian reality. That is, each one, instead of alienating himself, had to confront the Brazilian problem with his whole body and soul, on questions not only about the university but also about its social, political, and economic aspects. Although not all of them had the same level of experience, they all knew the derogatory meaning that used to be attached in Brazil to the label 'intellectual,' and they did not hide their disposition to change it through the active transformation of our social and political process."[35]

The modernization of the Facultad de Ciencias Exactas y Naturales of the Universidad de Buenos Aires, after the end of the first Peronist period in 1955, followed a similar inspiration. In 1966 its director, Rolando V. Garcia, presented a paper to the Fifth Pugwash Conference containing one of the stronger and more explicit endorsements of the notion that science should develop through the universities. Comparing Latin American with northern universities, Garcia said that "Latin American universities are much more complex living organisms. They are, on many occasions, the vanguard of the most progressive forces in the country. Historically, they have always taken an active part in every important political or social struggle. No wonder that most governments, the armed forces, and the Church are afraid of the universities."[36] The political turbulence of the

---

[33]Fuenzalida, "Institutionalization of Research," pp. 51–52.

[34]Ribeiro, A Universidade Necessária, p. 245 (my translation).

[35]Heron de Alencar, "A Universidade de Brasilia," p. 272 (my translation).

[36]Garcia, "Organizing Scientific Research," p. 12. For a historical view of the Universidade de Buenos Aires and its sociopolitical context up to this period, see Halperin Donghi, Historia de la Universidad de Buenos Aires.

Latin American universities contrasted with the serenity of Harvard, Oxford, or the Sorbonne, "quiet places where students are given regular doses of academic wisdom and provided with a detached attitude toward those problems which are the concern of professional politicians."[37] This turbulence was a good thing, according to Garcia, and implied a continuing two-front struggle. One side of the conflict was political, external to the university, and was to change the social, economic, and political conditions that were responsible for underdevelopment. The other was internal, a conflict against the "sacred cows" who did not allow for the development of institutions that could be fully aware of their responsibilities. The internal task was, essentially, "the process of transforming an institution dominated by lawyers and physicians into an institution where physicists, mathematicians, chemists and biologists share with specialists in social science and public health the highest priority." This transformed university should work according to a global plan that should be established as "a body at the highest governmental level where economists, scientists and technical officers of all (technical) branches of government meet to consult and to lay down the scientific policy of the country. The participation of the universities is here of primary importance."

The Modern Crisis

It is obvious that these different projects included individuals with different ideologies and visions of the role science, higher education, and the universities should play in the transformation of their societies. More seriously, experience has shown that it was relatively easy to improve the quality of small graduate programs, much more difficult to change the higher educational systems as a whole, and almost impossible to make significant improvements beyond that. Besides, the expansion and modernization of the economy in the region after the war were based in large part on the introduction of foreign capital and ready-made technology from outside, with little demand for local advanced research and highly trained manpower. In fact, the changes required the services of only a limited portion of the region's population, leading to increased differentiation between its "modern" and "traditional" sectors. Chile and Argentina, which already had a sizable and modernized middle sector from prewar days, witnessed a process of slow educational obsolescence and professional downgrading of large sections of their urban and educated populations; this led to potentially explosive cleavages between the latter and the smaller sectors that followed more closely the postwar pace of change. In the first few years it was probably hard to foresee the difficulty of bringing native technologi-

---

[37]On student political activism, see Albornoz, *Ideologia y Politica*; Lipset, *Student Politics*; Altbach, "The International Student Movement."

cal and scientific resources to bear on the industrialization and modernization process through higher education. As time passed, however, an ideological cleavage emerged between those who believed that science, technological research, and education should play a central role in the creation of a new, autonomous, and more egalitarian society and those who accepted the realities of a limited, dualistic, less autonomous, and dependent model. This cleavage eventually led to left-right, or liberal-conservative, confrontations.

Scientific research in and institutional modernization of the Latin American universities benefited extensively from North American influence or support, ranging from the Ford Foundation grant to the Chilean Convenio to large fellowship programs given to Latin American scientists by the United States Agency for International Development and by the Ford, Rockefeller, and other foundations. North American influence on the organizational model of the new Universidade de Brasilia was obvious. The American support, however, did not preclude the nationalist and often anti-American perspective of many of those engaged in these projects, for the United States was perceived as the main source of the region's foreign dependency and internal balkanization and dualism. As political life became more polarized in the late 1960s, ideology increased its weight. This contradictory situation was expressed very clearly by Felipe Herrera Lane, a Chilean who was for many years president of the Interamerican Development Bank, which played an important role in the financing of educational projects throughout Latin America. "In several countries there were those who considered . . . [the bank] to be a mere agent of the United States attempting to gain control of the higher education systems in Latin America, in spite of a Latin American 'image' we tried to develop with much sacrifice. I remember that, in my constant travels through the continent, one of the most stimulating challenges was the dialogue with the academic communities, explaining to them how Latin America was the true inspiration of the bank, and that the resources at the universities' disposal were meant to make them effective instruments in a task that included not only our economic independence, but also the affirmation of our traditions and cultural values."[38]

Crisis struck at these optimistic experiences with differing degrees of intensity and violence during the sixties. The intellectuals responsible for the organization of the Universidade de Brasilia entered into confrontation against the military regime that took power in 1964 and were forced to resign. Several of the organizational innovations of the Universidade de Brasilia, however, were later adopted in a nationwide university reform movement which introduced the departmental structure, set up the credit system for courses, and abolished the system of "chaired" professorships in

---

[38]Herrera Lane, "Dinamica Social y Desafios Educacionales," p. 30 (my translation).

Brazil. The following years saw sweeping changes in Brazil's higher education system, not only because of the reform, but mainly as a result of an extremely rapid increase in enrollments, which went from 142,000 in 1964 to 900,000 ten years later, and then to about 1.5 million in 1980. This expansion was followed by the creation of a huge system of graduate education: with only six graduate programs in the country before 1960, 123 were created between 1960 and 1970 and 620 in the ensuing decade.[39] The establishment of graduate schools, however, coincided with political mobilization and repression at the universities, which culminated in extensive student mobilization in 1968 and in the forced retirement, in the next two years, of dozens of the most talented professors and scientists at the country's leading universities and research centers.

Argentina was next. In 1966, the year in which the military government took power, it intervened in the Universidad de Buenos Aires with a violent invasion of the Facultad de Ciencias Exactas y Naturales. As a consequence, thousands of professors in all departments of the university—but mostly in the physical and social sciences—resigned.

This occurrence is still hotly discussed in Latin America: some believe that the university suffered because it was involved heavily in politics; others think exactly the opposite. Looking back at these events from the perspective of 1980, one of the major participants, Professor Manuel Sadosky, concluded that "our main weakness was that we did not do enough politically, in the best sense of the word, to convince the students that they were making a commitment to the country which they had to fulfill by placing their knowledge to work for the socioeconomic change that was indispensable for breaking the structures of the status quo." He partly accepts the charge of "scientificist" when he says that "we raised the requirements for study and work so much that, unwillingly, we contributed to the isolation of the students from political life." He believes, however, that it was the consciousness-raising activities that finally brought on the wrath of the conservative sectors in his own country and also in the United States: "Not only the local reactionaries considered us their enemies; in the North American Congress itself some representatives expressed their concern for the impetus that some of the more progressive universities in Latin America were getting. It is certainly not a coincidence that the most brilliant achievements of the universities of Buenos Aires, Brasilia, Montevideo, and, later, Santiago de Chile were annihilated with similar methods and harshness."[40]

---

[39]Unpublished data from the Brazilian Ministry of Education, CAPES, 1982. For data on Brazilian graduate programs after 1975, see "Pósgraduação no Brasil." For a discussion of the crisis in the undergraduate system, see Schwartzman, "A Crise da Universidade," pp. 96–126.

[40]Sadosky, "Una Esperiencia Educativa Argentina," p. 108 (my translation). A similar view was expressed by another eyewitness of the events, Amilcar O. Herrera: "If any doubt remained that these were not mere irreflective acts, simple consequences of momentary

In Chile, the crisis was slower to come. The implementation of the Convenio with the University of California slowed down after the university reform in the last few years of Eduardo Frei's government, and activities were kept limited during the Salvador Allende years. After the intervention in Chilean universities which followed the 1973 military coup, the Ford Foundation's remaining resources were restricted to helping only Chilean students who were already at the University of California.[41]

The Convenio showed, in 1978, mixed academic results, with better scientific performance in the fields of agriculture, veterinary medicine, and the hard sciences than in the social sciences. But the links established by the program became a liability when funds started to dry up. "Not only current activities are affected. Since libraries are forced to cancel subscriptions to journals, and equipment cannot be repaired or replaced with up-to-date ones, new research projects cannot be developed by the Chileans. The researchers themselves, frustrated by their working conditions, which they find particularly unbearable because of their firsthand and detailed knowledge of the working conditions of their Californian counterparts, end up leaving the University, or the country altogether."[42] After so much effort and hope the final balance was rather dismaying: "Whatever the Convenio is able to create in the University of Chile in the area of science and technology lacks roots in the Chilean soil. If foreign support does not come to the rescue (in the form of grants of foundations other than from Ford) these activities are bound to disappear." "The new University of Chile that resulted is unable to keep its programs working in these areas (veterinary medicine, basic science, and engineering) without a constant flow of resources, people, and ideas from the center. Instead of producing a modern higher education institution capable of self-sustained growth, the Convenio contributed to the creation of a subsidiary of the international centers of higher education (particularly the University of California)."[43]

Out of the Ashes?

It is difficult to evaluate the impact of the crisis in the different higher education systems throughout the continent. Most of the confrontation and repression that occurred in these years had little to do with scientific research at the universities, but a great deal more with the radicalization

---

political passions, it can be dispelled by pointing out that all subsequent acts show the intention of keeping these scientific centers (Facultad de Ciências Exactas of the Universidad of Buenos Aires and the Universidade de Brasília) in the deplorable state they were in after the interventions" (Herrera, *Ciencia y Política en America Latina*, p. 40; my translation). The fact is, however, that the Universidade de Brasília was not destroyed in spite of its successive crises, and today it is well above average among Brazilian higher education institutions.

[41]Fuenzalida, "Institutionalization of Research," p. 74, n. 6.

[42]Ibid., p. 56.

[43]Ibid., p. 57.

that swept the continent when the expectation of social, political, and economic participation, which was generated partly by the educational system, was not realized.

In Latin America the universities have often been a training ground for political leaders, but this did not necessarily mean that they were as progressive and vanguardist in educational, scientific, and technological matters as they were in politics. In an overview of the role of universities in national development in Spanish American countries, John P. Harrison tried to show how "co-cobierno," the institution of student participation in the universities' decision-making bodies which has been a tradition in Latin America since the reform movement of 1918, tended, in fact, to be a conservative force in this specific sense. "I am not aware," he stated, "of any indication that the students differed from their professors in regard to modernizing the curriculum or placing any greater emphasis on research or technical training not tied to the practice of a licensed profession. The most obvious evidence is that thirty years after Cordoba, the internal structure of the few universities where *co-cobierno* operated did not differ materially from those where control of the university remained in the hands of the catedraticos" (chairholding professors).[44]

Broadly speaking, there seems to have been a correlation in each country between the capacity for reorganization of higher education systems and the possibility of economic expansion. Nowhere was the destruction more sweeping than in Uruguay, where the dismantling of the university coincided with massive migration of the young and educated to other Latin American countries, Europe, and even Australia. Argentina followed a similar, but less radical, process. In Venezuela, where the Universidad Central had been the center for and the basis of the urban guerrillas who shattered the country in the early sixties, the oil revenues allowed for a generous policy of co-optation which brought the radical leadership to legitimate political roles and allowed the universities to remain centers of intense political activities and relatively low academic standards. A similar pattern was followed in Mexico after the 1968 massacre before the Olympic Games.

Scientific research did not necessarily disappear in this process; rather, it often increased in quality and quantity, in spite of the somber predictions of those who directly suffered the blows of political repression. As new manifestations of institution building and program development started to appear in the seventies, it became clear that science and higher education could continue to grow and improve in some Latin American countries, even in the absence of sweeping social and political revolutions, and that they could even be fostered by some of the political regimes that were considered essentially anti-intellectual and antiscientific.

---

[44]Harrison, *University versus National Development in Spanish America*, p. 13.

One change, however, could be observed everywhere: Latin American scientists in the years after the crisis lost much of their traditional European image as savants seeking an intellectual leadership role and adopted the more Americanized one of professional and specialized researcher. It is possible to follow this change in some of its manifestations. The first, which began several years before the crisis became apparent, was to create new, elite institutions that could be developed outside the mainstream of the higher education system and maintain high levels of quality. There are several examples in Brazil: the Instituto Tecnológico da Aeronáutica created in the forties; the Universidade de Brasilia in the early sixties; the graduate programs in engineering at the Universidade do Rio de Janeiro (COPPE) in the mid-sixties; and the Universidade de Campinas in the seventies. All these institutions, organized outside the country's higher education system, tended toward a maximum concern for quality and a minimum regard for formal procedures of bureaucratic administration, corporate autonomy, and long-term stability for its faculty. They tended to attract young and aggressive professionals, with little patience for any encumbrances on their work. They were open to international standards of scientific work and provided their students with unusual learning opportunities. All these initiatives eventually suffered institutional crises that derived from their marginality and innovativeness and from the threat they presented to the established institutions. They never entirely disappeared, however, and at their peak they set new patterns of academic excellence which their students and teachers would later try to develop and implement wherever they went. There are several examples in other Latin American countries, including, for instance, the Fundación Bariloche in Argentina and the Universidad Simon Bolivar in Venezuela.

The second manifestation was the attempt to place scientific research as far away as possible from the educational systems. Writing in 1973, Edmundo Fuenzalida suggested that the Chilean university should completely give up the attempt to develop scientific research on its own, since its goals included the transmission of knowledge and skills but not the "production of new knowledge, scientific or otherwise."[45] In 1971 Amilcar O. Herrera, who believed that research in the universities was an irreplaceable casualty of the years of repression, proposed the establishment of national agencies for scientific and technological planning at the higher political levels, without looking back to the higher education systems as significant actors in this project. The experience of Argentina's National Atomic Commission, which was able to work continuously and successfully in spite of the crisis that shattered the Universidad de Buenos Aires, has certainly inspired these and similar projects. Possibly the most impressive Latin American attempt in this direction is the Instituto Venezolano de Investi-

---

[45]Fuenzalida, "La Universidad Chilena no debe hacer investigación científica," p. 202.

gaciones Cientificas, established in the outskirts of Caracas as a nucleus of pure and high-level scholarship and research. This alternative amounted to looking at scientific research from the standpoint of science and technology, and not from the perspective of the educational system, a shift that almost necessarily led its proponents to the conclusion that divorce was the best solution.[46]

The third approach was to insist on the presence of science at the universities and on its important, but not exclusive, role in social and economic development. Emphasis was to be placed not on intellectual leadership, social awareness, and responsibility, but simply on the benefits of science and technology's products. This view was fully adopted by the Brazilian government when, in 1974, it presented its National Development Plan II (1975–1979). The first part of the plan, entitled "Development and Greatness: Brazil as an Emerging Power," stated that "science and technology, in the present stage of Brazilian society, represented the driving force, the conveyer of the idea of progress and modernization." "In the economic field, technological development will have in the next stage the same driving and modernizing role that the emergence of industrialization played in the years after the war."[47] The plan distinguished technological from fundamental research; for the former, the National Council for Scientific and Technological Development was organized, as an outgrowth of the former National Research Council, and the ambitious National Plan for Scientific and Technological Development was established. The estimation was that $2 billion would be spent for science and technology during the 1975–1977 period.[48]

This ambitious project was conceived at the end of a period in which Brazil's economy grew at more than 10 percent a year in real terms; the resources poured by the development agencies into the educational and research institutions after the late sixties were more than the latter could absorb and still grow in a balanced way. One of the consequences was the extraordinary growth of new graduate programs and research institutions in Brazil, usually alongside mainstream programs in higher education. Whereas the education system had grown through private, isolated schools, graduate training and research developed at the public universities, and although the increase in enrollments was seen mostly in the social professions, resources tended to go to the technological and exact sciences. The

---

[46]For Latin American thinking on the matter in the postcrisis years, see Herrera, *Ciencia y Politica en America Latina*; Sabato, ed., *El Pensamiento Latinoamericano*; Suarez et al., *Autonomia Nacional o Dependencia*; Boeninger et al., *Desarollo Cientifico-Tecnologico y Universidad*. A partial history of the Argentinian atomic energy program may be found in Tanis and Sabato, "Desarollo de Recursos Humanos en Metalurgia."

[47]República Federativa do Brasil, *Projeto do II Plano Nacional de Desenvolvimento (1975–1979)*, p. 3 (my translation).

[48]See data in Schwartzman, "Struggling To Be Born," p. 574.

resources were provided directly to research and graduate program leaders, who gained autonomy from the administration of the university and were able to offer much better salaries and working conditions than other institutions in the higher educational system.

The situation was, at least in intention, almost ideal for those who, inspired by the ideas of J. D. Bernal, had for years defended the placement of science and technology at the center of national planning, although it came from a military (and supposedly right-wing) regime and not from a university-led social revolution, as had been expected by many in preceding years.

The oil shock of 1973 marked the beginning of the end of the so-called Brazilian miracle, and the project of national greatness had to be postponed for an indefinite period of time. It was replaced by policies of short-term troubleshooting, which made all long-term plans moot. A direct consequence was that programs of higher education and research which were geared to provide human resources and know-how to the big national project were left empty-handed. According to the director of the most outstanding advanced engineering course in this entire effort, located at the Universidade do Rio de Janeiro, his program was initiated in order to graduate a type of engineer who did not exist before, one with a master's or a doctoral degree: "We had the idea that this element, which was necessary for the technological development of the country, was missing from the professional picture." But he adds: "What we expected to happen did not happen. We were throwing a sophisticated product into the market which we believed was required by the country's technological development. We thought that, if we did our part in training MAs and PhDs in engineering, that is, creative people, they would be absorbed by a country that was really interested in the internal development of technology. But this did not happen."[49]

The crisis at the Graduate Engineering Program of the Universidade do Rio de Janeiro did not take on the dramatic overtones of the interventions at other places and times. Slowly, the program turned its efforts toward the more traditional fields of engineering, mainly civil engineering; it developed its competence in terms of routine technical assistance to the local industry; it trained students well at the master's level, although it enjoyed little success at the doctoral level; and having been created with independent resources and completely outside the administrative arm of the Faculdade de Engenharia, it gradually fell under its control and supervision.

Brazil, with probably the most ambitious program, certainly did not make the only attempt in the past decade to develop scientific research and

---

[49]Coimbra, quoted in Nunes et al., "Pós-Graduação em Engenharia," chap. 6.

to offer highly qualified training in Latin American universities; and its frustrations are not unique. A detailed case study of the areas of chemistry and chemical engineering in Venezuela suggests major pessimistic conclusions. "The project of developing a scientific Chemistry and Chemical Engineering in Venezuela was part of the long-term strategy, based on the expansion of the modern industrial sector, that was raised in the forties and redefined in the late fifties." Today, however, "the facade of international cooperation in science and technology can no longer hide the harsh reality lying behind it: the preoccupation of some of the most powerful governmental and corporate actors with using superiority in science and technology to force the poorer countries into a dependent relationship and thus maintain dominance and control. Thus, instead of being a training place for self-reliance, science and technology education constitutes, in fact, a major factor of dependence. The educational system produces overskilled qualified workers in the sense of being highly specialized watchdogs of 'automated factories,' just as deskilled ones, in the sense of being deprived of certain general purpose skills or of traditional innovative capacities that have been downgraded or abandoned."[50]

Thus the experiences of Argentina, Chile, Brazil, and Venezuela seem to lead to the same dead end: increased scientific and technological capabilities producing overskilled professionals and increasing dependency. Would these countries be better off and more independent with less science and technology, and with underskilled professionals? This conclusion would be only slightly more absurd than its opposite, that is, that science and technology, within or outside the university, could by themselves determine the socioeconomic development and the self-reliance of a country. The introduction of scientific research in Latin American universities did not play the revolutionary role that so many hoped for and others feared. Nor did it help to solve in a significant way the problems of technological backwardness and dependency which could not be solved through other means. When crisis came, it did not lead to an overall setback in development, but only to a period of more or less violent disruption and to some changes in emphasis, tone, and ideology. The actual effects of the huge investments in graduate training in scientific research in Brazil in the past fifteen years, and of corresponding efforts in other countries, should not be judged solely in terms of their avowed goals, but rather by a series of less obvious and long-range consequences which affected changes in the perspectives and world outlooks of the thousands of persons who are to play a central position in their countries in the years to come.[51]

---

[50]Vessuri, "Science, University and Graduate Education in Venezuela," p. 3.

[51]One of the main determinants of attitude change, in this connection, is the experience of studying abroad. There are innumerable differences among countries in the way this program is implemented, including the return of students to their countries of origin. Argentina and Colombia tend to lose a significant number to the host countries; in Brazil, on the contrary, the

CONCLUSIONS

There are no easy solutions to the problems of underdevelopment, inequality, and restricted social and political participation which plague, in different degrees, all Latin American countries. Science, technology, and higher education constitute just a small part of a broader picture, and they do not hold a privileged key to a country's transformation. We can, however, understand their interrelations and their broader social role a little better if we consider a few propositions, some of which follow from the preceding discussion; others are necessary for a proper interpretation.

First, science and technology, regardless of their effective content, play a legitimating role for the claim of autonomy, resources, and social prestige of the Latin American universities. This role, stated by Ben-David and quoted earlier in this essay, applies in Latin America as well as elsewhere.

Second, the institutional instability of Latin American higher education systems makes this ideological role not only a matter of institutional self-defense and protection, but also the basis of a claim for social, political, and ideological leadership that goes far beyond the boundaries of the educational systems. The instability does not result from any supposed Latin American "cultural trait," but rather it stems from the extraordinary rates of urbanization, demographic growth, and modernization these societies have experienced in past decades, with corresponding changes in labor structure, social and political roles, and cultural values and aspirations. Because of these changes, there is a poor fit between the educational system and the labor market, leading to a pervasive feeling of frustration and protest among the educated. This situation is not new, but it becomes more serious as higher education systems grow.

Third, the main actors in the higher education system—teachers and students—are unhappy not only with their own institutions but also with the nonacademic elites who hold the highest economic and political positions and who are blamed, often with good reason, for the precarious economic and social conditions of the region's population. This is fertile ground, as it was earlier in Europe, for the idea that science and technology can provide better socioeconomic conditions and, incidentally, a new elite.

Fourth, the educational systems have been much more amenable to change and growth than other institutions in Latin America. International cooperation provided well-defined patterns and resources for the creation of

---

return rates are very high. The rate of return depends, among other things, on who pays for study abroad, the proper fit of the students to the host country's educational system, and the attractiveness of work conditions in the country of origin. For a summary of an international study on the subject, see Glaser, *Brain Drain*. The most ambitious program of fellowships for study abroad in Latin America today is provided by Venezuela through the Fundación Gran Mariscal de Ayacucho, which awarded more than 3,000 fellowships for that purpose in 1980. Of these, only a third were for graduate training. See Mauch, "Studying Abroad."

the new graduate and research programs; enrollment can grow very quickly, if there is not much concern about educational quality; and new professions can easily be specified on paper and be given supposedly coherent academic programs in the schools. This situation contrasts very sharply with the saturation of the labor market for university-trained people, the decadence of the inflated urban centers, the increasing technological gap between these countries and the industrialized ones, and the growth of capital-intensive industries in Latin America to the detriment of labor-intensive ones. These factors are proving to be very difficult to change.

One consequence of this entire situation is the relative isolation of the educational system and its institutions from the rest of the society. This isolation has both positive and negative consequences. Positively, it eventually allows for the development of competent teaching and research within the higher education system, without the pressures for short-term adaptability to the low requirements of the labor market or the industrial system. Negatively, it produces people trained in obsolete professions, scientific institutions working in outdated subjects with outdated methods, and the substitution of status symbols and behavioral patterns associated with them for proper education and scientific and technological work. In the absence of external checks and controls, it is often difficult to distinguish one from the other.

They are not, however, the same thing. Given the difficult and often dramatic social conditions in many Latin American countries, it would be unfortunate if there were a good fit between the educational system and the scientific community in these countries, on the one hand, and the local conditions on the other. A scientific community working with standards of high quality and a broad view of other possibilities and alternatives for their roles can be a dynamic factor of change and innovation, provided that other conditions are forthcoming.

At the same time, the emphasis placed on the role of scientific research for education, even if properly done, may have a detrimental effect upon other important functions in the areas of general education and professional training which higher education systems might have. In Brazil, the assumption that teaching and research are inseparable has led to the downgrading of professional training without academic degrees, and the creation of still another tier in the educational life for those who enter the higher education system. In practice, the new academic, scientific-minded graduate programs often work as a way of postponing the student's entrance into the labor market and as a filter that partly compensates for the swelling of the undergraduate system. Thus, instead of helping to increase the quality of undergraduate courses, the strengthening of scientific education has helped to bypass and avoid a direct confrontation with the difficult problems of the system.

Scientific research is not a panacea for underdevelopment; it is not even a solution to the problems of higher education in its varied implicit and explicit functions. It may be detrimental, as when it loses its content and gains weight and relevance as sheer ideology; but it may also be a factor for change, innovation, and social awareness. What is needed if higher education is to play a better role, in this context, is not just more or less science, but more differentiation and complexity, so that different and frequently contradictory functions can be performed simultaneously. The sociology of science should help to uncover the uniformity that the ideological imagery of modern science often brings to higher education in conditions such as these and should open the way for a richer and less naive understanding of the different roles and possibilities of each.

POLICY IMPLICATIONS

What are the policy implications to be drawn from the above? It is clear, first of all, that there is a place for scientific research in some segments of the higher education system in Latin America, as elsewhere. But the role played by research universities today in setting the standards for an entire system in a country such as England or the United States, where there is room for institutional competition and innovation, can become detrimental in more rigid and less well-established contexts, where the real contents of research and teaching can easily be replaced by formalistic and bureaucratic impersonations of academic behavior.[52] From the standpoint of scientific research, as from that of higher education, it is advisable to limit scientific research to those centers that offer the necessary conditions for doing it, and to try to stimulate other educational values and goals, more related to teaching and community services, in the remaining, larger part of the higher education system.

What are the chances of scientific research really taking hold in a social and cultural context that is without a previous scientific tradition? We may start by brushing aside some extreme misconceptions: there is nothing in the "Latin culture" which is intrinsically inimical to modern science; there is no future in the attempts to develop an "alternative" science that would be more congenial to Latin (or other) cultures and might compete with "Western" science in any significant way; and injections of money, fellowship programs, and visiting professorships are not sufficient, and they may even be counterproductive.

In the underdeveloped countries of today, as in western Europe centuries ago, modern science was brought in from outside. If we compare the

---

[52]On the role of the research universities as models for higher education systems, see Martin Trow's paper (chap. 5, above). For different interpretations of academic roles in an underdeveloped context, see Ilchman, "Hybrids in Native Soil," pp. 85–114.

conditions of the growth of science in Latin America with those of the early years of the European universities, we see that in both instances scientific knowledge was perceived as an instrument of social advancement for a relatively marginal group of people, who railed against the entrenched positions of the traditional universities. There are, however, important differences. One is that the scientistic movements in Europe occurred when "science" was relatively simple and the university culture was extremely complex and elitist, based on the mastery of formal logic and the classical languages. This situation permitted the emergence of the amateur scientist, the nonprofessional scientific societies, and the stereotype of the self-taught and slightly crazy, scientific genius which is still today part of international folklore. The contemporary situation is completely reversed: science is an extremely complex activity, requiring the mastery of advanced mathematics, a large literature, and a knowledge of foreign languages, whereas the system of formal education is mass-oriented and tends toward standardization and democratization of access. The Latin American scientist is marginal in the sense that he or she does not follow either the traditional paths of elite education in the traditional professions of law, medicine, and engineering, or the more popular lines of mobility through the new technical or semiprofessional careers. While his early European counterpart participated in a widespread movement for social mobility which was part of the bourgeois and rationalistic revolution, the Latin American scientist is much more isolated as a member of an emerging learned aristocracy.

How the scientist defines his social role, and how this definition is related to his social origins, might be an intriguing research topic for the future. Some scant information available on the Brazilian experience suggests that scientists in the biomedical field tend to be recruited from higher social strata and to define their role as members of the medical profession aristocracy. The physical scientists, on the other hand, are more likely to be recruited from immigrant and upwardly mobile sectors and tend to play a more active role as part of their country's new intelligentsia. Researchers in more applied fields are likely to define themselves as part of emerging new professions, who possess specialized knowledge and who assume appropriate rewards for their work. Social scientists are closer to those in physical science than to other types.[53]

The future of scientific research in this context will depend on the possibilities of institutionalizing science as a permanent and relatively stable professional career, without depriving it of its aura as a prestigious and socially meaningful activity and without submerging it completely in the mainstream of the higher education teaching population. The aura of prestige and social relevance is necessary if science is to recruit the best-qualified people and extract from them their greatest efforts, since other

---

[53]See Schwartzman, "Foreigners in Their Country." See also Becher's approach to the different cultures of academic specialties (chap. 6, above).

gratifications, those of a more material kind offered by other professions, are seldom forthcoming. Moreover, a complete identification with the professional teacher may mean a decreasing involvement with the scientist's academic community. Institutional questions and trade-union and professional (but nonacademic) concerns might easily lay claim to most of his or her social commitments and interests, an attachment that might be harmful for scientific work.[54]

Professionalization of science depends on a complex combination of economic, political, and institutional elements; we need, then, to consider the different activities that are usually brought together under the name of "science." The consolidation of technological research, for example, requires an economic and industrial policy that includes a significant volume of autonomous technological development and adaptation, if not creation. These policies may take different shapes, from military buildups to barriers to imported technologies. If this requirement is fulfilled, the next one is to create an educational system that will respond to this demand in terms of qualified education.

More academic and "basic" research may survive much more easily without direct industrial counterparts, if the necessary institutional ingredients are forthcoming. The most obvious one is money for salaries, equipment, office space, and the like. Then, the resources must get to the right people. Because of its limited size and political strength, scientific research tends to be organized as small sections of large educational or governmental institutions, units that receive low priority and are unable to marshal their own criteria of priorities, excellence, and organizational procedures. Brazil has been quite successful, in past decades, in establishing a series of financing institutions that go directly to the scientist or to his department or research group, bypassing the educational or ministerial hierarchy.[55] The corresponding increase in volume and quality of scientific research, however, combined with budget limitations, is leading to attempts to centralize

---

[54]The identification of the university teacher with his union or professional association adds another dimension to Clark's "moving matrix" of academic and institutional affiliation, which is for him a central element in higher education organizations. The distinction between academic and professional associations is not very clear in fields where the professions are defined in terms of their academic contents. In the Latin American context, however, there is an obvious difference between professional associations of lawyers, economists, statisticians, psychologists, and the like, which are mainly concerned with the corporative rights of their constituents, and associations in the corresponding academic institutions, which are more oriented toward the advancement of knowledge and the exchange of information. When these two functions are not clearly distinguished, the second tends to suffer. (See Clark's chap. 4, above.)

[55]These institutions include the Coordenação de Aperfeiçoamento de Pessoal de Ensino Superior (CAPES) in the Ministry of Education; the Financiadora de Estudos e Projetos (FINEP) and the Conselho Nacional de Desenvolvimento Científico e Tecnológico in the Ministry of Planning; the Fundação de Amparo à Pesquisa in the state of São Paulo; and several permanent, single-purpose research programs and agencies, such as the Instituto Nacional de Estudos Pedagógicos, in the field of education, and the Programa Nacional de Pesquisas Economicas, in economics.

and coordinate the available resources for research, and such centralization is being perceived, with good reason, as a threat to the previous ability of effectively getting the resources to the right persons.

There is a final and unavoidable political aspect. The development of scientific, technological, and educational prowess takes time and requires institutional stability. These conditions are impossible to meet when society is subject to constant oscillations between social mobilization and political repression, combined with successive and sweeping attempts at institutional reform. This view is not necessarily conservative, since it is obvious that not all forms of stability are conducive to good science and education and there are other social values and goals aside from these. However, it does explain why it is common for people engaged in educational and scientific institution building in contexts of political instability to become exasperated with the futility of their work and to decide that only politics can open the way for everything else. Unfortunately, this is a self-defeating prophecy, since overpoliticization contributes further to the weakening of the scientific and educational institutions, making them still more vulnerable to political uncertainties.

In short, institution building in the field of scientific research and higher education is a difficult and risky adventure. It deals with activities that are very different from one another, and even conflictful in many ways, but which cannot be fully disconnected. It may have unexpected and contradictory results. And it depends on variables that are usually out of the control of those who try to undertake it. Scientific research, however, is a necessary condition for knowledge, and no human society can willingly renounce it. That is why, like Sisyphus, we must persevere.[56]

---

[56]There are those, of course, who support the notion that both scientific research and higher education should be abandoned as significant goals for Latin America and that they should be replaced by other forms of cultural and emotional participation in society which are more direct, less westernized, and often more mystic and more hedonistic. As the promises of higher education grow dimmer, this view tends to take a stronger hold on better-educated people. The importance of this phenomenon, which in a way replicates the counterculture movements of the 1960s in the United States and Europe, is becoming increasingly evident.

BIBLIOGRAPHY

Albornoz, Orlando. *Ideologia y Politica en la Universidad Latinoamericana*. Caracas: Instituto Societas, 1972.

Altbach, Philip G. "The International Student Movement." *Comparative Education Review* 2 (October 1964):131−137.

Azevedo, Fernando de, ed. *As Ciências no Brasil*. 2 vols. Rio de Janeiro: Ed. Melhoramentos, 1955.

Babini, José. *La Evolución del Pensamento Científico en la Argentina*. Buenos Aires: Ediciones la Fragua, 1954.

―――. *Las Ciencias en Argentina*. Buenos Aires: Eudeba, 1963.

Balán, Jorge. "Social Sciences in the Periphery: Perspectives on the Latin American Case." In *Social Sciences and Public Policy in the Developing World*, ed. Laurence D. Stifel, Ralph K. Davidson, and James S. Coleman. Lexington, Mass.: D. C. Heath, 1982. Pp. 211−247.

Barber, Bernard, and Walter Hirsch. *The Sociology of Science*. New York: Free Press, 1962.

Ben-David, Joseph. *The Scientist's Role in Society: A Comparative Study*. Englewood Cliffs, N.J.: Prentice-Hall, 1971.

―――. *Centers of Learning: Britain, France, Germany, United States*. New York: McGraw-Hill, 1977.

Bernal, John D. *Social Function of Science*. New York: Macmillan, 1939.

―――. *Science in History*. 4 vols. Cambridge: MIT Press, 1971.

Boeninger, E., et al. *Desarollo Cientifico-Tecnologico y Universidad*. Santiago: Corporación de Promoción Universitaria, 1973.

Böhme, Gernot. "Models for the Development of Science." In *Science, Technology and Society*, ed. Ina Spiegel-Rösing and Derek de Solla Price. Beverly Hills: Sage Publications, 1977.

Brasil, República Federativa do. *Projeto do II Plano Nacional de Desenvolvimento (1975−1979)*. Brasília: Serviços Gráficos do IBGE, 1974.

Carvalho, José Murilo de. "Political Elites and State Building: The Case of Nineteenth Century Brazil." *Comparative Studies in Society and History* 24 (July 1982):378−399.

Crosland, Maurice, ed. *The Emergence of Science in Western Europe*. New York: Science History Publications, 1976.

De Alencar, Heron. "A Universidade de Brasília: Projeto Nacional de Intelectualidade Brasileira," *In* Darcy Ribeiro, *A Universidade Necessária*. 2d ed. Rio de Janeiro: Paz e Terra, 1975.

Falcão, Edgar Cerqueira, ed. *Oswaldo Cruz Monumenta Historica*. 3 vols. São Paulo, 1973.

Fonseca Filho, Olympia da. "A Escola de Manguinhos." In *Oswaldo Cruz Monumenta Historica*, ed. E. C. Falcão. Vol. 2. São Paulo, 1973.

Fuenzalida, Edmundo. "La Universidad Chilena no debe hacer investigación cientifica." *In* E. Boeninger et al., *Desarollo Cientifico-Tecnologico y Universidad*. Santiago: Corporación de Promoción Universitaria, 1973.

————. "The Institutionalization of Research in Chile's Universities." Paper presented to the session on "Science Development and Graduate Education," at the annual meeting of the Latin American Studies Association, Washington, D.C., March, 1982.

Garcia, Rolando V. "Organizing Scientific Research." *Bulletin of the Atomic Scientists* 22 (September 22, 1966):12–15.

Gilpin, Robert. *France in the Age of the Scientific State*. Princeton: Princeton University Press, 1968.

Glaser, William A. *Brain Drain: Emigration and Return. UNITAR Research Report 22*. Oxford: Pergamon Press, 1978.

Graciarena, Jorge. *Formación de postgrado en ciencias sociales en America Latina*. Buenos Aires: Ed. Paidos, 1974.

Graham, Loren. "The Formation of Soviet Research Institutes." *Social Studies of Science* 5 (1975):303–329.

Halperin Donghi, Tulio. *Historia de la Universidad de Buenos Aires*. Buenos Aires: Eudeba, 1962.

Halsey, A. H. "The Changing Functions of Universities." *In* A. H. Halsey, Jean Floud, and A. Anderson, *Education, Economy and Society*. New York: Free Press, 1962.

Halsey, A. H., Jean Floud, and A. Anderson. *Education, Economy and Society*. New York: Free Press, 1962.

Harrison, John P. *The University versus National Development in Spanish America*. Hachett Memorial Lecture, Institute of Latin American Studies, University of Texas, Austin, 1968.

Herrera, Amilcar O. *Ciencia y Politica en America Latina*. Mexico City: Siglo XXI Editores, 1971.

Herrera Lane, Felipe. "Dinamica Social y Desafios Educacionales: Perspectivas de dos Décadas." In *Universidad Contemporánea: Antecedentes y Experiencias Internacionales*, ed. Lavados Montes. Santiago: Corporación de Promoción Universitaria, 1980.

Ilchman, Warren F. "Hybrids in Native Soil: The Social Sciences in Southeast Asia." In *Social Sciences and Public Policy in the Developing World*, ed. Laurence D. Stifel, Ralph K. Davison, and James S. Coleman. Lexington, Mass.: D. C. Heath, 1982. Pp. 85–114.

Kuhn, Thomas S. *The Copernican Revolution: Planetary Astronomy in the Development of Western Thought*. Cambridge: Harvard University Press, 1957.

Lavados Montes, Ivan, ed. *Universidad Contemporánea: Antecedentes y Experiencias Internacionales*. Santiago: Corporación de Promoción Universitaria, 1980.

Lipset, S. M. *Student Politics*. New York: Basic Books, 1967.

Love, Joseph L. "Centro-Periferia e Troca Desigual: Origens e Crescimento de uma Doutrina Econômica." *Dados* (Rio de Janeiro) 19 (1978):47–62.

McGucken, William. "Scientific and Technological Advice in the United Kingdom during the Second World War." *Minerva* 17, no. 1 (1979):33–69.

Mason, Stephen S. *A History of the Sciences*. New York: Macmillan, 1956.

Mauch, James E. "Studying Abroad: The Fundación Gran Mariscal de Ayacucho." School of Education, University of Pittsburgh, March, 1982. Mimeo. 22 pp.

Mayr, Otto. "The Science-Technology Relationship as a Historiographic Problem." *Technology and Culture* 17, no. 4 (1976):663–673.

Merton, Robert K. *Science, Technology and Society in Seventeenth Century England*. New York: Harper and Row, 1970.

————. *The Sociology of Science: Theoretical and Empirical Investigations*. Chicago and London: University of Chicago Press, 1973.

Needham, Joseph. *The Grand Titration: Science and Society in East and West*. London: Allen and Unwin, 1969.

Nunes, M. B. de Melo, N. V. T. Souza, and S. Schwartzman. "Pós-Graduação em Engenharia: a Experiência da COPPE." In *Universidades e Instituições Científicas no Rio de Janeiro*, ed. S. Schwartzman. Brasilia: Conselho Nacional de Desenvolvimento Científico e Tecnológico, 1982.

Organisation for Economic Cooperation and Development. *L'Avenir de la Recherche Universitaire*. Paris: OECD, 1981.

Parsons, Talcott. *The Social System*. Glencoe: Free Press, 1951.

"Pós-Graduação no Brasil." *Revista Brasileira de Tecnologia* Brasilia 13 (January–March 1982):53–57.

Prebisch, Raul. *Transformación y Desarollo: La Gran Tarea de America Latina*. Santiago, Chile: Instituto Latinoamericano de Planificación Economica y Social, 1970.

Ribeiro, Darcy. *A Universidade Necessária*. 2d ed. Rio de Janeiro: Paz e Terra, 1975.

Sabato, Jorge A., ed. *El Pensamiento Latinoamericano en la Problematica Ciencio-Tecnologica—Desarollo—Dependencia*. Buenos Aires: Paidos, 1975.

Sadosky, Manuel. "Una Esperiencia Educativa Argentina." In Universidad Menéndez Pelayo, *La Lucha por la Democracia en America Latina*. Madrid: Universidad Menendez Pelayo & Ministerio da Educación y Ciência, 1981.

Schwartzman, S. "Struggling To Be Born." *Minerva* 16, no. 4 (1978):545–580.

————. "Universidade, Ciência e Subdesenvolvimento." *Dados* (Rio de Janeiro) 19 (1978):63–83.

————. *Formação da Comunidade Científica no Brasil*. São Paulo e Rio de Janeiro: Cia. Editora Nacional/FINEP, 1979.

————. "Foreigners in Their Country: Three Generations of Brazilian Scientists." Paper presented to the annual meeting of the Society for the Social Studies of Science, Washington, D.C., 1979.

————. "A Crise da Universidade." In *Ciência, Universidade e Ideologia*, ed. Simon Schwartzman. Rio de Janeiro: Zahar, 1981.

————. *Ciência, Universidade e Ideologia: a Política do Conhecimento*. Rio de Janeiro: Zahar, 1981.

————. "A Universidade de Padrão." *In* Simon Schwartzman, H. Bomeny, and V. Aderaldo, *Tempos de Capanema*. Forthcoming.

Schwartzman, S., ed. *Universidades e Instituições Científicas no Rio de Janeiro*. Brasilia: Conselho Nacional de Desenvolvimento Científico e Tecnológico, 1982.

Schwartzman, Simon, H. Bomeny, and V. Aderaldo. *Tempos de Capanema*. Forthcoming.

Silvert, Kalman, ed. *The Social Reality of Scientific Myth: Science and Social Change*. New York: American University Field Staff, 1969.

Spiegel-Rösing, Ina, and Derek de Solla Price, eds. *Science, Technology and Society*. Beverly Hills: Sage Publications, 1977.

Stepan, Nancy. *Beginnings of Brazilian Science: Oswaldo Cruz, Medical Research and Policy*. New York: Science History Publications, 1976.

Stifel, Laurence D., Ralph R. Davidson, and James S. Coleman. *Social Sciences and Public Policy in the Developing World*. Lexington, Mass.: D. C. Heath, 1982.

Suarez, F., et al. *Autonomia Nacional o Dependencia: la Politica Cientifico-Tecnologica*. Buenos Aires: Paidos, 1975.

Tanis, S. V., and J. Sabato. "Desarollo de Recursos Humanos en Metalurgia: Balanço de una Experiencia." Buenos Aires: Comisión Nacional de Energia Atomica, Programa Multinacional de Metalurgia, 1980. Publication PMM/I-287. Mimeo.

Vessuri, Hebe M. C. "Science, University and Graduate Education in Venezuela: The Cases of Chemistry and Chemical Engineering." Paper presented to the Latin American Studies Association annual meeting, session on "Science Development and Graduate Education in Latin America," Washington, D.C., March 3–5, 1982.

8. THE POLICY PERSPECTIVE

Ladislav Cerych

The development of higher education in the past ten to twenty years has been marked by an exceptionally large number of new policies and reforms,[1] but most of these have resulted in much less change than was originally envisaged. Examples abound in virtually all European countries and elsewhere as well.[2] A large number of the universities founded in Germany in the 1960s—Konstanz, Bochum, and Bielefeld, for example—are now part of the university establishment instead of having become models for the organization, content, and methods of the country's higher education. The nine new universities founded at the same time in the United Kingdom have similarly converged upon traditional forms, procedures, norms, and values. Furthermore, new institutional sectors set up to provide alternatives to traditional higher education, such as the polytechnics in Great Britain, the Norwegian regional colleges, and the French *instituts universitaires de technologie* (IUTs), either have tended increasingly to resemble the traditional university model or to fall short of their projected size and place in the national system.

At the global level, the situation is much the same. The German *Gesamthochschule* (comprehensive university), once expected to serve as the new general organizing principle for the whole of German higher education, has only partly materialized in two of the eleven *Länder*. Meanwhile, in France, the three goals of the well-known *loi d'orientation* of 1968—multidisciplinary teaching, student participation, and institutional autonomy—have been achieved only to a very limited degree or, some might say, not at all. Policies concerning specific aspects of higher education have not fared much better. New admissions policies designed to widen university access for students from underprivileged social strata have rarely resulted in a significant increase in their proportion of total enrollments, and even less so for those in regular full-degree programs. This applies to eastern European countries, to the relatively radical Swedish 25/5 admissions scheme (later called "25/4"), and, in part, to the British Open University.

---

[1]Conceptually the terms "policy" and "reform" have different meanings but I use them here interchangeably because I assume that every higher education reform implies or reflects a policy (while the reverse is not necessarily true).

[2]Although my discussion here centers on European experiences, I believe it has a much broader validity.

These partial achievements or limited outcomes are often explained in a rather simple way: universities are conservative institutions; academics resist change; higher education can develop only gradually; the reform goals were overambitious. There is certainly some truth in these statements but, without saying (for the moment) that they are not necessarily true, they do not, in fact, constitute any explanation at all. Why are universities conservative (if they are so) and why does higher education usually change by accretion and only very slowly?

In this paper I attempt to show that policy analysis can provide some meaningful answers to these and similar questions, thereby throwing light on the nature and functioning of higher education. I first discuss the nature of policy analysis and its relations with other social science perspectives, and I then turn to a comparison of a number of case studies of specific reforms which were developed in a major study of policy implementation in European systems of higher education.

THE FIELD OF POLICY ANALYSIS

Most of the disciplinary views presented in this volume stress the interconnections and the overlap with other disciplines. To some extent, specialists in any one of them might even be justified in thinking that their own discipline underlies, cuts horizontally across, or constitutes a common denominator for the others. This idea applies to policy analysis as much as to history, sociology, economics, and so on, but here an additional problem arises. The content and specific nature of policy sciences are indeed very imprecise, particularly in the way they relate to or differ from political science. In this respect, it is perhaps significant that many languages have no distinct term for "politics" and "policy." In French, for example, the word *politique* means both, as does the German *Politik* or *politika* in most Slavic languages. Moreover, even in English-speaking countries, many of those who pursue policy studies are political scientists by academic background and affiliation.

Yet policy studies or policy sciences are by no means the exclusive domain of political scientists.[3] Since they are primarily concerned with causes, content, and consequences of public policies, and since such policies have or might have almost any dimension—for example, economic, sociological, organizational—any tool or any perspective on social inquiry may be useful or even indispensable. And policy studies may, I suggest, make an important contribution to the understanding of higher education, particularly to the process of its change (or resistance to change). To do so, a relatively recent offspring of policy studies, implementation analysis, has to be taken into consideration and perhaps even emphasized. In concrete

---

[3] I am indebted to Rune Premfors for several points made in this section.

terms, such analysis means essentially an assessment of the extent to which policy objectives have been achieved, the reasons explaining their achievement, nonachievement, or distortion of original goals, as well as an assessment of the unintended effects of a given policy.[4]

Above all, implementation analysis is concerned with processes, rather than with the mere measurement of policy impacts, which is the proper concern of policy evaluation. Even if the boundary between implementation and evaluation analysis is often blurred, there is a major difference or emphasis with significant methodological and conceptual implications.

Policy and political sciences have, of course, always been concerned with implementation. In a sense, that is what the field of public administration is about and what philosophers, writers, and scientists from antiquity to modern times have dealt with. Along with the discussion of moral and other principles of government went also the means and conditions for carrying them through. The new interest in implementation analysis and its development into a more or less self-contained field of study, with its own methodology and vocabulary, is a response to at least three main factors. One is a consciousness of the growing complexity of almost any public policy implementation. This is the gist of what may be regarded as the classic starting point of all recent implementation analysis literature, and it is the subject of the book by Pressman and Wildavsky.[5] Second is the realization that implementation processes are essentially dominated by bureaucrats and that conflicts between bureaucrats and local implementers are always influenced by outside forces and clients. Third is the finding (or feeling) that the major cause of program failures may be found in the complexity and politicized nature of implementation processes. Again, the Pressman and Wildavsky classic or, more exactly, its subtitle illustrates this point: "Implementation: How Great Expectations in Washington Are Dashed in Oakland; Or, Why It's Amazing that Federal Programs Work at All, This Being a Saga of the Economic Development Administration as Told by Two Sympathetic Observers Who Seek to Build Morals on a Foundation of Ruined Hopes."[6]

By trying to evaluate the degree of achievement of policy objectives and to explain the frequent gaps between original aims and outcomes, implementation analysis has a twofold function. On one hand it provides

[4]Among the major works specifically dealing with policy implementation are Bardach, *Implementation Game*; Berman, "Study of Macro- and Micro-Implementation"; Elmore, "Organizational Models of Social Program Implementation"; Majone and Wildavsky, "Implementation as Evolution"; Mayntz, "Environmental Policy Conflicts"; Murphy, "Title I of ESEA"; Pressman and Wildavsky, *Implementation*; Rodgers and Bullock, *Coercion to Compliance*; Mazmanian and Sabatier, *Conditions of Effective Implementation*; Van Meter and Van Horn, "Policy Implementation Process"; Williams, *Implementation Perspective*; Ripley and Franklin, *Bureaucracy and Policy Implmentation*; Ingram and Mann, eds., *Why Policies Succeed or Fail*. (The major part of this selective bibliography was prepared by Paul Sabatier.)
[5]Pressman and Wildavsky, *Implementation*.
[6]Ibid.

information that should be practical for decision makers because it illuminates the factors and forces that favor or inhibit the success of particular policies and reforms. In this sense it constitutes an essential element of organizational learning as well as a tool for formulation of more effective implementation strategies and, if necessary, for reformulation of policy goals.[7]

From a more general theoretical point of view implementation analysis, by identifying factors of achievement and failure,[8] offers a particular insight into the functioning of a specific social subsystem (here, higher education) and into the interrelation among its various components and between them and forces external to the system.

Implementation analysis aims, therefore, both at better comprehension and more effective control. Its connections with other disciplines are obvious; the factors promoting goal achievement and the constraints inhibiting it indeed belong to a multiplicity of areas: economic, sociological, historical, legal, and administrative. Implementation analysis then is in itself an interdisciplinary approach; selecting elements of knowledge and information provided by a variety of fields, it orders or connects them within its own conceptual framework.

A particular and rather complex relation exists between implementation analysis and the stage preceding it, policy formulation. Earlier I pointed out the difficulty of distinguishing between political science and policy studies or sciences. For the purposes of the present paper I emphasize that policy implementation is part of the design and definition of a policy (including the motivations leading to policy formulation), its adoption and its subsequent reformulation, and its conversion into routine practice or its rejection. Whether and to what extent the policy implementation process can be analytically separated from the policy formulation process is a matter for discussion which cannot be pursued here. In any event the close relation between the two has to be kept constantly in mind.

The existence of a particularly close relation between implementation analysis and history should also be stressed. On the one hand, many of the factors in the implementation of a policy are determined by historical development and can probably be fully understood only in this perspective. Attitudes toward central authorities, the status of particular social groups, the interplay between the center and the periphery, the concept of local autonomy—all are more or less inherited from the past. On the other hand,

---

[7]Using the terms of Argyris and Schön, *Organizational Learning*, one might speak of "double-loop learning," implying the resolutions of incompatible norms not merely by correcting errors in implementation (called "single-loop learning"), but also "by setting new priorities and weighing of norms or by restructuring the norms themselves together with associated strategies and assumptions" (p. 24).

[8]We shall see later in this paper that the term "failure" (as well as the term "success") should be used with great caution, if at all.

since the implementation of a policy constitutes a process, its analysis automatically poses methodological problems with which history is particularly familiar. The implementation analyst certainly has much to learn from the historian, even if he usually deals with relatively short recent periods.

Two Analytic Questions

Two questions should be raised at this point, the discussion of which will complete the general treatment of policy analysis and implementation. First, is the implementation of policies of higher education fundamentally different from the implementation of any other public policy? Second, what particular contribution can implementation analysis of higher education reforms make to implementation analysis in general?

Any analysis of a particular social subsystem pursued in sufficient depth will reveal unique aspects as well as characteristics held in common with some or all other areas. Thus, while there may be some fundamental similarities to policies in other fields, we may at the same time argue that implementation of higher education reforms poses several special problems. The problems are set primarily by the inordinate complexity of the system: in particular, the large number of relatively autonomous actors and the diffusion of authority throughout the structure and in the various forms or types. Even in a centralized state, higher education as a system or organization is, to use Burton R. Clark's words, "bottom-heavy," more so than other social subsystems and certainly more than lower education levels. Policy implementation then becomes interactive, and implementation analysis becomes a study of the respective interactions. Of course, all this is not unique; a health system, for example, involves considerable multiplicity of actors and authorities, partly independent. But the range of differences and the diffusion of authority are not so wide. In higher education, within one system, there are autonomy-seeking clusters of professionals in law, architecture, education, business administration, physics, sociology, classics, and on and on, as well as in medicine.

In addition, the ambiguity of the goals and functions of higher education complicates policy implementation. Although higher education deals primarily with knowledge, it has been called upon, especially since the 1960s, to assume many new functions which are only indirectly related to its responsibility, as traditionally perceived, for extending and transmitting knowledge. It is supposed now to be an active agent in social equalization, to provide more vocationally oriented training, to serve as a pole for regional development, to cater increasingly to adults, and so on. There is no general consensus regarding these new functions and, if and when they become specific policy objectives, the latter are immediately questioned and are more or less openly contested. Implementation analysis may as its starting

point consider policy goals as those formally adopted by an act of parliament or a governmental decree and thus disregard their justification. In
that sense, it is neutral and the terms "success" and "failure" may be used in
their relative meaning only, that is, in relation to the given goals without
any implied judgment as to their desirability or instrinsic merits. The
questioning of the goals or their divergent interpretations, however, almost
always become an important factor in the implementation process and, as
such, have to be taken into account by implementation analysis.

I would therefore argue that the study of higher education can draw as
much benefit from policy and implementation analysis as the latter can
derive from the study of higher education policies and the way they unfold.
If my assumption is correct, policy analysis also provides a basis for an
answer to the second question. Implementation analysis in general can
probably benefit from the specific case of higher education, in that the latter
pushes, almost to an extreme, the evidence of complexity of policy implementation in a situation with a multitude of actors. All these different
related points should become clearer when specific recent higher education
policies and their implementation are considered.

COMPARATIVE CASE STUDIES

Implementation analysis has not often been applied to higher education
policies, but several recent books and articles about this topic are directly
relevant to it.[9] No less relevant are the numerous works of political scientists
and of organizational theorists or sociologists who do not speak explicitly of
implementation analysis but who deal extensively with various aspects of
"carrying through a policy," that is, with policy implementation.[10]

Implementation analysis was applied specifically to higher education in a
series of case studies conducted by the European Institute of Education and
Social Policy in Paris.[11] Information and findings from these studies consti-

---

[9]For example, Premfors, *Politics of Higher Education in a Comparative Perspective*; Kogan,
Educational Policy-Making; Clark, *Higher Education System*; Levine, *Why Innovation Fails*.

[10]Of the many works that might be listed, reference is made here to just a few of the more
recent ones: Crozier and Friedberg, *L'Acteur et le Système*; Crozier, *On Ne Change Pas la Société
Par Décret*; Wildavsky, *Speaking Truth to Power*.

[11]Case studies published within the framework of this project are, as of October 1982,
Woodley, *Open University of the United Kingdom*; Lamoure, *Instituts Universitaires de Technologie
en France*; Kyvik, *Norwegian Regional Colleges*; Bie, *Creating a New University*; Cerych et al.,
German Gesamthochschule; Kim, *Widened Admission to Higher Education in Sweden*. A volume
comprising summaries of all the case studies and a comparative analysis of their findings will be
published in 1983. It was prepared and the project as a whole was conducted jointly by Paul
Sabatier, University of California, Davis, and myself. Sabatier's extensive knowledge of the
literature on policy implementation and his own research and writings in this area helped me
greatly in my interpretation of the different findings of the project and in my work on the
present paper. He did not, however, have the opportunity to comment on any of its drafts and
is, therefore, in no way responsible for my formulations and conclusions.

tute the main empirical basis of the present paper. I investigated the following specific reforms along with their implementation and often refer to them in the course of my discussion:

1) Creation and development of the University of Tromsø in the far north of Norway. This institution was expected to differ in several respects from existing Norwegian universities: it was supposed to play a direct and important role in the economic and social development of its surrounding region and thereby help redress the imbalances between the south and the north; teaching and research were expected to be more interdisciplinary than in traditional universities; new fields of study not existing in other establishments of Norwegian higher education were to be introduced; the proposed system of university government presupposed participation of groups much less represented in traditional universities (students, nonscientific staff, etc.).

2) Creation and development of a network of regional colleges in Norway. These institutions represented a new type of "short-cycle higher education" with vocational courses as well as those leading to further university studies. Moreover, the colleges were expected to be directly relevant to their respective regions and play an important role in continuing adult education.

3) Creation and development of the University of Umea in the north of Sweden. The main objective of this university was similar to that of Tromsø: to help overcome imbalances between the southern and northern parts of the country. Its main contribution however, was to provide higher education opportunities in an area that had none. Teaching and research at this university were also to pay attention to specific regional needs and conditions, but they were not expected to be radically different from those in existing Swedish universities.

4) The introduction of the 25/5 admission rule in Swedish higher education. This rule implied that individuals twenty-five years or older, with at least five years of occupational experience, should be allowed to enter some of the liberal arts faculties, irrespective of their formal education background. (At a later stage the rule was changed to 25/4 and was applied to the whole system.) Equalization of educational opportunities, bridging the generation gap, and providing new vocational and professional training facilities were among the explicit goals of the scheme.

5) Creation and development of the British Open University. The main goals and features of this institution are well known: admission on a "first come, first served" basis; distance teaching through a combination of correspondence, radio, and television courses; special efforts in curriculum development; respect for established academic standards.

6) Creation and development of the university institutes of technology (*instituts universitaires de technologie*) in France. These institutes, constituting a new type of short-cycle (two years) higher education with vocational orientation, were expected to enroll, within six years of their launching, about a fourth to a third of the entire French student population.

7) Creation and development of the University of Calabria in Cosenza, Italy. This university, like those of Tromsø and Umea in Scandinavia, was expected to play an active role in the economic and social development of its region. Moreover, it was the first Italian university based on a departmental structure, the preferential admission of students of modest social and southern Italian origin, a full-time teaching staff, and a campus arrangement with the majority of students residing on campus.

8) The development of the German *Gesamthochschule* ("comprehensive university"). Originally this concept was envisaged as a model for a new organization of all West German higher education. It aimed at an integration of hitherto separated parts of the system, namely, universities and less prestigious technical colleges; at an equalization of the status of teachers and students in these two sectors; and at curriculum reform emphasizing a close relation between higher education and practical life. Ultimately, only six institutions were established with these formal objectives in two of the eleven German states.

9) The introduction of a "preferential point system" in admissions to universities in Poland. This system aimed at the facilitation of access to Polish higher education for students from workers' and peasants' families, thereby increasing their percentage and representation in total enrollments.

Clearly, the differences among these reforms are considerable: some concern single institutions, others deal with groups of institutions, and still others with the system as a whole either in one of its aspects (e.g., admission) or in a multiplicity of its features. They represent different political, administrative, and historical contexts, and they aim at different policy objectives, from social equalization to regional, economic, and structural goals. But all these differences are precisely of interest. They enable us to look at the implementation process with a more general perspective and thereby to formulate broader, more valid, conclusions than those reached by studying only one country or one policy.

I now consider such conclusions by examining five aspects of higher education policy implementation which resulted from a comparative view of the cases cited above. The discussion of a sixth and more general issue—the problem of change in higher education in the light of implementation analysis—serves as an overall conclusion to my analysis.

The Impact of Goals

Setting aside policies that represent mere legitimation of what exists or of what is expected to happen, most of the recent reforms in European higher education confirm a previously stated point: it is difficult to separate implementation from the process of policy design. Moreover, in many instances, the formulation of objectives has taken place in several stages, with priorities often changing from one stage to the next. For example, although the Swedish 25/5 scheme was initially based on economic considerations, including education as an investment and the demand for qualified manpower, the need to bridge the generation gap later became the prime objective, only to be displaced subsequently by social equalization. Also, the officially stated objectives are frequently ambiguous. Such ambiguity may be deliberate, either because more precise definition would have precluded the agreement of all interested parties (thus lack of precision is the price paid for essential political consensus), or because the legislature preferred to leave the detailed determination of goals to various types of planning or steering committees set up as a first step in implementation.

A single precise goal, however, does not guarantee better implementation. The Polish preferential point system had a clear single aim: to increase the proportion of students from working-class and peasant families in university enrollments. Yet it failed to a large extent.

Then, too, many higher educational reforms incorporated several seemingly conflicting goals. This point is well illustrated by the Norwegian regional colleges set up in 1969, for which two declared aims were regional relevance and the provision of a new type of higher education which would be of shorter duration and more vocationally oriented. Almost simultaneously, other virtually contradictory objectives were also implicitly or explicitly adopted. The regional colleges were supposed to lessen pressure on the universities while providing an education qualifying some students for subsequent university study, and also to respond to national needs, recruiting students and teachers from throughout the country. Unavoidably, the implementation process was strongly influenced by conflicts inherent in this goal structure, as well as by shifts of emphasis among differing and inconsistent aims. Yet conflicting aims were inevitable for the same reason as ambiguity was, in that it would have otherwise been difficult or impossible to reach a consensus on the proposed policy.

Finally, in many instances the implementation of reforms resulted in the achievement of unexpected and unintended goals. The Swedish 25/5 scheme, for instance, did not increase substantially the proportion of regular full-degree students from the lower socioeconomic classes, but it did contribute to increasing the number of students entering universities with a view to taking no more than a single course, thereby imparting to Swedish higher education an extension function of a kind generally associated with British and American universities.

In short, ambiguity and conflict in goals are, in most instances, unavoidable. Thus, also unavoidably, the door is left open to alternative developments in the implementation process, and often it is impossible to speak of a straightforward success or failure of a reform. Of vital importance is the question, "Which goals and whose?" since in view of the multiple objectives generated around every reform, both before and after its formal adoption, what is successful in one respect might be undesirable in another.

Moreover, success and failure obviously depend on expectations. As pointed out by Burton R. Clark, "the higher the expectations, the more likely the judgment of failure."[12] For example, the hopes for the German *Gesamthochschule* were so broad and so high that the outcome was almost bound to be disappointing, even if implementation had been much smoother than it actually was.

The Role of Assumptions and Evaluation

It is surprising how many of the reforms were based on assumptions that simply did not meet any criteria of already existing knowledge. Reforms aiming at social equalization fall into this category. Several of them have merely offered favorable conditions of access to higher education to underprivileged groups, without providing any special support measures. Yet it has been known for many years that merely widening formal access has limited effects and does not, in any event, lead to equality on the output side. Another example is that new types of higher education degrees and new contents of higher education programs do not help graduates obtain employment, for potential employers are not stirred to change their recruitment procedures. Of course, it can almost always be said after the fact that the nonachievement of a particular reform goal is owing to erroneous assumptions and thus to a wrong theory. Clearly, not everything can be foreseen in advance. Constraints emerge which could not have been predicted and individual and group behavior changes, often on nonrational grounds.

In theory, it is always stressed that evaluation should be an integral part of the implementation of reforms. In practice, even when it exists, evaluation is rarely used as a means toward correcting errors, identifying unforeseen constraints, or reformulating implementation strategies or, if necessary, even goals.[13] Evaluation has not been so used even in countries like Sweden, where "evaluation consciousness" is relatively developed. Yet many of the shortcomings and their reasons could have been relatively early and easily identified if the first outcomes of a reform had been analyzed and assessed. The fact that equalization policies primarily benefited the already

---

[12]Clark, "Implementation of Higher Education Reforms in the USA."
[13]See Argyris and Schön, *Organizational Learning*.

relatively privileged groups instead of the main target population, that certain incentives were insufficient, that new behavior emerged after socio-economic conditions had changed, could have been grasped early on and corrective measures possibly taken. The interesting question then becomes: Why was evaluation so little used? Aaron Wildavsky offers a simple answer: "Organizations do not want to rock the boat. . . . resistance to evaluation is part of self-protection. . . . scepticism clashes with dogma in organizations as well as in thought."[14] My analysis of the implementation of many recent reforms in European higher education confirms this interpretation.

Group Support and Resistance

In a sense, we may look at the whole policy implementation process in a perspective that focuses almost exclusively on group actors and on the power they can bring to bear on this process. As put by Burton R. Clark, "Innovations 'fail' because the innovators cannot acquire enough power to protect their new ways. They are allowed to start but unless they attach the interests of various groups to their own, persuading potential opponents at least to be moderate in their opposition, they can be tightly bounded—re-socialized or terminated—as others raise their own level of concern, clarify their own self-interests, and increase the bearing of their own weight."[15] This general finding, which draws on Arthur Levine's analysis of the effort of the New York state system to turn the University of Buffalo into "a Berkeley of the East,"[16] is largely confirmed by the different case studies mentioned above. The implementation is affected not only by groups directly concerned by the policy in question, but also by groups in those parts of the higher education system which this policy does not involve. Their perception of it as a potential advantage or threat to their established positions is often decisive in determining the behavior of those who are directly concerned. The misfortunes of the *Gesamthochschule* have been largely due to such relatively external reactions.

Also significant is the role of certain groups situated completely outside the higher education system and, in particular, that of the employers (or potential employers) of graduates produced by new institutions or different educational patterns. The improved image of the French IUTs, and of certain courses at the University of Tromsø, resulted in part from a favorable attitude on the part of employers.

Of interest are also the "compensatory strategies" adopted by groups that feel threatened by a particular reform if, for one reason or another, it apparently cannot be resisted or blocked, like the Polish preferential point

---

[14]Wildavsky, *Speaking Truth to Power*, pp. 5-6.
[15]Clark, "Implementation of Higher Education Reforms in the USA."
[16]Levine, *Why Innovation Fails*.

system in favor of working-class and peasant children. One of the explanations for the limited increase in the proportion of students from less privileged strata, a few years after the introduction of the scheme, was the special effort made by the children and families of the intelligentsia to overcome the relative disadvantage to which they were exposed. Special courses, private lessons, and similar forms of study became, for many, a means of improving examination marks and thereby compensating for the preferential points awarded to those from working-class and peasant families.

It is trite merely to say that a reform succeeds when there is enough support for it and vice versa. But this truism only poses the question: How should support be mobilized and resistance overcome? Obviously, the answer is, most frequently, by an adequate system of rewards and sanctions. These do not need to be, and often cannot be, financial in nature. Promotion, recognition, and similar rewards might be equally important. It is surprising how often this rather simple principle has been disregarded.

A good example is the goal of interdisciplinary teaching and research pursued by several of the new universities and, in particular, by Tromsø. This goal could almost never be fully implemented because the existing system of academic rewards was based largely on recognition provided by peers in established disciplines, and it so remained. Thus, even those most enthusiastic about an interdisciplinary structure at the outset, in order to safeguard their academic status and their career opportunities, eventually had to moderate their support of the new goal. Conversely, higher education institutions that hoped to develop consultant services for their surrounding regions were in general successful in doing so when such activities generated additional income for the individuals and departments involved.

It has also been noted, in certain instances, that absence of support or even latent opposition does not prevent compliance. Usually this is so when all those concerned believe that the new policy will be implemented anyway, and when they believe that there is a strong political will behind the reform which will make resistance useless. It is for this reason that for a long time there was no open resistance (even by very conservative groups) to the German *Gesamthochschule*. To again use Burton R. Clark's formulation, "potential opponents were persuaded at least to be moderate in their opposition."

In this context the role of leaders or strong personalities committed to the reform should also be mentioned. In general this role, as all implementation literature and common sense or practical experience shows, is crucial.[17] Such individuals participated in most of the reforms concerned with the

---

[17]Eugene Bardach uses the term "fixer," meaning thereby a person who monitors the implementation process, intervenes whenever necessary with authorities and agencies which might block or advance this process, and helps to "iron out" major difficulties (*Implementation Game*).

establishment of new universities, but much less in reforms related to the system as a whole. Usually their role was limited to policy formulation and adoption and to the very early phase of implementation. We might even wonder whether a number of difficulties, distortions, and conflicts that arose later could not have been overcome had real "fixers" been there long enough. Their absence might be explained by a certain climate surrounding European higher education after the early 1970s which did not attract strong personalities.

Environmental Changes

All the reforms mentioned here were adopted in the second half of the 1960s or the early 1970s, during the so-called "golden age of higher education," when new policies were not infrequently fueled by "the spirit of May 1968." However, much of the implementation of the policies took place under considerably different economic, political, and social conditions. The impact of the changed environment was not always detrimental to the achievement of initial goals. Indeed, in some cases, the apparent worsening of a situation has encouraged a policy that, in the years of euphoria, would not have gotten off the ground. For example, the French IUTs gained noticeably in prestige and popularity in the second half of the 1970s when the weakness of the labor market made vocationally oriented higher education more attractive. Similarly, the Swedish 25/5 scheme had the effect of compensating for a decline in traditional enrollments, thereby enabling many university departments to maintain an unchanged course capacity and teaching staff and causing them to look more favorably upon the reform.

Then, too, a lack of financial resources, compared with the larger supply in the 1960s, has not appeared to be a decisive factor in the failure to achieve or implement certain objectives. Similarly, inadequate or totally erroneous forecasts of policy costs have not necessarily inhibited implementation. When, in 1968, the Norwegian parliament decided to create the University of Tromsø, it approved an estimated investment cost for the project of some 200 million Kroner (at constant prices) for the pre-1980 period and, although the real cost has in fact amounted to some 500 million, the enormous overspending has never threatened the university's future.

At the same time, many of the policies I have reviewed were subject to some financial difficulties: the range of courses offered could not be sufficiently enlarged, as in Tromsø; the buildings of a new institution could not be completed according to the agreed schedule, as in Calabria; and the number of classes opened stayed well below the envisaged target, as in the French IUTs.

The most significant effects of a change in the socioeconomic climate seem to have shown up as differences in the priority given to one or another

of several objectives in a given policy. Sometimes this choice was deliberate, but more often it resulted from quasi-spontaneous pressures and led
to stronger emphasis on more traditional goals, as in the German *Gesamthochschule*, where academic recognition and respectability became more
important than curricular innovation. In short, there was no clear direction
in which the worsened socioeconomic environment influenced implementation of higher education reforms. In some instances the impact was
negative; in others it was not; and in still others it facilitated implementation. Even when it was negative, it was not the decisive factor in a failure
of implementation.

Centralized versus Decentralized Control

Can implementation analysis add anything to the vast existing literature on
this subject? Viewing comparatively the numerous higher education reforms adopted in Europe in the past twenty years, we certainly cannot say
that specific reform goals were better achieved in countries with centralized
systems than in those with decentralized ones. But neither can we say the
contrary.

In centralized France, the *instituts universitaires de technologie*, created as a
new type of short-cycle, vocationally oriented higher education in the
middle of the 1960s, got off the ground and achieved several of their original
goals, albeit with smaller enrollments than had been anticipated. But so did
the regional colleges in more decentralized Norway. The University of
Tromsø in Norway seems to be more innovative than the University of
Umea in centralized Sweden; but the technical University of Lulea in
Sweden differs from established patterns as much as Tromsø does. Central
control did not ensure significant progress in the distribution of students by
social origin, either in the Polish preferential point scheme or in the Swedish 25/5. But the British Open University, part of a more decentralized
system, was, in this respect, much the same. Both centralized and decentralized systems were relatively successful in achieving "regional relevance"
objectives, although both have encountered, and have not always overcome, conflicts between these objectives and general national and international norms.

In sum, what counts in implementation processes, and what influences
the relative ease or difficulty of implementation, is not just the centralized
or decentralized nature of a higher education system, but also the nature of
the goals to be implemented along with numerous other factors. A few
other examples are worth mentioning here.

One example is the reforms aimed at amalgamating new types and newly
created institutions with existing ones. Neither in centralized nor in decentralized systems was this goal ever achieved. Thus, the French IUTs were
expected to integrate and to replace the STSs (*sections de techniciens supé-*

rieurs), which were extensions of secondary schools with a strictly vocational orientation but much more specialized than the IUTs. In fact, the STSs grew as rapidly at the IUTs and no amalgamation took place. Almost the same happened in decentralized Norway. The initiators of the regional colleges strongly intended to make them umbrella organizations for all nonuniversity higher education. This objective had to be given up even before the colleges were formally created. Similarly, in Germany, neither the weak control at the federal level nor the much stronger powers of the *Länder* governments allowed the setting up of new institutions (*Gesamthochschulen*) which would integrate existing universities with other higher education establishments.

The *Gesamthochschulen* (GHS) point to another reason that the existence of central control might be unable to push through a particular reform. Even when speaking of centralized systems, we are facing not one but several sources of control and power, not just a ministry of education but also other ministries and authorities that may have different if not conflicting strategies. Thus, in Germany, the key prerequisite of the GHS—an integrated teaching staff—could not be implemented because the status of different categories of teachers as civil servants—their salaries and terms of promotion which were to be unified—was subject to rules established by a special section of the Ministry of the Interior. The policy of this particular ministry remained, for a long time, inconsistent with the GHS policy of the federal and several *Länder* ministries of education.

In brief, centralization of decentralization in itself does not often seem to be a decisive factor in implementation. Linked to other forces, however, it can be of strategic importance in amplifying either favorable circumstances or obstacles. In the case of the German GHS, as long as this reform was backed in the government by a strong political will, at both federal and state levels, all potential and natural opponents of the reform—in particular, the academic community—were ready to yield. As soon as this will disappeared the opponents won the battle. The development of the University of Tromsø in Norway was carried through, in spite of its very high cost and a certain "economic irrationality" in the project, because it corresponded to a strong central political will to establish a better balance between the north and the south of the country.

We may conclude that strong central control facilitates implementation of higher education reforms provided that other conditions are met: the achievement of reform objectives must not depend too heavily upon forces beyond the control of the central authorities; and the political will to pursue the policy must remain strong. But for many objectives of reforms there are forces beyond central control and a political will that is undependable. Then decentralized systems, more attuned to marketlike adjustments, may be equally or more successful. Finally, as put by Burton R. Clark, "the effect of each major form of order upon change will vary over time, facilitating in one period and constraining in another."[18] All forms of control, including the market, are subject to the accumulation of rigidities when they have long dominated a system. Alternative forms are then, for a time, facilitating.

THREE DIMENSIONS OF CHANGE

Implementation analysis can throw light on the central problems of change in higher education. Can change be only gradual? At what level of organization does change occur most easily? What are the conditions under which policies implying radical departures from existing patterns have a chance of being carried through successfully? In what aspects of higher education— for example, admission, curriculum, teaching methods, internal structures, management—is change most difficult? Such questions may be set within a framework of three dimensions of change which I call depth, breadth, and level. The three aspects are different meanings of the term "scope of change."

Depth of change indicates the degree to which a particular new policy goal implies a departure from existing values and rules of higher education. How congruent or incongruent with traditional patterns is this goal? For example, a policy that changes admission criteria by requiring three instead of two A levels, or further knowledge of foreign languages, implies a change of rather limited depth, whereas a policy postulating that the rule "first come, first served" be applied, irrespective of secondary school qualification, is a major one. We might also use the term "moderate" or "gradual" for the first and "radical" for the second of these policies. Breadth of change refers to the number of areas in which a given policy is expected to introduce more or less profound modifications, as in admissions, teachers' qualifications, or internal structures. Narrow breadth means that one or a very limited number of areas are to be directly affected by the new policy (possibly implying a change of great depth), whereas wide breadth means change in several or many areas. Level of change indicates the target of the reform: the system as a whole, a particular sector or segment of institutions, a single institution, or an institutional subunit. Any reform involves a combination of the three dimensions, and all kinds of combinations occur in practice: these might include a reform of great depth, narrow breadth, and affecting one institution, for example, the British Open University; or a reform that scores high in all three dimensions, such as the French 1968 reform; or the German *Gesamthochschule* policy in its original nationwide formulation.

---

[18]Clark, *Higher Education System*, p. 204.

I now deal briefly with empirical evidence about each of the three dimensions and their impact on the chances of implementation. As for depth of change, it is clear that implementing higher education reforms depends largely on the degree of consistency (congruence) or inconsistency of a given reform with rules and values already prevailing in the system. The strong continuous emphasis by the British Open University on following traditional university standards unquestionably facilitated the acceptance of this institution within the national academic community.

Similarly, the Swedish 25/5 scheme, although considered a radical deviation from established rules outside Sweden, was received by Swedish higher education and society at large without significant resistance because it was perceived as a continuation, if not an additional legitimation, of the country's long tradition of adult education. In Norway, too, the regional colleges were in general received very favorably and, in their development, encountered few problems common to other countries in the creation of nonuniversity higher education institutions. The prestige of such institutions in Norway, in contrast with other countries, was always high.

Conversely, the implementation of new policies that did not refer to a traditional base in their respective national contexts, or were even clearly inconsistent with "the rules of the game" in these contexts, was often extremely difficult if not impossible. The typical example here is the French higher education reform of 1968 which aimed, among other things, at making universities more autonomous in a system accustomed to a high degree of centralization and lacking any tradition of local autonomy. Another example is the German *Gesamthochschule* which aimed at integrating what had been, traditionally, quite distinct types of higher education institutions, the university and the technical college (*Fachhochschule*). The reform materialized to only a limited extent. None of this is surprising: an innovation is more easily carried through when it falls on fertile ground, when it is in tune with the system.

But the congruence argument cannot be pushed too far; congruence does not guarantee effective implementation. The Polish preferential point scheme was definitely not a radical innovation and even less a policy inconsistent with the prevailing rules of the Polish educational system which, since 1945, had pursued the goal of widening access to all forms of education for students of working-class background. Yet the scheme failed almost completely. And the specific contents of reforms, seemingly equally congruent, made a difference. As to the *Gesamthochschule*, policymakers proposed two alternatives in bringing under one roof hitherto separated and different types of German higher education. The alternatives were the integration of these different types (curriculum, staff, student body), or simply closer cooperation between them. The first formula was the one adopted, and that in a limited number of cases; the second alternative was not carried through at all, presumably because it was not considered worthwhile.

Another important limitation of the congruence argument arises from the interconnection between depth and breadth of change. It is not true that policies that postulate a radical departure from existing rules cannot be effectively carried through. Using the evidence of the British Open University, we may argue that such radical departures can be implemented provided that they are limited to one or very few areas of the higher education system and that most of the other prevailing traditions and standards are rigorously respected. Such reforms entail a great depth but a narrow breadth of change. The Open University brought a radical change in admissions conditions ("first come, first served" instead of a minimum of two A levels) and in the delivery system (distance teaching instead of daily student-teacher contact). Most of the other key aspects of the university's functioning, however, corresponded to established patterns, including degree standards and teacher qualifications. The Open University could innovate radically in certain fields by maintaining the status quo in others. In contrast, such broad reforms as the German *Gesamthochschule* or the French 1968 law aimed at radical changes in too many areas at once.

If my conclusion is correct, it calls for a revised formulation of the proposition that higher education can change only incrementally. Policies implying far-reaching changes can be successful if they aim at strictly selective parts of the domain of institutions and operational components.

The third dimension, level of change, has now been well specified in the research literature in two books by John H. Van de Graaff and associates[19] and by Burton R. Clark.[20] These two studies distinguish six levels of authority and decision making: (1) the department or the chair-institute combination; (2) the faculty or other subinstitutional aggregates of the units belonging to the first category; (3) the individual institution (university, college); (4) multicampus or regional groupings of institutions (alternatively, one might speak of sets of institutions of a particular type and academic level, such as all community colleges, *grandes écoles*, etc.); (5) local or regional authorities, essentially the main political subdivisions of a federation (states, *Länder*, etc.); and (6) the national government. To simplify and adapt this typology for my purposes, I refer to two levels only: (1) the individual institution as well as sets of institutions either within a particular geographic unit or nationwide, such as institutions of a particular type and orientation; and (2) the national system as a whole (or a major part of it, such as all French universities).

It is commonly assumed that a reform will succeed more easily if it concerns the institutional level rather than the system as a whole. On the

---

[19]Van de Graaff et al., *Academic Power*.
[20]Clark, *Higher Education System*.

same assumption it is said that a radically new pattern of university education can be developed through a single (preferably newly created) institution or through a limited group of establishments, rather than by changing all the existing ones. This theory seems logical, since the higher the level, the larger the number of implementers concerned. In the terminology of implementation analysis, a larger number of participants means an increasing number of "veto points,"[21] places where persons can block or delay implementation.

Much relatively successful reform in Europe and America has been in line with these assumptions. The Open University is certainly an example, as are, to some extent, the University of Tromsø and the regional colleges in Norway, as well as a number of other newly created or extensively reformed institutions on both sides of the Atlantic.

There are also, however, many examples of the reverse trend, such as the new German and British universities created in the 1960s. All of them have more or less (sometimes completely) yielded to the pressure of the global system to become, eventually, universities like any other. In Arthur Levine's terms, they have been "resocialized" or, at best, "enclaved."[22] A closer look at the implementation process clearly shows how this pressure operates. Members of the university, whether old or new, and particularly its academic staff, are subject to the same promotion rules. They must be loyal not only to their institutions but also to their national academic guilds. Students have to be aware of employment prospects, which are largely determined by the requirements and criteria of the national labor market. Such circumstances constitute a powerful force that makes the development of a completely different institution difficult and sometimes almost impossible, even if it is only a single establishment. In certain centralized countries such as France, this problem has occasionally been used as an argument in favor of a systemwide change and against a mere institutional reform.[23]

There is, therefore, no simple relation between the difficulty of change and the level at which it is envisaged, initiated, and implemented. Much depends on the two other dimensions of change, depth and breadth. An institution that is to be different in all or many of its functioning areas might face even more pressing problems than would the entire system in carrying

---

[21]For a further discussion of the notion of "veto points," i.e., points of decision and clearance necessary for completion of a program, see Pressman and Wildavsky, *Implementation.*

[22]Levine, *Why Innovation Fails.*

[23]This flexibility, incidentally, calls for a reformulation of the popular assumption that universities change very slowly because their key protagonists, the professors, are conservative and resist change. Many certainly do, but many do not, or at least they do not resist change per se. If an innovation is adopted only at the level of their institution, they may find themselves in a conflictual situation which they often resolve by yielding to the norms of the system, rather than to the originally subscribed-to, or supported, institutional reform.

through an even more radical reform which, however, is limited to a single area.

The relation among level, depth, and breadth of change may serve as a basis for a typology of the main categories of higher education reforms. In a simplified form, such a typology may be represented by a pair of identical two-by-two matrices: the first for policies implying a relatively limited depth of change, that is, those that are relatively congruent with established rules and traditions; and the second for policies requiring a great depth of change, a radical departure from prevailing patterns or criteria.[24]

TYPOLOGY OF CHANGE

		Policies implying a small depth of change				Policies implying a great depth of change	
		Level of change				Level of change	
		Institution	System			Institution	System
Breadth of change	Narrow	1	2	Breadth of change	Narrow	5	6
	Wide	3	4		Wide	7	8

Each square of the two matrices in the accompanying diagram corresponds to a policy implying change of a particular scope considered in its three dimensions. For example, the development of the Open University would fall in category five; the French 1968 reform, or the German *Gesamthochschule* in its original nationwide conception, in category eight; and the Polish preferential point system, in category two. The numbers are not a score for difficulty in implementing reforms or for chances that most of the policy goals will be achieved. But a few important relationships stand out. Reforms in category eight are extremely difficult and often impossible to implement fully. Almost the same is true of reforms in category seven (an institution wanting to be totally, and in too many respects, different, compared with the rest of the system). Surprisingly, policies in the second category, those with too limited a breadth and depth of change, are not necessarily easy to implement, whereas those in category five, such as the Open University, may often be successful.

The scope of change as measured by the 1-to-8 scale of the matrices in the diagram does not correlate closely with the degree of difficulty or the

---

[24]Ideally, of course, a three-dimensional matrix would be preferable. Moreover, none of the three dimensions is in practice dichotomous and at least three-by-three matrices would better correspond to reality. But that configuration would lead to twenty-seven categories instead of eight, a situation that is obviously too complex for the purpose of this discussion.

changes of successful implementation and can be easily explained: too many other factors besides the scope of change play a role in the implementation process. Several of them have been discussed under the preceding five subheadings. An additional one is the time dimension of the process: the difficulties of implementation of a particular policy vary, as we have seen, from one period to another. What looks like a failure or a relative failure after the first few years may appear as a success some years later (for example, the French IUTs), or vice versa. This, by itself, is another reason that it is almost pointless to speak of the success or the failure of a particular higher education policy. Reforms are usually a mixture of achieved, partly achieved, and unachieved goals, of intended and unintended effects, and of positive and negative results.

In conclusion, I want to stress again two points. In higher education, the difficulties of policy implementation are exacerbated by the natural complexity and "bottom-heaviness" of the system. Second, we do not explain the dynamics of academic change and, in particular, the limited successes of reforms when we turn to such simple answers as "universities are conservative," "academics resist change," "adequate financial resources are the primary condition of success," and "only gradual and slow change of higher education is possible." Rather, complex systems require varied and complex answers. Toward those answers, it helps to cultivate a policy perspective and to explore the interaction of various dimensions of reform and change.

BIBLIOGRAPHY

Argyris, Chris, and Donald A. Schön. *Organizational Learning: A Theory of Action Perspective*. Reading, Mass.: Addison-Wesley, 1978.

Bardach, Eugene. *The Implementation Game*. Cambridge: MIT Press, 1977.

Berman, Paul. "The Study of Macro- and Micro-Implementation." *Public Policy* 26 (Spring 1978):172–179.

Bie, K. *Creating a New University: The Establishment and Development of the University of Tromsø*. Oslo: Institute for Studies in Research and Higher Education, 1981.

Cerych, Ladislav, et al. *The German Gesamthochschule*. Paris: Institute of Education, 1981.

Clark, Burton R. *The Higher Education System: Academic Organization in Cross-National Perspective*. Berkeley, Los Angeles, London: University of California Press, 1983.

————. "Implementation of Higher Education Reforms in the USA: A Comparison with European Experiences." In volume edited by Ladislav Cerych and Paul Sabatier. Forthcoming.

Crozier, Michel. *On Ne Change Pas la Société par Décret*. Paris: Grasset, 1979.

Crozier, Michel, and Erhard Friedberg. *L'Acteur et le Système*. Paris: Seuil, 1977.

Elmore, Richard. "Organizational Models of Social Program Implementation." *Public Policy* 26 (Spring 1978):199–216.

Ingram, H. M., and D. E. Mann, eds. *Why Policies Succeed or Fail*. Beverly Hills, Calif.: Sage, 1980.

Kim, L. *Widened Admission to Higher Education in Sweden: The 25/5 Scheme*. Stockholm: National Board of Universities and Colleges, 1982.

Kogan, Maurice. *Educational Policy-Making*. London: Allen and Unwin, 1975.

Kyvik, S. *The Norwegian Regional Colleges*. Oslo: Institute for Studies in Research and Higher Education, 1981.

Lamoure, J. *Les Instituts Universitaires de Technologie en France*. Paris: Institut d'Education, 1981.

Levine, Arthur. *Why Innovation Fails*. Albany: State University of New York Press, 1980.

Majone, Giandomenico, and Aaron Wildavsky. "Implementation as Evolution." In *Policy Studies Review Annual, 1978*, ed. Howard Freeman. Beverly Hills, Calif.: Sage, 1978.

Mayntz, Renate. "Environmental Policy Conflicts." *Policy Analysis* 2 (Fall 1976):577–588.

Mazmanian, Daniel, and Paul Sabatier. *The Conditions of Effective Implementation*. Lexington, Mass.: D. C. Heath, 1980.

Murphy, Jerome. "Title I of ESEA: The Politics of Implementing Federal Educational Reform." *Harvard Educational Review* 41 (1971):35–63.

Premfors, Rune. *The Politics of Higher Education in a Comparative Perspective: France, Sweden, United Kingdom*. Studies in Politics, 15. Stockholm: University of Stockholm, 1980.

Pressman, Jeffrey, and Aaron Wildavsky. *Implementation*. Berkeley, Los Angeles, London: University of California Press, 1973.

Ripley, R. B., and G. A. Franklin. *Bureaucracy and Policy Implementation*. Georgetown, Ontario: Dorsey Press, 1982.

Rodgers, Harrell, and Charles Bullock. *Coercion to Compliance*. Lexington, Mass.: D. C. Heath, 1976.

Van de Graaff, John H., Burton R. Clark, Dorotea Furth, Dietrich Goldschmidt, and Donald F. Wheeler. *Academic Power: Patterns of Authority in Seven National Systems of Higher Education*. New York: Praeger, 1978.

Van Meter, Donald, and Carl Van Horn. "The Policy Implementation Process." *Administration and Society* 6 (Feb. 1975):445–488.

Wildavsky, Aaron. *Speaking Truth to Power*. Boston: Little, Brown, 1979.

Williams, Walter. *The Implementation Perspective: A Guide for Managing Social Service Delivery Programs*. Berkeley, Los Angeles, London: University of California Press, 1980.

Woodley, A. *The Open University of the United Kingdom*. Paris: Institute of Education, 1981.

9. CONCLUSIONS

Burton R. Clark

If the modern university is a powerhouse of knowledge, then a developed national system of higher education is a center of intellectual power many times over, containing dozens, hundreds, and sometimes even thousands of institutions, large and small, comprehensive and specialized, which are centers of knowledge creation, revision, and dissemination. What phenomenal social institutions these aggregations have become! Developing at an accelerating pace during the twentieth century from external need and internal impulse, these systems become major trading centers of the intellectual and innovative life of society. All the clichés of "the learning society" and "the knowledge society" contain the truth that knowledge is a crucial resource for nations as well as for individuals and organizations, moving the national structures for advanced learning to the front of the stage even as their characteristics become more varied, difficult to perceive, and resistant to direct manipulation. Economic recessions may depress the higher education system; smaller age-groups may reduce enrollment; political regimes may reduce budgets and even send in the troops. But to stay very long on the downslope of reduction or repression becomes dysfunctional for the state and the society, since the advancing division of labor depends considerably upon a more variegated and open system of higher education. The need for the products of the intellect, ideas and the fruits of research, steadily deepens.

With so much education, training, and research needed in modern society, the requisite work even spills over in large amounts to industry, the military, and other institutions. In the other sectors, individuals and whole enterprises gain advantage by enhancing and controlling knowledge; for example, the modern military establishment becomes a large school as recruits are instructed in hundreds of technical specialties and officers make their way up the hierarchy of command by attending seminars and instructional programs within the military and at universities. The future will see more postsecondary educational work develop within industry, within government, within the military establishment, and within still other sectors. But the need for advanced training is so demanding that there is more than enough work to go around. There seems little doubt that the main-line institutions, long chartered to be the core location for advanced study, will go on having the central role, even one deepened and extended.

The eight approaches set forth in this volume help us grapple with this understudied and easily misunderstood realm. Offering a particular vista, each uncovers ideas and produces facts that otherwise might pass us by. In the introduction I have taken note of the emphases adopted by each, and now that the perspectives have been spelled out and put to work, side by side, their particular utility has become more evident. This final chapter concludes on a convergent rather than a divergent theme, noting how these approaches can lead into larger frameworks that link rather than fragment. The first is the political economy of higher education, a larger approach designed particularly to link the political and the economic, with some grasp also of the organizational. The second framework is "institution and culture," which links structural components of higher education with symbolic aspects. Structure and culture are so closely related in reality that we should not allow our specialized approaches to long tear them apart. A third large topic, one located on a different logical plane from the first two, is the relation in modern society between "the Republic of Science" and the higher education sector. Here I enlarge upon the chapter by Simon Schwartzman, linking it more fully with the other materials and pointing to a nigh universal social problem that requires in itself a major line of inquiry.

Finally, in a concluding section I consider the relevance of these eight approaches to the thought and deliberations of practitioners. The implications vary widely in kind, but they are not of a direct "engineering" character. Even at its best, social science is an imprecise affair. In all its many branches, the existing bodies of ideas and techniques do not readily flow from "research" to "development," providing answers to specific problems faced in practice. But there is a certain enlightenment that can obtain when the perspectives of different disciplines, appropriately interpreted and simplified, are absorbed into the holistic thinking of those who govern. When the different visions of the disciplines are aimed toward action, they become ways of circling a phenomenon, to get a better fix on it, and to slice into a broad problem in search of its core and its linked components. In highly abbreviated form I spell out as clearly as possible the broad roads of analytical insight which are traveled by the specialties reported in this volume. These "ways of looking" can contribute importantly to the capacity of practicing professors, administrators, and other interested groups, inside and outside the system, to understand better the nature of what they are doing: where higher education has come from, what it is now about, where it is going, and how it will change.

POLITICS AND MARKETS

We may project a dimension that extends from tight to loose linkage in the parts of a social system.[1] The tight end is a unitary context in which all units are parts of an inclusive, integrated formal structure and have common goals. The next step down the continuum is a federative context in which the units primarily have some disparate goals but possess formal linkage for purposes they share. Farther along the line is a coalitional setting in which disparate intentions are so paramount that there is only informal or quasi-formal collaboration among the parts. At the loose end of the continuum appears the situation in which there are no inclusive goals and decisions are made independently by autonomous segments. This last context may still be thought of as a system, one whose outcomes stem from an aggregate of interactions. There are resultants—"social choices"—rather than planned or guided solutions.

National systems of higher education range along this continuum. Those in Communist-bloc nations tend toward the tight end. Those in the democratic nations of western Europe range farther down, beginning with such relatively integrated systems as those of Sweden and France and then moving on to less nationalized systems like those in the Federal Republic of Germany, with its federal structure, and the United Kingdom, with its long tradition of institutional self-control in such crucial matters as selecting students and hiring faculty. Farther down the continuum come the systems that have important private sectors in which many institutions independently pursue their own self-interests, as in Japan and Brazil, ending with the American system in which public as well as private institutions strive competitively to enhance status, position, and power.

A powerful body of thought is now developing between political science and economics which essentially confronts this dimension. Seen as an antithesis of the two ends, it becomes the choice between "politics" and "markets."[2] At the one extreme, the coordering of many parts is accomplished by state machinery, with the parts then dependent on "authority." At the other extreme, coordering is effected by market transactions, with subunits then dependent on "exchange." Exchange is seen as a way of controlling behavior and of organizing cooperation, without benefit of authority. The continuum is one of decreasing state-system inclusiveness and of increasing market interaction.

Developed at the societal level, the powerful metaphors of modern political economy may be applied to societal sectors, including the higher education system and its parts. At the broadest level, we can still speak globally of the political economy of whole nations as primarily driven by

---

[1]Based largely on Warren, "Interorganizational Field as a Focus for Investigation."
[2]Lindblom, *Politics and Markets.*

politics or by markets. But within each society, the major sectors need not, and typically will not, have the same amount of dependence on authority or exchange. The sectors vary considerably in their tasks and organization of work, with the overall type of coordination affected accordingly. For example, the command structure of higher education does not replicate that of the military establishment, but rather differs from it under virtually any major type of political regime and extensively so in the more democratic nations.

Political economists have also sought ways to put dynamics into this typology of state-market antithesis. One central idea developed in the recent literature speaks of "failure" of one form causing people to turn to the other; "state failure" causes a turn to the market, "market failure" produces movement toward state authority. We can also think of deficiencies or "lacks" rather than of outright failure, in one form or the other, leaving unmet needs that cause people to look for other answers. Such ideas may readily be put to work in the study of higher education, as in the major study by Daniel C. Levy on public and private sectors in Latin American systems of higher education, where unsatisfactory performance by public universities in many countries has produced a swing toward private universities and colleges.[3] Enlarging on the idea of failure beyond that of the state and the market, we may think of "form failure," the failure of institutional structures more generally, as a source of change.

A second idea developed in political economy in recent years locates disappointment as the social psychological mechanism behind swings from emphasis on the state or the market.[4] Societies oscillate between intense interest in public issues and almost total concentration on private goals because individuals and groups become disappointed as they fail to fulfill their expectations through state authority, and then, in turn, through privately sponsored programs. The state, the market, and institutional forms generally have a potential for disappointment in the gap between what we expect of them and what they seem able to produce.

Failure and disappointment are useful ideas for exploring change in the political economy of higher education, not only in shifting preferences for state control and markets but also in shifts along such dimensions as centralized and decentralized administration. The relatively centralized systems among Western democracies, like those found in Sweden, France, and Italy, have exhibited a strong interest in decentralization since the mid-1970s. In countries where state authority has clearly been dominant various groups have been disappointed in what has been achieved and have swung toward the idea of shifting power to initiate and act away from the chambers and offices of the national capital to provinces, cities, and local

---

[3]Levy, *The State and Higher Education in Latin America.*
[4]Hirschman, *Shifting Involvements.*

institutions. The "limits" of centralization are partly set by disappointment in the performance of central control, including the perception of inherent weaknesses which swings motivation toward arrangements that would permit diverse regional and local initiatives, thereby providing a somewhat more marketlike context. In contrast, relatively decentralized systems like those in the Federal Republic of Germany, Great Britain, and the United States have moved in recent decades toward stronger central direction, as numerous groups within and outside the system seek national action to compensate for perceived deficiencies of the more disjointed approach. Various groups in these countries have been unhappy about inequalities, duplications, underfinancing, and other perceived shortfalls against expectations of system performance, with disappointment turning them toward centrally controlled actions as possible remedies. In decentralized systems the search for improvement concentrates attention on the deficiencies of institutional aggrandizement, uncontrolled competition, and lack of articulated and perceivable order. Some shifting toward the state-authority pole of the original continuum is then the outcome.

Disappointment thus becomes a major problem for state-run systems of higher education, market-driven ones, and all combinations thereof. We expect more of higher education now than in the past: that it will be more of an instrument of social justice; that it will function competently in general education, liberal education, an ever larger number of fields of professional training, basic and applied research in more disciplines and subspecialties—all for a more heterogeneous input of students and more varied connections to job markets; that it will promote choice, liberty, individuality, and variety; that it will link with a wide set of state demands, from broad cultural relevance in inculcating common values that help integrate the nation to direct accountability and measurable effectiveness. As we expect more, we also heighten the potential for disappointment. Many of the values and interests conflict with one another in their implementation. They are internally pluralistic and contradictory: equality becomes a vast set of equalities; liberty a wide assortment of liberties. Hence swings in attention among promised large solutions are likely. Deficiencies grow as expectations enlarge. In contrast, moderate many-sided expectations reduce the swings of the pendulum which are produced by disappointment.

The political-economy mode of thinking becomes even more interesting and promising in its application to the higher education sector as we move from such contrasting ideal types as politics and markets, and such simplifying mechanisms as disappointment and failure, to mixed characterizations that come closer to the complexities of reality. Economists and political scientists who study higher education, as in this volume, constantly point to the interfusing and blurring of state authority and market exchange. All markets are state-framed, in one way or another. State officials even knowingly turn their backs on state authority and freely enhance certain markets, as when financial aid is given directly to students who then purchase their education at various institutions. In turn, all state-dominated systems contain some activity in consumer, labor, institutional, and other markets. And student enrollment remains the single most important criterion for state allocations around the world, one that is open to manipulation by departments and universities and is shaped by student preferences for fields of study and types of institutions, with "the state" thereby steered by academic personnel and consumers. There is a vast empirical world to be explored comparatively to find characteristic types of mixed systems and the specific mechanisms that allocate resources and other activities.

An additional way to bring high talk about politics and markets closer to reality is to concentrate on the machinery of state action and find whose hands are on it. The dominant groups need not be politicians or bureaucrats as we ordinarily understand them, or that vague entity called the ruling class about which many sociologists and political scientists like to speculate. When we probe the interest-group structures in this particular sector, three specific patterns are apparent. One is a corporatist relationship in which supposedly outside organized groups, particularly the organized arms of big business and big labor, gain formal rights inside the system to influence governmental and university decisions. There is an intimate, continuing relationship, as in Sweden: "Several hundreds of representatives of interest organizations participate in formal decision-making in higher education, from the board of management of the National Board of Universities and Colleges down to councils of admission in local institutions. . . . Simply put, the big interests of capital and labour have stepped in."[5] Will this form of influence spread in the Swedish system? Does it appear elsewhere? And does it shade down in degree to the informal but traditionalized expectations that certain groups should occupy given seats on controlling boards? Does it mean in the United States, for example, that there should be a "Catholic seat" or a "consumer seat" on a board of trustees? Creeping corporatism is a phenomenon readily overlooked when analysts travel only the high road in macropolitical economy.

A second pattern that is now equally clear is set forth in the essay on the organizational pespective (chap. 4, above): the system may be guilded in the sense that important seats of power within the central state machinery as well as within the local university are captured by inside professionals, that is, senior professors. The guild may co-opt the government, rather than vice versa. The phenomenon has been particularly widespread in the operation of national science agencies. It is indexed by the strength of peer review on the part of experts brought in from the field, as compared with

---

[5]Premfors and Östergren, *Systems of Higher Education*, p. 90. A general treatment of modern corporatism may be found in Olsen, "Integrated Organizational Participation in Government."

bureaucratic judgment and political dictate. It has characterized the working of the British University Grants Committee from its origin in 1920 to the late 1960s and early 1970s, the so-called Golden Age of the UGC. It has been typical in the many countries, such as Italy, in which advisory bodies staffed by professors, called by such names as "the superior council of public education," have acquired significant powers of initiation, approval, and veto. The inside professional constituency is then dressed in the clothes of government, even vested by law as a dominating interest.

Third, bureaucratic officials are themselves interest groups struggling against one another within the broad framework of state authority. "The state" is increasingly a diverse plurality of officials and offices whose interdependence requires mutual adjustment. Cadres of officials develop prerogatives in their own specific bureaus, within the major ministries and departments, and then must fit themselves into larger administrative domains by respecting one another's monopolies, or competing for jurisdiction and funding, or some of each. Bureau isolation and competition have been widely noted in central educational agencies in both developing and developed societies: in Mexico and Thailand as well as in Australia, Great Britain, France, and Sweden.[6] Thus higher education is subject to what we may call power markets, markets composed of governmental groups and enterprises struggling against one another within the broad frameworks of state authority.

It is increasingly necessary that we interweave the study of state authority with the study of economic forms and processes, in the higher education sector as well as in other sectors and in the general society. For this effort, newly sharpened tools are at hand. Both as approach and as empirical terrain, political economy offers considerable promise for future insight into the complex conditions of modern higher education. But its value will depend upon a recognition of the special tasks of the system and the many uncommon features that turn this sector into a unique part of society.

STRUCTURES AND CULTURES

There is some truth, but only a little, in the twin stereotypes that define sociology as the study of social organization and anthropology as the study of culture. Many sociologists analyze values, attitudes, norms, beliefs, ideologies—in short, the more symbolic side of social action. Many anthropologists study specific social structures, such as the clan, the factory, and the school, emphasizing the organizational side. The announced subject matters of these two fields are closely intertwined in social reality, to the

---

[6]See the summary account, with detail references, in Clark, *Higher Education System*, pp. 174–177.

point where each field adopts definitions that incorporate much of the supposed domain of the other. Thus, "culture" can virtually subsume "social organization," and vice versa.

The convergences of these two disciplinary perspectives are reflected in this volume. Chapter 4, which most directly pursues organizational components, also portrays knowledge, an ideational material, as the common substance of higher education systems. It emphasizes belief as one of the three basic elements of such systems, closely intertwined with structures of work and authority. Chapter 5, on the status of groups within the system, weaves back and forth between structures and values in order to explain the role of status hierarchies in the composition and performance of various national systems of higher education. Status arrangements become traditionalized in the values and norms of groups inside and outside the system, as well as institutionalized in patterns of resource allocation, task assignment, and power.

In turn, chapter 6, which highlights disciplinary cultures, also points to the "tribes" of academe, pursues the differentiation of these tribes internally and one from the other, and seeks to study intellectual "arenas." In his own "cultural" research, Tony Becher pursues such structural characteristics as the boundaries of disciplines and the degree of their internal unity. Chapter 7, on the interaction of systems of science with systems of higher education, links the traditional emphasis of sociologists of science on norms and values with a much needed emphasis on the building of institutions for the support of science inside and outside higher education. Simon Schwartzman brings broad structures back in, seeking to discover how they determine the fate of science as a set of ideas as well as a bundle of activities.

In short, to understand the social structure of higher education we must understand its culture. To understand its culture we must understand its structure. The blend is an institution-and-culture approach.

This combination of sociological, anthropological, and organizational concerns becomes a broad analytical stance that corrects some deficiencies of political economy. In stressing coordination and control achieved either by the command structure of the state or by the economic exchanges that follow from the pursuit of autonomous self-interest, "politics and markets" leaves out or radically subordinates other forms and norms of collective action. But, separate from state decisions and economic exchanges, a host of other forms are handed down over time, together with beliefs that define those patterns as the right way, even the only way, of proceeding. In a system in which many operating groups are authoritative, these other sources of coordination and control loom large. Science is one huge set of such procedures and shared assumptions, a veritable world of its own which is not captured well when one focuses on the command structure of the state or the play of markets. In addition, robust doctrines like freedom of research and freedom of teaching, reaching across the many roles of different types of professors, create and maintain powerful images of how academics should operate and especially how they should be treated by others. Notably, the guild forms of authority stressed in chapter 4 affect coordination from the bottom to the top of academic systems, but they are a part neither of state command nor of economic exchange. More than state officials or remote eyes of the market, academics witness and leverage one another's behavior as well as that of students. Their allocation of prestige becomes a steering mechanism.

As sociologists, anthropologists, organizational theorists, and others probe the institutions and cultures of higher education, they widen the framework within which we weigh causes and consequences. Because of its considerable analytical strength and promise, political economy may readily preempt attention. A necessary corrective, from the beginning of its use in analysis of higher education, is awareness of the other perspectives in social science which alert us to other basic structures and values, thereby offering supplementary and alternative explanations. If we focus on the polity and the market alone, we leave out "society"—the rest of social organization. As we add other perspectives, we bring "society" back in.

In this regard, comparative study of major traditions in higher education will be highly revealing. We learn much about the basic nature of higher education in any one country by comparing its social organization with that of another, for example, the United States with France, Japan with Britain. We shall also learn much about fundamental properties as we move to comparisons at an even broader level, such as the West and Islam. For example, what was it about Islamic social structure and culture, within as well as outside its higher learning, which so seriously retarded the development of higher education after the twelfth century, in contrast with the rise and success of universities in the West? Colleges had developed in Islam by the middle of the eleventh century, earlier than in the West.[7] But individual institutions and the higher education systems as a whole apparently were organized around specific forms and associated cultures that became static. Notably, they concentrated exclusively on legal and religious studies, becoming in effect colleges of religious law. They did not themselves develop corporate legal personalities, even though often endowed, but remained closely bounded by larger religious structures and tenets. The "idea of the university," as a separate body of masters or fellows, did not take root. The individual teacher or student remained closely constrained, and the college as a whole was restrained from moving into new areas of inquiry and professional practice. In contrast, universities in the West developed as a more independent form, able to maneuver for free space between church and state. The guild way of organizing academic work stressed autonomous control by small groups of masters over such distinc-

[7]Makdisi, *Rise of Colleges.*

tive territories as law, medicine, and theology. Especially after the Renaissance, such groups could become highly dynamic, stressing rational inquiry rather than traditional thought, incorporating new fields as well as altering old ones, and, in particular, limiting religious studies. The university became a form capable of considerable expansion and absorption, one that, beginning in the nineteenth century, could become the central place for the enormous specialization of scientific fields; and then, in the twentieth century, it became virtually a holding company comprising a host of schools and colleges that prepared professionals and semiprofessionals in an ever larger number of occupational specialties and offered instruction in many new subjects in the humanities, the social sciences, and the natural sciences.

In all such instructive cross-national and cross-cultural comparisons, institutional and cultural perspectives highlight features that are ignored or subordinated in political economy. The power of explanation is thereby increased.

SCIENCE AND HIGHER EDUCATION

If we want to increase the power of our explanations of how higher education works, we also have to grasp more fully the nature and organization of modern science. Scientific thought and activity loom ever larger in modern life. There is a huge complex of institutions, groups, and individuals which may appropriately be referred to as "the scientific estate."[8] This estate has a strong bent toward autonomy; for many of its members, it is an engrossing and encompassing community,[9] literally a world of its own. Its normative system can be quite compelling, amounting to a world view that rivals religion. Yet the scientific complex must of course relate to other institutions of society, especially to government as the principal source of funds and the center of public supervision. And it must have specific locales in which to do its work and house its members. In most nations, the most important locations are in the higher education system. In countries where this is not so, professors still play a key role in the scientific estate, occupying positions in outside research councils and academies as well as training scientific personnel. In short, higher education is always implicated, usually as the central arena.

How science and higher education interrelate then becomes a critical matter. The concept of matrix organization, introduced in chapter 4, on organizational analysis, highlights a basic aspect of their most common mode of intersection. The scientific disciplines are the most dynamic part of

---

[8]Price, *Scientific Estate.*
[9]Hagstrom, *Scientific Community.*

the disciplinary imperative. Each scientific field becomes a source of membership, commitment, prestige, and authority which slashes across institutions within the system and, finally, across national systems, powerfully conditioning higher education. However, the institutional imperative, in turn, cuts across the disciplines: each institution turning "their" members into "its" members, assigning them duties, offering them certain rewards and sanctions, allocating prestige, and exercising authority. Field by field and as a whole, science is thereby conditioned by higher education. Yet as noted in the introduction and highlighted by Simon Schwartzman in chapter 7, the conditioning connections between science and higher education have received relatively little attention. Two research literatures have constructed their own worlds, with the more powerful one, the sociology of science, developing a tunnel vision that has largely ignored the specific institutional locations in which scientists do their work. In the comparison of national systems, the studies of Joseph Ben-David stand virtually alone in focusing on how the structures of higher education shape scientific activity and progress.[10]

The general relation between science and higher education varies significantly across societies. The major dichotomy is between "science in" and "science out," that is, centered in higher education or outside the system. The leading system of the nineteenth century, the German, and the leading system of the twentieth, the American, have centered science in the system, following the belief that teaching and research should be closely coupled. Hallowed doctrines and practices have been at work here, especially in the elite sectors of these systems. In both countries, however, science increasingly locates also outside the system, particularly in the Federal Republic of Germany, where the numerous institutes funded under the Max Planck umbrella have become significant points of scientific concentration. Such centers amount to an effort to locate "best science" away from the demands for a uniform distribution of resources which are voiced in the higher education system. But the German and American systems remain significant models of "science in." In contrast, France institutionalized an arrangement in the nineteenth century, one continuing into the present period, in which science was mainly developed in a separate set of research academies. The dominant Communist model, that of the Soviet Union, goes even further in promoting "science out." Essentially, higher education does the teaching, research academies do the research.

Then, too, in those systems where "the Republic of Science" locates largely within the universities, its strength, relative to other modes of

---

[10]Ben-David and Zloczower, "Universities and Academic Systems"; Ben-David, *Scientist's Role in Society*; Ben-David, *Centers of Learning*, chap. 5, "Research and Training for Research." For an important analysis of science and education in France, Germany, and the United States, by a political scientist, see Gilpin, *France in the Age of the Scientific State*, esp. chap. 5, "The American Model of a Scientific State."

thought and fields of study, may vary considerably. The systems may be "science dominant," as in Germany, or "science subordinate," as in Italy, where a strong humanistic tradition, given renewed vigor in the half century between 1900 and 1950 by the towering influence of Benedetto Croce, tended to dominate the university system as well as Italian literary and philosophical life more generally.

Of growing importance in the intersecting of science and higher education is variation of the relationship across major subsectors within higher education systems, as both science and higher education become larger and more complicated sets of activities. The differentiation of sectors nearly always entails different emphases on science and research, with the crucial break usually occurring between "the university sector" and the "nonuniversity sector" or sectors. The university is seen as the proper place for science and the close coupling of research and teaching, even for the organization of teaching around the specific research activities of the professor. In contrast, the teachers college, the technical college, and the college of "further education" are seldom viewed as locales for scientific work. Their faculties teach what has been created and codified elsewhere, supplemented perhaps with a little "applied research" as time permits, on top of a heavy teaching load.

Where the differentiation of sectors is extreme, as in the United States, the variation in commitment to science becomes extreme. The leading fifty or so universities, increasingly known as "research universities," are large concentrations of research funds and scientific personnel. In contrast, the thousand or more community colleges have virtually no resources for scientific work. Leading liberal arts colleges provide conditions for some research and offer rewards for publication, but hundreds of average colleges within this sector give almost no support to research. State colleges vary between those that converge upon the ways of the universities—the clearest example of "academic drift" in the American system—and those that become fixed in character around conditions that do not support research.

Big science is a high-cost item. If spread throughout a system of higher education, it makes all parts of the system expensive, a condition that then in turn strengthens the hands of those who argue against expansion and wider access. Best science also requires top talent, usually in concentrated form, and hence is hard to scatter across a system. Thus, cost and talent encourage the location of science in certain parts of the system, with all that then follows by way of privilege and differential funding.[11] Indeed, power itself is thereby distributed in two basic ways: the institutions and personnel of the scientific sectors become powerful through the resources and reputations thereby gained; and some students gain access to the power of

---

[11]On the general need for "elite" components within "mass" universities and colleges, and modern systems in the large, see Trow, "Elite Higher Education"; Kerr, "Higher Education."

scientific knowledge while others do not. It is not hard to see why egalitarians become uncomfortable with science. Even when open and pluralistic in its internal organization, the Republic of Science pushes higher education toward a differentiation of institutions and sectors, which then will be ranked in a hierarchy of task, reward, and status. If the system does not differentiate extensively, then cost containment becomes size containment, sharply limiting access.

Hence, broad structural features of the higher education system, especially sector differentiation and institutional hierarchy, become fateful matters in the progress of science. The nature of governmental control of the system becomes crucial, together with the amount of competition permitted among institutions in the labor market of scientific talent. And those concerned about the fate of scientific programs and ideals will increasingly have to understand the support and resistance offered science by such seemingly mundane structures within higher education as chairs, departments, and graduate schools.

IMPLICATIONS FOR POLICY AND ADMINISTRATION

If these eight ways of thinking about higher education are beamed toward "policy" and "administration," is there any discernible relevance and enlightenment? One can recommend an unmediated immersion by individual policymakers and administrators in the broad subjects of the earlier chapters, a personal search for ideas and frameworks useful in grappling with practical problems. But life is short, and time this month much shorter, and compelling duties usually preclude such reading. We might also hope to have scholars closely associated with policymakers, connecting "truth" to "power" as they whisper advice in the ear of the prince. But this type of involvement also infrequently obtains. The movement of perspectives, ideas, and insights normally contains many steps, with much slippage and reinterpretation along the way. One reason for the writing of this volume was to reduce eight perspectives to chapter-length essays, each one clarifying an approach and showing its advantages. The volume in itself offers a definite economy of effort for those with the least time for reading, because they have the most to do administratively, and for those furthest from scholarship, because they are the closest to action.

Our final effort in integrating these eight approaches is to give a clear picture of their potential relevance to those who have practical concerns. Out of each perspective a central idea is extracted and presented as a guide to thought. Necessarily broad in formulation, and a far cry from the direct engineering of solutions, each of these ideas conveys a view of the higher education system which surely is not new to many practitioners but, just as surely, is new to others. And even for the most thoughtful policymakers and administrators, some of the expressed ideas may clarify what has been intuitively known. Together, the eight ideas become a battery of explicit thoughts that may help firm judgment amid the swirling disarray of everyday problems and pressures. If they serve only to point to crucial long-run features of the higher education system, for those whose obligations steadily pull attention to short-run decisions, they will be touchstones for informed judgment.

The eight large "truths" mined from the eight perspectives may be simply summarized:

1) The higher education system is rife with political action and hence may fruitfully be viewed as a political system. But the political processes of highest importance differ qualitatively at different levels. "Politics" at the bottom is different from "politics" at the top. Hence it is no longer useful to argue about whether the system as a whole is primarily a collegium or a bureaucracy, an open system or a closed system, and so on. At any one time, it may be professional politics at the operating level, bureaucratic politics at higher administrative levels, and corporatist politics, for example, at the level of state action. In any event, bona fide "interests," inside and outside the formal boundaries of the system, are always multiple, and they increase as the system becomes more complex. Hence, political processes are endemic and steadily multiple in number and type. The quality of politics in the system, conditioned by tasks and beliefs, is then a necessary object of observation and thoughtful evaluation by scholars and administrators alike.

2) Mechanisms of finance are central stabilizers of the higher education system and crucial levers of reform and change. They steer decentralized and loosely coupled parts that are otherwise difficult to touch. They make real the expression of state power, defining it broadly as guiding frameworks, when lump sums are disbursed, or narrowly as direct special controls, when categorical budgeting dominates. They become institutionalized particularly around enrollment, funding from higher to lower levels largely on the basis of number of students enrolled or anticipated. Hence, they can be manipulated by all parties concerned, not just by top formal coordinators, by attracting or repelling students or altering the ways in which they are counted. Thus, all chairs, departments, faculties, colleges, and universities, as entities, engage in "economic behavior," seeking to increase their share of resources. Among all the features discussed in this volume, the more economic ones come closest to the day-to-day problems of administrators and offer opportunities for some manipulation. There are good reasons why administrators see economists as the most relevant social scientists, even in settings where their predictions are

more wrong than right. At least they offer predictions, and in concrete numerical terms.

3) The individual disciplines and professional fields of study are authoritative segments in the social organization of any modern system of higher education. These "thought groups" fragment individual enterprises. They also fragment the academic profession, making it a conglomerate unlike other professions. Hence, no simple model of professional organization, any more than a bureaucratic model, points to the nature of the thought groups. Turning the understructure of the university and the system into a unique operating level, one characterized by fragmented professionalism and even guildlike arrangements, the disciplinary imperative demands that administrators be sensitive to the nuances of differences among subjects and their supporting groups. It also requires rejection of most of what a student learns about "management" while formally studying this art. More discriminating models of university organization, descriptive and normative, will develop as scholars and practitioners take seriously the imposing place of disciplinary organization among the unique features of the higher education system.

4) Prestige is a special coin of exchange in higher education, for individuals, groups, enterprises, and even whole national systems. The ambition and the work that go into winning a Nobel prize, or a less-known award in a scholarly field, are simply the extreme example of a more general phenomenon in which effort is tied to recognition more than to profit. Particularly in the more competitive sectors and systems, personnel exert and overexert themselves to increase their own status. Institutions do likewise, again especially in the more competitive settings, with higher status seen as the bridge to larger resources as well as a better life. Hence, institutional hierarchies become major mechanisms of allocation and coordination. Where they are somewhat open to status climbing by upwardly mobile institutions, or to central manipulation, they may be powerful mechanisms for change. If they are closed and fixed, they are grounds for resentment and despair. Key to the positive efforts of open status hierarchies is their encouragement of hope, a panoply of motivations in individuals, departments, and universities that things will be better if more strenuous efforts are deployed. Hence, sophisticated policy-makers and administrators are as sensitive to the meaning and use of prestige and hope as they are to the incentives of money and other material rewards. Prestige and hope are instrumental tools, means to important ends.

5) Beyond prestige, the symbolic side of organization has special power in a sector of society which is organized around bundles of knowledge, staffed by "men of ideas," and intensely professionalized. Only the

church among the major sectors of society is seemingly so laced with cultural imperatives. Each discipline or professional area of study becomes a subculture with self-elaborating and autonomy-seeking tendencies. The academic profession overall is permeated with such stirring ideologies as "freedom of research" and "freedom of teaching." Each institution develops symbolic representations of itself, in self-image and public image, which affect resources. Especially in competitive settings, these collective representatives are steadily cultivated, turned into powerful legends or sagas. Even in noncompetitive contexts, universities and colleges are readily transformed into romanticized objects of love and affection, more quickly converted into "communities" than are organizations in business and public administration. Thus, a sophisticated executive in this sector of society is one who understands the symbolic imperatives, especially the separate culture-building tendencies of disciplines and enterprises.

6) Science is increasingly a special world, a dynamic republic of special interests seeking favorable conditions outside as well as within higher education. The strain toward autonomy is pressing; the scientific sector develops hegemony that is not coterminous, or identical in interest, with that of higher education. The latter system has more to do, spreading its attention to activities that are nonscientific or only weakly scientific in nature. But science either has to be well accommodated within, spread throughout or centered in well-supported segments, or it will flow toward outside locales. If badly accommodated, research becomes divorced from teaching and the scientific norms of universalism are weakened within the academic profession and individual universities and colleges. Notably, higher education then loses the prestige and legitimacy conferred by modern science. Hence the care and feeding of science are enduring responsibilities for statesmen in all sectors of higher education as they concern themselves with the long-run status and effectiveness of the system.

7) Policy implementation is considerably more difficult than policy formation. Almost anyone can quickly formulate a policy—uninformed voters and preoccupied legislators do it all the time—but it takes sustained efforts and special competencies to implement effectively most policies that are enacted. The difficulties increase in systems where authority is diffused, purposes are ambiguous and contradictory, and the operating structure steadily grows more complicated. Higher education scores high on all such characteristics. The veto points are notably numerous; a host of interest groups can stand in the way. Hence, attenuation of policy is normal, and slowness in implementation is natural. And much incremental adjustment is the order of the day, pulling expectations of global change down to more modest level. To do otherwise is to multiply the unintended and undesired

consequences of policy and to excite major boomerang effects. Intelligent policy formation and implementation become step-by-step experimentation, zigging and zagging through unclear alternatives, pulling back from wrong starts, and finally blessing the small beginnings that prove they are worth larger application.

8) There is always history. All important phenomena within the higher education system are shaped by their developmental flow. Structures and processes laid down at any time tend to perpetuate themselves. In a sector with much diffusion of authority and a rich symbolic life, forms become deeply institutionalized in various parts of the system. They rarely need to prove comparative efficiency and effectiveness, for effective measures cannot be devised when significant outcomes are multiple, long-run, ambiguous, and intangible. The basic forms develop protected niches, even more under state authority than under market interaction, and become ends in themselves. Hence they project themselves powerfully into the future. They also shape what comes after them, since they occupy the domain of work and embody the common understanding of what higher education is and how it should proceed. A finely honed sense of historical development is extremely useful for those who practice, in politics and administration, the art of the possible.

At the same time, an existing set of structures and processes will develop deficiencies that help generate an interest in reform. The odds on disappointment particularly increase as we ask a system to do much more than previously in effecting contrary values and interests. The true believers in any one value are particularly prone to such disappointment and will seek changes that promise more of what they want. Forces for change are always operative in modern systems, in tension with the forces of stability and perpetuation.

* * * *

Our eight examinations of higher education offer no solutions to contemporary problems, but in providing perspectives they help make simple solutions and deep despair both seem less compelling. In common, they also make us realize that a national system of higher education is increasingly not a mere epiphenomenon, dependent for its direction upon the political order, or the economic forces of production, or "the world system."[12] There are decisive processes within as well as without, mechanisms for growth and qualitative change which are an integral aspect of the functioning of the system. There are abundant conflicts and contradictions,

---

[12]For a critique of such epiphenomenalism, see Archer, ed., *Sociology of Educational Expansion.*

forces and counterforces, to upset the status quo from within. There are beliefs that select and reinterpret environmental pressures and condition the responses of the system. There is room for autonomous initiatives, even for the adoption of ideas and forms taken from counterparts in other societies. The transferring of ideational materials from one society to another, long a major path of change, will loom ever larger as communication and learning across national borders increase. The agents of the higher education systems will do much of the exporting and importing, obeying their own logics and generally acting without asking anyone's permission.

The habit of thinking cross-nationally will soon be as important for those who administer higher education as for those who study it. Historians tell us appropriately that if you want to know where you are going, it helps to know where you have been. We may add: it also helps to know where you are. That sense of place depends on coordinates that locate one's own responsibilities and efforts in larger frames. Scholars can now help practitioners sense their latitude and longitude on an international grid, identifying on a broad and basic scale the universals and the particulars in their own systems and their own work. The comparative grasp can thereby help to clarify the destination of each system in the years to come. It also significantly adds meaning to a multitude of personal efforts, granting importance and even additional dignity to what must be faced in the office next Monday morning. A comparative capacity has become a rich resource in practical thinking as well as in scholarly analysis, and nowhere more so than in the practice and study of higher education.

BIBLIOGRAPHY

Archer, Margaret S., ed. *The Sociology of Educational Expansion*. Beverly Hills, Calif.: Sage Publications, 1982.

Ben-David, Joseph. *The Scientist's Role in Society: A Comparative Study*. Englewood Cliffs, N.J.: Prentice-Hall, 1971.

————. *Centers of Learning: Britain, France, Germany, United States*. New York: McGraw-Hill, 1977.

Ben-David, Joseph, and Abraham Zloczower. "Universities and Academic Systems in Modern Societies." *European Journal of Sociology* 3 (1962):45–84.

Clark, Burton R. *The Higher Education System: Academic Organization in Cross-National Perspective*. Berkeley, Los Angeles, London: University of California Press, 1983.

Gilpin, Robert. *France in the Age of the Scientific State*. Princeton: Princeton University Press, 1968.

Hagstrom, Warren O. *The Scientific Community*. New York: Basic Books, 1965.

Hirschman, Albert O. *Shifting Involvements: Private Interest and Public Action*. Princeton: Princeton University Press, 1982.

Kerr, Clark. "Higher Education: Paradise Lost?" *Higher Education* 7 (1978): 261–278.

Levy, Daniel C. *The State and Higher Education in Latin America: Private-Public Patterns*. Forthcoming.

Lindblom, Charles E. *Politics and Markets: The World's Political-Economic Systems*. New York: Basic Books, 1977.

Makdisi, George. *The Rise of Colleges: Institutions of Learning in Islam and the West*. Edinburgh: Edinburgh University Press, 1981.

Olsen, Johan P. "Integrated Organizational Participation in Government." In *Handbook of Organizational Design*, vol. 2, ed. Paul C. Nystrom and William H. Starbuck. Oxford: Oxford University Press, 1981. Pp. 492–516.

Premfors, Rune. *The Politics of Higher Education in a Comparative Perspective: France, Sweden, United Kingdom. Stockholm Studies in Politics 15*. Group for the Study of Higher Education. Stockholm: University of Stockholm, 1980.

Premfors, Rune, and Bertil Östergren. *Systems of Higher Education: Sweden*. New York: International Council for Educational Development, 1978.

Pressman, Jeffrey, and Aaron Wildavsky. *Implementation*. Berkeley, Los Angeles, London: University of California Press, 1973.

Price, Don K. *The Scientific Estate*. Cambridge: Harvard University Press, 1965.

Trow, Martin. "Elite Higher Education: An Endangered Species?" *Minerva* 14 (1976):355–376.

Warren, Roland L. "The Interorganizational Field as a Focus for Investigation." *Administrative Science Quarterly* 12 (1967):396–419.

PARTICIPANTS

Conference on "Systems of Higher Education: Eight Disciplinary
and Comparative Perspectives"

University of California, Los Angeles, July 26–31, 1982

Professor Philip Altbach, Director
Comparative Education Center
State University of New York at
Buffalo

Dr. J. Victor Baldridge
Senior Research Sociologist
Higher Education Research
  Institute
University of California,
Los Angeles

Professor Tony Becher, Chairman
Education Area
University of Sussex

Professor Robert Berdahl, Director
Institute for Research in Higher
  and Adult Education
University of Maryland

Professor Tessa Blackstone
Institute of Education
University of London

Dr. Barbara Burn, Director
International Programs
University of Massachusetts,
Amherst

Dr. Ladislav Cerych, Director
European Institute of Education
  and Social Policy
European Cultural Foundation
University of Paris IX—Dauphine

Professor Burton R. Clark
Allan M. Cartter Professor of
  Higher Education and Sociology
Graduate School of Education
University of California,
Los Angeles

Professor James S. Coleman,
Chairman
Council on International and
  Comparative Studies
University of California,
Los Angeles

Dr. Oliver Fulton
Department of Educational
  Research
University of Lancaster

Dr. Dorotea Furth,
Program Officer
Organisation for Economic
  Co-operation and Development
Paris

Dr. Roger Geiger,
Research Associate
Institution for Social and Policy
  Studies
Yale University

Professor Klaus Huefner
Institut für Wirtschaftspolitik
Free University of Berlin
Berlin

Professor Maurice Kogan, Head
Department of Government
Brunel University

Professor Harold J. Perkin,
Director
Center for Social History
University of Lancaster

Dr. Rune Premfors,
Research Associate
Group for the Study of Higher
  Education and Research Policy
Department of Political Science
University of Stockholm

Dr. Gary Rhoades,
Research Associate
Comparative Higher Education
  Research Group
Graduate School of Education
University of California,
Los Angeles

Professor Sheldon Rothblatt,
Chairman
Department of History
University of California, Berkeley

Professor Lewis Solmon
Graduate School of Education

University of California,
Los Angeles

Professor Simon Schwartzman
Instituto Universitário de Pesquisas
do Rio de Janeiro (IUPERJ)
Rio de Janeiro

Professor Ulrich Teichler, Director
Wissenschaftliches Zentrum für
  Berufs-und Hochschulforschung
Gesamthochschule Kassel

Professor Martin A. Trow,
Director
Center for Studies in Higher
  Education
University of California, Berkeley

Dr. Bjorn Wittrock,
Associate Professor
Department of Political Science
University of Stockholm

Professor Gareth Williams, Head
Department of Educational
  Research
University of Lancaster

Professor Morikazu Ushiogi
Faculty of Education
Nagoya University

INDEX